Education in a post-welfare society

Second edition

INTRODUCING SOCIAL POLICY
Series Editor: David Gladstone

Published titles

Perspectives on Welfare
Alan Deacon

Risk, Social Policy and Welfare
Hazel Kemshall

Comparative Social Policy: Theory and Research
Patricia Kennett

Education in a Post-Welfare Society
Sally Tomlinson

Social Security and Welfare
Robert Walker

Reconceptualizing Social Policy
Amanda Coffey

Education in a Post-Welfare Society: Second edition
Sally Tomlinson

Education in a post-welfare society

Second edition

SALLY TOMLINSON

Open University Press

Open University Press
McGraw-Hill Education
McGraw-Hill House
Shoppenhangers Road
Maidenhead
Berkshire
England
SL6 2QL

email: enquiries@openup.co.uk
world wide web: www.openup.co.uk

and Two Penn Plaza, New York, NY 10121-2289, USA

First published 2005

A catalogue record of this book is available from the British Library

ISBN10: 0 335 21753 2 (pb)   0 335 21754 0 (hb)
ISBN13: 978 0 335 217533 (pb)   978 0 335 217540 (hb)

Library of Congress Cataloging-in-Publication Data
CIP data has been applied for

Typeset by RefineCatch Ltd, Bungay, Suffolk
Printed and bound by CPI Group (UK) Ltd, Croydon, CR0 4YY

The first edition was dedicated to:

Fred Jarvis, General Secretary, National Union of Teachers 1975–89

This second edition is dedicated to:

My three granddaughters, Anna, Laura, and Emily

Plato grossly overestimated the power of education to reform
. . . Aristotle knew what Plato did not, that politics and good
intentions do not mix.

Heller, J. (1988) *Picture This*

Contents

List of boxes		xi
Series editor's foreword		xiii
Acknowledgements		xv
List of abbreviations		xvii
Introduction		1
Themes of the book		2
A post-welfare market society?		5
Human capital in a post-welfare society		6
Plan of the book		8
Notes		11
Further reading		12
1	**Social democratic consensus? Education 1945–79**	13
	Equalizing opportunity 1945–60	15
	Comprehensive struggles	18
	Demons of the 1960s	20
	The 1970s	23
	Ruskin and after	25
	Ideology in the 1970s	26
	Note	27
	Further reading	27
2	**Market forces gather: education 1980–87**	29
	Education Secretaries of State	31
	Shadow Education Secretaries	31
	Regressive vision	31

Selection and privatization 32
Special selection 36
Ethnic minorities 37
School governance 38
Centralizing control 39
Teacher control 41
Curriculum control 42
Vocational education 44
Towards serious reform 45
Notes 47
Further reading 47

3 **Creating competition: education 1988–94** 48
Education Secretaries of State 51
Shadow Education Secretaries 51
Education Reform Act 1988 51
Choice and diversity 54
Chaos and perversity 55
Legislation for inspection 58
The longest Education Act ever 58
Curriculum control 61
Curriculum critiques 62
Higher education 64
Teachers and their training 66
Labour education policies in the early 1990s 68
Notes 70
Further reading 71

4 **The consequences of competition: education 1994–97** 72
Education Secretary of State (from July 1995 Secretary of State for
    Education and Employment) 74
Shadow Education Secretary 74
Legislation 1995–96 74
The final Tory Act 76
The effects of market forces 77
Failing schools 79
Special educational needs 81
Curriculum issues 82
Ages 14–19 and the academic–vocational divide 84
Labour policies 86
Notes 88
Further reading 89

5   New Labour and education: 1997–2000   90
    Secretary of State for Education and Employment   94
    Shadow Education and Employment Secretaries   94
    School policies   94
    School Standards and Framework Act 1998   99
    Selection and specialization   100
    Tackling exclusion   104
    Centralizing governance   109
    Notes   114
    Further reading   115

6   Diversity, selection and privatization 2000–2005 117
    Secretaries of State for Education and Skills   121
    Shadow Education and Skills Secretaries   121
    Commitment to diversity   121
    Overt selection   123
    Specialist diversity   125
    Academies and admissions   127
    Five-year strategies   129
    Early years and childcare strategies   132
    Special educational needs   133
    Privatization in public education   134
    More modernization   136
    Notes   139
    Further reading   140

7   Centralizing lifelong learning 1997–2005   141
    Lifelong learning   144
    Learning to succeed   146
    Twenty-first century skills   149
    Policies and qualifications 14–19   151
    Higher education   154
    Continuity and change 1997–2005   158
    Notes   162
    Further reading   163

8   Education and the middle classes   164
    Changing class structures   166
    Meritocracy and attainment   168
    School effectiveness   170
    Middle class needs   171
    Private advantage   173
    Choice and advantage   174

Avoidance of the vocational   176
Avoiding the poor   177
Globalization and the middle classes   178
Class and the common good   179
Notes   180
Further reading   180

9 **Equity issues: race and gender**   182
Race and ethnicity   183
Gender   193
Girls' achievements   195
Boys' 'underachievement'   197
Notes   198
Further reading   199

10 **Education and the economy**   200
Recent history   201
New Labour ideologies   202
The labour market into the 2000s   204
Jobs and education   205
A new economy?   207
The global economy and education   208
Prospects for the poor   210
Notes   213
Further reading   213

Conclusion: education in a post-welfare society   215
Positive aspects   217
Negative aspects   218
Education in a post-welfare market state   220
The future   222
Notes   223

References   225
Index   253

List of boxes

Box 1.1	Chronology of Acts, reports and events 1945–79	14
Box 2.1	Chronology of Acts, reports and events 1980–88	30
Box 2.2	Education Act 1980: main sections	34
Box 2.3	Education (Special Education) Act 1981: main sections	36
Box 2.4	Education Act (no. 2) 1986: main sections	39
Box 3.1	Chronology of Acts, reports and events 1988–94	50
Box 3.2	Education Reform Act 1988: main sections	53
Box 3.3	Education Act 1993: main sections	58
Box 3.4	Further and Higher Education Act 1992: main sections	65
Box 3.5	Education Act 1994: main sections	68
Box 4.1	Chronology of Acts, reports and events 1995–97	73
Box 5.1	Chronology of Acts, reports and events 1997–2000	92
Box 5.2	School Standards and Framework Act 1998: main sections	99
Box 6.1	Chronology of Acts, reports and events 2000–2005	119
Box 7.1	Chronology of Acts, reports and events in post-16 education 1997–2005	143
Box 7.2	Higher Education Act 2004	158

Series editor's foreword

Welcome to the Introducing Social Policy series which is designed to provide a range of well-informed texts on a wide variety of topics that fall within the ambit of Social Policy Studies.

Although primarily designed with undergraduate Social Policy students in mind, it is hoped that the series – and individual titles within it – will have a wider appeal to students in other Social Science disciplines and to those engaged on professional and post-qualifying courses in health care, education and social welfare.

The aim throughout the planning of this series has been to produce a series of texts that both reflect and contribute to contemporary thinking and scholarship, and which present their discussion in a readable and easily accessible format.

I am delighted that Sally Tomlinson has agreed to produce a second edition of her popular and award-winning book in this series.

'Education, education, education' was a central theme of New Labour's successful election campaign in 1997. As Tomlinson shows, scarcely a year has passed since then in which there has not been some new Act of Parliament or guidance for some sector of education or other. This has created not only a growing diversity of types of schools – especially at secondary level, but also a political and professional debate about appropriate methods of assessment. It has also produced policy innovations: the developing interface between child care and school age education is one topical example. Another is the introduction of 'top up' fees in higher education.

As in her earlier edition, Sally Tomlinson provides an authoritative guide to such recent – and many other – policy changes, setting them against the changes of the past sixty years. It was a period that began with the 1944 Education Act, one of the centrepieces of the social legislation that created Britain's 'classic' welfare state. Her narrative provides a clear and concise introduction to the policy changes and the influences that have shaped them: between the vision of equality of educational opportunity enshrined in the 1944 Act and the increasingly diverse system of schooling that prevails midway through the first decade of the twenty-first century.

Over that sixty year time span, as Tomlinson points out, more people have become educated to a higher level. Yet at the same time the objectives and purposes of schooling have undergone considerable change. From being a strategy devoted towards social change and social inclusion, over the past quarter of a century educational policies have increasingly been directed towards maximizing individual opportunity – by preparing people for maximum economic productivity throughout their lives – and national output by enhancing the quality of the workforce and, therefore, economic growth and productivity.

All these – and many other themes – Sally Tomlinson discusses in this second edition with vigour, scholarship and personal commitment. In the process she provides an acute analysis of the past and the present and raises important questions about the future of education in a more competitive, globalized and post-welfare society.

David Gladstone
University of Bristol

Acknowledgements

Both editions of this book are the product of many discussions and debates with colleagues and students about the purpose and direction of education. Special thanks to Len Barton, John Fowler, David Pegg and Stewart Ranson, who were my critical readers, and to Richard Pring and John Furlong, who gave me the hospitality of the Department of Educational Studies, University of Oxford, to write. Thanks also to Stephen Ball, David Gillborn, A.H. Halsey, Christine Heward, Joan Lofters, Pat Mahoney, Peter Mortimore, John Rex, Peter Robinson, Roger Slee, Roy Smith, James Tooley, Brian Tomlinson, Margaret Tulloch, Carol Vincent, Geoff Walford and Geoff Whitty; to series editor David Gladstone, and to Laura Dent at McGraw-Hill for her advice and patience.

List of abbreviations

A level	Advanced level
AEN	Additional Educational Needs Index
ALI	Adult Learning Inspectorate
A/S	Advanced supplementary level
BSF	Building Schools for the Future
CACE	Central Advisory Council for Education
CASE	Campaign for State Education
CATE	Council for the Accreditation of Teacher Education
CCTA	City College of Technology and Arts
CNAA	Council for National Academic Awards
CoVE	Centre of Vocational Excellence
CPD	Continuing Professional Development
CRE	Commission for Racial Equality
CSE	Certificate of Secondary Education
CTC	city technology college
CVCP	Committee of Vice-Chancellors and Principals
DES	Department of Education and Science
DfE	Department for Education
DfEE	Department for Education and Employment
DfES	Department for Education and Skills
DoE	Department of Employment
EAZ	Education Action Zone
EBD	emotional and behavioural difficulties
EMAG	Ethnic Minority Achievement Grant
EOC	Equal Opportunities Commission
EPA	Educational Priority Area
EPPE	Effective Provision of Pre-School Education project
ESG	education support grant

FAS	Funding Agency for Schools
FE	further education
FEFC	Further Education Funding Council
FVASA	Foundation and Voluntary Aided Schools Association
GCE	General Certificate of Education
GCSE	General Certificate of Secondary Education
GDP	gross domestic product
GM	grant-maintained
GNP	gross national product
GNVQ	General National Vocational Qualification
GTC	General Teaching Council
HE	higher education
HEFC	Higher Education Funding Council
HMC	Headmasters' [and Headmistresses'] Conference
HMI	Her Majesty's Inspectorate
ICT	information and communications technology
IEP	individual education plan
ILEA	Inner London Education Authority
IPPR	Institute for Public Policy Research
ISC	Independent Schools Council
KS	key stage
LAPP	Lower Attaining Pupils Programme
LEA	local education authority
LMS	local management of schools
LSC	Learning and Skills Council
MFG	minimum funding guarantee
MSC	Manpower Services Commission
NC	National Curriculum
NCC	National Curriculum Council
NCVQ	National Council for Vocational Qualifications
NUT	National Union of Teachers
NVQ	national vocational qualification
OECD	Organisation for Economic Cooperation and Development
OFFA	Office of Fair Access
Ofsted	Office for Standards in Education
O level	Ordinary level
ONS	Office for National Statistics
PFI	Private Finance Initiative
PIRLS	Progress in International Reading and Literacy Study
PISA	Program for International Student Assessment
PRU	Pupil Referral Unit
PSHE	personal, social and health education
QCA	Qualifications and Curriculum Authority
RAE	research assessment exercise

RDA	Regional Development Agency
RSA	Royal Society of Arts
SATs	Standard Assessment Tasks
SCAA	School Curriculum and Assessment Authority
SEAC	School Examinations and Assessment Council
SEN	special educational needs
SENCO	special educational needs coordinator
SIs	Statutory Instruments
SSA	standard spending assessment
SSC	Sector Skills Council
TDAS	Teaching and Development Agency
TEC	Training and Enterprise Council
TES	*Times Educational Supplement*
TGAT	Task Group on Assessment and Testing
THES	*Times Higher Education Supplement*
TTA	Teacher Training Agency
TVEI	Technical and Vocational Educational Initiative
UfI	University for Industry
UGC	University Grants Committee
YTS	Youth Training Scheme

Introduction

This is the second edition of a book first published in 2001, which aimed to provide a critical overview of education policy since 1945, a period during which government in the UK moved from creating and sustaining a welfare state, to promoting a post-welfare society dominated by private enterprise and competitive markets. The first edition took readers through a descriptive review of Acts, reports and events in education between 1945 and 2000. This edition continues the policy story and covers two terms of a New Labour government, up to March 2005. The major purpose of the book is to provide a critical overview of educational policy over the past sixty years and a discussion of the relationship of policy to class, race, gender and the economy. Over the period there has been a shift from a relatively decentralized education system to a centralized system, in which funding, teaching and curriculum are centrally controlled, and the subjection of schools to market forces has increased social and academic divisions. Education was central to post-second world war social reconstruction, and the Education Act (1944), along with the National Insurance Act (1946) and the National Health Service Act (1948), was regarded as one of the three pillars of the welfare state. In the post-welfare society there has been a fragmentation of social welfare programmes via the introduction of market principles. By 2005, education, subject to these principles, had become a competitive enterprise and a commodity, rather than a preparation for a democratic society. Despite a plethora of reforms, the education system did not appear to serve either the needs of society or the needs of individuals satisfactorily. It could not be regarded as a pillar of a post-welfare society.

The justification for yet another book on education policy is that many people, teachers, students and parents in particular, remain confused by the welter of legislation – the Acts, circulars, regulations, the consultation and curriculum documents, and the 'initiatives' which have emanated from government, especially since the late 1970s. There is also confusion about the political focus and ideological purposes behind educational change. This is partly due to a rhetoric that the state has given more freedom to individuals, while in reality central control has tightened. Before the 1992 general election, a group of university professors, supported by Fred Jarvis, former General Secretary of the National Union of Teachers (NUT), declared in a letter to the *Guardian* that a modern society could not prosper with a narrow education base and socially divisive hierarchies of schools, that government should treat education as a public service and not as a commodity to be traded in the marketplace, and that high quality education should not be reserved for some children in some schools.[1] The professors, and countless others with an interest in education, were disappointed when a Conservative government, elected for a fourth successive term since 1979, moved even further to subject schools to the operation of market forces and centralize control of all aspects of the education service. There was even more disappointment and much disillusionment when a Labour government, elected in 1997, continued to pursue Conservative market policies, despite some more ameliorative policies which were intended to return a measure of social justice to an education system becoming increasingly divisive and divided. By the time New Labour won a second term in office in June 2001 it was clear that social democratic values were to be subordinated to neo-liberal values. Education was to become less of a public service, publicly funded, and more of a commodity. Selection of children by schools, under the rhetoric of 'diversity' was further encouraged. Marketization and privatization of educational services at all levels was to be further encouraged, taking precedence over equalized provision and more equally distributed public funding.

Themes of the book

The storylines in this book will be familiar to those with an interest in education. Since the late 1940s more people have been educated to higher levels than ever before, but education is constantly portrayed, especially by some sections of the media, as failing or in crisis. There has been continued antagonism to equity in education – elitists arguing for selection for superior and better resourced kinds of education, usually described as academic, for a minority, others to be offered a practical or vocational education. Some of those committed to equality continued to argue for a meritocracy based on equality of opportunity, which presumes an equal start, unencumbered by well-documented social class inequalities. The middle classes, who historically have always claimed more than their fair share of superior forms of education, discovered or were offered new ways to do this. Governments around the world, who were turning their welfare states into post-welfare societies, were rediscovering human capital theory, with individuals told to invest in themselves in a lifelong process of learning and re-skilling in order to get or retain any kind of job. Teachers were being gradually stripped of their professionalism and policed by new inspection regimes. Schools, teachers and local education authorities were increasingly held responsible not only for failing individuals, but also for failing to make the national economy competitive in global markets. The roles and responsibilities of local education authorities (LEAs) were increasingly diminished, and the role of private contractors and business entrepreneurs expanded. A language and practice of managerialism, of accountability, inspection, testing and targets, precluded debates about the purposes of education beyond preparation for the economy. It also precluded discussion as to why in all westernized systems education had become such a major site of struggle for esteemed forms of knowledge and for credentials which can be exchanged for employment, income and status. Discussion as to how unequal possession of economic, cultural and social capital gives different social classes unequal chances in the competition for high level knowledge, credentials and jobs was minimal (Tomlinson 2001).

For those who remembered Britain pre-1939, when 88 per cent of young people left school by 14, and those who grew up in the post-war period benefiting from the Education Act 1944 and free secondary education for all, the period of 1945 to 1979 was an optimistic one. Education policy was largely based on a social democratic consensus that governments should regulate and resource education to achieve redistributive justice, and provide equal opportunity. Although it soon became apparent that the educational opportunities offered by the 1944 Act largely benefited middle class children, along with a small number of selected working class children, and that the rich and influential did not attend state-maintained schools, the optimistic feeling persisted. It was encouraged by an expanding economy and relatively full and secure employment. It seemed that, for the first time in the history of public education, there was a real intention to educate the mass of young people to far higher levels than ever before. The development of comprehensive education from the 1960s appeared to signal an end to education as a vehicle for the perpetuation of social class divisions and raised the hope that the talents of the whole population could be put to new social and economic use.

From 1979, however, the radical restructuring of public welfare provision in the UK began to take shape. Reforms of the health and education services, and of housing, social and legal services, were undertaken by the Conservative governments of Margaret Thatcher and John Major, and continued under the New Labour government of Tony Blair. The introduction of market forces and competition, the license given to people to pursue personal and familial profit, and a diminished emphasis on redistribution, equity and social justice resulted, by the 2000s, in a dramatic increase in social and economic inequalities and enhanced disadvantages for particular groups (Hutton 1995; Smith and Noble 1995; Pantazis and Gordon 2000). Despite a rhetoric of 'inclusion' and policies designed to 'lift' poor children out of poverty, by 2004 the Institute of Fiscal Studies was able to demonstrate that the UK had become one of the most economically unequal countries in Europe, with poor people in Britain poorer than the worst off in more equal industrial societies (Brewer *et al.* 2004). Although from the 1960s western governments had focused on what were variously described as the disadvantaged, the underclass, and the socially excluded as victims of economic exclusion and poverty, for New Labour the 'social exclusion' of groups and individuals from full participation in society became a worrying legacy of an ideological commitment to the workings of market forces, and a focus for intense political attention (Blair 1998b; Institute for Public Policy Research 2003). Although economists continued to argue that economic inequality was the most important cause of social exclusion (Hill 2004; Jackson and Segal 2004), the government was more concerned to focus on supposed individual, educational and familial deficiencies of the poor. In the political and popular mind social exclusion became a metaphor for anxieties over crime, antisocial behaviour and welfare fraud. In education, people became fearful of their children attending schools with those bearing the hallmarks of social exclusion. It was also obvious that there was a massive contradiction between the achievement of a meritocracy, to which the Prime Minister had committed himself (Blair 1999) and the achievement of an inclusive society, to which the government was also committed (Blair 1998c).

By the turn of the century optimistic feelings about education had been replaced by anxiety and uncertainty among a growing number of parents and educators. Post-war public education policies based on the notion of partnership between central and local government and teachers had disappeared, and educational decision-making had moved from being largely decentralized to being located almost entirely in the central political arena. Enhanced central control and regulation encompassed the teaching profession. Almost every aspect of the education system had been reformed and restructured, and the belief that educational resources would be shared more fairly had shrivelled back to the pre-1940 belief that a good education was a prize to be competitively sought, not a democratic right. However, it was also becoming clearer that, since 1999 when the Scottish Parliament and Executive and the Welsh Assembly took responsibility for education and training, market reforms applied predominantly to England. In Scotland and Wales approaches to public services were more sceptical of the power of markets. Davies, commenting on the politics of public service in Wales, wrote that 'While Tony Blair stresses the role of markets, praises the efficiency of the private sector, and emphasizes consumer choice, politicians' language in Wales is more likely to refer to citizenship, equality of outcome, collaboration rather than competition and public rather than private provision' (Davies 2003: 1).

A post-welfare market society?

Reform of the welfare provision in countries rich enough to have offered social protection to those in labour markets and to those unable to work, and to offer universal education and training, has been in progress since the 1970s (Esping-Anderson 1996; Ellison 1997; Jordan 1998). In Britain and the USA, the agenda was primarily economic – the accepted political view was that welfare costs were prohibitive; supposed profligate tax and spending was unsustainable in countries competing in a global market economy, and a privatization of former state activities was necessary to open up markets and offer expanded choice (Baer 2000). There was also a moral imperative to welfare reform. It was to be impressed on individuals that they had a mutual obligation to work, become skilled and re-skilled and engage in community and civic life, or they could not expect public support. In Britain the New Labour government used the notion of a Third Way – an attempt to marry social democracy with market capitalism – as a theory to explain the diminishing of collective public welfare provision, the incursion of private business and capital, and the increasing expectation that individuals would provide for themselves. In the USA, in some ways a model for English reforms, Bill Clinton referred in his 1998 Presidential State of the Union address to America of having found a Third Way, with smaller but progressive government (Clinton 2004). A Third Way meeting on progressive governance in London in 2003 heard New Labour advisor Philip Gould discuss the methods that should be used to persuade voters of the value of greater private involvement in public services (Wintour 2003). Although the concept of a Third Way of governing in capitalist societies generated a large amount of literature, with major protagonist Anthony Giddens eventually complaining that there was a 'wilful refusal to face up to the changes the left must make to adapt to the world in which we find ourselves' (Giddens 2002: 3) the rhetoric of a Third Way never penetrated popular consciousness. Lawson, writing in 1999, labelled the whole notion 'designer drivel' (Lawson 1999), and Martin Jacques referred to the term as 'a grand way of ducking any kind of ideological engagement with the right' (Jacques 2005).

A more accurate description of what was happening in England can be found in Philip Bobbitt's (2002) description of a market state. Producing an historical typology of state forms he concludes that the latest forms are the 'Nation State' and the 'Market State'. A nation state is concerned to benefit the people it governs. A nation state 'with its mass, free public education, universal franchise and social security policies, promises to guarantee the welfare of the nation' (Bobbitt 2002: 211). But in undertaking the welfare of all citizens, it restricts opportunities for the most productive workers and ties the least productive into a cycle of dependency. Bobbitt argued that there had been a shift in expectations of what people could expect from the state, and governments could no longer agree to improve the welfare of all citizens, with the result that 'It may be that we can expect . . . the sharp and permanent diminishment of the welfare state with its safety net' (p. 241).

In place of a welfare state comes a market state, which promises to maximize opportunities, to privatize many state activities, and to make government less influential and more responsive to global markets. In a market state there is deregulation, privatization and contracting out. It encourages a meritocracy where 'no-one can remember what the moral basis for merit were, but where it can be ruthlessly assessed and quantified' (Bobbitt 2002: 232). This will encourage competitive dynamism in the whole society. Bobbitt's market state is not an appealing one for those still in favour of welfare states. It is not a good setting for mutual assistance, as once the state has 'off-loaded' some of its former responsibilities 'there is the alternative of privatization' (p. 241). Education is singled out for profound change and Bobbitt forecasts that the days of universal mass public education are probably unlikely to continue. It may be significant that David Blunkett, Secretary of State for Education and later Home Secretary in the Blair governments, was reported to have found Bobbitt's thesis on the remaining role of governments very appealing (Pollard 2005: 42). Ainley (2004) discussed the implications for further and higher education functions in the new market state, and Pollack (2004) offered a compelling account of how the National Health Service, in which health care was established as a right for all within the nation state, has been progressively dismantled and privatized over the past twenty-five years.

Human capital in a post-welfare society

A characteristic of post-welfare society is the de-personalization of people as human beings into consumers, human resources and human capital. Those travelling by rail in the UK were surprised to hear, after rail privatization in the 1990s, that they were no longer passengers, they were customers. The emphasis on the creation of an adaptable, employable workforce, with benefits for those unable to work dependent on discretionary reviews, has focused attention on the way in which individuals, as human capital, can be prepared, encouraged and if necessary compelled, to work. Post-industrial governments, notably in the USA and UK, had by the 1990s put the work ethic and competition in the labour market at the policy centre (Jordan 1998). Policymakers were aware that the needs of global capitalist economies were a major influence on local and national economies and assigned education a major role in improving national economies. Institutions and individuals were required to 'learn to compete' as never before (Department for Education and Employment (DfEE) 1996a). Governments of varying political persuasions around the world rediscovered human capital theory (Vaizey 1958; Becker 1964), a theory which suggested that improving people's skills and capabilities makes them act in new productive ways, and assumed that investment in education will improve the quality of the workforce, which will in turn improve economic growth and productivity. By the 1990s government was firmly committed to the belief that only greater investment in human capital would enable the country to compete in the new global economy. As the DfEE pamphlet put it, 'Investment in learning in the 21st Century is the equivalent of investment in the machinery and technical innovation that was essential to the first industrial revolution. Then it was capital, now it is human capital' (DfEE 1996a: 15).

There was certainly an argument to be made for regarding young people as human capital and persuading them that continuous education, re-skilling and lifelong learning were in their own best interest, as evidence mounted that the educational and vocational qualifications of young British people were lower than in countries considered as economic competitors (Green and Steedman 1997; DfES/DTi 2003). Although P. Robinson (1997, 1999) consistently pointed out that there was little evidence on the actual relationships between school performance, credentials and national economic competitiveness, and work often moved to where labour was cheapest (Lloyd and Payne 2003) the notion that educating and training all young people to higher levels might help them to face an uncertain globalized future, slowly became more acceptable in Britain. However, a report in 2000 for the EU Presidency, pointed out that if individuals were required to reach certain educational and skill levels, governments had a responsibility to ensure levels of employment and income (Ferrera *et al.* 2000).

The New Labour government, elected in 1997, made education, training and work central to its politics, claiming that work was crucial in the attempt to unite individual liberalism with a measure of social justice. Prime Minister Blair declared in 1998 that 'The Third Way approach to the challenge of modern employment is about extending welfare to work . . . and investing in the skills people need in a more insecure and demanding labour market' (Blair 1998b: 9). Two terms of New Labour government saw a relentless emphasis on the duties and responsibilities of individuals to retrain, reskill and engage in lifelong learning, although there was eventually a greater recognition that factors beyond national government control made investing in one's own human capital a risky business. A White Paper jointly produced by the Department for Education and Skills, the Department for Trade and Industry, HM Treasury and the Department for Work and Pensions noted that 'The global economy has largely made extinct the notion of a job for life. The imperative now is employability for life' (DfES/DTi 2003: 11). The government had certainly made it clear that in a modernized

Britain the young human capital was to regard education as a preparation for the economy and not much else.

However, no government up to the turn of the century came near to resolving the contradictions involved in greater investment in education and training for all, in a society that still regarded educating the working class and socially excluded with ambivalence and had not yet managed to come to terms with the moderate success of welfare state education. The status division between academic and vocational education persisted. Expanded secondary and tertiary education, which allowed more people to acquire credentials, created anxiety among the middle classes, who feared increased competition and manoeuvred for the positional advantage described by Hirsch (1977). Disadvantaged groups found raised hurdles and moved goalposts in the struggle to acquire qualifications. The increasingly competitive nature of education meant further control of the reluctant, the disaffected and those 'special needs' groups who were unlikely to join the economy at any but the lowest levels, but whose presence might interfere with the prescribed education for the majority. As Ellison delicately commented: 'The stress is on individual achievement underscored by a state whose enabling role masks a certain coercive dimension' (Ellison 1997: 55).

Plan of the book

The first seven chapters of the book offer a descriptive review of Acts, reports and events in education between 1945 and 2005. As an aide-memoire to readers, these are summarized in a list near the beginning of each chapter, and the main sections of major Acts are summarized in boxes. Finch (1984), examining education as social policy in the 35-year period 1944 to 1979, summarized major events in a table that contained only three Education Acts, one of these being an Act by which Thatcher, then Secretary of State for Education, removed the entitlement of free school milk for all children – a move which earned her the label 'Mrs Thatcher, milk snatcher'.[2] During the twenty-five-year period from 1980 to 2005 some 34 Education Acts were passed, with hundreds of accompanying circulars, regulations and statutory instruments.[3] After the Education Reform Act 1988, described by one journalist as a gothic monstrosity of legislation, literally thousands of curriculum documents, working group reports and other documents were produced. The New Labour government promised that 'Education, Education, Education' would be a major focus of government, and continued the pace of reform and the avalanche of documentation. No one book can do justice to all this activity, and the review of events is necessarily selective.

Chapter 1 briefly overviews education as central to the creation of a welfare state attempting to redistribute social goods and resources more equitably, charting the development of comprehensive education and the persistence of opposition to non-selective schooling. The chapter notes that the 1960s, actually a period of considerable educational advance and innovation, have been consistently demonized by right-wing politicians and sections of the media as a period of liberal anarchism, and an important aim of the Thatcher governments in the 1980s was to reverse the democratic and egalitarian education policies of the 1960s. By 2004, both the New Labour Prime Minister and his Chief Inspector of Schools were also blaming the 1960s for problems in education.

Chapter 2 overviews the education policies of the incoming Conservative government from 1979 to 1987, the period when liberal individualism, moral authoritarianism and nostalgic imperialism translated into a partial dismantling of a democratically controlled education system and its eventual replacement by schools with centrally controlled funding and curricula. The chapter notes policies on selection and privatization, special educational needs, ethnic minorities, school governance, teachers and curriculum.

Chapter 3 documents the period 1988 to 1994, a period when one or more Education Acts were passed each year and when those working in education began to be overwhelmed by the reforming zeal of the Conservative government. Long-term strategies to change the whole system of education from nursery to higher education became apparent during this period. The chapter reviews the Education Reform Act 1988 and the 1992 White Paper which extolled 'choice and diversity' in schooling and decided that schools as well as individuals could be labelled as 'failures'. The Education Act 1993 (the longest Act ever), legislation for new inspection regimes and higher education reform, including teacher training, are described. This chapter and the following one conclude with a comment on Labour policies being developed in opposition.

Chapter 4 covers the period from 1994 to 1997, describing the attempts to recreate a selective system of schooling via grant-maintained (GM) schools and a three-track route for pupils from 14 into academic, vocational or work-oriented courses. The increasing educational divide along social class lines, exacerbated by 'choice' and the publication of league tables of examination results, is noted. The chapter covers the consolidating Acts passed on the recommendation of the Law Commission to clarify the spate of legislation, and the final legislation by the Conservatives, some of which was repealed by the incoming Labour government; the effects of market forces, especially on failing schools and those with special needs and disabilities; and the political convergence of plans to boost literacy and numeracy and education 14–19.

Chapter 5 covers New Labour's policies for schools between 1997 and 2000, which exhibited considerable continuity with Conservative policies. In particular it notes the retention of market principles of 'choice' and competition between schools fuelled by league tables, the policing of schools by Ofsted, an emphasis on standards of basic literacy and numeracy, and a relabelling of existing schools. This, together with the creation of specialist schools, ensured the continuation of a divided and divisive school system. The chapter covers the 1997 White Paper and the Schools Standards and Framework Act 1998, policies for the poor, the disaffected and those with special educational needs, and policies directed towards 'modernizing' LEAs – particularly by privatizing services – the teaching force and the curriculum.

Chapter 6 continues to track New Labour's education policies in its second term of office, a period which saw the resignation in 2002 of a Secretary of State for Education who explained her reasons for doing so in an article entitled 'Why I said sod it' (Ward 2003). The chapter covers the continuing commitment to a diversity of secondary schools and notional parental choice – in reality an expansion of selection of pupils by schools – the creation via the 2002 Education Act of state-subsidized Academies, and more 'modernization by privatization' initiatives which further diminished the role of local education authorities. The continued emphasis on assessment targets, managerialism, and the expansion of early years education and childcare policies is noted, as is policy on special education needs. The chapter includes an examination of the DfES *Five Year Strategy for Children and Learners* – a plan for a third term of a New Labour government (DfES 2004a) – presented to Parliament without any consultation in July 2004, and in the week before Labour's National Policy Forum met, supposedly to agree the education policy to be included in the 2005 election manifesto. The chapter also notes the final Act of a second term New Labour government passed in April 2005, and which turned out to be the fifth longest education act ever.

Chapter 7 documents post-14 and further and higher education policies from 1997 to 2005, noting again the continuities from previous governments, with investment in human capital and the subordination of education and training to the needs of the economy being dominant themes. The chapter covers policies on lifelong learning and training noting particularly the Learning and Skills Act 2000, and the 2003 White paper *21st Century Skills: Realising Our Potential* (DfES/DTi 2003). The chapter covers 14–19 policies, as the search for a more coherent phase of learning that would incorporate academic and vocational courses in both schools and colleges of further education continued. It notes the final report of the Working Group chaired by Mike Tomlinson[4] suggesting a common format and a unified diploma for this phase of education, a plan rejected by the government almost immediately. Higher education (in particular the 2004 Higher Education Act which allowed Universities to charge up to £3000 per annum for their courses) is covered, and the chapter concludes with a comment on continuity and change in education policy 1997–2005.

Chapters 8, 9 and 10 briefly review the effects of education policy changes and reforms in terms of social class, ethnicity and gender, and considers links between education and the economy. There is a very large literature in all these areas and the chapters are intended to provide an overview and guide to further reading. Chapter 8 discusses changing class structures and the effect of reforms on the middle classes. The advantages conferred on middle class and aspirant groups by choice policies and policies which enable an avoidance of the poor are noted, and the consequences of the effects of globalization for the education of the middle classes considered. Chapter 9 reviews the partially successful efforts to eliminate racial and gender inequities in education since the 1940s, the negative effects of choice policies on minorities generally, and the increase in xenophobia and racism towards Muslims and asylum seekers despite amended race relations legislation. The moral panic over the achievements of working class boys and the enhanced school achievements of girls are noted. Chapter 10 reviews links between education and the economy affected by global economic factors, takes a critical stance on the 'knowledge economy' and looks at the prospects for the poor in an increasingly socially divided society.

The book concludes with a brief assessment of the positive and negative impacts of educational policies since the late 1940s and the effects of the short- and long-term educational agenda in the UK into the twenty-first century. It asks whether it is possible to envisage politicians and the public embracing an education for the common good, especially as democracy itself had become a contested concept. It suggests that in the longer term there may be a reaction against meritocratic selection, a centrally imposed curriculum, never-ending assessment and inspections, control of educational institutions and a narrow economic view of the purpose of education, but that the preponderant influence of right-wing ideologies in the early twenty-first century will make this difficult. An overall conclusion is that education has moved from being a key pillar of the welfare state to being a prop for a global market economy and an instrument in the development of a market state.

Notes

1 The *Guardian* letter was followed up by the publication by the fourteen professors of *Education: A Different Vision* (1993) edited by Ted Wragg and Fred Jarvis. In early 2005, as a general election approached, Wragg and Jarvis mobilized some of the original professors, and others, to write a series of *Letters to the Prime Minister* (Wragg 2005)

2 A number of other Education Acts between 1945 and 1979, specified the responsibilities of LEAs and schools, set up middle schools, and established teacher negotiating procedures. An Employment and Training Act in 1947 established the Careers Service, a London Government Act created the Inner London Authority in 1963 and a Local Government Act in 1966 established the rate support grant and allocated funds for the education of New Commonwealth immigrant children.

3 Statutory Instruments (SIs) are used to make orders of general application. They need not go before Parliament although Parliament can object to them. Regulations can be made and imposed by the Secretary of State. Circulars are documents circulated by government departments for information and comment. In this book legislation referring to England, Wales and Scotland is noted; Northern Ireland is not covered.
4 Mike Tomlinson (no relation to the author) was appointed Chief Inspector of Schools after the resignation of Inspector Woodhead in 2000. He was appointed in 2002 to chair a working group to reform curriculum and assessment arrangements for 14–19-year-olds, and knighted in 2004 for services to education.

Further reading

Chitty, C. (2004) *Education Policy in Britain*. London: Palgrave-Macmillan. A review of education policy since the 1970s with particular emphasis on the impact of devolution, as Scotland and Wales pursue different policies to those being imposed in England.
Jordan, B. (1998) *The New Politics of Welfare*. London: Sage. This important book analyses the emerging politics of welfare, which stresses the importance of a work ethic in a global context. Chapter 4 suggests ways of restraining competition for positional advantage in education.
Lawton, D. (2005) *Education and Labour Party Ideologies 1900–2001 and Beyond*. London: Routledge/Falmer. This book demonstrates that over the twentieth century and into the twenty-first, the Labour Party has lacked unity and ideological coherence about education. It examines New Labour policies and the 'Third Way' and concludes with some suggestions for change New Labour could follow.
Philips, R. and Furlong, J. (eds) (2001) *Education, Reform and the State: Twenty-five Years of Politics and Practice*. London: Routledge. This edited collection examines different aspects of education policy and practice since 1976, clarifying factors which have shaped contemporary education provision and debate.
Whitty, G. (2002) *Making Sense of Education Policy*. London: Paul Chapman. The Director of the Institute of Education, London, uses the resources of sociology and the politics of education to make sense of education policy changes.

chapter

one

Social democratic consensus? Education 1945–79

This chapter overviews education as central to the creation of a welfare state which was intended to redistribute social goods and resources more equitably and to encourage economic growth and productivity. The post-war education system developed in Britain did, for the first time, and way behind other developed countries, begin the attempt to educate the mass of young people to levels hitherto reserved for elite groups. Despite continual antagonism to the expansion of education for the 'common man' – the headmaster of Manchester Grammar School for example, claimed that the development of comprehensive schools would be a 'national disaster' (James 1947) – offering a secondary education to all children did provide the base for a slow but steady raising of standards. Before the 1944 Act, nearly 90 per cent of young people left school at 14, having largely attended all-age 5–14 schools, only 10 per cent achieved passes in public examinations and less than 5 per cent went into higher education. Forty years later 100 per cent of young people were in school until 16, 70 per cent until 17, over 80 per cent achieved passes in public examinations, and 33 per cent went into higher education.

There is a very large literature documenting educational policy, practice, ideology, development and change over the period 1945–80 (see for example Banks 1955; Floud *et al.* 1956; Benn and Simon 1970; Halsey 1972; Karabel and Halsey 1977; Silver 1980; Lowe 1988; Knight 1990; Gordon *et al.* 1991; Simon 1991; Lawton 1994; Benn and Chitty 1996; Carr and Hartnett 1996; Lawton 2005). Despite the educational successes and advances that could be recorded, a major theme in the literature is that any expectations that more access to education would lead to a more equal society rapidly gave way to disillusionment. Education persisted as a means by which inequalities were created, legitimized and justified, and privileged groups continued to use the divisions and distinctions of schooling to confirm and reproduce their own position. Private schools, keeping a low profile during the post-war Labour government, continued to give the upper and middle classes access to positions of power and influence in ways which bypassed the beliefs that equality of opportunity would create a genuine 'meritocracy' of the most able. Belief in meritocracy supported the principle of selection, which sanctioned the differential treatment of the supposedly able, less able and disabled. This was enough to hinder the development of a fair system, which served the needs of all young people.

This chapter discusses attempts from 1945 to equalize opportunities and resources, particularly through the development of comprehensive schools, the persistence of opposition to non-selective schooling, and events and issues during the 1970s that set the scene for the Conservative educational policies from 1979. The educational reforms of the 1980s, as Carr and Hartnett (1996) have pointed out, did not appear out of a political vacuum. They were a central aspect of the Thatcher revolution, which aimed to create a non-interventionist state in which individual freedoms were guaranteed by the market, and state intervention to create a more democratic and egalitarian society, particularly by education policies, was to be reversed (Carr and Hartnett 1996: 11).

Box 1.1 Chronology of Acts, reports and events 1945–79

1944   Fleming Report, *Public Schools and the General Education System* (Ministry of Education)
1944   Education Act
1945   Labour elected
1945   *The Nation's Schools* pamphlet argued for a tripartite system and against comprehensive schools (Ministry of Education)
1947   Central Advisory Council for Education (CACE) Report *School and Life* (Ministry of Education)
1947   School leaving age raised to 15
1951   Conservatives elected
1951   General Certificate of Education (GCE) Ordinary (O) and Advanced (A) level examinations replaced the School Certificate
1952   Labour adopted comprehensive schooling as a policy
1954   CACE Report *Early Leaving* (Ministry of Education)
1955   Conservatives re-elected for a second term of office
1959   Conservatives re-elected for a third term of office
1959   Crowther Report *Fifteen to Eighteen* (Ministry of Education)
1960   Campaign for State Education (CASE) set up[1]
1962   Certificate of Secondary Education (CSE) examinations introduced
1962   LEAs to provide grants for higher education (HE) students
1963   Newsom Report *Half Our Future* (Ministry of Education)
1963   Robbins Report *Higher Education* (Ministry of Education)

1964	Labour elected; Ministry of Education becomes Department of Education and Science (DES)
1965	Circular 10/65 requested LEAs to reorganize their schools on comprehensive principles
1967	Plowden Report *Children and their Primary Schools* (DES)
1968	*Public Schools Commission* first report (DES)
1969	*Black Paper One* attacks comprehensive schooling and child-centred education (Cox and Dyson)
1970	*Public Schools Commission* second report (DES)
1970	Education (Handicapped Pupils) Act 'The last to come in'
1970	Conservatives elected
1970	Circular 10/70 issued (10/65 withdrawn); LEAs no longer expected to go comprehensive
1971	Education (Milk) Act
1972	School leaving age raised to 16
1972	White Paper *Education: A Framework for Expansion* (DES)
1973	Manpower Services Commission (MSC) set up
1974	Labour elected
1974	Centre for Policy Studies set up by Keith Joseph and Margaret Thatcher
1975	Thatcher becomes Conservative Party leader
1975	Direct grant schools abolished by cessation of grant
1975	Bullock Report *A Language for Life* (DES)
1975	Sex Discrimination Act
1976	Auld Report on William Tyndale School Affair
1976	Race Relations Act
1976	Education Act (repealed by 1979 Act)
1976	Ruskin College speech by James Callaghan, Yellow Book and 'Great Debate'
1977	Taylor Report *A New Partnership for our Schools* (DES)
1977	Green Paper *Education in Schools* (DES)
1977	Fifth Black Paper attacks comprehensive education and 'Marxist infiltration' in education (Cox and Boyson)
1978	Warnock Report *Special Educational Needs*
1979	Labour government's Education Bill suggests admission by parental choice and parents and teachers on governing bodies
1979	Conservatives elected and Labour Education Bill falls

Equalizing opportunity 1945–60

The Education Act 1944 emerged out of a democratic consensus between the coalition wartime government, the churches and the education service. Primary and secondary education were separated and among other ancillary welfare services, free school milk and meals, school transport and clothing grants were introduced. Secondary education was made compulsory to 15, but children were to be separated at 11 on the basis of 'age, ability and aptitude' into grammar, technical and modern schools. This legislation was based on the report of the Norwood Committee (1943), which accepted the administratively convenient and educationally spurious notion that there were three types of mind, the academic, the technical and the practical, and that children could be separated at 11 by their measured abilities and aptitudes. This notion has cast a long and pernicious shadow over the education of less privileged groups throughout the twentieth century. The use of group intelligence tests to measure ability at 11 was soon challenged by research, which demonstrated that coaching and intensive tuition, used by the middle classes, improved test scores (Heim 1954). But from 1946 some 80 per cent of mainly working class children were placed in secondary modern schools with inferior resources and less well qualified staff. The post-war Labour government compounded the inherent inequalities in the school structure by arguing against the development of comprehensive schools, reduced grammar school places, prevented secondary modern pupils from entering for external examinations and openly stated that these schools were for children 'whose future employment will not demand any measure of technical skills or knowledge' (Ministry of Education 1945: 13). Despite the promise inherent in secondary education for all, the government accepted the apparently meritocratic argument that Britain needed the 'finest trained brains from whatever class of society they come', overlooking mounting evidence, even at that time, that the finest brains appeared to come disproportionately from the middle classes. Simon has argued that 'Even under a Labour government elected with a massive majority the mediation of class relations was still seen as a major function of the education system' (Simon 1991: 115).

The interconnections between social class, economic needs and school structures became more obvious as secondary level education was opened up to the mass of young people. The post-war government was concerned to provide the workforce desperately needed for economic reconstruction and it made economic sense to hurry as many working class young people through their education and into waiting jobs at 15 as possible. This happened despite the conclusion in 1947, of the first report from the Central Advisory Council for Education, that schools should educate pupils and not prepare them for particular jobs (Ministry of Education 1947). At the other end of the social scale the education of the upper and middle class young, particularly those attending the prestigious Headmasters' Conference (HMC) public schools, continued to ensure their reproduction into positions of power and influence. The recommendations of the 1944 Fleming Report, that public schools should gradually be integrated into the state system, were quietly forgotten (Ministry of Education 1944).

Certainly neither Prime Minister Clement Attlee nor subsequent Labour leader Hugh Gaitskell, both educated at public schools, showed interest in challenging the influence of these schools. Tony Benn recorded in his diary on 2 October 1953 that Gaitskell 'still wants an educated elite learning Latin verse' (Benn 1994: 172) and they were also satisfied that grammar schools should continue to educate small selected groups despite the adoption by the Labour Party of a policy of comprehensive schools in 1952. The ideology of meritocracy (discussed in Chapter 8) has always had a strong appeal for Labour leaders, and their attitudes towards private schooling have always been ambivalent.

Research from the early 1950s demonstrated clearly that grammar school intakes remained, as pre-war, schools for the middle classes, and that social class was a major influence on educational achievement (Floud *et al.* 1956). Middle class parents continued, as they had done throughout the century, to ensure that their children were more successful in competitive examinations for the best state schools. The few working class children who made it to grammar schools soon disowned their backgrounds and were pleased that their education had separated them from the 'dim ones' (see Jackson and Marsden 1962: 192). The practice of streaming primary school children, widespread from the 1940s, worked as a form of social selection. Brian Jackson's study in the early 1960s demonstrated clearly that the children of professional and managerial workers went into A streams, the children of semi-skilled workers into B streams and those of unskilled manual parentage into C streams (Jackson 1964). Jackson even noted that in the streamed schools he observed, the A stream children were taller and better fed than the C streams (Jackson 1964: 116).

Defenders of selective education used the argument that parity of esteem was intended to operate between the three types of secondary schools, but Olive Banks (1955) in a seminal study demolished supposed notions of parity of esteem between the different kinds of schools. Grammar schools prepared children for professional and good white-collar jobs, modern schools directed their male pupils to manual work and females to factories or offices; few LEAs invested in technical schools, with only about 6 per cent of the pupil population ever attending such schools. The restriction of educational opportunities and access to professional and managerial employment to those of supposed higher ability nicely paralleled both perceived economic need and the social class structure.

The grammar school curriculum of the 1940s and 1950s was based on the subjects laid down by the 1904 Board of Regulations, which derived from the nineteenth-century public schools curriculum. There was early specialization and an arts–science divide; the subject content was Anglocentric and anti-European and reflected an imperial Britain. Although the intentions were to offer a broad curriculum relevant to the pupils who attended the secondary modern schools, beliefs in 'a distinction of mind imposed by nature' led to inferior resourcing, teaching and status of these schools, and the curriculum was oriented to practical and craft subjects. In his thorough study of secondary modern schools, McCulloch concluded that the curriculum, resourcing and discipline in most of them 'radiated uncomfortable reminders of working class elementary education and even of the Victorian workhouse or prison' (McCulloch 1998b: 90).

Evidence that the 1944 Act was not actually promoting equality of opportunity either for working class children to enter grammar schools, or receive a balanced and well-resourced education mounted during the 1950s. A government report on *Early Leaving* (Ministry of Education 1954) noted that children from lower socio-economic groups were more likely to leave school early, whatever type of school they attended, and recommendations were made for maintenance grants for poor boys and girls. The Crowther Report (Ministry of Education 1959) on the education of 15–18-year-olds drew attention to a 'wastage of talent' among working class leavers. The report recommended an expansion of further education (FE) (which did not occur until the 1980s when youth unemployment was high), a coherent national system of technical and vocational training (still to happen) and new external examinations for secondary modern schools (the Certificate of Secondary Education exam was introduced in 1962). In 1963 the report of the Newsom Committee on the education of 13–16-year-olds again argued against a wastage of talent among the 'average' pupils and against the prevailing notions of fixed ability and intelligence, of which the working classes always appeared to have less! 'Intellectual talent is not a fixed quantity but a variable that can be modified by social policy and educational approaches' (Ministry of Education 1963a: para. 15).

The Newsom Report recommended raising the school leaving age to 16 (which happened in 1972), a redistribution of spending towards the less able, and a more stimulating curriculum in secondary modern schools, albeit one directing boys to the labour market and girls to domesticity.

Comprehensive struggles

By the early 1960s a study of Liverpool schools suggested that there were now 'two nations in education', with an unbridgeable divide separating grammar and secondary modern schooling (Mays 1962). Given the realities of the unequal education system that had developed, it was unsurprising that the middle classes demonstrated early on their disquiet about selection at 11, when it became apparent that their children might be displaced from grammar schools by limited numbers of 'bright' working class children. The Conservatives, in office for the whole of the 1950s, feared that Labour was serious in its intentions on comprehensive schooling, and intent on the abolition of selection and of grammar schools. They were also concerned that Labour had plans to abolish private education or integrate private schools into the maintained system. David Eccles, Conservative Minister of Education from 1954, who famously told teachers that 'we are all working class now' despite his education at Winchester school and Oxford University, did approve the setting up of comprehensive schools in new towns and other locations that did not displace existing schools. He believed that grammar schools gave parents 'choice' and that secondary modern schools should develop specialisms. It is noteworthy that the themes of choice and specialist schools became Tory education policies in the 1980s and were adopted by Labour in the late 1990s.

However, it was now becoming apparent that governments around the world were beginning to recognize the need for expanded education systems, offering more and extended education to people who had previously been excluded. It was also admitted that this would involve more public expenditure, especially in science and technology, which sustained economic growth and development. The Conservative government of the early 1960s recognized that educating more young people to higher levels was an economic necessity. This coincided with the views of some Labour politicians that egalitarianism – specifically, educating all children together, rather than equality of opportunity for a few to be selected for a superior education – was a desirable aim. A broad consensus was established at this period, encouraged by Tory Minister Edward Boyle and Labour's Anthony Crosland, that comprehensive schools should be established, and higher education expanded (Simon 1991: 222).

On the latter point there was little Conservative objection. The Tory Prime Minister Alec Douglas-Home accepted the recommendations of the Robbins Committee (Ministry of Education 1963b) that higher education should be expanded, on the day their report was published. The report rejected the prevailing notion that there was a limited pool of ability in the population, and recommended the expansion of higher education to cater for up to 17 per cent of young people. The evidence gathered for this report was important in the struggle to break away from beliefs that only a small number of young people had the academic ability to attend universities, and that they had to come from grammar or public schools. Jean Floud (1963) produced evidence to show the socially determined production of 'intelligence', arguing that intelligence, as measured by the IQ tests which were used to separate children into different schools, was strongly affected by home environment. She pointed out that primary education had expanded from 1870 and secondary education from 1945 despite assertions that large numbers of young people lacked the ability to benefit. There was no reason why higher education could not expand in the 1960s as there was 'no iron law of the national intelligence imposing an upper limit on the educational potential of the nation' (Floud 1963: 57).

The Robbins Report rejected deterministic theories of intelligence, and Minister of Education Boyle referred to children being offered an 'equal opportunity to develop intelligence' (foreword to Newsom Report, Ministry of Education 1963a), but many opponents of comprehensive schools continued to argue that selective education was best suited to different abilities. Teachers found it hard to divest themselves of what later became known as low expectations, particularly when the effects of streaming in primary schools compounded pupil performance. Despite evidence that all children progressed more rapidly in unstreamed schools (Rudd 1960; Daniels 1961) a majority of teachers in the early 1960s believed in streaming and selection as a form of 'natural selection', despite their awareness that the processes produced a situation of social selection. Teachers told Brian Jackson that 'In the training of racehorses and athletes we are most careful to cream and train, why not with children?' and 'streaming gives middle class children the chance their parents had in private or prep schools now that state schools are more widely used' (Jackson 1964: 45). Working class parents and pupils internalized the message that they were not 'educable'. O'Connor recalled the first year girls she taught in a secondary modern school in 1964 telling her: 'You don't need to bother about us, Miss; all the bright ones have gone up the road to the grammar school' (O'Connor 1990: 1).

But by 1964, before Labour won the general election of that year, some 90 out of 163 local authorities had submitted plans to reorganize their schools. The new government made the introduction of comprehensive schools a priority, issuing circular 10/65, which requested all local authorities to submit plans for reorganization. Benn and Chitty (1996: 29) have pointed out that the mistake made by the government was to request, not require, this to happen, which allowed some authorities to procrastinate until as late as 1979, and fifteen authorities to retain selective schooling into the 2000s. Labour also rashly promised to preserve 'all that is best' in grammar school education, which led to a reinstatement of grammar and modern streams within some comprehensive schools. Simon (1991) has argued that Labour's decision not to legislate for nationwide change ensured piecemeal development school by school, some retaining streaming, some planning for mixed ability teaching. The CSE examination, introduced in 1962, imposed a threefold division of O level pupils, CSE level and 'non-exam' children, although the Schools Council was by 1970 pressing for a single exam at 16 for all students. Evidence subsequently demonstrated that the three levels of examination soon correlated with social class, with middle class pupils entered for O levels, working class pupils for CSE or non-exam (Smith and Tomlinson 1989).

Demons of the 1960s

By the 1960s the principle that a democratic society should educate all its young people rather than selected elites, and that modern economies needed more and better educated people, was beginning to shape policy and practice.

The Labour government moved tentatively towards comprehensive education and curriculum reform, and robustly towards higher education expansion. Harold Wilson, as prime minister from 1964 to 1970, may well be best remembered for setting up the Open University.

But to right-wing Conservatives the decade of the 1960s was, both at the time and subsequently, regarded as a period of liberal anarchism when traditions were wantonly destroyed and educational standards lowered. The ending of selection was presented as a destructive process and campaigns sprang up to 'save our grammar schools' (see Benn and Simon 1970). The idea of educating all young people in the same kind of school was attacked as a levelling down, as social engineering and as a destruction of high academic standards. Headteachers of established grammar schools and their associations were to the forefront in these campaigns, a situation to be repeated in the 1990s when the more recently established grant-maintained (GM) schools felt under threat. The national media largely took the side of the pro-grammar lobby, depicting comprehensive schools as 'blackboard jungles' staffed by lefty teachers. As O'Connor (1990) pointed out, comprehensive schools had barely had time to become established before grammar school had become synonymous with 'good' school, and comprehensive with 'bad' school – a message still around in the late 1990s. The demon of lowered academic standards was presented in fearsome and often inaccurate detail in a series of 'Black Papers' published by right-wing academics and policy groups between 1969 and 1977, in which articles resurrected deterministic theories of intelligence, used the student unrest of 1968 as proof that academically unfit young people had been admitted to universities and proposed measures to raise standards which included retention of corporal punishment (not abolished in schools until 1986), streaming, setting and regular testing from the age of 7 (Cox and Boyson 1977).

One area in which the demons of the right and left met was that of home background. The right could draw on a long tradition in western societies of explaining poverty, disadvantage and associated poor school performance with the working classes' innate incapacities and feckless behaviour, perpetuating the Victorian view that urban slum conditions and the ineducability of slum children were the result of 'stagnant pools of deteriorated men and women, incapable of work and demoralising their children' (Webb 1926: 172). Eugenic views of the poor emerged again during the 1960s – a decade when poverty was rediscovered in the USA and in Britain. The left's recognition that children were caught up in cycles of disadvantage (Rutter and Madge 1976) and cultures of poverty (Lewis 1968) sparked positive liberal policies to alleviate the influence of poor home background on children's education but perpetuated the view that family factors were responsible for the poorer educational performance of working class children.

Thus the Headstart programmes in the USA and the Educational Priority Areas (EPAs) in the UK (see Halsey 1972) were attempts to direct attention and resources to children whose education was affected by poverty, but without much discussion of the macro-economic conditions that create poverty, or the political failures over redistributive social justice. The report of the committee examining primary education, chaired by Lady Plowden (DES 1967) came out in favour of positive discrimination for children in deprived areas and justified EPAs on the grounds that as 'the homes and neighbourhoods from which the children come provide little support and stimulus for learning, the schools must provide a compensating environment' (DES 1967: 57). A focus on the inability of poor parents to provide a stimulating background for their children was used by the liberal left to argue for compensatory education, and by the right to reassert the innate incapacities of the lower classes (Cox and Dyson 1969). The disordered lives of the poor and their supposed inability to support their children's education, whether blamed on poverty, cultural disadvantage or low intelligence, continue to be recurrent themes in welfare and educational literature and policy.

The Plowden Report provided the right with a third demon by its advocacy of a progressive curriculum. Progressive education, with connotations of child-centred education as opposed to didactic teaching methods, became a focus for attacks by eminent and influential right-wing politicians, think-tanks and academics into the 1990s, usually linked in media reporting to the teaching methods adopted by 'trendy' teachers. Evidence that most teachers were never particularly innovative in their teaching methods, and that the didactic teaching of the 1940s and 1950s produced much failure and demotivation, has never troubled those who have demonized the 1960s as a decade when progressive education supposedly caused irreversible decline (see Jarvis 1995; Walden 1996). The demonization of education in the 1960s continued into the twenty-first century. In July 2004 Prime Minister Blair introducing a new crime policy remarked that the policy 'marks the end of the 1960s liberal consensus on law and order' and that the decade 'spawned a group of young people who were brought up without parental discipline and without any sense of responsibility' (Toynbee 2004). In October 2004, David Bell, Chief Inspector of Schools and born in 1959, claimed that much of the teaching in the 1960s had been 'plain crackers' and he had seen 'too many incoherent or non-existent curriculums . . . and too much of the totally soft-centered beliefs that children would learn if you left them to it' (Smithers 2004).

The right-wing revisionist history of the 1960s can be counterbalanced by those involved in education at the time. For many teachers and parents, the 1960s were a time of some innovation, with modest but positive changes in the primary school curriculum, the setting up of the Schools Council for the Curriculum in 1964, which had considerable teacher input, and changes in secondary school organization which pointed the way towards a more equitable education for all. There was also an opening up of the public examination system with the introduction of the CSE in 1962, and an expansion in higher education. It was a decade in which serious consideration began to be given to the education of all children in a system designed to give elites priority, and, with the arrival of children from former colonial countries, began to consider how to educate racial minorities in a system designed for white children (see Chapter 8). Also in 1970, before the Labour government fell, the Education (Handicapped Children) Act brought the last group of children, those with severe disabilities, into education. Labour had failed to tackle the divisions created by the private sector, despite setting up a Public Schools Commission, which produced two reports (DES 1968, 1970). The decade ended with a general expectation of an expansion of non-selective secondary education, further innovation, and higher levels of expenditure on education. As Simon commented:

> To many, the traditional educational structure of the past seemed ripe for a new break-out where educational forms embodying a new humanist perspective might be made a reality.
>
> (Simon 1991: 405)

The 1970s

Events in the 1970s signalled a retrenchment from egalitarian and innovative educational policies. Global economic developments put schooling under stress as the effects of a rise in oil prices and a recession in the early 1970s affected wage structures and employment of young people. Advocates of selective education and traditional teaching made headway against the principles of comprehensive education and curriculum innovation, and the fragile consensus that non-selective education was the way forward began to crack. This decade set the scene for the Conservative educational reforms in the 1980s.

A Conservative government was elected in 1970, with Thatcher as Education Secretary. Her first action was to cancel circular 10/65 and issue circular 10/70, which left LEAs free to choose whether to go comprehensive. Her second action was to cancel free school milk and impose charges for museums. The antagonisms accompanying comprehensive reorganization and the resulting ideological battles have been documented in detail in Knight (1990), Simon (1991) and Benn and Chitty (1996). According to an early biography of Thatcher, the opposition to attempts to retain selection caused her such distress that her husband suggested she resign from politics (Cosgrave 1978)! By the end of her tenure as Education Secretary the number of comprehensive schools had doubled and over 60 per cent of secondary age children attended them. But the retention of grammar schools in some areas meant that only half were genuinely comprehensive; the grammar schools continued to be presented as the only schools which could preserve high standards.

Although Thatcher published a White Paper on educational expansion (DES 1972) which included promises of an increase in educational spending, an expansion of nursery education, higher education and teaching degrees, massive cuts in the education budget were imposed in 1973 as a result of the oil crisis and other problems that Edward Heath's government faced. The school leaving age was raised to 16 in 1972, which partly took care of rising youth unemployment, and both the governments in the 1970s did attempt to deal with the dramatic expansion of unemployed youth – from 10,000 in 1974 to 240,000 in 1977 – by a series of Youth Training Schemes (YTS) run by the Manpower Services Commission, a body set up in 1973.

A Labour government was elected in 1974 and despite economic problems did revert, to some extent, to an egalitarian agenda. In 1976 education spending represented some 6.2 per cent of gross national product (GNP), the highest point it was ever to reach in the twentieth century. The Sex Discrimination Act and the Third Race Relations Act were passed in 1975 and 1976 respectively, outlawing direct discrimination against women and ethnic minorities, education being included in both Acts. LEAs were now required to reorganize along comprehensive lines; the Education Act 1976 laid down that admission to secondary schools was to be non-selective and children with disabilities should be integrated in mainstream where possible. In 1975 the 154 direct grant schools were abolished. These schools, educating mainly middle class children, had since 1925 received central government grants in return for educating 25 per cent of 'scholarship' children free. Two-thirds of these schools promptly went private. The Labour government supported the recommendations of the Bullock Committee, that all schools should have a policy for 'language across the curriculum' and that minority languages should be recognized and supported (DES 1975b). The government also accepted the Taylor Committee recommendations that school governing bodies should be expanded and given more powers, with parents, school staff and even pupils being represented (DES 1977a). More powers for governing bodies and more parental choice of school were incorporated into a Labour Education Bill in 1979, which fell with the government, although Simon took the view that this was a belated attempt to steal Conservative clothes (Simon 1991: 460). The Conservative Education Act 1980 did in fact adhere to these policies.

The Conservatives continued to attack non-selective education, linking it to lowered standards and denial of parental choice; choice and standards now became important ideological and policy concepts. A new target became 'extremists of the left'. Margaret Thatcher and Keith Joseph, Minister of Education 1981–6, set up the Centre for Policy Studies in 1975, which emerged as a vocal opponent of non-selective and progressive education. Joseph made a speech in 1975 in which he asserted that 'bully boys of the left' were responsible for a decline in educational standards, delinquency, truancy and vandalism; left-wing intellectuals were responsible for a decline in national pride; and for good measure, the lower classes were over-producing and threatening the national stock (Joseph 1975). Rhodes Boyson, an ex-comprehensive school headteacher and right-wing Member of Parliament (MP), claimed that London comprehensive schools housed Marxists and Maoists (Boyson 1975). They were given ammunition in 1976 by the events at the William Tyndale primary school in London and a subsequent inquiry into the running of the school (Auld 1976). Teachers at the school operated a progressive curriculum which was not popular with parents. The Inner London Education Authority (ILEA) eventually held a public inquiry and teachers were dismissed. The affair called into question teacher influence on the curriculum, and encouraged calls for greater teacher accountability.

Ruskin and after

By the end of 1976 an education system which most politicians, and those who had benefited from an academic education, regarded as adequate while there were unskilled and semi-skilled jobs to fill, was condemned as inadequate by politicians of all parties. It was, ironically, Labour Prime Minister James Callaghan who decided that the time was ripe for a public debate on education, but did this in distinctly right-wing terms. DES officials produced a 'Yellow Book' – a briefing paper which concluded that it was time that the Department for Education and Science should 'give a firmer lead' in what went on in schools. Callaghan, in a speech at Ruskin College, Oxford, in October 1976 attacked what he called the 'educational establishment', who were not adequately preparing children for the world of work, and had not yet realized that higher standards of education were needed in a complex world (see Simon 1991: 446–51). He called for a Great Debate on education, which took the form of a series of conferences around Britain. There was a notable lack of enthusiasm for what Lawton later described as 'not a debate and not very great' (Lawton 1994: 39) and one result of prime ministerial intervention was to demoralize teachers. Wide publicity was given to employers and business people who argued that comprehensive schools did not serve the needs of British industry, and from this time educational practices were to become more closely linked to industrial regeneration. Callaghan's criticism of the education service, which delighted Black Paper writers (see Cox and Boyson 1977: 5) was regarded as an own goal by other Labour politicians, including Neil Kinnock, Shadow Education Secretary from 1979 and subsequent leader of the opposition to Margaret Thatcher. He said later:

I found the speech dismaying, but what I said to Jim is that it was innocently dismaying. He is a man with an enormous respect for scholarship who saw education as the great avenue of liberation but was frustrated by the fact that it didn't appear to be taking place despite the fact that since 1944 there had been a replacement of the old system by a much more accessible system and since the 1960s a gradual removal of selection. The great shame is that if he had got in touch with a host of people-practitioners – generally called progressives, he would have found they all shared his frustrations and they would have had constructive suggestions to make about higher standards.

(Kinnock, personal communication, 12 October 1992)

In fact, despite persistent accusations of lowered standards, the 1977 Green Paper *Education in Schools* (DES 1977b) issued by Shirley Williams, Labour Education Secretary, made it clear that there was no evidence that education standards had fallen and that more children were better educated than those in 1945. But this did not prevent education becoming a scapegoat for a troubled economy.

Ideology in the 1970s

On the surface the debates of the 1970s were about how education should be managed and organized, and what curriculum, methods and assessment were most appropriate to prepare young people for the world of work. Non-selective education and progressive curriculum change, barely established, had become by the mid-1970s the focus for the charge that educational standards were too low and that schools were failing to produce a literate and compliant workforce. Underlying these charges was a concern voiced by those on the political right, that social democracy itself, by encouraging groups hitherto destined for lower status jobs and lower levels of education to claim equal treatment, was undermining the authority of the state (see Gamble 1988). Changes in the traditional family and in gender relationships, and the decline in Britain's economic fortunes, were blamed on demands for citizenship rights and opportunities. The arrival of immigrant minorities from former colonial countries and Britain's dwindling influence in the world were creating something of a crisis of national identity and there was a growing resistance to still embryonic notions of multicultural education. Carr and Hartnett (1996) rightly noted that it was against a confused background of social and economic change that schooling acquired particular significance for the political right. Education was to return to its role as an allocator of occupations, a defender of traditional academic values, teaching respect for authority, discipline, morality and 'Englishness' and preparing a workforce for the new conditions of flexible, insecure labour markets. But it was to do all this under new liberal commitments to eventual market competition between schools and a drastic reduction in local authority influence on schooling.

The political left had never managed to develop the democratic egalitarian ideals that were inherent in extended secondary education in common schools, an equalizing of opportunities and resources, and progressive education. Instead, as has been observed, the Labour leadership was until the 1960s content with a version of meritocracy which was consistent with selection, and indulged in scapegoating the education service when it became apparent that comprehensive education was neither fulfilling its egalitarian ideals, nor preparing a modern workforce. During the 1970s, although there was still a commitment to comprehensive principles, there were no coherent plans for the education of working class children to higher levels, or for dealing with a private sector which sustained division and privilege. Young working class unemployed people were to be offered a variety of low-level training schemes with no guarantee of permanent work. Thatcher's government offered a more coherent ideological approach centred around notions of a free economy and deregulated markets, promising choice, competition and excellence along with respect for tradition and hierarchy. Those on the left were slow to realize the implications of this and were taken aback at the speed with which the Thatcher government set about changing the direction of the whole education system.

Note

1 Originating in a parents' group in Cambridge in 1960, and first named the Confederation for the Advancement of State Education, the Campaign for State Education has campaigned over the years against selection, for more resources, nursery provision, adult education and parental involvement. Lifelong campaigners Joan Sallis and Margaret Tulloch kept this organization running successfully for many years (see Sallis 1994).

Further reading

Benn, C. and Chitty, C. (1996) *Thirty Years On: Is Comprehensive Education Alive and Well or Struggling to Survive?* London: David Fulton. This book, based on a survey of over 1500 comprehensive schools and colleges, tells the real story of a successful education reform. It is an antidote to the many attempts to denigrate comprehensive education.

McCulloch, G. (1998) *Failing the Ordinary Child.* Buckingham: Open University Press. This book describes the second-class education offered to children 'selected' for secondary modern schooling. It clearly demonstrates why comprehensive schooling was an advance for the majority of children in England and Wales.

Simon, B. (1991) *Education and the Social Order 1940–1990*. London: Lawrence and Wishart. This seminal text is the final volume in Brian Simon's documentation of the history of education from 1780. It is crucial to understanding the detail of educational policy 1944–90.

Market forces gather: education 1980–87

This chapter overviews the educational policies of the incoming Conservative government from 1979 to 1988. During this period ten Education Acts were passed, two with reference to Scotland, reaffirming the separate legal status of Scottish education. Incoming governments are keen to imprint their ideological beliefs on social policy via legislation, but there is usually also a process of policy borrowing from the previous government when particular policies are strongly embedded, suit future plans or are electorally popular. The new government immediately passed two Acts which reflected right-wing desires to return to selective education in state schools, to support private education, to introduce market forces into education via parental choice, and to reduce the costs of education overall. But it also borrowed some policies developed by the previous government on parent governors, vocational training and special education. Policy themes continued from the Labour government related to political needs to make effective uses of financial resources, to improve the quality and standards of education, to link education more closely to industrial requirements and to take firmer control of teachers and their practices. Some progress was made in the area of multicultural education, despite opposition from New Right groups.

Education, as Thatcher herself noted in her memoirs, was not an initial priority of the government (Thatcher 1993), although a continuing recession, efforts to control the money supply and reduce public sector pay and costs affected all social welfare and educational services. But education was now open to influence and intervention by powerful groups. What became known as the 'New Right' – a coalition of neo-liberals interested in free markets, competition and control of public spending, and Conservatives interested in preserving nineteenth-century notions of tradition, hierarchy, authority and order – was able to influence the direction of the education service considerably. Influential civil servants in the Department for

Education and Science and idiosyncratic secretaries of state for education were able to centralize and consolidate influence over the curriculum, examination and teaching methods and notions of teaching as a profession staffed by responsible and reflexive practitioners came under attack (see for example Chitty 1989; Ball 1990; Knight 1990; Lawton 1992; Tomlinson 1994; Carr and Hartnett 1996). Over the next seventeen years few areas of education were to escape the government's reforming zeal. The relationship between central and local authorities, school structures and governance, funding and resourcing, curriculum, pedagogy and assessment, modes of inspection, teacher autonomy and training, early years and post-16, ancillary services, relationships with parents, higher education and vocational training, were all to be subject to scrutiny, criticism and legislation. The lawyers who edit the Butterworth Laws of Education ultimately regarded the amount and weight of legislation with amazement. The editors of the 1998 volume wrote that:

> Upon the foundations of the 1944 Act, there was erected over the ensuing 50 years a more and more ramshackle statutory edifice, as the role of LEAs was elaborated or diminished by one amending Act after another ... The pressure of some thirty amending Acts eroded the foundations of the 1944 Act, which could hardly have been expected to survive the addition of a penthouse, the 1988 Act, more extensive than the foundations themselves. These crumbled under the heavier burdens [of further Acts].
>
> (Liell *et al.* 1998: 4)

Box 2.1 Chronology of Acts, reports and events 1980–88

1980–1 Local Government Acts
1980   Education Act
1980   *A Framework for the School Curriculum* (DES)
1981   Rampton Report *West Indian Children in Our Schools* (DES)
1981   Race riots in Brixton and Toxteth
1981   Education (Special Education) Act
1981   Education (Scotland) Act
1981   Reduction of university grant
1981   White Paper *The New Training Initiative* (Department of Employment)
1982   Cockcroft Report *Mathematics Counts* (DES)
1982   Technical and Vocational Educational Initiative (TVEI) introduced
1982   Scarman Report on the *Brixton Disorders*
1982   Schools Council for the Curriculum abolished
1983   Conservatives re-elected for a second term of office

1983	School Curriculum and Development Committee and Schools Examination Council set up
1983	Lower Achieving Pupils Project (LAPP) for 'bottom 40 per cent' of pupils
1983	White Paper *Teaching Quality* (DES)
1984	Education (Grants and Awards) Act
1984	Council for the Accreditation of Teacher Education (CATE)
1984	Green Paper *Parental Influence at School* (DES)
1984	Honeyford controversy in Bradford
1985	Swann Report *Education for All* (DES)
1985	White Paper *Better Schools* (DES)
1986	Education Act (no. 1)
1986	Education Act (no. 2)
1986	Social Security Act
1986	City technology colleges (CTCs) set up
1986	National Council for Vocational Qualifications (NCVQ) set up
1986	White Paper *Education and Training: Working Together* (DES)
1986	General Certificate of Secondary Education (GCSE) replaced O levels and CSE
1987	Teachers' Pay and Conditions Act
1987	Task Group on Assessment and Testing (TGAT)
1987	Conservatives re-elected for a third term of office
1987	Consultation on Education Reform Bill
1988	Local Government Act (Section 28)

Education Secretaries of State

Mark Carlisle 1979–81
Keith Joseph 1981–86
Kenneth Baker 1986–89

Shadow Education Secretaries

Neil Kinnock 1979–83
Giles Radice 1983–87
Jack Straw 1987–92

Regressive vision

The core focus of Conservative educational policy under Thatcher was an emphasis on the use of markets and free enterprise to produce and to distribute, with a minimum of regulation, the goods and services wanted by consumers. Although in the 1980s other developed countries were experimenting with the introduction of market forces in education, dismantling local bureaucracies, and allowing schools much more autonomy to manage their resources (see Whitty *et al.* 1998), the vision underpinning the British Conservative government reforms was that of a nineteenth-century liberal individualism, in which ostensibly free consumers embraced the laws of the market and the values of self-interest and personal and familial profit. This vision was supplemented by a traditional conservative appeal to a moral authoritarianism and a nostalgic imperialism in which individuals were expected to accept a hierarchical understanding of their class, gender and racial position, and by a distinctly Victorian view that those who did not help themselves by making the right choices, were unworthy of state help. As Thatcher expressed this:

> I never felt uneasy about praising Victorian values . . . or virtues . . . because . . . they had a way of talking, which summed up what we are now rediscovering – they distinguished between the deserving and the undeserving poor.
>
> (Thatcher 1993: 627)

In the regressive Conservative vision of the 1980s, fairness and justice were not visible attributes. In education the vision translated into an economic market doctrine that a precondition for consumer choice was the partial dismantling of a democratically controlled education system and its replacement by individual schools with centrally controlled funding and curricula. Education was in future intended to be a commodity, with parents supposedly free to choose the quality, location and amount, and the best quality education was, as in pre-war Britain, to be a positional good which must be competitively sought. Values of competitive individualism, separation and exclusion were to be extolled and knowledge itself regarded as a commodity for private consumption. But knowledge was, by 1988, to be regulated and controlled by central government via a national curriculum, which in the event was largely based on a version of the nineteenth-century public school curriculum, with distinct barriers between academic, practical and technical learning.[1] In effect, education remained a preparation for a class-divided hierarchical society in which those destined for skilled work or places on the margins of the economy received a different and inferior education to those destined for professional and managerial jobs and positions of power and influence.

Selection and privatization

The Education Act passed in 1979 by the incoming government reflected the traditional desire to return to a selective education system and slow down moves towards comprehensive education for all. Thatcher led the attack on a common education with an open assertion that the aspirant middle classes now had less access to a more privileged education.

> It is my passionate belief that what had gone wrong with British educa-tion is that since the war we have strangled the middle way. Direct Grant and grammar schools provided the means for people like me to get on equal terms with those from well-off backgrounds.
>
> (Thatcher 1993: 578)

Her first Education Secretary, Mark Carlisle, declared that comprehensive education was from October 1979 no longer national policy. Local author-ities were to be free to retain their selective grammar and secondary modern schools or return to this pattern. Several authorities did this, notably Kent and Essex. Others attempted the reversal, notably Bolton, Solihull and Thameside, but were defeated by changed local politicians or parental objec-tions. The movement towards comprehensive schooling did continue throughout the 1980s, but now this form of education was on the defensive, and various forms of selection and specialization were to creep in over the decade.

The successes of comprehensive schooling and an expanded examination system were glossed over or regarded by some as dangerous. Education Secretary Carlisle recorded his resistance to suggestions that educational standards were dropping, as 'the number staying on in higher education, the number passing O and A levels showed an upward trend. To claim they were diminishing in real terms seemed to me to fly in the face of available evi-dence' (Carlisle quoted in Ribbins and Sherratt 1997: 76). Carlisle was soon sacked by Thatcher. In 1984 Ranson interviewed senior civil servants at the DES and recorded one as worrying that:

> We are beginning to create aspirations we cannot match. In some ways this points to the success of education in contrast to the public mytho-logy that has been created . . . so we have to select, to ration the educational opportunities . . . people must be educated once more to know their place.
>
> (Ranson 1984: 241)

During the 1980s various strategies to ration educational opportunities emerged, leading, unsurprisingly, to a reassertion of social class as the major determinant of opportunity. Those with what Thatcher described as 'well-off' backgrounds had usually made sure that their children attended private schools, yet the conservative impulse to protect and enhance the role of private schooling was evident in the second Education Act passed by the new government in May 1980.

Box 2.2 Education Act 1980: main sections

1 LEAs to assist the attendance of able pupils at private schools on a means-tested basis. All independent schools to be registered.
2 Parents allowed to express a preference for a school providing it was compatible with efficient education and use of resources. Appeals committees set up by LEAs and voluntary aided schools for parents refused schools. LEAs to provide information on admissions criteria, numbers, examination results and curriculum.
3 Every school to have its own governing body with two parent governors and at least one teacher governor.
4 Education of under-5s to be discretionary, not compulsory, by LEAs.
5 Removal of any requirement on LEAs to provide school milk and meals (except for means-tested free school meals). Nutritional standards abolished.
6 Rights of LEAs to refuse places for pupils out of their area restricted.

A major provision of the 1980 Act was 'to enable pupils who might not otherwise be able to do so to benefit from education at an independent school' (Edwards et al. 1989: 1) or, as one head of a private school interviewed by Edwards and his colleagues in their research on the assisted places scheme put it, 'to pluck embers from the ashes of the comprehensive schools'. The scheme was partly intended to revive the principle of direct grant schools, and was intended to select pupils from poor homes by academic merit. As research by Edwards and his colleagues subsequently demonstrated, low income was no measure of educational need, and the majority of children who took assisted places came from homes with 'educationally advantaged' parents. The scheme which reinforced the view that comprehensive state education was unable to offer all children an adequate education, bolstered the private sector considerably (some schools which market forces would have closed, stayed open by public funding) and increased the percentage of pupils staying in private schools post-16. The scheme, according to Simon (1991: 475) was a means of siphoning off public money with no public control, some £70 million being spent over the first seven years. The Labour Party pledged to abolish the scheme, which happened in 1997.

In order to save money the 1980 Act also removed the obligation on LEAs to provide free school milk and meals for children, except for those from families on supplementary benefits. The Social Security Act 1986 removed even this obligation although LEAs were left with powers to provide free meals for children whose families received Income Support. LEAs (and later schools) put meals services out to tender, and as nutritional standards had also been abolished, the era of chips with everything was ushered in. One consequence of this seemingly educationally unimportant decision was to be seen later in the growth of health inequalities (Acheson 1998); nutritional standards were reinstated in 1999. The principle of privatizing services hitherto supplied by local authorities had also been established.

The Education Act 1980 also enhanced the notion of parental 'choice' of school, by allowing parents to express preferences for schools and setting up appeals committees for dissatisfied parents. This provision increased covert selection between comprehensive schools and began the sharp social and academic polarization between 'popular' schools and less popular schools. By the mid-1990s 'choice' processes had virtually ensured that in urban areas the social classes were educated separately, rural areas having less scope for 'choice'. By the later 1990s research was demonstrating that the secondary school system was systematically becoming more academically and socially divisive than ever before (Gibson and Asthana 1999).

In the early 1980s, however, Conservatives were still searching for ways of continuing selection of the few for academic education, and basic education and training for the rest. Keith Joseph, Education Secretary 1981–6, was a strong supporter of what he termed 'differentiation' between pupils, and together with his junior ministers, would have welcomed a return to grammar and secondary modern schooling. When the Conservative controlled borough of Solihull attempted a return to grammar schooling, but was defeated by parental pressure in the attempt, Joseph argued that 'Since differentiation between schools is largely out, then there must be differentiation within schools' (see Simon 1991: 500). Simon has noted that it was around this time that New Right supporters began to consider the strategy of new types of schools to circumvent the comprehensive system. A national network of 'Crown schools' directly funded by the government, magnet schools similar to those in the USA, and specialist schools set up by parents and teachers were all suggested by Conservative ministers and their advisers (see Brown *et al.* 1985). Joseph was also urged by his advisers to set up voucher schemes by which parents would be given vouchers worth a cash value to be exchanged for their educational choices. He was enthusiastic but, as he recorded in an interview, 'producer forces were unanimously hostile and I was forced to tell the 1983 Conference that, at least in the foreseeable future, the voucher is dead' (Joseph quoted in Ribbins and Sherratt 1997). But as Lawton (1992: 49) pointed out, parental choice plus a cash value for each pupil, more or less the same as a voucher, did become official policy in 1988. One supporter of vouchers was Alan Howarth, director of the Conservative Research Department and later a Conservative MP. Howarth changed his allegiance to Labour in 1995 and was made a Labour Education Minister in 1997.

Special selection

The Education (Special Education) Act 1981, which changed the law on special education, appeared as something of an anomaly, given the pressures for selection by 'ability'. The Act followed the report of the Warnock Committee in 1978, a committee originally set up by Thatcher in the early 1970s, which had argued that children formerly segregated by 'categories of handicap' into special schools should progressively be integrated into mainstream schools, and all children with special educational needs (SEN) should be integrated on a functional, social or locational basis with other children (Warnock 1978). Although Labour's Education Act 1976 had specified the principle of educating all children in mainstream schools as far as possible, it was not until the 1980s that debates and practices surrounding integration and inclusion became widespread. Warnock herself wrote in 1980 that 'ordinary schools must expect to cater for more children with special needs and the whole concept of children with peculiar difficulties, or indeed peculiar talents, must be a natural part of the comprehensive ideal' (Warnock 1980). This expressed an egalitarian belief that a common school should be inclusive of children of all abilities and disabilities and clashed both with beliefs that 'natural' abilities and disabilities needed separate schools, and also with the needs of teachers to get rid of 'pupils who may present insuperable problems for teachers in the ordinary classroom situation' (National Union of Teachers 1979). As pressure on teachers to raise standards increased, the need to remove any pupil who was in any way troublesome was intensified, and led to considerable professional and political conflict. Much of the 1981 Act was repealed and replaced by the Education Act 1993.

Box 2.3 Education (Special Education) Act 1981: main sections

1 Categories of handicap replaced by the concept of special educational need, defined as present when a child has significantly greater difficulty in learning than the majority of children of his/her age, or has a disability which prevents or hinders the use of educational facilities normally provided.
2 Local authorities to have the duty of identifying and assessing children with special educational needs, and for making and maintaining a statement of special educational needs for some children.
3 Parents to have rights to be consulted, to appeal against statements and to request assessments.
4 Children with special needs to be educated in ordinary schools providing that their needs can be met, the education of other children is not affected, and there is an efficient use of resources.

Ethnic minorities

A second anomaly in Conservative education policy concerned the education of ethnic minorities. Race and ethnicity had a higher profile in education during the first half of the 1980s than at any other period. This was
partly due to race riots, or urban disorders as they were termed, in various
parts of Britain, notably Brixton in London and Toxteth in Liverpool in
April 1981. Lord Scarman, appointed by the government to examine the
causes of the riots, concluded that young black people did not feel politically,
socially or economically secure in Britain, and made a number of recommendations, including suggestions for improving educational provision for
minorities (Scarman Committee 1982: 204).

The criticisms of the education service made in the report were not new.
The education of children from racial and ethnic minorities had become a
serious policy issue during the 1960s and 1970s, based on assumptions that
some form of assimilation into the majority society would take place. By the
later 1970s it had become obvious that the education system was not
equipped to offer equal opportunities to acquire qualifications and credentials to minorities, and that there were no curriculum strategies to ensure
that young white people learned to understand and respect their fellow
pupils. Policy aims articulated by Roy Jenkins, Labour Home Secretary in
1968, were that there should be 'not a flattening process of uniformity, but
cultural diversity, coupled with equal opportunity, in an atmosphere of
mutual tolerance' (Rex 1986: 32). However, racial and ethnic minorities
were regarded as a 'problem' by many schools. Minorities had mainly
settled in urban areas served by poorly resourced schools developed from
secondary modern status, but the populist white view, encouraged by the
xenophobic attitudes of New Right groups (see for example Hillgate Group
1986; Palmer 1986), was that it was the presence and cultures of minorities
that 'lowered standards'. Minority groups, especially African-Caribbean
parents, quickly became concerned that the system was not offering their
children equal opportunities, and both the Conservative and Labour governments of the 1970s were aware of anxieties about minority educational
achievements. The Labour government was also concerned that

> Our society is a multicultural and multiracial one, and the curriculum
> should reflect an understanding of the different cultures and races that
> make up our society ... the curriculum appropriate to our Imperial
> past cannot meet the requirements of modern Britain.
>
> (DES 1977b: 41)

In response to a House of Commons Select Committee (1977) report on *The
West Indian Community*, Shirley Williams, Secretary of State for Education,
agreed to set up a committee to inquire into the underachievement of West
Indian children in school. Under the chairmanship of Anthony Rampton this

committee issued an interim report in 1981, which suggested that the education of minority children must be considered alongside the education of all children for a multiracial and culturally diverse society (DES 1981a). Thatcher, who remained consistently hostile to any initiatives designed to make the education system more suitable for a racially and ethnically diverse society, sacked Anthony Rampton.

Despite this antagonism, and the publicity given in 1984 to a Bradford headteacher, Ray Honeyford, whose attitude to multicultural education brought him into conflict with his employers and Asian parents (Honeyford 1988), the early to mid-1980s was a period in which initiatives were put in train by both central and local government which did improve the education of minorities and raised awareness and knowledge levels of teachers around Britain. Initiatives included a requirement that intending teachers would receive some training for a multicultural society: making 'teaching and the curriculum in a multiethnic society' an in-service priority for two years in 1986 and 1987; requiring the new GCSE examination boards to take account of cultural and linguistic diversity; offering support to schools from Her Majesty's Inspectorate (HMI) and local advisers; and providing education support grants (ESGs) in predominantly white areas for curriculum development projects. Despite pressure from educational nationalists (Tomlinson 1990: 36), Thatcher did allow the Committee of Inquiry into the Education of Ethnic Minority Children to continue its work under the chairmanship of the liberal Lord Swann. The report of this committee (DES 1985a), with its 71 recommendations on the role of education in a complex and diverse multiracial society, was the high point of positive policy thinking about race issues. Thereafter what Apple (1999) has termed the 'absent presence of race in educational reform' characterized educational discourse.

School governance

Following the report of the Taylor Committee (DES 1977a) whose recommendations on parental representation on school governing bodies had been accepted by the Labour government, the 1980 Act required every school to have its own governing body, which should include two parent governors. The Conservative government decided to make governing bodies major agents in the running of schools, and to reduce the domination of LEAs in governor appointments. Schools, according to the White Paper *Better Schools* (DES 1985b: 63) 'need to recognize themselves as more than an agency of the LEA'. A Green Paper on *Parental Influence at School* (DES 1984), together with the White Paper and the subsequent Education Act 1986, changed the composition of governing bodies, and gave governors responsibility for the conduct of the school and major influence over the curriculum. In particular, reflecting right-wing anxieties over the introduction of such areas as world studies, peace studies, urban studies and health and sex education (Scruton *et al.* 1985), governors were to determine the curriculum policy for their schools, take specific responsibility for sex education and for ensuring that any political education was balanced and not 'indoctrination'. Governors were also to report annually to parents, their reports were to be published and they were given more responsibility for excluded pupils. This Act also abolished the use of corporal punishment in state schools from 1987.

Box 2.4 Education Act (no. 2) 1986: main sections

1 Maintained schools to have between two and five elected parent governors, one or two teacher governors, two to five LEA appointees, and three to six co-optees and the headteacher. Some variations for voluntary aided and controlled schools.
2 Governors given responsibility for the conduct of the school, for any funding delegated by the LEA, for staff appointments and the curriculum.
3 LEAs to provide training for governors.
4 New provision for exclusion of pupils and parental appeals.
5 Corporal punishment abolished.
6 Teacher appraisal schemes introduced (not implemented until 1992).

A major effect of the 1986 Act was to accelerate the process of removing powers, duties and control of education from LEAs. The government did not, however, appear to be entirely clear about the powers it had removed. In 1988 an amendment was inserted into a Local Government Act forbidding LEAs to 'promote teaching in any maintained school of the acceptability of homosexuality as a pretended family relationship' (Section 28), despite the fact that school governors, not LEAs, had been responsible for sex education in the curriculum since 1986. In 2000 the New Labour government attempted to abolish Section 28 but, although there had been no prosecutions of LEAs and the law was meaningless, the House of Lords voted to retain the section. The New Scottish Assembly voted for abolition. The Section was finally abolished in England via a 2003 local government act.

Centralizing control

The period from the early to mid-1980s saw 'new modes of control developed and brought into play' (Simon 1991: 504). Central government – politicians, their advisers and officials – took over functions formerly carried out or shared in partnership with local government and teachers. Ideological paradoxes abounded. While individual freedom, market choice and power for consumers rather than 'producers' of education were extolled, the central state took tighter central control of finance, curriculum and examinations, teachers' practice and training. Part of what became a continuing political agenda was to remove power from institutions and groups, which were bases for dissent, criticism or independent advice. Thus, in 1982, the Schools Council for the Curriculum, an independent body set up in 1964, which had considerable teacher influence, was abolished by Keith Joseph. Two government appointed committees ostensibly giving independent advice on curriculum and examinations replaced it. Universities suffered under a combination of cuts and greater government control in 1981, with reductions in student numbers and staffing, and were gradually pushed towards greater industrial and commercial relevance, responsiveness to economic needs and the world of business (Silver 1990: 94). In 1983 subsidies for overseas students coming to Britain were removed. One result of this was that students from poorer countries, particularly from Africa, went to other countries for their higher education, thereby reducing possible British influence on elites in these countries, and universities began to search the world for richer students.

Local authorities had their responsibilities for decision-making reduced by a Local Government Act passed in 1980, whereby central government decided on a standard level of service for each LEA and gave a block grant, usually less than local authorities, particularly urban authorities, needed. At the same time local authorities had their powers to raise extra money through local rates cut (rate capping). The Education (Grants and Awards) Act 1984 further reduced local authority control over spending by taking money from the block grant to allocate to ESGs for projects that the Education Secretary considered important. While ESGs did support some important projects, central government was making it clear that local authorities were in future to 'bid' for money which central government would decide to give or withhold. A further instance of central government removal of local decision-making power was exemplified by the Education Act (no. 1) 1986, which required LEAs to submit their plans for the in-service education of teachers to the secretary of state for approval, national priority areas for such training having been laid down by central government. Local authorities continued to apply for money under Section 11 of the Local Government Act 1966, for money to employ staff for teaching 'Commonwealth immigrant children', although local decisions on how this money was to be spent were progressively eroded. Overall, by 1987 educational expenditure, as a proportion of the gross domestic product (GDP) had fallen from 5.5 per cent in 1981 to 4.8 per cent; local autonomy over spending and decision-making on schools and other educational expenditure had been greatly reduced.

Teacher control

Moves to curtail the professional autonomy of teachers and the influence of their educators and unions were made during the early 1980s. By the end of the decade teachers were well on their way to becoming a technical workforce to be managed and controlled rather than a profession to be respected. Those who had argued that teachers should become reflexive practitioners, and that theory and practice in teaching should be inseparable, were presented by the radical right as enemies of good practice (Lawlor 1990). The nineteenth-century view, that teachers should simply be 'trained' to reproduce a set of technical operations and transmit subject knowledge at primary and secondary level without a professional input, was resurrected. Central government took control of teachers and their training by the abolition of independent advisory groups and committees, by detailed prescription of teacher training courses and by control of teachers' pay.

The Association of Local Authority Education Committees was abolished in 1983, an Advisory Committee on the Supply and Education of Teachers was abolished in 1985, and the English and Welsh Central Advisory Councils for Education, established in 1944 to advise ministers, were abolished via the Education Act 1986. It has already been noted that the Schools Council, a body through which teachers could express their views on the curriculum, was abolished in 1982. A 1983 White Paper on *Teaching Quality* set out policies on the size, management and training of teachers (DES 1983), and in 1984 government issued criteria for the approval and review of all teacher training courses. A Council for the Accreditation of Teacher Education (CATE) was set up in 1984, its chair being a government appointment, to carry out this review, effectively removing responsibility for developing teacher education courses from institutions of higher education.

Teachers' pay had been falling behind other professional groups since the early 1970s, and teachers and their unions had not claimed any large salary increases. But Keith Joseph angered teachers considerably when he suggested in a 1985 speech that pay should be linked to appraisal and to performance. He also suggested that as there appeared to be an adequate supply of teachers, pay must be adequate (Joseph 1985)! A bitter pay dispute ensued, which was not resolved until 1987. In 1986 Joseph was removed as Secretary of State for Education and replaced by Kenneth Baker. Baker was particularly antagonistic to the teacher unions and their negotiating rights over pay; in November 1987 he introduced a Bill which abolished the negotiating procedures set up in 1965 in the Remuneration of Teachers Act (the Burnham Committee). The resulting Teachers' Pay and Conditions Act 1987 set up an advisory committee appointed by the secretary of state, which could impose pay structures and conditions on teachers (the Pay Review Body).

Conservative education policies were at this point not popular with voters; the chair of the Conservative advisory group on education wrote that 'The Conservatives have managed to alienate almost every group of people involved in education' (Argyropolu 1986). But despite this, teachers, their trainers and unions, LEAs and higher education were by now dancing to a Thatcher government tune.

Curriculum control

Control of the school curriculum has always been a political issue. As Lawton pointed out in 1980, curriculum planning is 'making a selection of the most important aspects of culture for the next generation. The crucial cultural question is "what is worthwhile", the crucial political question is "who makes the selection"' (Lawton 1980: 6). Post-1945 teachers came to have considerable influence over the curriculum, guided by the Norwood (1943) doctrine of 'types of mind'. Grammar schools continued to offer a traditional academic education and secondary modern schools attempted to develop post-elementary, pre-vocational schooling. Comprehensive school curricula became in the 1960s a mixture of the two traditions, although many comprehensive schools did attempt to implement a common curriculum, and teachers began to search for ways in which courses for pupils previously written off academically as 'secondary modern material' could be offered as equally challenging an education as those selected for grammar schools.

During the 1980s central government and the DES gradually asserted centralized control over the curriculum, with teacher input and influence scaled down. Mark Carlisle proposed *A Framework for the School Curriculum* (DES 1980) which identified a core curriculum of English, maths, science, modern languages, religious education and preparation for working life, with further papers from the DES and HMI appearing in support of a common curriculum (DES 1981b; HMI 1981). HMI was in favour of a curriculum theorized as areas of experience rather than subjects – verbal, mathematical, scientific, ethical, aesthetic and physical – with an Assessment of Performance Unit sampling pupil performance to check standards. However, ministers and DES officials clung to the traditional format of single subjects. A single exam at 16, unifying O levels and CSE, was envisaged, under DES control. This came about in 1986, when the GCSE was introduced.

During Keith Joseph's time as Education Secretary, the development of a common curriculum for all pupils gradually slipped backwards towards a differentiated curriculum, based on the familiar notion that some children were unsuited to an academic curriculum. He used findings from the Cockcroft Report on mathematics (DES 1982), which had pointed out differences in maths attainment at 11, to argue that 'there should be careful differentiation: what is taught and how it is taught need to be matched to pupils' ability and aptitudes' (DES 1985b: 15). Joseph later claimed that he invented the GCSE examination, and that 'I invented the differentiation. I said I'd only agree to unify the two examinations (GCE and CSE) provided we established differentiation' (Joseph quoted in Ribbins and Sherratt 1997: 24). In 1983 he initiated a Lower Attaining Pupils Programme (LAPP) directed towards the 'bottom 40 per cent of the ability range' (some 2.5 million children) who were to be offered a curriculum suitable for the less able, and in September 1983 a technically and vocationally oriented curriculum for 14–18-year-olds was piloted in 14 schools. David Young, head of the MSC, later Secretary of State for Employment and ennobled by Margaret Thatcher, claimed the credit for initiating TVEI, a 'Dawn Raid on Education' as he put it in his memoirs (Young 1990: ch. 7). Funding for TVEI came via the MSC, LEAs being required to bid for money for local projects. Although the stated intention of TVEI was that it would cater for all abilities, it appeared that a tripartite curriculum was being resurrected within comprehensive schools. Eventually over £1 billion was made available to schools and colleges to create technical and vocational courses; the funding was wound up in 1991. Pring (1995) later took the view that the prevocational courses developed during the 1980s, including TVEI, could have bridged the academic–vocational divide in the English curriculum, but the defence of an academic curriculum for elites was too strong.

The White Paper *Better Schools* (DES 1985b) set out government views on the purpose and nature of education by the mid-1980s. Some of these views clearly resonate into the twenty-first century. 'Raising standards at all levels of ability' became a major aim, qualified by an acceptance that definitions of standards change over time and that British society had become more complex and diverse, particularly as the pace of technological change quickened and unemployment became more widespread (DES 1985b: 1). The White Paper was clear that a major task of schools should be to 'create the human capital which is the raw material for industry', providing via a differentiated curriculum a differentiated but versatile workforce, suitably prepared for management or labour, which would possess skills, attitudes and technological competence equal to international economic competitors (DES 1985b: 15). Thus:

> Education at school should promote enterprise and adaptability in order to increase young people's chances of finding employment or creating it for themselves and others.
>
> (DES 1985b: 3)

> It is vital that schools always remember that preparation for working life is one of their principal functions . . . Industry and Commerce are among the school's main customers.
>
> (DES 1985b: 15, 82)

In familiar vein, the paper also set out reductions in expenditure on education and expected local authorities to reduce costs by 'rationalisation and efficiency', phrases which became familiar as the decade progressed as meaning no pay rises and a reduction in the teaching force.

Vocational education

Government policies dealing with youth unemployment within an economy in which unskilled labour was no longer needed, and an enterprise culture which demanded fewer but more highly skilled workers, were laid out in a Department of Employment (DoE 1981) White Paper, *The New Training Initiative*. This envisaged a national training policy for all those who left education for unemployment at 16, a revised apprenticeship system and adult retraining. There was no suggestion that any vocational training could be developed into the well-funded, employer-backed, comprehensive vocational training system that other European countries, notably Germany, had developed; vocational training courses and schemes continued to be low-status courses for working class young people. But the need to provide employers with recognized qualifications did lead to the setting up, in 1986, of a National Council for Vocational Qualifications, which was given the task of developing national vocational qualifications (NVQs). A DES (1986) White Paper *Education and Training: Working Together* envisaged that the Education and Employment departments would work together to develop NVQs, but in the event the two departments continued to work separately, with sometimes conflicting results. For example, the NCVQ designated five levels of vocational performance at the same time that National Curriculum assessment was developing ten levels of school performance (see Stanton 1997). The basis of NVQs was that of competence in the performance of work tasks, and by the 1990s a three-track system for young people post-16 had become embedded, with NVQs accrediting the occupational route. According to some critics, NVQs have proved an expensive addition to a 'jungle' of vocational qualifications and embody the separate traditions of academic education versus vocational training endemic in English education. Responsibility for most youth training schemes was devolved to Training and Enterprise Councils (TECs), employer-dominated regional organizations created by government in 1986 and abolished in 2000.

A further attempt to provide a separate vocational and technical education for the 'less academic child', and link the education system more firmly to the needs of industry, was made in 1986 with the creation of city technology colleges (CTCs). The CTCs were presented as an extension of the technical and vocational educational initiatives already in place, and the government hoped that industry would provide most of the funding. In the event, employers were reluctant to provide funding and most of the money for the

15 CTCs that were eventually set up came from the taxpayer. The ideology supporting CTCs, as Walford and Miller (1991) suggested, was that of diversity of provision with selection of children for and education appropriate to their 'aptitudes and abilities', and the creation of the CTCs allowed private and grammar schools to continue to offer an academic education to selected 'able' children.

Towards serious reform

In 1985 the president of the Society of Education Officers had warned that government predispositions towards centralization and control of education, together with managerial and market models of organization, had alienated teachers and removed the historic partnership between government, local authorities and teachers. The views he articulated at that time would be appropriate for a number of years.

> The sustained public criticisms over the past decade, the inadequate public funding of the service, the erosion of its status and the general uncertainty about the future, have reduced morale to a disabling level and the relationship between the historic partners is at an all-time low.
>
> (Hall 1985)

However, the government, under pressure from HMI about the deteriorating state of school buildings as well as pressures from teachers and parents, sought new pragmatic alternatives to spending more money and returning to partnerships. Alternatives were to find private and more 'efficient' ways of funding education, and to put into practice ideas emanating from the right wing of the party for competition between schools, and for further control of teachers and the curriculum. The recommendations in a pamphlet by the No Turning Back Group of MPs, *SOS Save our Schools* (Brown *et al.* 1985), appeared in the Conservative election manifesto in 1987. This suggested that schools opt out of local authority control, and be directly funded by the DES and in competition with one another, with governors and heads given powers to hire and fire teachers. In early 1987 Baker announced that he would legislate for a national curriculum in named subjects with tests at 7, 11 and 14, and that financial control of schools would be devolved to headteachers. A Task Group on Assessment and Testing reported in December 1987 on possible national arrangements for assessing children's learning.

The Conservatives won the election in June 1987 and in July Baker issued four 'consultation documents' on the National Curriculum, financial delegation to schools, grant-maintained schools and school admissions; replies were to be sent in by September. Despite the derisory period allowed, some 20,000 responses were made to the documents, and to a proposed Education

Bill. De Haviland (1988) edited the replies in 'A Selection of Advice on the Government's Education Reform Bill which the Secretary of State invited but decided not to publish', and demonstrated that replies were overwhelmingly opposed to most of the reforms, particularly the proposed subject-based structure of the National Curriculum (NC). Consultation replies were disregarded and the Education Reform Act was on the statute books by July 1988.

The goals of government policy during the 1980s were underpinned by a desire to reinstate selection and move away from a comprehensive education system. This should not be surprising in a party traditionally committed to defending a hierarchical social structure. Reynolds (1989), in summing up education policy 1979–87, pointed out that while the previous Labour government had sought to transform education, the Conservative government was firmly committed to education for the reproduction of existing social divisions. This meant a continuation of an academic–vocational divide, which paralleled social class divisions, and aimed to maximize class advantages for some groups while minimalizing the prospects for groups already disadvantaged (Reynolds 1989: 193). Already by 1987 selective divisions between schools were in place with private, grammar and comprehensive schools in middle class areas taking advantaged pupils and producing better exam results. A competitive market between schools was about to exacerbate this.

As at the end of the 1970s, the political left, towards the end of the 1980s, still had no clear educational policy alternatives. Despite a continued increase in the numbers of pupils taking and passing public examinations – girls especially beginning to achieve well at GCSE level – and an increase in numbers staying on in further education and entering higher education, Labour produced no coherent defence of comprehensive schooling, although the 1987 election manifesto did promise a comprehensive tertiary system of post-16 education, and a restoration of teachers' collective bargaining rights. By the end of the decade the Labour Party had adopted the Conservative language of falling standards and was promising that Labour's commitment to comprehensive education would help to ensure raised standards for all children.

The party also took over research on effective schooling and used it to present the argument, used consistently throughout the 1990s, that because the performance of children in schools serving similar areas differed, schools and teachers must be at fault.[2] Developing a critique of less effective schools and low teacher expectations helped set the Conservative agenda for attacks on 'failing schools' in the 1990s. In other policy areas, notably parental choice and representation, National Curriculum, vocational training, special education, and centralization of control over local education authorities and teachers, there was considerable policy agreement, as New Labour policy in the later 1990s was to demonstrate.

Notes

1 Nicholas Stuart, a civil servant at the DES and himself educated at Harrow public school and Oxford University, was a major architect of the Education Reform Act 1988. He later became director general for employment, lifelong learning and international director at the DfEE.
2 Labour particularly used research by Smith and Tomlinson (1989) to argue that 'If the below average schools were simply brought near the best 25 per cent, standards would be transformed' (Labour Party 1990: 30; Smith and Tomlinson 1989: 301).

Further reading

Ball, S.J. (1990) *Politics and Policy-making in Education*. London: Routledge. This book offers a thorough analysis of the practice of policy-making in education, with particular reference to the 1980s and the influence of the New Right.
De Haviland, J. (1988) *Take Care, Mr. Baker*. London: Fourth Estate. This is a selection from some of the 20,000 critical replies to Education Secretary Kenneth Baker's consultation on the Education Bill 1987, which were presented in the two-month period allowed. Those drafting the 1988 Act subsequently ignored any critical responses.
Knight, C. (1990) *The Making of Tory Education Policy in Post-War Britain 1950–1986*. London: Falmer. This book documents in intense detail the personalities, vested interests and conflicts which characterized Conservative policy-making over 36 years.

chapter

three

Creating competition: education 1988–94

During the period 1988–96 the Conservative government appeared to be gripped by a frenzied need to legislate on every aspect of education, with an Education Act arriving on the statute books almost every year. Those working in education were overwhelmed with the reforming zeal with which every aspect of education, from early years to higher education, through changes to school structures, funding, curriculum, assessment, parental influence, inspection, ancillary services and teacher training, were all subject to scrutiny, criticism and legislation. It was not, however, the piecemeal approach that it appeared to be at the time. It was part of a developing, longer term strategy to change the whole system of education. Aims of legislation included consolidating a market ideology to be achieved by parental choice, establishing central government control over curriculum and assessment, further eroding the powers and responsibilities of local authorities, teachers and their trainers, demanding accountability from individuals and institutions, especially universities, and encouraging selection under a rhetoric of diversity.

Reform was rationalized by constant criticism, from all quarters, of both the products and the producers of education, right-wing groups and conservative politicians and industrialists having throughout the 1980s subjected schools and teachers to continual criticism. Low standards, particularly in comprehensive secondary schools, and incompetent teachers were favoured targets (Thatcher 1993: 590). A former ambassador to the USA, Oliver Wright, blamed the 'cocoon of the welfare state' which he thought discouraged effort by university and school staff (Critchfield 1990). Teachers were also criticized for allegedly poor pupil behavioural standards, although a committee set up to examine *Discipline in Schools* (Elton Committee 1989) did not support right-wing portrayals of schools as 'blackboard jungles' and offered balanced and sensible policies to schools. The influence of right-wing individuals and organizations who influenced the Prime Minister, other politicians, and even strong-minded civil servants into the destruction of a national state education system moving slowly towards egalitarian structures and outcomes, and replacing it with a competitive, fragmented and divisive system, has been well documented (see, for example, Ball 1990; Knight 1990). Even the chair of the Conservative Education Association (Dimitri Coryton) conceded that Thatcher drew to herself 'some fairly bizarre and peculiar individuals' (quoted in Ball 1990: 42), whose personal agendas were concerned more with self-interest than improved education.

However, left-wing and liberal commentators were also castigating low levels of educational performance achieved by the mass of young people, albeit with rather more historical understanding. The Labour Party, with Jack Straw as Shadow Education Secretary, had, by the late 1980s, decided to attempt to outdo the government and stress policies to raise standards, counter low teacher expectations and promulgate effective schools.[1] The then Warden of Wadham College, Oxford, Claus Moser, observed in a speech celebrating the twenty-fifth anniversary of the 1963 Robbins Report that despite an opening up of higher education, 'we may be one of the least educated advanced countries' with 40 per cent of young people leaving school at the first opportunity with minimal qualifications. Moser went on to set up a National Commission on Education when the government refused, despite the support of many eminent educationists and scientists, to set up a Royal Commission on Education (National Commission on Education 1993).

Whether the spate of legislation over this period – which handed to the Secretary of State for Education over a thousand new powers and created a more divided and divisive school system than at any time since the Second World War – was responsible for raised standards in education is still a debatable proposition. As Chapter 2 has noted, standards, as measured by entry and success in public examinations, had been slowly but steadily rising since the 1960s, when a majority rather than a minority of children began for the first time to be taught for and entered for such examinations. There is certainly a case to be made for the view that more carefully planned change in real consultation with all partners in the education process might have seen much more improvement. Lawton (1994), summarizing the Conservative education legislation to 1994, took the view that legislative changes could have been part of a process of building a 'magnificent modern system'. Instead,

the legislation has been a mixture of attempts to enforce ideological prejudices, and out-of-date traditions, and then more legislation to patch up earlier over-hasty drafting ... The result is a system with demoralised teachers who have had to cope with too many changes in too short a time.

(Lawton 1994: 104)

This chapter takes the form of a chronological discussion of the Acts and reports over the period 1989–94, most of which relate to issues raised in Chapter 2.

Box 3.1 Chronology of Acts, reports and events 1988–94

1988   Education Reform Act
1988   National Curriculum Council (NCC) and School Examinations and Assessment Council (SEAC) set up
1989   Children Act
1989   Self-Governing Schools (Scotland) Act
1989   Elton Report *Discipline in Schools*
1990   Education (Student Loans) Act
1990   Training and Enterprise Councils set up
1991   Teachers' Pay and Conditions Act
1991   Parents' Charter *You and Your Child's Education* (DES)
1991   General National Vocational Qualifications (GNVQs) to be introduced.
1991   White Paper *Education and Training for the 21st Century* (DES/DoE)
1992   Transfer of Functions Orders: Department of Education and Science (DES) to become Department for Education (DfE)
1992   Further and Higher Education Act
1992   Howie Report *Upper Secondary Education in Scotland*
1992   Further and Higher Education (Scotland) Act
1992   Conservatives re-elected for a fourth term of office
1992   White Paper *Choice and Diversity* (DfE)
1992   Education (Schools) Act
1992   Office for Standards in Education (Ofsted) set up
1992   League tables of GCSE results first published in newspapers
1993   Education Act
1993   NCC and SEAC replaced by School Curriculum and Assessment Authority (SCAA) (Ron Dearing as chair)
1993   Dearing Report *The National Curriculum and its Assessment*
1993   National Commission on Education Report *Learning to Succeed*
1994   Updated Parents' Charter *Our Children's Education* (DfE)
1994   Code of Practice for Special Educational Needs
1994   Education Act
1994   Teacher Training Agency (TTA) set up

Education Secretaries of State

Kenneth Baker 1986–89
John MacGregor 1989–90
Kenneth Clarke 1990–92
John Patten 1992–94

Shadow Education Secretaries

Jack Straw 1987–92
Ann Taylor 1992–94
David Blunkett 1994–97

Education Reform Act 1988

The Education Reform Act 1988, described by its supporters as a great education reform and one of its opponents as a 'Gothic monstrosity of legislation', made the decisive break with the welfare state principles which had underpinned the education service since the Butler Education Act of 1944. Butler himself, speaking in the 1960s, said that he had hoped that his Act would have wide social consequences, creating one nation and offering equal opportunities, and to some extent by the 1960s he saw this happening. The Baker Act, in contrast, was about individual entrepreneurism and competitiveness, achieved through bringing education into the marketplace by consumer choice. It was not concerned with principles of equity and a fully comprehensive state system. It was also, paradoxically, about increasing the influence of the central state on education by reducing local powers and taking control of what was to be taught in schools. The opposition to much of the suggested reform during a consultation period has already been noted (De Haviland 1988); a number of commentaries critical of the early working of the Act, and wary of the changes it made to the power structure in the education system, had appeared by the early 1990s (see MacClure 1988; Chitty 1989; Flude and Hammer 1990; Ranson 1990; Lawton 1992; Bowe *et al.* 1992).

The Act, with its 238 sections and 13 schedules, took up 360 hours of parliamentary time and gave the secretary of state 451 new powers. A major feature of the Act was the introduction of a ten subject National Curriculum for all pupils 5–16, to be assessed at four key stages, key stage 4 (KS4) being the GCSE examination. A National Curriculum Council and a School Examinations and Assessment Council were to oversee the arrangements, but the Secretary of State was granted the powers to decide ultimately on actual curriculum content. The major feature was the open enrolment or parental rights to choose schools and financial management of budgets by schools. Local authorities could no longer fix admission limits, and schools were to publish examination results. Taken together, this was intended to ensure that popular schools would expand and unpopular schools close. A competitive market was to ensure that consumers of education gained market power over producers. Education was to become a product. Choice was to be enhanced by the reintroduction of schools directly funded by central government, breaking the monopoly of local authorities. Legislation for these grant-maintained schools, to be introduced after parental ballots, was extremely complex and strongly opposed by those who feared that the schools would seek to re-emerge as selective and, with extra money promised, would become prestigious schools in a tiered system of schools. Simon (1991) has commented on the importance of the success of this initiative to the government: Margaret Thatcher appeared on television to say that she hoped all schools would opt out of LEA control (Simon 1991: 550). A Grant-Maintained Schools Trust, financed largely by business, was launched before the Act received royal assent and circulated all schools with a brochure announcing *The New Choice in Education*. This told headteachers that 'Grant-Maintained status gives to governors, heads and parents the opportunity to improve the quality of education at their schools unhindered by local authority pressure' (Grant-Maintained Schools Trust 1989).[2] Between 1989 and 1991 the DES issued a series of coloured booklets on 'How to become a grant-maintained school'. Other important features of the Act were those relating to further and higher education, whereby via a new planning and funding system, central government extended its control to these sectors of education, and the abolition of the ILEA, a body set up in 1964 to provide an integrated education service for inner London, and its replacement by twelve boroughs and the City of London, responsible for education.

Baker himself wrote that he 'wanted to steer this major piece of legislation through parliament around all the obstacles which the vested education interests would throw in its way' (Baker 1993: 164). He considered those defending their vested interests to include teachers, their unions, LEAs, universities, senior civil servants at the DES, and HMI. He had already voiced his suspicions in a speech at the 1987 Conservative Party conference in Brighton that the 'educational establishment simply refuse to believe that the pursuit of egalitarianism is over' and that 'tolerance of the smug complacency of many educationalists, which has left our educational performance limping along behind our industrial competitors' was about to end. If the reminiscences of retired politicians are to be believed, Baker, in an interview over ten years later for the *Guardian*, claimed that his agenda was to 'punish the teacher unions, kill off the local education authorities, and wipe out comprehensive schools by stealth' (Davies 1999: 1). Baker was reportedly pleased that giving schools their own budgets in local management of schools (LMS) diminished the power of teacher unions and LEAs, and created a competitive market that left some schools struggling to survive while others prospered. There was, as Davies (1999) commented, no research demonstrating that organizing schooling in this way actually improved education for all children. Before the Act was passed Campbell *et al.* (1987) had suggested that a more mundane explanation than melodramatically breaking the power of vested interests, was simply that more central control means that governments could control spending better.

Box 3.2 Education Reform Act 1988: main sections

1 *National Curriculum and assessment* All maintained schools to provide a broad and balanced curriculum for pupils 5–16 which includes the National Curriculum (NC) and religious education. The secretary of state to specify attainment targets, programmes of study and assessment. Information on the curriculum and assessment to be provided for parents (Sections 1–25).

2 *Open enrolment* School admission procedures changed to ensure that schools enrol pupils up to a 'relevant standard number' (based on numbers in 1979–80). LEAs or governors could fix higher limits (Sections 26–32).

3 *Local management of schools* Schools to be delegated their total budget through a formula worked out by each LEA and approved by the secretary of state. Governors given powers to manage the school budget and hire staff (Sections 33–51).

4 *Grant-maintained schools* The secretary of state to be given the responsibility to maintain GM schools, financed directly by central government. Ballots of parents to be held to decide whether the school should opt out of LEA control (Sections 52–104).

5 *City technology colleges* The secretary of state to be given powers to enter agreements with (private) sponsors of CTCs and colleges for arts and technology (Section 105).

6 *Higher and further education* Polytechnics and some large colleges of higher education removed from local authority control. A Universities Funding Council and a Polytechnic and Colleges Funding Council set up. Local authorities to have a duty to provide further education (FE) and to delegate budgets to FE colleges. Academic tenure to end (Sections 120–38).

7 *Abolition of ILEA* The Inner London Education Authority to be abolished by April 1990 and local control of education to pass to twelve new LEAs and the City of London (Sections 162–96).

8 *Miscellaneous* A number of other provisions included a redefinition of free education. The duties of local authorities and governors with regard to payment for school extras were clarified and permission given for voluntary contributions to schools (Sections 106–11).

Choice and diversity

The most far-reaching effects of the 1988 Act derived from the open enrol-ment and LMS provision whereby funds follow parental choice of school. Choice, in reality only the right to express a preference, as many parents discovered when LEAs wished to direct children to specific schools, was the mechanism which made some schools richer and others poorer. This led to massive diversion of funds into marketing and public relations (Bowe *et al.* 1992), encouraged parents to become 'vigilantes' and complainants rather than partners in schooling (Tomlinson 1991) and 'crippled some perfectly good schools by rumour and innuendo' (Tim Brighouse quoted in Simon 1988: 61). The operation of market choice, as Ranson (1990: 15) argued, and which was subsequently shown to be the case, would also prove a crude mechanism for social selection (Gewirtz *et al.* 1995). Ideological belief that all parents desired and would benefit from choice between schools was not borne out by research, which into the 1990s had indicated that apart from those parents seeking private or selective schools, what most parents wanted was a good local comprehensive school, well resourced and staffed and offering equality of treatment of all children (Adler *et al.* 1989; Bright *et al.* 1998). Nevertheless, choice was what parents were going to get, and unremitting propaganda, plus the very real aspirations and fears about edu-cation that developed during the 1990s, led to eventual parental acceptance of a marketplace in schooling. The Children Act 1989, which clarified the concept of parental responsibility, including responsibility to ensure regular school attendance, possibly also influenced more parents into considering 'the best interests of their child' as the Act put it. The comment by Tawney, eminent Labour philosopher in the 1920s, that 'What the best and wisest parents want for their child, the state should want for all its children', was forgotten by the 1980s (Tawney 1931: 146).

For parents to exercise their choices, the legislation introduced diversity in the form of GM schools. These were to be schools financed, as were the old direct grant schools, by central government, and run by their governing bodies without LEA representation. Parents were to be balloted before their children's schools could go grant-maintained. This section of the Act, as MacClure (1988: 64) noted, aroused much hostility from local authorities and from teachers, who feared that the measures were intended to reintroduce selection or lead to privatization. City Technology Colleges and schools specializing in arts or technology were to offer further choices, although at this time there were only some eight CTCs in operation. In 1989 all parents in Britain were sent a booklet *Our Changing Schools* (DES 1989a), which described their rights to school preference and school infor-mation, appeals procedures if their choice was disregarded, and new choices through diverse kinds of school. Voluntary aided and controlled religious schools, Anglican, Catholic and Jewish, which educated some 23 per cent of children at this time, also had the right to go grant-maintained and opt out of LEA control.

In 1991 all parents were sent a copy of a Parents' Charter, which was updated and sent out again in 1994 (DES 1991; DfE 1994a). This told parents that they had a right to a free school place, noting GM schools, CTCs, independent schools and assisted places, but not LEA comprehensive schools, which were later disparagingly referred to as 'council schools'. The Charter promised much more information for parents including the proposed publication of public examination and National Curriculum test results and truancy rates. In 1992 these duly appeared, being eagerly published in most national newspapers as 'league tables' of schools from best results to worst, and becoming an annual media event. Despite objections that such results would demonstrate the social class composition rather than the educational performance in an area, league tables of school performance were to become a political weapon for subsequent claims that effective schools and bad schools could be easily identified (see Slee *et al.* 1998). Schools topping the league table list were, unsurprisingly, private schools, especially the top girls' private schools, remaining grammar schools and other selective schools. Grant-maintained schools were also paraded as 'doing better' than local authority comprehensive schools despite their different social class composition. The 1994 Parents' Charter also published national targets for education and training, which at that time targeted 80 per cent of young people to gain five good GCSE passes or an equivalent by 1997 and 50 per cent of young people to achieve the equivalent of two A levels by 2000. These targets were wildly over-optimistic, and were later scaled down by Labour to target 50 per cent of 16-year-olds to achieve five good GCSE passes by 2002. The notion of potential school leaving examinations which only one-half of all young people 'pass' satisfactorily has been regarded with some surprise by European educationists (McClean 1990; European Commission 1997).

Chaos and perversity

The five years following the 1988 Act were characterized by Lawton (1994) as moving from 'confusion to chaos'. The creation and imposition of a National Curriculum and its assessment on an unconsulted teaching force, the working out of further central controls on local authorities, teachers and higher education, the increased spending despite promises of reduction – National Curriculum and test development costs alone amounted to some £800 million – and ideological interventions by ministers, including John Major, the Prime Minister from November 1990, did not augur well for creating a promised 'stable system of education that sets international levels of excellence' (DfE 1992: 64). Education ministers moved on rapidly, with

John MacGregor taking over from Baker in July 1989, but, having gained a reputation for niceness, MacGregor was moved after a year in the job to make way for Kenneth Clarke, a party heavyweight. Clarke declared that his aim was greater *Choice and Diversity* in education; this became the title of the DfE (1992) White Paper, which was reputedly known to some education officials as 'chaos and perversity'. Prime Minister Major made some interesting interventions, recommending a back-to-basics curriculum, telling the 1992 Conservative Party conference that 'teachers should learn how to teach children to read, not waste their time on the politics of gender, race and class', and writing that 'the problem of low standards stems in large part from the nature of the comprehensive system Labour ushered in the 1960s' (Jarvis 1995). Even the Minister of State, Chris Patten, soon to go on to be Governor of Hong Kong, spoke at the 1992 conference of 'voodoo teaching methods that have blighted chances of a generation of school children'. After the Conservatives won a fourth election in April 1992, John Patten, a former university teacher, became Secretary of State for Education, but continued confrontational policies and attacks on teachers, teaching methods and theorists. His major contribution was the 1992 White Paper, which formed the basis of the Education Act 1993, an Act even longer than that of 1988. His belief that 'Good schools that attract most pupils will get most money. Poor schools that cannot attract pupils must improve standards or wither and perish' was set out in a Conservative magazine (Patten 1992).

The White Paper claimed that since 1979 five great themes had characterized educational change: quality, diversity, parental choice, school autonomy and greater accountability. Its key objectives, encapsulated in the 1993 Act, were to increase the number of GM schools – tactics to bring this about included the remarkable ruse of creating 'failing schools' which ultimately would become grant-maintained – and allowing special schools and clusters of school to opt out. The government had been disappointed that there had been no rush, over the preceding four years, to opt for GM status, especially in Labour-controlled local authorities. By 1992 only 422 out of some 24,000 schools had voted to opt out and in 32 local authorities no parental ballot had been held. In Scotland, despite a 1989 Act allowing opting out, no school had gone grant-maintained. There was thus a need to rescue a failing policy.

The paper also signalled a further reduction in LEA powers, proposing a Funding Agency for Schools (FAS), with members appointed by the secretary of state, which would share control of school admissions with the LEA once 10 per cent of schools had opted out. It suggested a school inspectorate working for the government, rather than independent HMIs, and proposed the abolition of the NCC and SEAC to create a government appointed School Curriculum and Assessment Authority (SCAA). It also developed the idea of education associations, bodies to be set up by the government to take over schools regarded as 'at risk' of failing pupils.

Associations were to act as GM governing bodies in running schools and either recommend closure or bring the school into the GM fold. In the 1990s only one such body was set up, and its actions were questioned in the High Court (O'Connor *et al.* 1999). Under the language of diversity, the White Paper also suggested more selection of pupils by schools, particularly for specialist schools, by both ability and aptitude, but asserted that 'The government wants to ensure that there are no tiers of schools ... but rather parity of esteem between different schools' (DfE 1992: 19). Clearly the evidence that demonstrated that parity of esteem (like the American doctrine of 'separate but equal schools' for black and white pupils) was an impossibility, had been forgotten. In addition, at this time all school-aged children of members of the government's Cabinet were in private school. The limited research into the working out of 'choice' at this time suggested that parental school preferences were constrained by what was offered locally, and that diversity 'inevitably leads to fragmentation, segregation and selection' (Brain and Klein 1992: 46). As the 1990s progressed, a major effect of choice, especially in metropolitan areas, was a 20 per cent increase in road traffic as parents drove their children around cities to non-local schools.

Choice and Diversity was not well received. An astonishing response from the Conservative Education Association (chaired by Lord (Mark) Carlisle) noted that

> The government's present emphasis on grant-maintained schools is something we have grave doubts about ... In effect, the government is nationalising the schools of England and Wales ... if more schools do opt for GM status an even larger part of the £14.5 billion spent annually on schools will be spent by bodies that are not democratically accountable.
>
> (Conservative Educational Association 1992)

An editorial 'Four lies to tell parents' in the *Independent on Sunday* asked:

> Do politicians think we are all stupid? Last week's White Paper, possibly the most dishonest and intellectually incoherent document to emerge from a government department for 50 years, suggest they do. The White Paper is a political document and it is full of lies.
>
> (*Independent on Sunday* 2 August 1992)

The editorial went on to point out that allowing more schools to select by ability, or by aptitude for specialist schools, would create selective ghettos within the comprehensive system. It also pointed out that there was still no evidence that comprehensive schools had lowered standards: more children were taking and passing exams and going on to higher education than ever before.

Legislation for inspection

The White Paper had ended with the grandiose statement that 'This White Paper details the final stages of a great transformation in education which will take at least a decade to work through' (DfE 1992: 64) and promised that legislation to achieve this was already in train. The Education (Schools) Act 1992 and the 1993 Education (School Inspections) Regulations set up an Office for Standards in Education (Ofsted), independent of the DfE, and with chief inspectors of schools appointed by the secretary of state in England and Wales. Although some 250 of the old HMI, who had traditionally conducted school inspections independently and given advice to ministers, were retained, they were to have an administrative and supervisory role. Actual inspections were to be conducted by teams of private inspectors given contracts by Ofsted and paid for by the school or colleges being inspected. All schools were to have a four yearly inspection, and inspectors were to report on the quality of education, standards achieved, financial management and spiritual, moral, social and cultural development of children. The retiring Chief Inspector, HMI, Eric Bolton, in a careful assessment of the new inspection arrangements, noted that despite international interest in the work of HMI and admiration for their independent advice to government, 'In Britain by an act of careless vandalism, driven by ideology and ignorance, we have enacted a small but important tragedy and destroyed it' (Bolton 1994: 127). The Chief Inspector of Schools appointed by the government, retained by the Labour government after 1997, was Chris Woodhead. He proved to be a controversial figure whose political stance on school inspection, and whose willingness to criticize schools and teachers, proved useful to both Conservative and Labour governments. Under his regime, however, the inspection service was later judged by some to have had a harmful effect on schools, and caused 'a grave distress to the teaching profession on which we rely for the care of our children' (Fitz-Gibbon and Stephenson-Foster 1999). Woodhead resigned his post in November 2000 and announced his intention to become a writer on educational matters, initially in the *Daily Telegraph* newspaper and later for the *Sunday Times*.

The longest Education Act ever

Box 3.3 Education Act 1993: main sections

1 *Funding Agency for Schools (FAS)* Funding authorities to be set up in England and Wales with members appointed by the secretary of state. Funding authorities to carry out 'value for money' surveys of schools (Sections 1–11).

2   *Responsibility for education* The secretary of state to decide responsibility for school admissions between FAS and LEA (shared after 10 per cent of schools were GM, responsibility of FAS after 75 per cent had gone GM) (Sections 12–21).

3   *Grant-maintained schools* Encouragement of schools to opt for GM status by changes in balloting rules for parents, expenses for governing bodies arranging ballots, new funding arrangements for the schools, independent schools, special schools and clusters of schools able to opt for GM status, religious education in GM schools (Sections 22–155).

4   *Special educational needs (SEN)* Most of 1981 Act repealed, but LEAs to retain primary responsibility for children who have SEN. A Code of Practice to be issued to LEAs and schools, and a Special Educational Needs Tribunal to be set up with chair appointed by the Lord Chancellor. Governing bodies able to decide that state special schools shall go GM (Sections 156–91).

5   *School attendance* Attendance of children at schools to be secured by attendance orders. Parents to be guilty of an offence if their child does not attend school regularly (Sections 191–203).

6   *Failing schools* Clarifies procedures for the identification of schools judged after inspection as failing to give an acceptable standard of education. Schools to be placed under special measures, and regulations made to ensure that measures to improve standards are monitored. LEAs to appoint additional governors and take over the school budget. Secretary of state to appoint an education association to take over if no improvement, and recommend discontinuance of school or GM status (Sections 204–28).

7   *Miscellaneous* Includes provision to dissolve NCC and SEAC and set up a School Curriculum and Assessment Authority, regulates in respect of sex education, proposals for nursery schools, and rationalization of schools places, allows for the incorporation of governing bodies, lays new duties on LEAs for religious education, and for the setting up of Pupil Referral Units (PRUs) for pupils excluded from school or otherwise not in school. Abolition of any requirement to have an Education Committee in an LEA (Sections 229–98).

The Education Act 1993 was the largest piece of educational legislation ever enacted in the UK, containing 308 sections, 21 schedules and many last-minute amendments (Morris *et al.* 1993). Its major purpose was to put in place the key objective of the 1992 White Paper and increase the number of GM schools. Funding agencies for schools were to be set up in England and Wales to distribute central government money, and share allocation of school places with LEAs. Parents were to be balloted annually on seeking GM status and their ballot expenses paid, while local authorities were to be restricted in their spending on persuading schools to stay with the democratically elected local authority. Clusters of schools and religious schools could opt for GM status and 'failing schools' were to provide a further boost to GM figures. Schools identified as failing to give an adequate standard of education were to be put under special measures and although the LEA initially had powers to help the schools improve, an education association, or 'hit squad' as the press dubbed it, could be appointed to manage such schools. The 'normal expectation was that at the end of their stewardship the school will become GM'. Since failing schools were likely to be found in Labour-controlled poor and disadvantaged areas, the LEA could be weakened and schools turned GM without a parental ballot, thus killing two birds with one stone! In the event the only education association to be appointed to go into a school (Hackney Downs in 1995) had its actions questioned in a judicial review (O'Connor *et al.* 1999). However, it is noteworthy that a member of this association was Michael Barber, a former NUT education officer and a university professor from 1993, who was appointed by the Labour government in 1997 to head the new School Standards and Effectiveness Unit at the DfEE.

After the 1993 Act the number of GM schools did increase slowly, schools tempted as much by the extra funding offered as by freedom from LEA control. By 1997 some 1000 out of 3500 secondary schools in England were grant-maintained but only two in Scotland. Howson (1999) has noted that for much of the 1990s, GM schools enjoyed direct funding levels well above those of local authority controlled schools, on average £120 more per pupil, plus capital grants; in 1999, when the Labour government ended grant-maintained status and attempted 'fair-funding' policies, there were howls of protest from GM headteachers. GM schools did fulfil the Conservative desire for selection, as most became overtly or covertly selective, while still remaining comprehensive in name, and becoming sought after schools by the middle and aspirant classes. The leader of the Labour Party, Tony Blair, decided to send his eldest son to the grant-maintained Catholic London Oratory School in 1994, which prompted accusations of hypocrisy from various quarters (Bosely 1994; Hughill 1994). Prime Minister Major, in a speech to the Grant-Maintained Headteachers' Conference in Birmingham in 1994, 'looked forward to the day when all schools will become GM', an ambition restated by the Conservative leader William Hague at the Conservative Party conference in 1999.

A further purpose of the 1993 Act was to clarify responsibility for children regarded as having special educational needs: although the 1981 Act had specified that such children should be educated in mainstream schools if possible, there had been a dramatic increase, particularly after 1988, in parental requests for statements and extra resources. The Audit Commission (1992) had identified a lack of clarity about what constituted special educational needs, about the respective responsibilities of schools, LEAs and government, and whether the £2.5 billion spent on SEN in 1992 constituted value for money. The Act introduced a statutory Code of Practice for schools and LEAs, implemented in 1994, for the identification and provision for such children, and which included the need for a special educational needs coordinator (SENCO) in every school, set up a Special Educational Needs Tribunal for parental appeals, and introduced the undemocratic notion that governors of special schools could alone decide that the school should become GM. The Act also introduced fines for parents whose children did not attend school regularly, legislated for the setting up of Pupil Referral Units for excluded and troublesome pupils, and allowed heads more freedom to exclude pupils. Among other miscellaneous provisions it required LEAs to review their agreed syllabi for religious education and made sex education part of the basic (but not the national) curriculum, from which parents could withdraw their children. Teaching about AIDS, HIV or other sexual diseases was to be excluded from National Curriculum science.

Curriculum control

In 1988 central government took substantial and unprecedented control of the school curriculum. The first 25 sections of the 1988 Act legislated for a national curriculum and its assessment, the place of religious education, and disapplication for some children. An NCC was to oversee the development of three core and seven foundation subjects, which were uncannily similar to the subjects laid down by the Board of Education in 1904. Extensive political interference in the development of the National Curriculum created bitter conflicts and disputes; eventually there were substantial changes and a 'slimming down' of the curriculum in 1993 (Dearing 1993). Duncan Graham was appointed as chair of the NCC by Kenneth Baker, who welcomed him with a malt whisky (Graham 1993: 1); Graham left three years later utterly frustrated by the level of political interference by ministers and their advisers, whose mission was a return to 'traditional teaching and Victorian values' (Graham 1993: 5). The National Curriculum, itself an unfortunate title at a time when globalization and internationalism were becoming key words in the economy, was to occupy some 70 per cent of school time in state schools, but private schools were to be exempt and could continue to devise their own curricula. A booklet put out by the DES (1989b) *Your Child and the National Curriculum* attempted to explain to parents the working out of the NC, although it is doubtful how many parents at that time understood the new curriculum language of levels, stages, courses and the graphs of 'average attainment'.

Although there had been and continued to be considerable support for a common curriculum to which all children were entitled, many teachers, parents and others were dismayed at the levels of prescription over both content and assessment, and the removal of any influence on curriculum development by teachers, parents, governors, LEAs and independent bodies. Subject working groups, appointed by the secretary of state, were to devise the programmes of study and attainment targets for each subject; children were to be set Standard Assessment Tasks (SATs) in four key stages at 7, 11, 14 and 16. The ten levels of performance drawn up by the Task Group on Assessment and Testing (TGAT 1987) were to cover the range of progress by individual children, and although the TGAT had given as much weight to teacher assessments as to any tests, these assessments were soon to be ignored. In the three years following the Act an avalanche of curriculum documentation, guidance, circulars and regulations descended on primary and secondary schools; teacher stress and frustration mounted, and 'death by a thousand ring-binders' as one head put it (Graham 1993: 102) became the norm. Although the evidence was that teachers struggled to put in place the new curriculum and its assessment, they soon became aware that it was teachers and schools who were being assessed, and that schools with children who did not appear to be performing well would lose out on resources. Forcing teachers to put in place market-oriented strategies which were largely at odds with their own beliefs about their work led, during the 1990s, to high levels of stress and illness, lower teacher morale, early retirements, and recruitment problems as young people eschewed teaching as a career.

Curriculum critiques

Much criticism of the NC eventually centred on the influence of right-wing bodies and individuals whose confused neo-conservative and neo-liberal agendas ensured that the curriculum became a virtual battleground (see Whitty 1989; Graham 1993; Cox 1995; Phillips 1998). A multicultural working group, set up at Baker's instigation by the NCC, to ensure that multicultural and global perspectives were spread across subjects, received short shrift from ministers of education (Tomlinson 1993). Graham recorded that 'it was made starkly clear to NCC by Ministers that whatever influence it might have would be rapidly dissipated by entering what was widely seen as a no-go area' (Graham 1993: 132). Ray Honeyford, the Bradford headteacher who became noted for his views on the education of ethnic minorities in the early 1980s, wrote in the Conservative journal *The Salisbury Review* that continued references in the NC to cultural diversity, equality for women and handicapped people, and to personal and social education, was evidence that the curriculum was still dominated by left-wing extremists and progressive zealots (Honeyford 1990). Cox, one of the original authors of the early 'Black Papers' (Cox and Dyson 1969; Cox and Boyson 1977) and thought to be safely traditionalist, was put in charge of the working group developing the English curriculum. He became concerned by the 'rhetoric of the right' which incorporated 'myths and fantasies' about left-wing influence and declining standards (Cox 1995: 34–6) and was particularly incensed when false evidence purporting to show a decline in reading standards fuelled a takeover of the NCC by right-wing appointees in 1991. 'How was it possible for Kenneth Clarke to hand over control of NCC and SEAC to a small, extreme, right-wing group?' he asked (Cox 1995: 29).[3] The interference of politicians in the development of the history curriculum has been documented by Phillips (1998), who considered that this period saw the most blatant attempts by the central state to control and influence the subject. Thatcher wrote in her autobiography that she was appalled when the history working group delivered its report (Thatcher 1993: 596) and she attempted to influence the group in a more nationalistic direction, in a manner that was reminiscent of totalitarian regimes of the 1930s. Even the music curriculum became an ideological battleground as the government attempted to divert the curriculum towards classical music and away from popular rock and folk music, complaining that schools were using electric keyboards and guitars, while at the same time policies were removing funding for LEA services for orchestral instrument teaching (Shephard and Vulliamy 1994).

Thatcher eventually expressed 'thorough exasperation' at the complexity of NC proposals, blaming Kenneth Baker, civil servants and teachers who were attempting to carry out unworkable directives; there were other attempts by politicians to distance themselves from the prescriptive and bureaucratic curriculum they had created. Even politicians began to crack under the strain of attempting to force through unworkable measures. By 1993 the NCC was writing that overload was causing 'superficial teaching', especially in primary schools, and teacher frustration was high. Teachers, with the support of parents' organizations, boycotted Key Stage 3 tests, and the then Education Secretary John Patten, voted in an *Observer* survey the worst Education Secretary of the decade, took time off to be ill (Cox 1995: 146). Sir Ron Dearing, a former chairman of the Post Office, who had been appointed the first chair of the new SCAA following the 1993 Act, was appointed to conduct a complete review of the NC; his final report in December 1993 recommended a simplification and slimming down of the whole curriculum. Sir Ron was made a Lord in 1998 by Tony Blair.

The 'levels of performance' for children, now reduced to eight, were no longer to apply after pupils were 14, as 'schools had been given more flexibility to develop courses appropriate to pupils' aptitudes and needs' (Dearing 1993). This meant that some pupils were offered short courses and entry to lower tiers of GCSE, and also that another attempt had been made to develop vocational courses. These were to be general national vocational qualifications (GNVQs), flagged in the White Paper *Education and Training for the 21st Century* (DES/DoE 1991) and developed hastily and at ministerial request by the National Council for Vocational Qualifications, not the DES. The Dearing curriculum review suggested that post-16 there should be a three-track system: an academic route leading to A levels, a vocational route leading to GNVQs and a craft or occupational route leading to NVQs. The report suggested that an occupational or vocational element could be introduced post-14, offered by FE colleges or employers as well as schools, to 'better develop some young people into capable and sensible young men and women' (Dearing 1993: 19). This was, as Tomlinson pointed out, the academic–vocational divide along class lines so familiar in the educational system.

> It is safe to assume that students offered these new courses will be from lower socio-economic and disadvantaged groups, the groups known to be at risk of educational failure, and targeted for low-level training as early as possible.
>
> (Tomlinson 1997c: 6)

Higher education

Further and higher education also came under greater central control during the early 1990s. Higher education had expanded considerably since the recommendations of the Robbins Report (Ministry of Education 1963b) were put into operation and polytechnics created. But universities had been left relatively autonomous, funded by a university-dominated organization, the University Grants Committee (UGC). Polytechnics and HE colleges were the responsibility of local authorities, and their degrees awarded by a Council for National Academic Awards (CNAA). Students on both sides of what became known as the binary line were entitled to state funds for fees and maintenance. The 1988 Act had removed some 30 polytechnics and 50 colleges from local authority control and set up a government-controlled Polytechnic and Colleges Funding Council, while the UGC was replaced by a Universities Funding Council. From 1989 universities were pushed into adopting managerial methods, enhancing their role as entrepreneurs and measuring their performance on quantitative indicators. Vice-chancellors became chief executives of their institutions and senior academics became middle managers. Research and teaching output and quality were increasingly to be measured and funds distributed accordingly. As Barnett put it,

> there was a level of trust in the 1960s towards a relatively small and homogenous sector, that gave way to a determination on the part of the State in the 1990s, to exert a close interest in the re-shaping of higher education and to extract maximum value for money.
>
> (Barnett 1999: 295)

In 1990 an Education (Student Loans) Act was passed which empowered the secretary of state to issue regulations for students to receive loans for maintenance, and the maintenance grant was frozen. Loans were to be repayable when a student's subsequent earnings reached 85 per cent of the national average wage. In 1992 a Further and Higher Education Act ensured that funding for all HE courses was unified and that all HE institutions would in future compete for funding for teaching and research.

Box 3.4 Further and Higher Education Act 1992: main sections

1   FE colleges to become corporations independent of local government and funded by a Further Education Funding Council (FEFC).
2   Sixth-form colleges to leave LEA control and be funded through the FEFC.
3   All HE funding to be unified and funded through Higher Education Funding Councils for England and Wales.
4   Polytechnics and other institutions to become degree-awarding bodies and take the title of university (subject to agreement by the Privy Council). The Council for National Academic Awards to be abolished.
5   Colleges of education would not be permitted to award degrees but could have their degrees validated by a university.

The 1992 Act removed yet more responsibility and financing from local authorities, and set up a centrally controlled Higher Education Funding Council (HEFC) to distribute money to universities in England and Wales and hold them accountable for spending. The HEFC was to be

> an arm of government and an instrument for the implementation of government policy on the universities, which, in the government's view are by their nature and their traditions recalcitrant and tend to defend their own parochial interests against the national interest, as defined by the government of the day.
>
> (Trow 1994: 13)

Polytechnics took advantage of a perceived rise in status by taking the title university and joining the competition for funding, although in the subsequent 'research assessment exercise' (RAE) that allocated research money, 'new' universities took some time to catch up with 'old' universities. A pecking order quickly appeared among the universities, and a group of research-dominated old university vice-chancellors calling themselves the Russell Group (after the hotel they met in) claimed to be at the top. The government had successfully instituted the tactic of divide and rule in higher education.

Teachers and their training

Further control of teachers as a workforce and new modes of teacher management continued to be a feature of government policy and legislation during the 1990s. New management regimes were being put in place in private business, where 'human resource management' was changing organizational cultures, and the development of a market in education demanded new managerial regimes in schools (Hatcher 1994). Teacher pay negotiating rights had been removed in 1987, but there were still national pay scales. In 1990 John MacGregor attempted to create the conditions for local pay scales, and in 1991 his successor Kenneth Clarke introduced the notion of linking appraisal of teachers' performance to their pay, an issue that was taken up enthusiastically by the Labour government at the end of the decade. A Teachers' Pay and Conditions Act 1991 established a review body, with members appointed by the secretary of state to make recommendations about school teachers' pay and conditions. The first chair of this group was Graham Day, a businessman from Rover cars, who had brought total quality management and inter-factory competition to Rover. (Rover was later sold to the German firm BMW; in 2000 sold again after BMW had threatened closure; and called in the receivers in 2005.) The first report from the review body recommended that heads and governors should use appraisal information for promotions and pay increases.

As teachers were gradually stripped of their role as professionals, and were becoming more of a technical workforce to be managed, there was a corresponding focus on their performance and competence in the classroom. Newly qualified teachers were to be subject to profiling and competence-based assessment, and new schemes for training teachers were to be developed, including school-based initial training. A focus on teacher training institutions, which by the 1990s were situated mainly in university departments of education and some HE colleges, with HEFC funding, was inevitable. Much publicity was given to right-wing beliefs that these institutions were hot-beds of left-wing theory, teaching progressive, child-centred methods and producing incompetent teachers who neither knew their subjects nor could keep order in classrooms (Lawlor 1990; Thatcher 1993). Teacher supply, teacher education and quality of teachers were taken seriously and less ideologically by international bodies, and educationists on the left were researching new modes of teacher education and ways of improving quality (Ross and Tomlinson 1991; Barton *et al.* 1994). However, Kenneth Clarke (in a speech to the North of England Conference in January 1992) accepted the view that teacher trainers promoted 'dogmatic orthodoxies' and training should be handed over as far as possible to schools, mostly in partnership with higher education, but with school-centred initial teacher training being advocated as a policy which would minimize HE influence. In 1993 the government published proposals for the reform of teacher training, which in essence were to remove funding for initial teacher education from the HEFC, and hand it over to a Teacher Training Agency (TTA) whose chief executive and members would be appointed by the secretary of state. The education and training of teachers would thus become largely detached from higher education. The Council for the Accreditation of Teacher Education was to be abolished and Ofsted, another quasi-government agency, was to inspect teacher training institutions. The concept of teacher education had by now disappeared from official documents. Proposals that money for educational research be distributed by the TTA were partially defeated after consultation, although the British Educational Research Association recorded its worry that research done under a government directed agency would be unlikely to be impartial.

There was, unsurprisingly, a concerted negative reaction to the proposals and the notion of a Teacher Training Agency from the University Council for the Education of Teachers, all the teaching and lecturers' unions, the Labour Party and shadow ministers, a majority of the House of Lords, and other influential bodies. The Committee of Vice-Chancellors and Principals (CVCP), a body not noted for extreme views, wrote that

> The proposed establishment of a teacher training agency is a further example of the proliferation of government by appointed, unrepresentative bodies. The establishment of such an agency would set a sinister precedent for the future fragmentation of the HE sector.
>
> (CVCP 1993)

The then assistant education secretary at the NUT, Michael Barber, wrote that the TTA would lack political independence, institutions would be subject to political interference, and that Ofsted was an inappropriate body to inspect teacher training (NUT 1993). His views changed considerably when he became a government adviser. Education professors Bolton, Brown and Tomlinson also wrote expressing 'a general concern about the apparent increase in political control which a TTA would bring' (Pyke 1993). Both the NUT and others were strongly in favour of a General Teaching Council to regulate teacher education. Despite opposition, a Bill proposing such an agency was drawn up and became law in 1994, this time as one of the shortest Education Acts passed in the 1990s. The Bill also included a section on the abolition of compulsory membership of student unions, which drew much opposition from students and during debate in the House of Lords. In the Lords debate on the whole Bill (*Hansard* vol. 550, no. 11, 1993) some 37 peers spoke against the Bill and only three were in favour. Lord Glenemara declared that

> The teachers of this country will never forgive the Conservative government for depressing their qualifications, for allowing laymen to organize training courses and to inspect and report on their work. They

will never forgive the government for taking training out of the mainstream of higher education and pushing their profession downmarket.

(*Hansard* vol. 550, no. 11, 1993: 842)

Box 3.5 Education Act 1994: main sections

1 A Teacher Training Agency to be set up, with eight to twelve members appointed by the secretary of state to fund teacher education courses, including school-based courses, the secretary of state giving general directions to the agency (Sections 1–10).
2 The agency to carry out or commission research on training and standards of teaching (Section 11).
3 Schools to be involved or to offer courses in initial teacher training with grants (Sections 12–13).
4 Student unions, their meaning and requirements in relation to such unions to be clarified (Sections 20–22).

Labour education policies in the early 1990s

It is important to ask what alternative policies the Labour Party was developing during the early 1990s. Given the obvious confusion of many of the Conservative reforms, the time was ripe for the presentation of more coherent alternatives. There was no shortage of advice and assistance from educationists and academics who were seriously concerned about the divisive structures of schooling emerging, and the consequent effect on educational performance. The Institute for Public Policy Research (IPPR), a left-of-centre body set up in 1989 by Baroness Blackstone and James Cornford,[4] published a series of education papers between 1990 and 1994, and in 1993 a group of fourteen university professors and a former general secretary of the NUT, Fred Jarvis, published *Education: A Different Vision* (Wragg and Jarvis 1993) as an alternative to the 1992 White Paper. Tomlinson, organizing a seminar on alternative education policies for the IPPR in 1993, wrote that

> a new system of education will express and create the values of an educated democracy; such a system must be truly public, being more than the sum of individual choices, transcending crude, class-based opportunism that competitively seeks education to gain and sustain privilege.
>
> (Tomlinson 1994: 5)

However, Labour politicians were realizing that the Tory electoral success was partly due to the attention paid to the new and aspirant middle class groupings to whom collectivist and egalitarian notions had little appeal, and who could rightly point to the way that upper and middle class groups had always used education to sustain privilege. In 1989, the Labour Party, under Neil Kinnock's leadership, was making a serious attempt to shed its 'militant union cloth-cap image' and begin its campaign, successful in 1997, to capture the middle ground of British politics, speaking to middle class and aspirant working class groups (Gould 1998). The Labour Party (1989, 1990) published Policy Review documents in 1989 and 1991, and began to develop a series of education policies, which would focus on raising educational standards, but in partnership with teachers, parents, and local government rather than as antagonists. Between 1990 and 1994 over 30 policy documents on education were published, some in-house and some glossy documents for press attention.[5] Jack Straw, Shadow Education Secretary 1987–92, was influenced by 1980s research into effective schooling, and his advisory group spent much time developing the idea of an Educational Standards Council or Commission, which by 1997 became a DfEE-based Schools Standards and Effectiveness Unit. Labour's problem was that it could not be seen to be against choice and the workings of the market, but was well aware of the inequalities this produced. Until 1994 it was policy to attack the underfunding of state education, and selection and privatization, promising the return of GM schools and CTCs to the local authority fold.

There was particular concern for early years education, for the education of 14–16-year-olds and for reform of post-16 education and training. In 1991 Jack Straw and Tony Blair, then Shadow Employment Secretary, produced a paper on *Today's Education and Training: Tomorrow's Skills*, in which they argued for a unified qualifications structure leading to an advanced certificate in education and training for all young people at 18, with NCVQ and SEAC merged to become a Joint Qualifications Board, and a flexible curriculum from 14 which avoided 'the development of selection at 14, with a hard academic model of the national curriculum for the brighter children and a softer version for others' (Straw and Blair 1991: 10). They were concerned that the government at this time was encouraging a two-tier system of the grammar and secondary modern schools to be recreated in comprehensive schools. Also in 1991 Neil Kinnock set up a European Inquiry Team to study the post-16 arrangements of other European countries. Derek Fatchett,[6] who chaired this group, produced coherent proposals for a 14–19 curriculum embracing both academic, vocational and work-related courses for all students, leading both to the advanced certificate in education and training, and to higher education.

But the fourth successive defeat of Labour in 1992 caused some reappraisal of policy, including the possibility that Labour would drop its opposition to GM schools. In an invited selection of comments on Labour education policy published in the *Times Educational Supplement* (*TES* 15 May 1992) the principal of Cheltenham Ladies' College warned that Labour should accept the continued existence of schools which 'enjoyed considerable popular support' – private and GM schools. However, David Miliband, then an IPPR researcher, later to become head of the Downing Street Policy Unit, commented that Britain still educated elites and that selection and hierarchies of schools should be abolished. Ann Taylor, Shadow Education Secretary 1992–4, did consult widely on policy, and did attempt to marry 'old Labour' beliefs in comprehensive education with new ideas, but her 1994 consultative paper on education, *Opening Doors to a Learning Society* (Labour Party 1994), was disliked by Tony Blair (elected party leader in July 1994)[7] who, with his new Shadow Education Secretary David Blunkett, set about suggesting ways in which GM and specialist schools could continue under different guises. At the October 1994 party conference Blair avoided policy promises, but did move towards the Conservative agenda of attacking schools and teachers for educational problems, claiming that education would be a 'passion' in his administration, and that he 'would not tolerate children going to run-down schools, with bad discipline, low standards, mediocre expectations or poor teachers' (Hackett 1994). The party was about to enter a period when Labour education policies would be carefully geared to 'middle England' voter aspirations, which proved electorally successful for the party in 1997, but which led to antagonisms between Old Labour supporters of non-selective schooling and New Labour policies. The latter continued to espouse a market in schooling and new forms of specialization which inevitably encouraged selection.

Notes

1 The author was a member of Shadow Education Secretary Jack Straw's Advisory Group 1990–2 and a member of Neil Kinnock's European Inquiry Team; she assisted Ann Taylor 1992–4.
2 The director of the Grant-Maintained Schools Trust was Andrew Taylor, a former Conservative education researcher. He appeared ten years later at the 1999 Conservative Party conference still confident that all schools would eventually be allowed to opt out of LEA control.
3 In 1991 David Pascall, an oil executive who had been a Thatcher policy adviser, replaced Duncan Graham as chair of NCC, and the chair at SEAC went to Lord (Brian) Griffiths, a former head of the Downing Street Policy Unit.
4 Baroness Blackstone became Minister for Higher Education in 1997 and James Cornford was an adviser in the Cabinet Office.
5 Many of the papers were written by Richard Margrave, adviser to Jack Straw 1989–92 and later Head of Communications for the Association of Teachers and Lecturers. The advisory group was coordinated by Paul Corrigan, a former Head of Sociology at the University of North London and Labour Education Officer until 1994.
6 Derek Fatchett became a Foreign Office minister in 1997 but died in 1998.
7 Denis Lawton later wrote that 'Ann Taylor's Green Paper was a serious and

successful attempt to combine Labour Party ethical values and principles with the needs of a modernising society' (Lawton 2005: 120).

Further reading

Gewirtz, S., Ball, S.J. and Bowe, R. (1995) *Markets, Choice and Equity in Education*. Buckingham: Open University Press. Based on excellent research, this book examines the complexities of parental choice and school responses to the introduction of market forces.

Lawton, D. (1994) *The Tory Mind on Education 1979–1994*. London: Falmer. This book summarizes and comments on Conservative education legislation to 1994, and points out that ideological preferences for outdated traditional education led to missed opportunities for positive educational reform.

Tomlinson, S. (ed.) (1994) *Educational Reform and its Consequences*. London: Rivers-Oram Press for IPPR. The contributors to this book question whether educational reforms to 1994 would improve standards or distribute resources fairly and describe a vision of an educated democracy in which a good education would form the basis for an inclusive economic, political and cultural order.

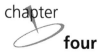
The consequences of competition: education 1994–97

This chapter continues to describe the attempts made during the 1990s by the Conservative government to recreate a selective system of school education, as it tried to move more schools into the GM sector, with a three-track route for pupils from 14 between academic, vocational and practical work-oriented courses, and an expanded but more tightly controlled HE sector. The chapter notes the increasing educational divide along lines of social class which market force was exacerbating. Despite a trade in political insults – the secretary of state declared in 1994 that the Labour Party had had no coherent education policies for fifteen years and were opposed to changes designed to raise standards (Gillian Shephard quoted in Ribbins and Sherratt 1997: 208) – by the mid-1990s there was considerable overlap between Conservative policies and those being developed by the shadow Labour government, now styling itself 'New Labour'. Both parties were committed to the notion of raising standards, which since the publication of league tables of public examination results was now largely defined as an increase in pupils obtaining five GCSEs at A to C grades, to targets for education and training, and to improving basic literacy.

Although retaining a commitment to the abolition of assisted places in private schools, Labour had become equivocal on the outright abolition of selection, although the Shadow Education Secretary, David Blunkett, did ensure some future embarrassment for himself by declaring in a speech at the 1995 Labour Party Conference: 'Let me say this very slowly, in fact if you can watch my lips – no selection either by examination or interview under a Labour government'. He later claimed that he had said no 'more' selection. The Opposition had also become equivocal on the fate of the remaining grammar schools and the future of GM schools, and had embraced the notion of specialist schools. Both parties were committed to teacher appraisal and control of teachers' work, and although Labour supported the creation of a General Teaching Council, originally envisaged along the lines of the General Medical Council, it had abandoned previous opposition to the Teacher Training Agency and to Ofsted as a method of policing schools and teachers. Both parties, for different political reasons, were focusing on the development of early years education, the 'naming and shaming' and possible closure of 'failing' schools, and further reduction in LEA powers. This chapter details some of the policies developed by shadow ministers 1994–97, as the Labour Party did have a raft of policies, initiatives and legislation to put into place after winning the general election on 1 May 1997.

Box 4.1 Chronology of Acts, reports and events 1995–97

1995   (June) *Diversity and Excellence: A New Partnership for Schools* (Labour Party)

1995   (June) *Performance in City Schools* (House of Commons Education Committee)

1995   (July) Department for Education merged with Department of Employment to become Department for Education and Employment (DfEE)

1995   Disability Discrimination Act

1995   (December) *Excellence for Everyone: Labour's Crusade to Raise Standards* (Labour Party)

1995   National targets for education and training revised

1996   (February) *Education and Training for 14–19 Year Olds* (House of Commons Education and Employment Committee)

1996   (March) Dearing Report *Review of Qualifications for 16–19 Year Olds*

1996   Ofsted Report *The Implementation of the Code of Practice for Pupils with Special Educational Needs*

1996   (March) *Aiming Higher: Labour's Proposals for the Reforms of the 14–19 Curriculum* (Labour Party)

1996   Education (Student Loans) Act

1996   (July) Nursery and Grant-Maintained Schools Act

1996   (November) *Early Excellence: A Headstart for Every Child* (Labour Party)

1996   (November) Education (Schools) Act (consolidating Act)

1996   (November) Education (Schools Inspection) Act (consolidating Act)

1996   (December) *Learning to Compete: Education and Training for 14–19 Year Olds* (DfEE)

1996   White Paper *Self Government for Schools* (DfEE)

1996   (November) Education Bill

1996   National Literacy Project proposed

1997   (March) Education Act

1997   (May) Labour government elected

Education Secretary of State (from July 1995 Secretary of State for Education and Employment)

Gillian Shephard 1994–97

Shadow Education Secretary

David Blunkett 1994–97

Legislation 1995–96

The year 1995 was a quiet one as far as educational legislation was concerned. Apart from a merger between the Department for Education and the Department of Employment, the whole to be known as the DfEE, with one secretary of state in overall charge, no new legislation appeared on the statute books. However, in 1996 the lawyers appeared to go into overdrive as four Education Acts were passed. The first of these was a second Education (Student Loans) Act. The 1990 Act had allowed for the setting up of a private Student Loans Company, to provide loans to HE students out of public funds; the 1996 Act allowed for private sector bodies, such as banks and building societies, to lend money for student maintenance, but not for fees. A Teaching and Higher Education Act effectively repealed much of this Act in 1998. Two further Acts were consolidating Acts,[1] passed on the recommendation of the Law Commission, which was of the opinion that there had been so much change to education law that certain functions needed clarification. Jonathan Robinson (1994), lecturer in law at Buckingham University, had pointed out that the pace and change in the law of education had led to a substantial increase in litigation and complaints to the secretary of state and to the local Ombudsman.

Disquiet about the extent and consequences of educational change was also expressed by the all-party House of Commons Education Committee, which published its inquiry into educational expenditure in England and Wales in 1995. The report noted that in real terms expenditure on education had not increased since 1992 and that local authorities were to have their Standard Spending Assessments reduced by 2 per cent up to 1998.[2] The committee expressed the view that since there were to be cuts in resources, efforts should be made to 'avoid sudden and unreasonable change in education' (House of Commons Education Committee 1995a: 6).

The first consolidating Act, passed in November 1996, clarified the stages of education as primary, secondary and further education, and reiterated the duties of the FEFC with respect to further education. It laid out that the duty of secretaries of state, as in 1944, was to 'promote the education of the people of England and Wales', but that they were now empowered to transfer their funding powers to Trusts and governing bodies of GM schools, CTCs and City Colleges of Technology and Arts (CCTAs). LEAs were to 'contribute towards spiritual, moral, mental and physical development by securing effective primary, secondary and further education to meet the needs of local populations' and also promote high standards of education (Education (Schools) Act 1996 Chapter 3). LEAs were also reminded that they had a responsibility (but not a duty) to establish maintained nursery schools and classes for under-5s, provide suitable full- or part-time education for children who were ill, excluded or otherwise out of school, either in schools, at Pupil Referral Units (PRUs), or with home tuition, and LEAs were also to arrange for the education of some children at fee-paying schools. This last requirement was meant to take care of the growing number of cases where parents whose children were designated as having special educational needs were requesting private education. The duties of the FAS were also clarified, although this was to be abolished in 1998. Further consolidation measures clarified the establishment of county and voluntary schools and their funding. LEAs were now to assist in setting up new voluntary schools, as under the 1993 legislation, religious groups other than Catholic, Anglican and Jewish could be funded to set up schools. There was still equivocation, however, concerning the setting up of state-funded Muslim schools. Much of this was repealed or negated by Acts and regulations after 1997.

A further consolidating Act was the Education (Schools Inspection) Act 1996, which clarified the functions of the chief inspectors for schools for England and Wales, and that of the registered and specialist inspectors. It reiterated the procedures for inspection, destination of inspection reports, the powers over schools thought to require special measures, the responsibility of LEAs to make a statement of proposed action for these schools, and the function of education associations, the only one set up under the 1993 Act, having (as noted) been challenged in the High Court. Although the Secretary of State for Education, Gillian Shephard, denied that Ofsted was a politicized body (Shephard quoted in Ribbins and Sherratt 1997: 224), Ofsted had in fact become an important tool for the government in driving the choice agenda, as knowledgeable parents studied Ofsted reports to discover the 'best' schools, and also as an ally in criticizing the mainly Labour-controlled LEAs which incorporated most of the schools considered to be 'failing'. Thus, the 1994–5 annual report by the Chief Inspector of Schools, Chris Woodhead, named and praised 32 schools which had achieved 'excellent GCSE results sustained over a number of years', the majority of these schools being existing grammar schools and other selective schools, while criticizing 'schools serving areas of disadvantage where pupils continue to perform below their capabilities' (Ofsted 1996b: 17). This report, presented in all seriousness, presumably unwittingly parodied the differential resources available to schools serving different social classes with different histories of resources and opportunities. Thus, a college in Sussex was praised for its musical links with Glyndebourne, and a CTC funded by both public money and business was praised for its links with industry, which included 'business breakfasts'.

The Nursery and Grant-Maintained Schools Act, passed in July 1996, was intended to be important legislation in the continued drive towards more GM schools. These schools were to be enabled to borrow money from private sources and offer security for their borrowing, thus increasing their resources and autonomy. The Act also saw the return of the voucher in the form of nursery vouchers, which were to be exchanged for pre-school education in state, voluntary or private provision. A scheme to offer vouchers to parents had been piloted in several areas during 1995–6 and a DfEE publication in January 1996 outlined *Nursery Education: The Next Steps* (DfEE 1996c). The Act allowed grants to LEAs for schools with nursery education and to 'other persons' in respect of nursery education for 4-year-olds. The LEA was to offer parents a 'piece of paper, which for convenience sake we will call a voucher', as a minister described it during the passage of the Bill, which could then be exchanged for either state or private nursery education. The pilot schemes had already begun to create the intended competition between private, voluntary and state pre-school providers as schools planned more nursery provision to attract the vouchers, and some voluntary pre-school playgroups closed down (Blackburne 1996). The Labour Party pledged to end the voucher scheme, integrate the education and care of under-5s into an early years service, and set up pilot Early Excellence Centres. The incoming Labour government scrapped the voucher scheme, intended to be in operation nationally by April 1997.

The final Tory Act

At their October party conference in 1996 the Conservative government, embarking on what turned out to be its final parliamentary session after eighteen years in power, promised yet another Education Act and produced a White Paper which proposed that schools be able to select larger numbers of pupils without seeking approval from the secretary of state, with GM schools able to select up to 50 per cent of pupils, specialist schools 30 per cent and local authority schools 20 per cent. Comprehensive schools would be enabled to set up grammar school streams and governors would be required to consider annually whether to increase selection in their schools (DfEE 1996b). The proposals were opposed by all the teacher unions and the Society for Education Officers, the main objection being the 'nightmare for parents' of admissions procedures, especially if they made multiple applications to schools and appealed on rejection (Hackett 1996). The Secondary Heads

Association described the proposals as 'incoherent, unfair, divisive, cost ineffective, administratively burdensome and potentially gender-biased . . . with sink schools filled with disaffected and demoralized boys' (Young 1996: 3). Undeterred, the government produced a Bill intended to increase selection, boost private education by extending assisted places to private preparatory schools and further reduce LEAs' powers by allowing for their inspection by Ofsted. Labour opposed much of the Bill during debate over the winter of 1996–7, and then incorporated parts of it into its own legislation and policy after the 1997 general election.

The Act notionally became law in March 1997. Part 1 of this Act (never implemented) referred to the assisted places scheme, at that time costing the taxpayer some £100 million, and proposed extending the scheme to pupils at private preparatory schools where parents were already paying for their children, much being made in debate of the sacrifices of holidays and other treats by these parents! Part 2 laid out rules on school discipline, legislating on such issues as restraint of pupils, detention, and the use of exclusion from school. During debate on this section of the Bill the reintroduction of corporal punishment was sought by some Conservatives, and even Gillian Shephard gave her personal view that 'corporal punishment can be a useful deterrent' (Gardiner 1996b). Part 3 incorporated much of the White Paper's proposals on selection and school admissions. Part 4 introduced the notion of baseline assessment for children entering school reception classes at 5, a proposal accepted by Labour, and which led some parents, who did not understand that such assessment was not intended as a test, to vie with each other as to whether their child had 'passed' the baseline assessment.[3] Part 5 was concerned with the curriculum and qualifications and proposed that the SCAA and the NCVQ be merged. Labour too supported this and the two organizations became the Qualifications and Curriculum Authority (QCA) in October 1997. Part 6 allowed the Chief Inspector of Schools to inspect LEAs if required to do so by the secretary of state, a move also eagerly accepted by the incoming Labour government.

The effects of market forces

By the mid-1990s inequalities in income had accelerated and it had become commonplace to speak of a widening gap between rich and poor families. The Thatcher government had encouraged income inequality as a supposed incentive to work, with the result that poverty, on any definition, had increased. On a European Community definition, the proportion of individuals in poverty in Britain rose from 8 per cent in 1979 (4 million people) to 19 per cent in 1993 (10.7 million people; Walker and Walker 1997: 20). Low income families were increasingly concentrated in certain geographical areas, especially disadvantaged estates in inner cities and outer rings, while other urban and suburban areas became steadily more prosperous. John Major had claimed, in a foreword to *Choice and Diversity* (DfE 1992), that he was 'not prepared to see children in some parts of the country having to settle for a second-class education'. But the creation of a market in education, driven by the self-interest of knowledgeable parents and the competitive strategies of schools which had been forced, with varying degrees of reluctance, to market their schools to attract desirable customers, was ensuring a first and second class division in state schooling.

The Child Poverty Action Group, examining access to educational resources, access to provision by choice policies, the outcomes of education, and the costs to families (meals, clothing, school trips and so on) demonstrated that the much hyped policies of choice and diversity were being translated into divisions and inequalities in provision. It concluded that 'many children in poor areas continue to receive far less than a first class education' (Smith and Noble 1995: 136). A study by HMI on *Access and Achievement in Urban Areas* had also concluded that, although schools could do much to improve their own effectiveness,

> schools in disadvantaged areas do not have the capacity for sustainable renewal . . . beyond the school gates are underlying social issues such as poverty, unemployment, poor housing, inadequate health care and the frequent break-up of families.
>
> (Ofsted 1993: 45)

This was also the view of the House of Commons Education Committee (1995b) who examined performance in city schools in the session 1994–5. The committee pointed out problems of the choice policies, especially the poorer exam results of some schools which, when published in league table form, 'creates a poor reputation, leading to the flight of more mobile, better-off parents, which creates empty places filled by pupils excluded from other schools' (House of Commons 1995b: 1 vii).

Evidence from around the world was demonstrating that choice policies increased social class segregation in schools (Organization for Economic Cooperation and Development (OECD) 1994) and academic studies, notably the seminal studies carried out by Stephen Ball and his colleagues at King's College London (Ball 1990; Bowe *et al.* 1992; Gewirtz *et al.* 1995; Ball *et al.* 1996) were demonstrating the advantages that choice policies gave to middle class parents, and the resulting 'de-comprehensivization' of secondary schools, as schools increasingly sought to select desirable pupils (see Chapter 6). In England and Wales these effects should not have been surprising, as they were a logical result of policies intended to demonstrate that the pursuit of equality was indeed over.

However, influential figures on the left were also now extolling choice policies, blaming schools, teachers and the 'educational establishment' for failure to improve education and arguing that a selective schools system, with streams within schools, was the key to raised standards. Stephen Pollard, director of research at the Fabian Society, historically the intellectual but compassionate arm of the Labour Party, produced a diatribe for the right-wing Social Market Foundation in 1995, arguing that inner city schools fail because the schools and staff are 'simply incapable of doing the job required of them' (Pollard 1995: 3) and that 'Middle-class *Guardian*-reading liberals continue to worship at the shrine of their comprehensive ideals, whilst bemoaning the fact that their local school is unfortunately not good enough for Amanda or Henry so, much as it pains them, they have to send them to private school'. Pollard later co-authored a book with Andrew Adonis, suggesting that pupil selection in comprehensive schools would bring back the Amandas and Henrys (Adonis and Pollard 1997). Adonis, a former journalist, was appointed in 1998 to advise the Downing Street Policy Unit on education.[4] Will Hutton (1995), author of the best selling *The State We're In*, also argued that 'grammar schools and grammar school streams need to be revived in order to attract members of the middle class back to the state system' (Hutton 1995: 311). Whether promising small numbers of well-off middle class parents that they could get a good free education separated from undesirable children was the way to raise standards for all, had always seemed a curious argument.

Failing schools

Policy convergence between Conservative and Labour governments was most observable over one of the cruellest and most pointless policies developed in the wake of the Education Act 1993 – that of attacking so-called 'failing schools'. These were demonized individual schools, most of which were former secondary modern schools or comprehensives serving disadvantaged working class areas, whose heads, teachers and governors were held to be personally responsible for the underperformance of pupils. Press coverage of failing schools was negative and derisory, as the media competed to discover 'the worst school in Britain', an accolade handed out to different schools every few months (Brace 1994). Politicians, particularly as the 1997 general election approached, competed to demonstrate their 'zero tolerance . . . of school failure' (Blair 1996: 12). The failing schools legislation was set out in a DfE circular which explained that the Education (Schools) Act 1992 and the 1993 Act could lead to special measures being taken when a school is 'failing or likely to fail to give its pupils an acceptable standard of education'. Criteria for failure were set out in the Ofsted *Framework for the Inspection of Schools* and in *Technical Paper 13 of the Ofsted Handbook for the Inspection of Schools* (Ofsted 1995). Deficiencies included poor standards of achievement in NC subjects, poor quality of education (measured by low expectations, demoralization and disenchantment among staff and high staff turnover), inefficiency in the running of the school (including resources and budgets), and also disruptive behaviour, truancy, and high levels of racial tension. Failing schools were officially regarded as operating divorced from historical, economic, social, political and educational contexts, and staff in post at 'failing time' were held responsible for the effects of long-term central and local political decisions plus most of society's problems (Tomlinson 1997a).

Although the notion of the failing school was a deliberate policy invention, it was also a result of the introduction of market forces, as parental choice was to be the mechanism by which schools gained or lost pupils, money and resources. Schools which lost desirable customers or, ironically, took in those pupils regarded as undesirable – notably pupils with special needs, disaffected pupils, those excluded from other schools and second language speakers – became easy targets for the failing label. The first survey of 92 failing schools did show that the majority of the schools served areas of poverty and deprivation. This survey, produced for an OECD seminar held at the London Institute of Education, noted that 'there is certainly a link between socio-economic deprivation and the likelihood of a school found to be failing'. Only 17 per cent of schools nationally had disadvantaged pupils, while some 70 per cent of failing schools educated such pupils (Ofsted/ OECD 1995: 12). Attacking failing schools was a convenient way for the Conservative government to shore up its failing policy of persuading more schools to go grant-maintained. As noted in Chapter 3, schools not improved by their governing bodies or local authorities could be put under an education association, a body appointed by the secretary of state to be 'effectively in the position of a grant-maintained governing body. At the end of its stewardship the normal expectation is that the school will become grant-maintained' (DfE 1992: 50–1). It was also envisaged that an education association would 'control as many schools in an area including neighbouring LEAs as were found to be failing'. However, after the first education association to be appointed had its recommended closure of Hackney Downs School questioned in the High Court (O'Connor *et al.* 1999) and the council in neighbouring Haringey promised court action when similarly threatened by the North East London Education Association (Gardiner 1996a) the government abandoned this form of political intervention.

The failing schools policy was, however, embraced by the Labour Party, which continued to support the 'naming and shaming' of individual schools (Carvel 1997a). The policy was defended by both Conservative and Labour policymakers, who used academic research into school effectiveness (see Sammons *et al.* 1995) to demand lists of factors which made schools effective – not to develop policies to assist weaker schools, but to castigate those which did not measure up on effective factors. By the mid-1990s schools were expected to improve, develop and manage themselves effectively, to reach government targets for examination passes and improve on these year by year. Schools which found themselves in financial difficulty, had problems with their pupil intakes or could not raise exam results were likely to be put, at the instigation of Ofsted, under special measures. Hamilton suggested in 1996 that politicians had adopted a Social Darwinist view of schools: 'Some schools have become sick institutions, they are regarded as a threat to the health of the economic order' (Hamilton 1996: 1). It had begun to appear that politicians who attacked the deficiencies of individual schools and their personnel were attempting to deflect attention away from more basic political and economic concerns. Structural changes in the economy had led to the need to ensure that, for the first time in Britain, all young people were educated to higher levels than ever before. It had become easier to blame schools than to concentrate on restructuring the economy to ensure that all young people had an economic future.

Special educational needs

In contrast to the harsh policies directed towards failing schools, and with a curious disregard that many of these schools contained disproportionate numbers of children with special educational needs, SEN policies during the mid-1990s were more coherent and humane. Reasons for this were complex, but the expansion of the sub-sector of special education, despite a rhetoric of integration and inclusion, was partly a result of 'de-comprehensivization': if selection of the able was permissible, so was selection of the less able or disabled. It was also a result of market forces which encouraged schools either to get rid of such children or to claim the resources to keep them in mainstream, which, under the 1993 Act, LEAs were expected to provide for children with SEN. Middle class parents, who until the 1970s had usually objected to their children entering most forms of special education, began to claim additional help and resources, notably for the specific learning difficulty known as dyslexia, first recognized under the Employment Act 1970.

Claims for rights and resources for children with SEN were enhanced by the global lobby for *Equal Rights for Disabled People*, as a paper commissioned by the Institute for Public Policy Research put it (Bynoe *et al.* 1991). This paper argued that there should be 'a framework of enforceable citizens rights, as the basic structure around which welfare services and facilities can be organised' (Bynoe *et al.* 1991: 3). Public services should not be seen as privileges conferred by the judgements of experts, but as equal rights. International claims for basic civil rights influenced the government in drawing up a Disability Discrimination Act in 1995. Disability was defined as 'A physical or mental impairment, which has a substantial or long-term effect on a person's ability to carry out normal day-to-day activities'. *Booklet D100* (Minister for the Disabled 1996) laid out the requirements of the Act for schools, further and higher education, echoing the 1993 Act that LEAs had a duty to place children in mainstream schools if it was appropriate to the child's needs, did not conflict with the interests of other children, and was an efficient use of the LEAs' resources. Schools must continue to publish their SEN policies and explain how they would ensure equal treatment for disabled children.

The Disability Discrimination Act had an overt focus on physical and sensory disability, although the majority of children regarded by the mid-1990s as 'having SEN' were children with learning and behavioural problems, which many schools would have liked to see moved out of mainstream education, but which government, mindful of the cost of any form of special education, wished to see retained in schools. The Code of Practice, which from September 1994 all schools were required to 'have regard to', was an attempt at a national policy to ensure that schools took as much responsibility for all children as possible, and that LEAs carried out their statutory obligations. There was considerable potential for conflict here as LEAs did not have enough money to fund the increasing demands for extra resources. The basic principles of the Code were that there was a 'continuum of needs and provision'; all children should have access to a broad and balanced curriculum, including the NC; most children should stay in mainstream with or without a statutory assessment and statement; and that there should be partnership between schools, LEAs, other services and parents. There were to be five stages of help for children with special educational needs, the first three based in schools with external help if needed, the last two bringing in the LEA and its specialists (DfE 1994b). Identified children should have an individual education plan (IEP) drawn up for them, and under the Education Act 1988, could have their curriculum modified or be disapplied from following the National Curriculum and its assessment. The DfE issued a booklet *Special Educational Needs: A Guide for Parents* in 1994 and in 1996 Ofsted carried out a survey of 62 schools in 8 LEAs to report on the implementation of the Code of Practice. This found that most of the schools were having regard to the code and had appointed the required SENCO from among existing staff to identify and make arrangements for children with SEN, but school governors were poorly informed about SEN, schools were still excluding disruptive children (Ofsted 1996a) and there were problems with curriculum provision.

Curriculum issues

Whether or not children with special educational needs were being offered the broad and balanced curriculum that the 1988 Act had promised all children, the mid-1990s saw a distinct convergence of curriculum policy between the Conservative government and New Labour. Up to 1994 Labour was attacking the National Curriculum as 'an educational straitjacket which confines and dictates what can and cannot be taught' (Hansard 1993: vol. 194, 20 April), and supporting teacher boycotts of testing. However, the slimmed-down NC suggested by Ron Dearing (1993) was acceptable to both parties as a way of saving political face and avoiding any return to basic questions about the kinds of knowledge all young people in a democracy were entitled to have access to, the organization and transmission of knowledge, and the interactions between teachers and learners.

Policy convergence between the Conservative government and the ensuing Labour government was most clearly demonstrated over the imposition of detailed frameworks for the teaching of literacy and numeracy. The Conservative approach, still heavily influenced by right-wing traditionalists (Chew 1990; Turner 1990) was based on the unprovable assertion that literacy standards had been lowered by trendy teaching and progressive methods. A report on the teaching of reading in three inner London boroughs, produced by Ofsted in May 1996 (Ofsted 1996b) was 'amended' by Chris Woodhead, the Chief Inspector of Schools, who deleted sections noting that factors outside school control – poverty, bilingualism, high staff turnover – affected pupil progress, but left in criticisms of teachers and their methods. Professors at the Institute of Education in London pointed out methodological weaknesses in the Ofsted report, and the chairman of council of one of the boroughs surveyed observed that 'Mr Woodhead is as much use in the battle for higher standards as a chocolate teapot' (MacCleod 1996: 2). However, the government had developed a National Literacy Project by December 1996, prescribing the teaching of reading and number in detail, setting up pilot centres for literacy and numeracy in 25 LEAs, and planning the training of consultants and key teachers in the preferred methods (Hofkins 1996). All this was to be incorporated into the policy of literacy and numeracy hours for all primary schools after Labour came to power.

Labour had set up its own Literacy Task Force in May 1996, appointing as the chair the ubiquitous Michael Barber.[5] The Task Force recommended new national targets for reading: Barber enthused about how this could be done in his book *The Learning Game* (Barber 1996). At the Labour Party conference in October 1996, party leader Tony Blair set out the three main priorities for his first government. They were to be 'Education, Education, Education' with promises of literacy summer schools and raised targets for reading and maths in national tests (Blair 1996).

Labour had by now done a U-turn on its promises to abolish national league tables of exam results based on raw scores at GCSE level, and had converged with the Conservative view that international comparisons of numeracy and literacy levels, particularly with economically competitive countries, demonstrated a failure of teaching methods. Both major political parties and their advisers had become adept at selectively drawing on international data on literacy and numeracy, for example three large-scale international maths and science surveys and an international assessment of educational progress, drawn together by Reynolds and Farrell (1996) in an Ofsted commissioned report. Margaret Brown (1998), Professor of Mathematics Education at King's College London, later pointed out that this report did not mention a major finding of the surveys reviewed, which was that no effect on attainment in maths due to different teaching methods had ever been detected and also that in some aspects, logic and problem-solving, English pupils did better than all others. She also pointed out that 'in spite of misleading ways of presenting results, especially the league table rankings, the reality is . . . that England tends to perform in maths in a similar way to most European/Anglophone countries' (Brown 1998: 43).

By 1996 the proportion of pupils gaining five GCSE A–C grades was 44.5 per cent, a 1 per cent increase from the previous year, and there were suggestions that schools were concentrating on D-grade students in efforts to boost their league table rankings (Pyke 1996). However, reactions to even this modest evidence that more pupils were achieving to higher levels brought accusations that standards were being lowered and exams made too easy. Faced with more competition the Headmasters' Conference, representing top private schools, demanded a higher level academic exam and more vocational qualifications 'for the weaker brethren, to avoid the erosion of the A-level gold standard' (Bright 1996).

Ages 14–19 and the academic–vocational divide

Throughout the 1980s and early 1990s the government had attempted to deal with the growing number of young working class school leavers for whom, as manual work disappeared and manufacturing industries contracted, there were no jobs. A plethora of youth training schemes, provided by the MSC, the Training Agency and TECs, were offered in place of any unified coherent system of education and training. Education for young people post-14 and particularly post-16 continued to develop in the 1990s as a divided, fragmented system in curricula, assessment, institutional, organizational and funding terms. Development was hampered by a legal school leaving age of 16, despite the fact that some 70 per cent now stayed in some form of education as jobs disappeared; by a jungle of competing qualification offered by bodies with vested interests; by the market system developed after the Higher and Further Education Act 1992, which set FE and sixth-form colleges and schools with sixth-forms against each other in competition for funds; and by the determination to retain the A level exam as a 'gold standard'. This was despite a plethora of calls from an astonishing number of organizations calling for reform of the post-14 curriculum and its assessment (see Finegold *et al.* 1990; Hodgson and Spours 1997; Tomlinson 1997b).

Money given for TVEIs in schools between 1984 and 1991 was used creatively by many schools and colleges in an attempt to bridge the academic–vocational divide, which was the inevitable consequence of the selection of elites for a liberal academic education and the provision of a practical vocational education for the mass (Pring 1995). GNVQs continued to be developed by the National Council for Vocational Qualifications, in addition to occupationally oriented NVQs. But, mindful of the votes of the middle and aspirant middle classes, a political consensus emerged across left and right to preserve A levels as a major route into higher education, and encourage the young 'non-academic' working class youth on to work-related courses from 14. These views did not go unchallenged. A report by the Royal Society of Arts in February 1995 called for a common core curriculum for all young people from 14 to bridge the academic–vocational divide, with a modular framework and with a unified qualifications system (White *et al.* 1995). A House of Commons Education and Employment Committee (1996) report noted that the government was now talking about a 'learning society' and continuous education and training throughout life but the structure of the education system with the break at 16 impeded this.[6]

In April 1995 Ron Dearing, who had 'slimmed down' the NC in 1993, was asked by the secretary of state to review qualifications for 16–19-year-olds, while 'maintaining the rigour of A levels'. His report (Dearing 1996) recommended a national framework for qualifications at advanced, intermediate, foundation and entry level, and a consolidation of the three-track system of the academic route of A, advanced supplementary (A/S) and GCSE, the route of GNVQs and that of NVQs. The introduction of such courses as NVQ catering and construction for 14-year-olds and of work-related part one GNVQs in schools, and suggestions that lower achievers leave school to attend FE colleges, were all, as was the secondary modern curriculum in the 1940s, defended as desired by and more suitable for the children of the old manual working class. The children of politicians, civil servants and government advisers continued, as always, on academic routes in either state or private education.

A DfEE White Paper (published in December 1996) summed up what was expected of all young people 14–19 in its title, *Learning to Compete: Education and Training for 14–19 Year Olds*. According to this paper, all young people, due to reforms in schools, in post-16 education and training, especially output-related funding (paying colleges by results) 'now have every opportunity to reach their potential' (DfEE 1996a: 10). Young people were exhorted to make themselves employable by acquiring skills and knowledge, especially the key skills of working with others, improving their own learning and performance, being adaptable and managing their own careers throughout their lives. Employers, the beneficiaries of 14–19 learning, were only, in contrast, 'invited' to take some action to improve education and training.

Labour policies

The remaking of the Labour Party as New Labour under the leadership of Tony Blair has been documented in numerous books (see for example Anderson and Mann 1997; Brivati and Bale 1997; Driver and Martell 1998; Gould 1998) and much of the comment on education reflects a mixture of despair and admiration as the politicians took over and reworked many of the Conservative education policies, ditching as 'Old Labour' commitments to free comprehensive education from nursery to higher education, and under a rhetoric of 'standards, not structures', retaining the divisive school structures and funding mechanisms of the education market. Ann Taylor's *Opening Doors to a Learning Society* (Labour Party 1994) was the last Old Labour document, and she was moved from her post as Shadow Education Secretary as soon as Blair was elected party leader. A significant feature of the three years before Labour won the general election in 1997 was the way in which the Shadow Education Secretary David Blunkett took a lead on policy initiatives and prepared the outlines of policies that were speedily implemented, usually with support from the Treasury, as soon as the new government came to power.[7] Hodgson and Spours (1999) were to remark that the party took different positions on compulsory and post-compulsory education – education up to 16 being characterized by a continuation of Conservative measures to centralize, regulate and control, post-16 education and training policies being more cautious and voluntarist (Hodgson and Spours 1999: 2), at least until 2000.

Party policy in the mid-1990s was cautiously critical of the three-track qualification routes and the academic–vocational divide. Just before his election as party leader Blair, speaking at Manchester College of Art and Technology (4 July 1994), 'wondered whether the A-level system, which condemns two-thirds of pupils to vocational courses deemed second class, is at odds with the demands of a modern economy and society', and 'instead of asking 15-year-olds to choose between education and training, A levels or NVQs, we should be offering an opportunity to balance general and vocational study'. However, A levels were to prove politically tenacious. Post-16 policy, not a political front-runner at the time, was set out in March 1996 in *Aiming Higher: Labour's Proposals for the Reform of the 14–19 Curriculum* (Labour Party 1996a). This document criticized the three qualifications pathways and the 'confusing, complex and fragmented qualifications structure', and recommended an advanced diploma – a unified overarching qualification bringing together academic and vocational studies with learning organized on a modular basis, and a merger of SCAA and the

NCVQ into a National Qualifications Council. It promised a continuation of general education as well as specific vocational education to those leaving school at 16 and converged with the 1996 Dearing Report in suggesting that young people disaffected with schooling could leave at 14 and follow work-related courses in FE colleges. Liz Allen, Labour Education Officer during these years, reported that Blunkett distanced himself from this paper, as 'there were no votes in the abolition of A levels'.[8]

The ideological context in which New Labour's education policies were to be set was well developed by the mid-1990s. As with right-wing think-tanks in the 1980s, the leftist Institute for Public Policy Research provided many of the ideas that influenced policy. David Miliband, an IPPR researcher, was appointed as a policy adviser to Tony Blair in 1994, becoming head of the Downing Street Policy Unit in 1997, and an MP in 2001. Education and training were to be the way in which Britain would be transformed from a low-skill, low-wage economy to a high-skill, high-wage and technological economy. In opposition New Labour used dubious evidence to support its assertions, familiar since the 1970s, that educational providers had failed. Ministers repeatedly used a figure from a 1995 report on *World Competitiveness* compiled by the World Economic Forum, which put Britain in thirty-fifth place out of forty-eight countries for the adequacy of its education system. The professor who compiled this report later explained that the statistic actually represented the views of 500 business executives working in the UK, none of whom were necessarily knowledgeable about the British state school system. Nevertheless a paper on *Learn as You Earn* (Labour Party 1996c) promised individual learning accounts and a University for Industry, while a paper on *Lifelong Learning* (Labour Party 1996d) reiterated that continuous education was the key to economic success and social cohesion. Individuals were responsible for their own learning and 'the young unemployed have a responsibility to seek work, accept reasonable opportunities and upgrade their skills' (Labour Party 1996d: 7). However, at this point those in higher education were still to be subsidized, Shadow Minister Bryan Davies being sacked when he presented a paper suggesting more student loans and possible fees. In March 1997 the paper *A New Deal for New Britain: Proposals for Youth and Long-term Unemployment* (Labour Party 1997) foreshadowed the New Deal policy.

Labour's main problem in the run-up to the general election of 1997 was, however, that of GM schools, the unfair funding policies which favoured these schools, and the fact that by 1996, almost a thousand schools had opted for grant-maintained status, and had significant support from middle and aspirant middle class voters. In May 1995 Blunkett published *Diversity and Excellence* (Labour Party 1995a) which cleverly suggested three types of comprehensive secondary schools – community, aided and foundation. Although the paper promised fair funding and a fair admissions policy, it opened the way for most GM schools to opt for foundation status, most religious schools to opt for aided status and both to retain many of their privileges, including appointing staff. This was followed in December 1995 by *Excellence for Everyone* (Labour Party 1995b) a paper which set out many subsequent policies and initiatives: the establishment of a General Teaching Council, a Standards Unit at DfEE, a national qualification for headteachers, advanced skills teachers, home–school contracts, homework levels, education development plans and targets for improved performance from LEAs, baseline assessment for children starting school, literacy programmes, setting in schools, specialist schools, disciplinary measures, exclusions, inspections and 'fresh starts for struggling schools'. The paper also signalled recognition that new technologies were to be of crucial importance in the future, something the Conservatives had missed, and promised links to the information superhighway and access to computers. Liz Allen's view was that these documents were early examples of 'spin'. 'They caused agony to old Labour supporters who thought Blair had sold out to the Tories, but were in fact clever documents'.[9]

The political parties went into the general election campaign in March 1997 with education manifestos that were remarkably similar, and differences rapidly became similarities. The main differences were that Labour promised an end to the assisted places scheme, a reduction in class sizes and the scrapping of nursery vouchers. Both major parties were promising higher educational standards and rigorous appraisal of teachers, the Conservatives were promising more specialist schools and more pupil selection, both of which were to continue after Labour took over. Prime Minister Major went into the campaign promising 'a grammar school in every town'. The retention of a market in education was to ensure that in most towns there were de facto grammar schools, and the de-comprehensivization movement continued. Education policy indicated more continuity than discontinuity after May 1997.

Notes

1 Consolidating Acts gather together existing legislation and present it in a more coherent form. No new substantive points of law are introduced in such Acts.
2 The Standard Spending Assessment is central government's estimate of what is adequate for all local authority spending.
3 Personal interviews with mothers.
4 Roy Hattersley, writing in the *Independent* (23 November 1998: 5) on the appointment of Andrew Adonis, noted that 'When a Number 10 political adviser is an established opponent of official government policy, the fact is worth mentioning'.
5 See Anderson and Mann (1997: 417) for a résumé of Barber's career, from Education Officer at the NUT in 1993 to head of the new DfEE Standards and Effectiveness Unit in 1997. He stood as a Labour candidate in 1987 against Michael

Heseltine in Henley-on-Thames, and during the 1990s mixed educational journal-
ism, academic jobs and political advisory work with skill. He was appointed to
the education association which recommended the closure of Hackney Downs
School by Conservative Minister Gillian Shephard, and was criticized in the press
in 1996 when he sent his daughter to a private school.

6 This report reprinted a figure from Cantor *et al.* (1995) showing the major
   categories of awards from 14 upwards.

7 Anderson and Mann (1997) have detailed how Blunkett, born blind in Sheffield in
   1947, worked to become Leader of Sheffield City Council and then became an MP
   and later Secretary of State for Education and Employment in 1997. Pollard
   (2005) wrote a new biography *David Blunkett.*

8 Personal interview 16 February 1999.

9 Personal interview 16 February 1999.

Further reading

Barber, M. (1996) *The Learning Game.* London: Cassell. This book lays out the
personal views on education of the influential head (from 1997) of the DfEE
Standards and Effectiveness Unit.

O'Connor, M., Hales, E., Davies, J. and Tomlinson, S. (1999) *Hackney Downs: The
School that Dared to Fight.* London: Cassell. This book tells the story of the only
school to be closed on the advice of the education association created by the
Education Act 1993. It demonstrates the injustice of the 1990s policy of labelling
schools as failing and raises serious questions about ways of improving schools in
Britain.

Ribbins, P. and Sherratt, B. (1997) *Radical Educational Policies and Conservative
Secretaries of State.* London: Cassell. This fascinating book includes personal
interviews with seven Conservative Education Secretaries from Mark Carlisle to
Gillian Shephard, reporting their backgrounds and views on their policies, colleagues and civil servants.

chapter

five

New Labour and education: 1997–2000

New Labour settled into office in May 1997 and continued the avalanche of education-related policy initiatives, legislation and advice which had characterized 18 years of Conservative rule. As Stephen Ball (1999: 195) remarked two years later, 'Whatever else one would want to say about Labour's education policies there is certainly no shortage of them'. This chapter and Chapter 6 document continuity and change in the education policies pursued post-1997. Much continuity derives from an acceptance and elaboration of Tory reforms post-1988; indeed a pursuit of some of these policies passed the point that Tory ministers had been willing to go. There was an acceptance of the Conservative faith in choice and competition, with education developing as a market commodity driven by consumer demands, demonstrated by the retention of market competition between schools, and fuelled by league table publication, school choice, specialist schools and failing schools. There was a continued rhetoric of 'raising standards' with a weakening of the commitment to end academic selection as more subtle policies for distinguishing between the more able and less able, and the academic and vocational, were developed. There was an adherence to the belief that all education institutions should be effectively managed along the lines of private business, with enhanced business funding and influence. There was a continued emphasis on state regulation and control of the curriculum, its assessment, teachers and their training and local authority activity. The driving force behind the 'epidemic of policy-making' (Levin 1998) continued to be the perceived need to respond to a competitive global economy by improving the skills and qualifications of young people. The key to a successful economy was to be knowledge and education. Investment in human resources via lifelong learning, the subordination of education to the economy, and the scapegoating of schools and teachers for failing to deliver enough high quality products underpinned New Labour education policy in the 1990s.

There were, however, changes in the approach to education policymaking. More emollient approaches to partners in the education enterprise were apparent, with a stress on new kinds of cooperation and partnership with local authorities and with private business. More public money was made available, particularly after the Treasury Comprehensive Spending Review in 1998, which promised that £19 billion would be spent on education, lifelong learning and work-related measures.[1] There was also a declared commitment to a measure of social justice. In 1994 new party leader Blair, writing in a Fabian Society pamphlet, had claimed that he did not want to 'run a Tory economy with a bit of social compassion . . . the public is once again ready to listen to notions associated with the left, social justice, cohesion, equality of opportunity, and community' (Blair 1994: 2). On 8 December 1997 Prime Minister Blair launched a Social Exclusion Unit attached to his Cabinet Office, declaring in his speech that he wanted 'a Britain from which no-one is excluded from opportunity and the chance to develop their potential' and that 'we should make it our purpose to tackle social divisions and inequality'.

Politics and good intentions, however, as Joseph Heller, the writer of the novel *Catch-22* pointed out, do not mix. Recognition of powerful vested interests, which need conciliation or compromise, perceived electoral advantage and financial considerations constrain even the best intentioned politicians. The contradictions of pursuing competitive market policies in education while affirming commitment to social justice continued to create major problems. While New Labour was preaching inclusiveness and developing palliatives to mitigate disadvantage, market and selective forces were demonstrably excluding large sections of the working and non-working class, plus many ethnic minority children and those with learning difficulties, from the more desirable schools and universities. On the wider welfare front, a range of policies to reduce poverty, particularly among those on low wages, was accompanied by continued disparities in wealth and income.

New Labour education policies and initiatives were accompanied by familiar assertions that standards needed to be raised, targets met, and incompetent teachers sacked. The *Britain 1998: An Official Handbook* (ONS 1998) solemnly declared in its education section compiled by civil servants that 'despite the reforms which have taken place to date, test results show . . . that standards of literacy have not changed significantly since 1945' – a manifest economy with the truth. There were no literacy test results which compared standards in the 1940s with the 1990s. The evidence, as Michael Barber pointed out in 1996, was that in the UK educational standards may be low compared to other European countries but 'it is important to recognise that for many young people they are rising and have been rising for a number of years' (Barber and Dann 1996: 8). Mortimore (2000: 8) added that until the late 1980s it was governments who led the way with low expectations of the academic potential of most school pupils. Yet the unremarked situation in the 1990s was that British society was actually benefiting (although still unequally) from the relative success of the education policies of the 1960s and 1970s. For the first time, a generation of people under 35 had experienced five years of secondary schooling and had had the opportunity to take public examinations. Higher education had expanded dramatically as young people from comprehensive schools qualified for entry. Surveying indicators such as book sales, especially scientific books, museum entries and internet access in 1999, journalist Andrew Marr (1999: 6) noted 'the continued rise of a very well-informed and literate population'. But there were contradictions of educational improvement for the majority alongside an increasingly disadvantaged minority.

Box 5.1 Chronology of Acts, reports and events 1997–2000

1997   (May) Labour government elected
1997   (May) Cabinet sets up Welfare to Work Committee
1997   Standards and Effectiveness Unit set up in the DfEE
1997   (June) Launch of New Deal for unemployed young people 18–25; summer literacy schools initiative announced
1997   (July) Education Act; abolition of assisted places scheme and nursery vouchers
1997   (July) White Paper *Excellence in Schools* (DfEE); National Literacy Strategy announced; a literacy hour to be in place in all primary schools by September 1998
1997   Committee on *Computers in Schools* set up (chair Lord Stevenson)
1997   (October) Green Paper *Excellence for All Children: Meeting Special Education Needs* (DfEE)
1997   (December) School Standards and Framework Bill
1997   (December) Social Exclusion Unit set up in Cabinet Office
1997   Muslim schools given state funding as voluntary aided schools
1998   (May) Standards Fund set up
1998   Ethnic Minority Achievement Grant (EMAG) to replace Section 11 of Local Government Act 1966 (EMTAG – the additional T referring to Travelling pupils from 2000)
1998   (May) House of Commons Education and Employment Committee Fifth Report *Disaffected Children*
1998   (May) National Childcare Strategy launched
1998   (June) Education Action Zones: first 25 announced; interim guidance on school admissions published by DfEE
1998   (July) School Standards and Framework Act
1998   (July) Teaching and Higher Education Act
1998   (July) New Opportunities Fund set up (National Lottery money)
1998   Plans for a University for Industry (UfI)
1998   Expansion of Specialist Schools Initiative; beacon schools to be identified

1998	National Grid for Learning to be set up (agreements with British Telecom and cable companies)
1998	(September) Guidance on national childcare strategy and early years development and childcare partnerships
1998	(September) Literacy hour in all primary schools advised; Numeracy Task Force set up
1998	(September) National Year of Reading launched
1998	(September) Crick Report *Education for Citizenship and the Teaching of Democracy in School*
1998	DfEE published homework guidelines; plans announced for a network of school study centres in *Extending Opportunity: A National Framework for Study Support* (DfEE 1998)
1998	(October) *Supporting Families: A Consultation Document* (Home Office)
1998	(November) *Meeting Special Educational Needs: A Programme for Action* (DfEE); consultation on a revised code of practice for SEN
1998	(December) Green Paper *Teachers: Meeting the Challenge of Change* (DfEE)
1999	(January) *Sure Start: A Guide for Trailblazers*: programmes for 0–3-year-olds in areas of deprivation (DfEE)
1999	(March) Blair and Blunkett announce action plan for inner city education, including an expansion of specialist and beacon schools and a new approach for gifted children
1999	(March) *Excellence in Cities* (DfEE)
1999	(May) Revised National Curriculum put out for consultation; report on creative and cultural education: *All Our Futures* (Robinson)
1999	(September) White Paper *Learning to Succeed* (national and local Learning and Skills Councils to be set up) (DfEE)
1999	(September) Numeracy strategy suggested for all primary schools
1999	(November) National Curriculum (to be followed by all schools from September 2000) published
1999	A 'Black' Seventh Day Adventist school and a Sikh school given state funding
1999	(December) Learning and Skills Bill
2000	(January) Blunkett announced tests for 12-year-olds, summer camps for 16-year-olds and changes to enrolment in specialist schools; Blair reiterated commitment to specialist schools
1999	(January) Commission on Childcare set up (chair Harriet Harman)
2000	(March) Blunkett announced creation of centrally funded 'city academies' modelled on USA charter schools
2000	(July) Comprehensive Spending Review promised an extra £5 billion for education over three years
2000	(September) Statutory code of admission for all maintained schools

Secretary of State for Education and Employment

David Blunkett 1997–2001

Shadow Education and Employment Secretaries

David Willetts 1997–99
Theresa May 1999–2001

School policies

Policies 1997–98

The New Labour government wasted no time in developing a raft of policies and initiatives designed to achieve the first prime ministerial promise of a 'world class education service' (Blair's first speech after election victory, 2 May 1997), although the new Secretary of State for Education, David Blunkett, asserted that the Conservatives had operated a scorched earth policy before leaving office, paring down the education budget to the minimum. The new government left in place the Conservative appointments at the major quangos, Anthea Millet at the TTA, the controversial Chris Woodhead at Ofsted and Nicholas Tate at the QCA, although he resigned in 2000 to head Winchester, a major public school. Any notion of abolishing the TTA – Labour policy in 1994 – had long been abandoned, and no moves were to be made to undermine the privileged position of private education.

To underline the promise that 'standards not structures' were to be a major goal, a Standards and Effectiveness Unit was set up at the DfEE, headed by Michael Barber. Task forces and groups rapidly became a favoured way of debating if not instigating policy, with members invited or co-opted. A Standards Task Force was set up to promote good practice and guarantee the 'delivery' of literacy and numeracy targets. The appointment of two antagonistic vice-chairs to this group may have impeded progress. Tim Brighouse, Chief Education Officer in Birmingham and left-wing defender of teachers, LEAs and disadvantaged pupils, clashed with Chris Woodhead, right-wing critic of teachers, LEAs and progressive methods. Woodhead had strong support from the Prime Minister and from the Prince of Wales, who despite his own private education and sending his sons to Eton took a critical interest in state education. Brighouse eventually resigned from the group (Carvel 1998). A Literacy Task Force was set up to raise primary literacy standards and a Numeracy Task Force to assess teaching in numeracy. These groups influenced the development of the literacy hour and numeracy strategy in all primary schools, set periods in which each minute of teaching time was centrally dictated, although the notion of a literacy hour was originally suggested by the Conservative National Literacy project in 1996.

A Continuing Education Advisory Group was created to advise on adult and lifelong learning and to develop a University for Industry, assisted by a University for Industry Working Group. A Special Needs Advisory Group was set up to help produce a paper on SEN and advise on action, and a Schools Framework and Consultative group to develop policy on the new framework for schools. A New Deal Task Force was to oversee new policies for youth and unemployment with help from a New Deal Advisory Group. There was even a Red Tape Working Group, to advise on ways of cutting bureaucracy and reducing teachers' stress! The appointment of unelected members to these groups was queried in the *Times Educational Supplement* (3 October 1997).[2] Conflicts and alliances between ministers, advisers and civil servants at the DfEE and between personnel at the Downing Street Policy Unit were apparent over the creation of new policies, illustrating the fact that 'policies are not simply abstractions, they carry traits of the personalities of their producers' (Lawrence 1992: 3).[3] There were also anxieties that policies were stamped by a 'macho' image with continued reference to tough policy, zero tolerance and pressure (McKie 1997).[4]

The new government continued the previous government's policy of 'naming and shaming schools', 18 schools being named as 'failing' almost at once; Blunkett defended the policy as demonstrating that 'persistent failure will not be tolerated by this government'. Although politicians in the later 1990s competed to demonstrate their zero tolerance of school under-performance, and the media coverage of failing schools was negative and derisory, two-thirds of schools labelled as 'failing' were schools attended by the children of the poor, of minority ethnic origin and children with special educational needs, not wanted in other schools. Market forces were helping to create failing schools (Tomlinson 1997a). It was not until October 1998 that the public humiliation of schools and teachers was abandoned. The head of one named school, an inner city school serving a poor, largely black intake, noted bitterly that 'we have had a Herculean task to improve in a climate of hostility' (Gardiner 1997: 7).

Legislative priority in the first few weeks of the new government was given to implementing the manifesto promise that the assisted places scheme would be abolished and money used to fund reduced class sizes for 5–7-year-olds. An Education (Schools) Bill was introduced in May 1997 and became law in July 1997. Assisted pupils already in private schools had their education guaranteed, although Standards Minister Stephen Byers estimated that £100 million would be diverted from the scheme by 2000. There was no immediate money to pay the extra 2400 teachers the Institute for Public Finance estimated would be needed to reduce infant class sizes to 30, and schools were continuing to make teachers redundant as their funding decreased.

By 7 July the new government had produced its first White Paper *Excellence in Schools* setting out the educational agenda for 3–16-year-olds (DfEE 1997a). Although historian Richard Aldrich (1997) was impressed with the speed with which the paper was produced, many of the policies (as noted in Chapter 4), had already been formulated. At a Labour Education Summit in April 1997, Blair had outlined his educational vision – 4 principles and 21 chief policy proposals – for his government. There was, however, a distinct difference in tone between documents produced in opposition and those produced in office. The White Paper opened with an emollient foreword by Blunkett, noting that the government was committed to high standards, partnerships with schools, LEAs, governors and parents, changing the educational culture from complacency to commitment to success, overcoming the spiral of economic and social disadvantage, valuing teachers while ensuring the best classroom methods, and above all to an economic imperative. 'We are talking about investing in human capital in an age of knowledge. To compete in the global economy . . . we will have to unlock the potential of every young person' (DfEE 1997a: 3).

The paper then adopted a prescriptive and more confrontational style, threatening in the first section that there would be 'unrelenting pressure on schools and teachers for improvement' albeit with the 'right balance of pressure and support' (DfEE 1997a: 11) and setting out six principles on which policy would be based. These were that education would be at the heart of government, that policies would be for the many, not the few, there would be a focus on standards not structures, intervention (by inspection) would be in inverse proportion to success, there would be zero tolerance of under-performance and government would work in partnership with those committed to raising standards. Most government White Papers indicate a broad sweep of policy. This paper set out highly prescriptive, detailed policies, most of which after a period of consultation appeared in legislation.

The second section covered early years education, requiring baseline assessment for children starting school, national standards for the early years, and national targets for 11-year-olds – 80 per cent were to reach standards expected of their age (level 4) in English and 75 per cent in mathematics. A structured literacy hour was to be in place in all primary schools by September 1998 and a Numeracy Task Force was to advise on a structured period of mathematics which would include interactive whole-class teaching, differential group teaching and learning times tables by heart to prevent over-reliance on calculators (DfEE 1997a: 21). Local authorities were to set up early years forums and 25 early excellence centres were to be piloted.

The third section promised yet more performance data from primary and secondary schools for parents and presumably the media, required LEAs to provide schools with local comparative data and schools to set targets for their own improvement. LEAs were to draw up education development plans by April 1999 with guidance from the Standards and Effectiveness Unit and were to monitor and support schools, demonstrate improvements and 'tackle failure'. Schools not recovering from failure could be closed and reopened with a Fresh Start. The role of Ofsted was to be enhanced by inspection of LEAs from January 1998, and it was to identify excellent and failing schools. DfEE enhanced its influence and was to 'play a crucial role in leading and creating a climate for change' (DfEE 1997a: 32). The Standards Task Force was to lead a 'crusade' for higher standards. Raising the achievements of ethnic minority pupils and pupils with special needs concluded the section. Each section of the White Paper included case studies of schools already demonstrating the successful implementation of suggested policies. This could rebound. An illustration of a failed school, Phoenix High, which had been closed and reopened with generous extra resources under a Fresh Start, was praised for improving standards. In fact, by 1998 the school recorded 11 per cent of pupils obtaining 5 A–C GCSE passes, the same as that obtained by pupils (without extra resources) at the reviled Hackney Downs School closed on the advice of the education association in 1995 (O'Connor *et al.* 1999). By March 2000 the head, William Atkinson, appointed to turn the school round, was blaming the pupils – the 'low ability of the raw material we started with' – for low examination results (Dodd 2000: 11).

The fourth section of the White Paper described how the government intended to modernize the comprehensive principle, asserting, despite evidence to the contrary (see Boaler 1997; Sukhnandan and Lee 1998), that mixed ability teaching had failed. Modernizing was to take the form of selection by ability in sets, target groups, fast tracks, accelerated learning groups and support for the able, gifted and talented. For the disadvantaged the development of Education Action Zones (EAZs) was to raise standards and hope in urban areas. A pilot programme of 25 zones would be set up by September 1998 incorporating two or three secondary schools, primary and special schools, each run by an action forum which would include parents and representatives from the local and business community. Zones were to be given flexibility in staffing, organization and curriculum. A major purpose would be to motivate young people in tough inner city areas. Although the government was 'deeply committed to equal opportunities for all pupils . . . we want to encourage diversity' (DfEE 1997a: 40). Schools could therefore bid to be specialist schools focusing on technology, languages, sports or the arts, providing they also raised money from private sponsors. Families of schools could bid for specialist status by sharing facilities and teaching materials. The paper noted that £54 million was spent annually on the fifteen CTCs, and indicated that their funding would be levelled down. The section concluded with the promise of a National Grid for Learning whereby pupils would have access to information and communications technology (ICT) and schools would be connected to the internet and each other with help from British Telecom and cable companies. The fifth section promised teachers a 'new deal', but dependent on improvement in their achievements;[5] new core requirements for all teacher training courses with a focus on the most effective teaching methods, especially in literacy, numeracy and ICT; national training for headteachers and a professional headship qualification; a new grade of advanced skills teacher; more appraisal; streamlined ways of 'dealing with incompetent teachers'; and a General Teaching Council. The sixth section explained how schools and parents could work together to raise standards and provide an orderly learning environment. Parents were to sign home–school contracts, there would be national guidelines for homework, more family learning schemes, a national framework for extra-curricular activities, more parental representation on governing bodies and support for pupils with behaviour problems, and national nutritional standards for school meals were to be reinstated.

The final section asserted that the government's priority was standards, not school structures, then reiterated the divided and inevitably divisive new structural framework of foundation schools, aided schools and community schools, with schools free to choose 'which status will best suit their character and aspirations' (DfEE 1997a: 67). Schools choosing the foundation label were to continue to own their own capital assets and premises and appoint their own staff, as were aided schools, a virtual continuation of existing voluntary aided schools. Foundation schools were to have at least two LEA governors and the White Paper referred to fair funding between schools, and left admissions to foundation and aided schools with these schools but with possible referral to an admissions adjudicator. Specialist schools would be allowed partial selection by aptitude. In the Act which followed the White Paper the notion of aided school became voluntary school, comprising existing voluntary aided and voluntary controlled schools.

Barber and Sebba (1999), looking back on two years of New Labour education policy, rightly noted that 'within 67 days of being elected the White Paper *Excellence in Schools* was published in which plans for the whole five year Parliamentary term were laid out' (Barber and Sebba 1999: 185). The style of the paper owed much to Barber: 'intervention in inverse proportion to success', for example, comes from his book *The Learning Game* (Barber 1996: 149).[6] Many, but not all, of the proposals in the White Paper appeared in legislation or statutory instruments over the two years. Some initiatives, for example government advice on homework, were issued in the form of non-statutory guidance. The new government had made clear that there was to be no return to a decentralized system or attempts to build democratic partnerships with LEAs and teachers. The curriculum was to remain centralized. Teachers were to be even more heavily policed, with management of their performance based on private sector models, parents were to remain vigilantes in scanning league tables and acting as extra hands in classrooms, and government-appointed bodies and individuals were to control major educational decision-making and spending.

School Standards and Framework Act 1998

The first major Education Act of the New Labour government was introduced into Parliament in December 1997 and became law in July 1998. In seven parts, it contained 145 sections and 32 schedules. Despite the insistence that standards not structures mattered, the Act was mainly concerned with structures, 89 of the 145 sections being concerned with the new categories of maintained schools, their establishment, financing, staffing, admissions and selective nature. The words comprehensive school or comprehensive education do not appear in the Act at all.

Box 5.2 School Standards and Framework Act 1998: main sections

1   Limits on infant class sizes (Sections 1–4).
2   Duty laid on LEAs to promote high standards in primary and secondary education, and to prepare education development plans to be submitted and approved by the secretary of state, secretary of state to intervene in failing LEAs, parent governors to be appointed to LEA Education Committees (Sections 5–9).
3   Education Action Zones to be established consisting of groups of schools, together with an Education Action Forum whose object will be to improve education at the schools. Disapplication of Section 3 of the Teachers' Pay and Conditions Act 1991 in the schools (Sections 6–13).
4   LEAs' powers of intervention in schools with serious weaknesses or requiring special measures extended and clarified, intervention by the secretary of state clarified including power to close a school (Sections 14–19).
5   New categories of schools to be community schools, foundation schools, voluntary schools (comprising voluntary aided and controlled) and community and foundation special schools. Clarification of foundation and voluntary schools; duty of LEAs to maintain the schools; continuing charitable status of foundation and voluntary schools. All LEAs to establish a school organization committee including an LEA officer and nominees from the Church of England and Roman Catholic Church and prepare a school organization plan approved by the committee or referred to an adjudicator (Sections 20–7).
6   Proposals for establishing the new kinds of school and any alteration or discontinuance, including special schools, for the rationalization of schools places (where there are too many or too few places in an area)

and for schools changing from one category to another (Sections 28–35).

7 Governing bodies' functions and responsibilities clarified, including reporting to parents and parents' meetings (Sections 36–44). Schedule 9 laid out the composition of the governing body for all schools, foundation and voluntary aided schools now to have two LEA governors.

8 Financing of maintained schools laid out, all schools to have a delegated budget. LEAs required to prepare a financial scheme, certified if necessary by the Audit Commission, mismanagement of budgets and powers of governing bodies to spend dealt with (Sections 45–53).

9 Staffing appointments and dismissals at all types of schools including teachers of religious education; responsibilities of governing body and headteacher for school discipline; school attendance and exclusion of pupils and duties for religious education and a collective act of worship set out. Further provisions relating to land, including playing fields, trust deeds and employment in the new schools made (Sections 54–83).

10 School admission arrangements dealt with. The secretary of state to issue a Code of Practice on admissions, appeals panels and adjudicators to be appointed. Admissions authorities to be set up, LEAs to enable parents to express a preference for schools except where the school is foundation, voluntary aided or wholly selective or a child has been excluded from two schools. LEAs given powers to direct pupils to specified schools, nursery and special school admissions noted (Sections 84–89).

11 Selection of pupils reviewed. Pre-existing selection and selection for banding permitted, selective admission by aptitude up to 10 per cent of intake, procedures set out for balloting to retain (the 164) grammar schools (Sections 90–109).

12 Other provisions include home–school agreements, an extension of work experience for KS4 pupils (aged 14–16), provision for these pupils in FE College, reinstatement of nutritional standards for school meals, duties of LEAs in respect of nursery education including preparing early years development plans (Sections 110–24).

13 Further provision refers to arrangements in Wales, a Code of Practice for securing effective relations between LEAs and schools, payments for pupils at non-maintained schools, corporal punishment as constituting battery, Dissolution of the Funding Agency for schools, the Education Assets Board to become the Education Transfer Council and other transitional provision (Sections 125–45).

Selection and specialization

The new school structures set up by the 1998 Act – a clever relabelling rather than an actual change of structure – together with permitted levels of selection, ensured a continuation of a divided and divisive school system. Some 1000 of the 4460 state secondary schools in the UK had opted for GM status by 1997 (only two schools in Scotland);[7] a majority had taken up permitted levels of selection by ability. In the London Borough of Wandsworth, two nominally comprehensive schools were selecting 50 per cent of pupils. By 1999 most GM schools, enriched by several years of privileged funding and intakes, had opted for foundation status, and most voluntary aided and controlled religious schools had opted for voluntary status, although voluntary aided schools which had also gone grant-maintained had to make a choice. A major reason for the separate legal status of GM schools and their control of their own admissions, as Margaret Thatcher had always made clear, had been to revive selection in the long term (Benn and Chitty 1996: 138). New Labour, as has already been noted, was equivocal over selection, preferring to reduce percentages rather than insist on non-selection. Thus, despite interim guidance on admissions issued in July 1998 (urging cooperation between schools over admissions, setting up local forums, local adjudicators and appeals committees, with a chief adjudicator (Sir Peter Newsam) at the DfEE, foundation and voluntary schools were to retain control of their admissions. The selective juggernaut rumbled on into 2000 as some local adjudicators did try to reduce selection. Tory-controlled Wandsworth challenged the decision of its adjudicator to reduce selection in three schools to 25 per cent in court, and the Conservative Shadow Education Secretary Theresa May objected to 'Labour's plan to end selection by stealth' (Smithers 2000a: 2).

To enhance their difference, the heads of foundation and aided schools promptly formed a Foundation and Voluntary Aided Schools Association (FVASA) to look after their own interests. The chair of this association argued at one point that failing schools should be closed and their money diverted to 'leafy suburbs . . . where parents may not be wealthy but have stretched themselves to buy houses in the catchment areas of the schools' (Smithers 1999b: 13). The Funding Agency for Schools, which had distributed money to GM schools from central government, was closed down in April 1999 and a policy of 'fair funding' for all schools via LEAs instigated. The FVASA then argued for cash contributions from parents, even the Prime Minister being asked for £30 per month for his sons at the London Oratory School. Choice policies had, by 1998, become something of an absurdity: in some areas children were taking selective examinations or being interviewed at several schools and denied entry to their local school. Journalist Jon Hardy wrote at the end of 1997 that almost every school in his area of south London was selective and humorously suggested those selectors should honestly tell children why they were not selected.

Face it kid, we don't want you here. It's not that you're stupid, which incidentally you are – you were nervous. What good is that in today's world? It's a global economy out there, nervous won't cut it!

(Hardy 1997)

Another group of journalists noted that 'even middle class parents are losing out in the fierce competition for state schools high up in league tables' (Bright *et al.* 1998). In Dulwich, south London, children travelled to 40 different secondary schools, and local parents had formed an association to demand a new local comprehensive. In Bristol, where 60 per cent of good A levels were obtained by pupils at the 12 private schools in the city, middle class parents who were not able or wanting to pay sent their children to schools in Somerset and Gloucestershire rather than to city state schools. Peter Mortimore, head of the London Institute of Education, reiterated many times to ministers, to no avail, that a key factor associated with school success for all children was an academic balance among pupils (Mortimore 1998). Choice policies were creating or exacerbating the unbalanced academic and social mix in inner city schools. There was thus a certain amount of hypocrisy, or playing for electoral advantage, when the Prime Minister announced in January 1999 that 'when I look at some of the inner city schools it is no wonder that parents feel they have to move their children out or make other arrangements' (Blair interview on *Today* BBC Radio 4, 19 January 1999).

Fierce battles ensued over the fate of the remaining 164 grammar schools, whose selective policies affected some 500 other schools. A lengthy and complex balloting of parents at feeder schools as to whether the schools should remain selective ensured that the debates over elite versus mass education of the 1960s were rerun. In March 2000, after a bitter campaign, parents in Ripon, North Yorkshire, voted to keep their grammar school; the ballot allowed 772 parents with children at private schools to vote as their children had been at 'feeder' primary schools (Hattersley 2000). The Campaign for State Education argued vigorously for an end to grammar schools and noted their skewed intake. Government figures showed that in the schools only 1 per cent of children were eligible for free school meals, the major indicator of poverty. The argument that grammar schools provided an escape from poverty or a ladder of opportunity was untrue (Carvel 1999a).

Arguments also developed over the policy of specialist schools. Introduced by Conservative legislation in 1993, by January 1998 100 LEAs had bid for specialist status, and there were 210 technology colleges, 50 language, 17 sports and 13 arts colleges, all partly sponsored by business. The 1998 Act permitted specialist schools to admit up to 10 per cent on 'aptitude' and specialist schools had quickly become over-subscribed. An extension of specialist schools, each offered £100,000 matched by private money, was defended by David Blunkett as 'diversity within a modernized school system catering for individual strengths rather than a bland sameness' in a speech to the Technology Colleges Trust annual dinner in February 1998. By June 1999 Higher Education Minister Blackstone (1999), claimed that 330 specialist schools had received private sponsorship of at least £100,000. The designation and extra funding of some schools as 'beacon schools' was also controversial. The schools were intended to offer examples of good practice to other schools, but a major result of such designation, reported by estate agents, was that house prices rose near beacon schools. Nevertheless, by March 1999 the Prime Minister and Secretary of State for Education had jointly announced a radical extension of the specialist and Beacon school programme: 800 specialist and 1000 beacon schools were planned for by 2002. This was despite evidence provided by Edwards (1998), in a commissioned review of specialist schools, which concluded that there was no parental demand for a specialist curriculum. The traditional academic curriculum continued to be the most popular, but 'even the appearance of being partially selective seems both to increase the attractiveness of a school to ambitious, better educated and confident parents and skew the intake in their direction', with low-status parents channelled towards neighbourhood schools that have no specialized curriculum offerings and poor resources (Edwards 1998).

In an effort to moderate the selective effects of specialist schools – now renamed specialist colleges – Blunkett announced in January 2000 that secondary pupils should have individual education plans, and be able to study at specialist colleges even if not enrolled. Margaret Tulloch, chair of CASE, pointed out the unfairness of extra funding for one school in four. It is instructive to note the hierarchy of thirteen kinds of schooling, which the Act now supported:

- private (independent) schools
- city technology colleges
- grammar schools (ballots on retention)
- foundation specialist schools
- voluntary specialist schools
- community specialist schools
- foundation schools
- voluntary schools (voluntary aided and voluntary controlled)
- community schools
- foundation special schools
- community special schools
- Pupil Referral Units
- Learning Support Centres

In addition, in March 2000 the secretary of state announced that 'city academies' would replace seriously failing schools. These would be run by central government, voluntary, church or business sponsors, with no LEA input (Blunkett 2000).

The Conservatives promised *Choice and Diversity*, New Labour promised *Diversity and Excellence*. The reality was that structural differentiation was ensuring a hierarchical pecking order of schools, which unsurprisingly, given the history of English schooling, continued to mirror the social class structure.

Tackling exclusion

Special educational needs

By the late 1990s some 3 per cent of children had statements of SEN, and schools claimed 18 per cent as having learning or behavioural difficulties – some 1.6 million children overall. LEAs were allocating one-seventh of their budget, £2.5 billion annually, to provision for those with SEN. The modernized comprehensive system now sanctioned selection and differentiation, the education market encouraged schools to avoid or exclude children who were difficult to teach and an increasing number of parents were claiming entitlement to extra resources for their statemented children, all of which meant higher costs. The government faced the 150-year-old dilemma over the costs of educating young people who might not be economically profitable to society and who did not fit into a human capital equation (Tomlinson 1989: 195).

New Labour was possibly more open and pragmatic about SEN dilemmas than previous governments. A National Advisory Group on SEN began work in the summer of 1997, chaired by the minister responsible for SEN, Estelle Morris. By October 1997 a Green Paper *Excellence for All Children: Meeting Special Educational Needs* (DfEE 1997b) had been put out for consultation, receiving 3600 replies. The paper laid out a 'tough-minded determination to show that children with SEN are capable of excellence' (DfEE 1997b: foreword) and that as many as possible should be included in mainstream schools and budgets managed more effectively. As many children as possible were to be prepared to 'contribute economically' as adults.

By November 1998 a further paper, *Meeting Special Educational Needs: A Programme for Action*, had been produced and £37 million promised from the Standards Fund to support SEN in 1999 (DfEE 1998a). The Action Programme was directed towards reducing parental demands for resources and dealing with any subsequent disputes. It required LEAs to develop partnership schemes, set up conciliation arrangements, publish more information and monitor their SEN policies, include information on inclusion policies in the education development plans, help develop links between mainstream and special schools and ensure that children with SEN were treated fairly in school admissions. A simplified code of practice was to be in place by 2001, promoting school-based support and preventive work. More money was to be made available for professional development of teachers and support staff and the role of educational psychologists scrutinized. From April 2000 there was to be regional coordination of SEN provision and training, new duties of partnership between local authorities and the health services, and information on school and college leavers with SEN was to be collected and the young people 'helped more effectively for adult life'. In 1998 the TTA was required by the secretary of state to consult on national standards for training specialist SEN teachers – those working with children with severe and complex SEN – and the Special Needs Educational Training Consortium was advised to improve the training of SENCOs in mainstream schools. Teachers' responses to the Green Paper, action programme and training consultation stressed their concern that inclusion would mean the retention of more children with emotional and behavioural difficulties in mainstream – children whom historically teachers have always wished to exclude.

Exclusions from school had become, by the 1990s, a major way of removing troublesome or difficult pupils from schools more speedily than through special education referral processes, and large numbers of pupils were being excluded from schools at all ages. By 1993 the number of permanent exclusions from schools was over 10,000 per year. Both Conservative and Labour governments in the 1990s were concerned to persuade schools to keep their troublesome pupils to reduce the costs of their education outside the mainstream, but market forces dictated that teachers, supported by their unions, were reluctant to take pupils who might disrupt their task of credentialling other pupils. The Education Act 1993 limited the power of headteachers to exclude on fixed or permanent terms and allowed LEAs to set up PRUs. The 1997 Act extended the permissible period for fixed-term exclusions to 45 days but the 1998 Act further limited the power of headteachers and extended the duty of governors to scrutinize exclusions. However, the first report of the Social Exclusion Unit (1998) examined truancy and school exclusion, setting a target for one-third reduction in exclusions by 2002. The DfEE (1999a) issued a circular, *School Exclusions and Pupil Support*, laying down procedures to be followed before pupils could be excluded and by 2000 headteachers had their scrutiny of exclusions returned. The over-placement of black male pupils in EBD schools (for pupils with emotional and behavioural difficulties) and the high numbers excluded from school was particularly worrying to black parents and teachers – a race issue that governments had preferred to ignore if possible, although the Social Exclusion Unit report had drawn attention to the issue (Commission for Racial Equality (CRE) 1996; Gillborn and Youdell 2000).

Policies for the poor

New Labour came to power in 1997 promising an attack on poverty and social exclusion. The economic inequalities of the 1980s had left what

Jordan (1996) described as a legacy of alienated and dispossessed people, mainly living in inner cities and outer city council estates where jobs had disappeared. A major thrust of policy was to identify and target groups and areas, produce policies and offer some redistribution of resources. Since welfare-to-work was to be a major way of reforming the welfare state, an initial target was young people who had left school, and who were unemployed but claiming benefits. In opposition Labour had pledged to remove the 250,000 unemployed young people aged 18–24 off benefit, but by 1997 the number of young unemployed had fallen to less than 200,000. The 1997 New Deal for 18–24-year-olds became a major employment policy. Young people aged 18–24 who had been unemployed for six months were required to take up subsidized employment with a company, enrol for up to 12 months' full-time study, work for six months with an environmental task force or in the voluntary sector, or lose their benefits. By early 2000 ministers were claiming that 170,000 people mainly lacking basic educational skills had been 'helped' from unemployment to work and were even proposing to offer job applicants funds to buy or borrow interview suits to impress potential employers (Hetherington 2000). But critics argued that 40 per cent of participants failed to find lasting jobs and the New Deal failed to help the most disadvantaged.

Women with children living on benefits were also to be a major target in the reformed welfare state and there was early recognition that working mothers needed childcare. A National Childcare Strategy was launched in May 1998 with the five-year goal of creating a million new childcare places, 20,000 after-school childcare projects, 60,000 new childcare jobs and enabling 250,000 families to move off benefits. The government encouraged partnerships with LEAs (already developing their own Early Years Development and Childcare Partnerships), with the Benefits Agency, which appointed 17 'Childcare Champions', with charities such as Education Extra and the Kids Club Network,[8] and with local Training and Enterprise Councils. The government claimed it was offering £470 million for the National Childcare Strategy which included money from the New Opportunities Fund (from the National Lottery) and money promised to LEAs for the Early Years Initiatives (Hodge 1999). A further major investment was to be the Sure Start Programme (DfEE 1999b), a £425 million project for 0–3-year-olds offering home visits and services from a range of health, education and social services professionals to help families and carers in disadvantaged areas. Sixty trailblazer programmes started after April 1999, and unusually, there was a promise that applications for Sure Start projects would not be competitive providing they met standards (DfEE 1999b). A Treasury deputy director, Norman Glass, took a particular interest in this programme, possibly ensuring its funding. Sure Start was one of the few policies based on sound research findings: the Headstart programmes in the USA had demonstrated that in the long term early intervention did have individual and social gains. As with many of the government initiatives in education, health and childcare, with New Deals, partnerships and forums, Sure Start appeared to provide good employment possibilities for a large number of qualified professional people. There was also an irony in the encouragement of mothers to take low-paid jobs while equally low-paid carers looked after their children.

Locating areas or 'zones' where the unemployed and disadvantaged were concentrated quickly became a major policy focus, partly modelled on the Educational Priority Areas (EPAs) developed in England in the 1960s and Social Priority Areas set up in France in the 1980s. In February 1998 five Employment Zones were identified for helping the long-term jobless move into employment or 'neighbourhood regeneration work' and a New Deal for Communities which promised £800 million for deprived neighbourhoods was launched (Home Office 1998). In April 1998 eleven Health Action Zones were set up for health promotion, and in September 1998 the first of 25 Education Action Zones began to operate (Gewirtz 1999). Halpin (1998) viewed these zones as attempts to ameliorate the more negative effects of Conservative policies by offering more resources, and by harnessing local collective action and encouraging cooperation between schools, parents, business, communities and schools. The zones, intended to encompass two or three secondary schools and their feeder primaries and special schools, were to be innovative and experimental, run by Education Action Forums, and to promote a 'business-like approach to educational management' (Halpin 1998). Each zone was to run for three years, with £750,000 from the government and other funding from business. Some initial business partners in the zones were large companies such as Shell, Tate and Lyle, Research Machines and General Electric, but by 1999 'the idea that private business was going to be leading zones has simply not been fulfilled' (Barnard 1999: 10). Bids for most of the first zones were led by local authorities, which did not please the Chief Inspector of Schools.[9] The Teachers' Pay and Conditions Act could be suspended in the areas, teachers could be paid differently and the National Curriculum could also be suspended. This last prompted the chair of the Commission for Racial Equality to express concern that pupils in the zones, encompassing large numbers of young ethnic minorities, could be offered a second class curriculum rather than the full entitlement of the National Curriculum (Maden 1999). There was certainly some concern expressed that the problems of the poor could not be solved by the market solution of competitive bidding for action zones, and also that the status of being a designated zone might be seen as a stigma by communities.

Disaffection and excellence

The long association of inner city schools with disadvantaged, disaffected and disruptive pupils continued to be regarded as a major public policy challenge by New Labour. Dealing with the children of those whom the Victorians had called the 'feckless poor', now known as 'disrupted families', who constituted a major reason why aspirant parents wished to move their children away from inner city schools, took priority. The government was caught in the contradictions of market policies, which encouraged schools to get rid of troublesome pupils, the costs of educating pupils outside the mainstream, and fears of nurturing a criminal underclass. A report by the House of Commons Education and Employment Committee (1998) on *Disaffected Children* attempted to calculate the economic cost of disaffection to the public purse. It pointed out the strong link between low attainment, truancy, school exclusion and crime – 30 per cent of daytime burglaries were committed by 10–16-year-olds. They attempted to quantify the disaffected, arriving at a figure of some 190,000 16–17-year-olds who were in 'status zero' (Rees *et al.* 1996) neither in education, work nor training and not covered by the New Deal programme. The committee recommended an expansion of voluntary agencies to deal with the young people, creating local forums to establish action plans, and encouraging schools to minimize exclusions and be responsible for excluded pupils. The committee also returned to the familiar solution that the disaffected children of the poor needed a vocational curriculum to engage their interest and recommended 'high quality vocational education including workplace experience which would be of enormous value to those disaffected with the more traditional school curriculum' (House of Commons Education and Employment Committee 1998: 37). Children should be allowed to leave school at 14 and 're-engage' at FE college. By August 1998, regulations had been made allowing schools to set aside two NC subjects to allow the disaffected to take up their work-related curriculum.

In March 1998 the Prime Minister and his Secretary of State for Education launched an action plan for inner city education and appointed Estelle Morris as Minister for Inner City Education. *Excellence in Cities* (DfEE 1999c) deplored the low standards, aspirations and failure in inner city schools and promised immediate measures to improve things, including 'an improvement in parental confidence in the capacity of city schools to cater for ambitious and high-achieving pupils' (DfEE 1999c: 1). This was to be achieved by an expansion of beacon and specialist schools in inner cities, extending opportunities for the gifted and talented – including special programmes for the top 5–10 per cent, and the new 'world class' tests, more setting in schools, separating out the less able and disruptive into learning support centres, learning centres with modern IT facilities, low cost leasing of home computers, learning mentors, and new small EAZs. Although race and ethnicity were mentioned only in recruitment of staff, much of the policy was directed towards aspirant ethnic minorities who were not able to move out of inner cities and had been vocal critics of the poor city schools their children had entered. The paper briefly mentioned the variety of social and economic problems in inner cities, including unemployment and poverty, but rather than embarking on an analysis of these, enthused over measures to raise standards, offer challenging opportunities and achieve excellence with diversity.

Centralizing governance

Modernizing LEAs

Excellence in Cities also promised to modernize and improve LEAs, although the six LEAs to be involved in the action programme were informed, not consulted, about their participation (*The Education Network*, May 1999: 1). Improvement was to be brought about by accelerating the inspection of LEAs, and intervention where LEAs were failing. Intervention, unsurprisingly, was to be 'in inverse proportion to success' (DfEE 1999c: 17). Inspection of LEAs by Ofsted had been signalled from 1996, and in October 1997, before there was statutory provision for such inspection, an 'improvement team' had been sent into the London Borough of Hackney. The School Standards and Framework Act 1998 gave the Secretary of State the unprecedented power to intervene in local authorities, effectively ending any notion of democratic pluralism and partnership between central government and locally elected councillors. Within a year three authorities, Hackney, Calderdale and Manchester, had been publicly named as inadequate; the Labour leader of Manchester City Council called for the resignation of the Chief Inspector Chris Woodhead, after he released his inspection report to the press before releasing it to Manchester (Prestage 1998).[10]

In opposition, the Labour Party had opposed measures to remove local authority powers, particularly when the creation of GM schools threatened the existence of LEAs, and the 'demise of LEAs' had been widely discussed (Ranson and Tomlinson 1994). In power New Labour made it clear that local authorities, if they were to survive, were to be delivery agents of central government policy. Tony Blair signalled this in a speech in 1998: 'If you [local government] are unwilling to work to the modern agenda, then the government will have to look to other partners' (Blair 1998a). Although LEAs were key agents in implementing national strategies, and had a statutory duty to secure high standards in their maintained schools, they were 'not to meddle in the day-to-day running of individual schools', as Standards Minister Stephen Byers put it (*Hansard* 1998, col. 795, 3 March), and the DfEE (1999d) issued a *Code of Practice on LEA–School Relationships*. Fair funding of all maintained schools was to be instigated, but the finance regulations made it clear that central government was to dictate how local authorities allocated the funds. LEAs were to operate under direction, licence and scrutiny (Hannon 1999: 210).

In moves which the previous Conservative government had rejected as too radical, New Labour was willing to privatize both LEAs and schools deemed to be 'failing'. By May 1999 the DfEE had named ten consortia willing to take a lead in partially privatizing state education. These included CEM Consortium, a firm set up by Sir Robert Balchin, former head of the Grant-Maintained Schools Centre and a key supporter of Thatcher's education policies; Nord Anglia, the first education company to be listed on the stock exchange; and Capita, a company that ran the Conservative nursery voucher scheme (Carvel 1999b). In the event, a private company set up by the first city technology college became the first company to take over a 'failing school' (Kings Manor school in Surrey) and Cambridge Education Associates became the first private company to takeover the day-to-day running of a local education service in Islington, London. This company contracted to lose profits if it failed to raise standards in the local schools, but the legal responsibility for raised standards remained with the LEA (Hackett 2000). The LEA newsletter *The Education Network* noted in September 1999 that there was no evidence that privatization would solve the problems of lower educational performance in urban areas, and that 'macho privatization could sap commitment of other more positive, government initiatives' (*The Education Network*, September 1999). A month later, at a fringe meeting of the Conservative Party conference, Chief Inspector Woodhead supported Tory policy to remove *all* schools from local authority control, saying that 'much of the work done by LEAs was not of democratic significance' (Ward 1999).

Early in 2000, the Prime Minister reiterated that if LEAs were not 'doing the job' private contractors would be employed. He did not 'want the whole system privatized' but the role of LEAs was to raise standards, intervene in schools where necessary and 'pass' on to schools the money given by central government (St John-Brooks 2000: 5).

Modernizing teachers

The modernization of the teaching profession continued to be a major theme of government between 1997 and 2000, to be achieved by the carrot and the stick.[11] Modernization meant a new career structure for teachers with performance-related pay, improved management and leadership from headteachers (armed with a compulsory headship qualification) and the sacking of incompetent teachers. Chief Inspector Woodhead, who claimed that the profession included some 15,000 incompetent teachers, had amended this to 13,000, plus by 1997 some 3000 headteachers offering poor leadership (Judd 1997). Wragg and his colleagues, researching incompetent teachers, pointed out that when trust in a profession is low, demand for accountability increases, but accusing teachers of incompetence at a time when so much was expected of the profession did little for teacher morale or recruitment (Wragg *et al.* 2000). Poor recruitment was not helped by the head of the Teacher Training Agency, who, now that funds for teacher training were channelled through the TTA rather than the HEFC, declared in a letter to the *Times Educational Supplement* that 'initial teacher training is not an academic study and therefore not an intrinsic part of H.E.' (Millett 1997).

The TTA had by 1997 taken over most stages of teacher training and professional development, producing a framework of national standards for newly qualified teachers, for advanced skills teachers, for subject leaders, for SENCOs and for a national professional qualification for headship (Mahoney 1998). The Conservative government had suggested a compulsory headship qualification and this became New Labour policy, great faith being placed in the charismatic school leader, whose vision and managerial skills would raise teacher and pupil performance. By 1999 a National College for School Leadership, dubbed a 'Sandhurst for Heads' by the press, had been agreed with the University of Nottingham, and much was expected of outstanding headteachers to lead a reformed teaching profession. However, the policy suffered a setback when, early in 2000, three 'superheads' appointed to Fresh Start schools resigned their posts.

Despite emollient assertions that teachers were to be valued – 'our schools depend, above all, on the skills, commitment and dedication of our heads, teachers and support staff' (DfEE 1998b: 1) – and initiatives such as teaching awards for outstanding teachers and knighthoods for headteachers, teachers mostly remained sceptical of government initiatives. Teachers felt pressurized by new schemes, initiatives and requirements dictated by ministers, civil servants and advisers and they felt undervalued by government and the public. Recruitment to the profession remained problematic, particularly in 'shortage' subjects. By the end of 1998 the TTA and DfEE had spent £1 million on advertising to recruit teachers and the DfEE was offering financial and other incentives and was pleading for the return of former teachers (DfEE 1998c). Perversely, the government did not appear to make the connection between criticism of teachers, unpopular reforms and low morale, and recruitment. At the 1999 Labour Party conference, and in a subsequent speech to new headteachers, the Prime Minister berated the 'forces of conservation' – teachers and local authorities who were resistant to modernization (Wintour 1999: 3). In a subsequent interview, the editor of the *Times Educational Supplement* noted that he exhibited a key characteristic of his government: difficulty in believing that anyone would genuinely disagree with his policies, particularly on performance-related pay for teachers (St John-Brooks 2000: 4).

The new government did, in 1997, move quickly to implement a key election promise, the creation of a General Teaching Council for England and for Wales (Scotland had created a GTC in 1965) and the Teaching and Higher Education Act became law in July 1998.[12] Sections 1–17 of this Act set out the aims and functions of the GTCs, major functions being the maintenance of a register of teachers, the production of a code of conduct for professional practice and via Schedule 2, disciplinary powers over incompetent teachers. By the end of 1998 the media were publishing league tables of training courses – university departments and colleges of HE were labelled as 'very good, good, average or poor' – and a virtual national curriculum for teacher training was in place. In December 1998 a Green Paper *Teachers: Meeting the Challenge of Change* (DfEE 1998b) set out a new career and pay structure for teachers. The paper proposed two pay ranges for classroom teachers with a performance threshold to be crossed via a new appraisal system. Teachers would be reviewed annually against agreed objectives and those crossing the threshold would receive higher pay – some £2000 to start with, and more responsibility. A School Performance Award Scheme would encourage achievement by whole schools, and a national fast-track scheme would help talented trainees and teachers to progress with better use of, and training for, support staff. The new framework for headship training was detailed, together with the National College for School Leadership, and possible fixed-term contract for heads and a School Support Fund would encourage small schools to work together. Unsurprisingly, the notion of performance-related pay, with echoes of the Victorian payment-by-results system, was resisted by many teachers and teacher unions, concerned that competitive differential pay scales would threaten collegiality and by the possibility that parents would want their children taught only by higher-grade teachers. Concern mounted when it became clear that the DfEE intended to hire private consultants to assess teachers' bids to cross the performance thresholds. Cambridge Education Associates, already busy in Islington, was chosen to recruit over 2000 assessors, whose pay levels prompted the general secretary of the National Association of Schoolmasters and Union of Women Teachers to remark that 'there is more to be made out of telling teachers how to do the job than for doing the job' (Barnard 2000: 1). In July 2000 the High Court ruled that the 'threshold standards' and changes to teacher contracts for performance-related pay were unlawful and introduced too hastily. The secretary of state was required to rethink the procedures for assessing teachers (Woodward 2000a).

Modernizing the curriculum

Under New Labour, private schools continued outside the National Curriculum, and within the constraints of public examinations, decided their own curriculum. In state schools, despite pre-election criticism of the narrow subject-based curriculum, and promises of a more flexible curriculum framework, the NC, slimmed down by Ron Dearing in 1993, was left substantially in place, with additional assessment and testing. The major modernization was to narrow the curriculum at Key Stages 1 and 2 to allow for more time for literacy and numeracy teaching, to narrow the early years of secondary schooling for the same reason, and to reduce the entitlement of disaffected pupils by allowing pupils 14+ to take up work-related learning in FE colleges.

Two genuine modernizing initiatives were the introduction of citizenship teaching and a more stringent focus on ICT. In November 1997 an Advisory Group on Citizenship, chaired by Bernard Crick, was set up to advise on education for citizenship; the brief of this committee was to teach pupils how to participate in a democracy, their duties, responsibilities and the value of community activity (Crick 1998: 4). The group reported in September 1998, recommending that citizenship education be part of the National Curriculum at all key stages and from September 2000 5 per cent of the NC was to be devoted to the area. Groups advising on personal, social and health education (PSHE) and creativity and culture were also set up; most schools were already devoting time to PSHE, but the creative arts had been cut back since 1993. The National Advisory Committee's report on creative and culture education fared less well than the Citizenship Committee. The new-look curriculum to be put in place from September 2000 was denounced by the theatre director, Sir Peter Hall, and by Sir Herman Ouseley, Chair of the Commission for Racial Equality, as 'culturally bereft and multi-culturally inadequate' (Smithers 1999a: 9).

Following instructions from the secretary of state, the QCA consulted on possible changes to the curriculum from May 1999. Changes were to ensure concentration on teaching literacy, numeracy and key skills, to prepare pupils to be good citizens and to encourage good practice, particularly via the National Grid for Learning – an online access for schools to share ideas and materials (QCA and DfEE 1999). Education was to ensure that all pupils 'respond as individuals, parents, workers and citizens to the rapid expansion of communication technologies, changing roles of employment, and new work and leisure patterns resulting from economic migration and the continual globalisation of the economy and society' (QCA and DfEE 1999: 3). A major policy decision by New Labour was to attempt to catch up with the worldwide spread of ICT and encourage its use in schools. A committee to examine the use of computers in schools was set up in 1997, chaired by Lord Stevenson, the architect of the National Grid for Learning. Eventually a £1 billion programme of investment in ICT was promised, all teacher training courses were to include computer literacy and all pupils were expected to learn to use the new technologies via key skills qualifications in A/S courses and other lower-level courses. By September 1999 guidelines for a revised National Curriculum and its assessment had been issued; schools were to follow these by September 2000.

The early acquisition of literacy and numeracy skills was encouraged from 1997 by a number of schemes and initiatives – summer literacy schools, holiday schemes, homework clubs and guidelines, after-school activities – and by the expectation that parents would do more to complement the work of the school. The New Opportunities Fund (money from the National

Lottery) provided much of the funds for these initiatives. The government and its inspectorate were concerned to meet the targets laid down in manifestos and White Papers, and by 2000 were announcing that primary school targets for literacy and numeracy were being met and there could now be a concentration on more of the same in secondary schools. Whether this traditional curriculum and pedagogy were actually meeting the requirements of children or society remained problematic. Davies and Edwards (1999) noted that for a significant number of young people, the school curriculum remained a source of alienation and failure rather than enlightenment and empowerment.

New Labour's school policies 1997–2000 constituted a mixture of the 'standards' agenda first set by Keith Joseph and Margaret Thatcher in 1975, adherence to Conservative beliefs in a market in education, and partial privatization of former public services, plus some attempts to alleviate inner city and outer council estate disadvantages and aim for a measure of social justice. However, the number of overt and covert selective policies, designed to ensure privileges for the middle and aspirant classes, ensured that familial self-interest and the scramble for 'good' schools continued. School education continued to be a divisive rather than a cohesive force.

Notes

1 It is difficult to decide how much money was actually made available for education, as New Labour adhered to Conservative policies to hold down public expenditure. Travers (1999) estimated that expenditure of education as a percentage of GDP fell from a high of 5.2 per cent in 1992/3 to less than 4.7 per cent in 1998/9, and that extra money given after the Comprehensive Spending Review was unlikely to make a radical difference to average spending on education over the period 1997–2000 (HM Treasury 1999).

2 *TES* reporters noted the influence of Michael Barber over appointments to task forces. They asked 'does the future of Britain's education system rest with groups of Michael's friends and friends of his friends, or is this new style a genuine attempt to draw together people from different groups?' ('The powers behind Blunkett's throne', *Times Educational Supplement*, 3 October 1997). In 2000 Anthea Millett, head of the TTA, was replaced by Ralph Tabberer, a senior adviser in the Standards and Effectiveness Unit.

3 The DfEE under its heavyweight permanent secretary Michael Bichard enjoyed an unprecedented period of influence in the centralized education system, but policy was also heavily influenced by the Downing Street Policy Unit, headed by David Miliband, a young former researcher at the IPPR who was knowledgeable about education. Miliband became an MP and a Schools Minister in 2001, and a Cabinet Minister in 2005.

4 The first New Labour government, with a record number of female MPs elected, had two women in the education team, Baroness (Tessa) Blackstone for higher

education, and Estelle Morris. There were no women in the Downing Street Policy Unit and no women in senior positions at the DfEE.

5 Teachers' 'achievements' were to be the improved test performance of their pupils, a situation reminiscent of the payment-by-results system in the late nineteenth century.

6 Barber's work was resonant with that of Fullan (1991), a Canadian expert on educational change, Caldwell and Spinks (1988), Australian advocates of self-managing schools, and the literature on school effectiveness.

7 The Scottish Office Education and Industry Department was responsible for education in Scotland, parliamentary control being devolved to a Scottish Parliament in 1999.

8 Education Extra, the foundation for after-schools activities, was set up in 1992 by Lord Michael Young and directed by Kay Andrews, a former personal assistant to Neil Kinnock. By 1998 it was a major 'deliverer' of DfEE Study Support policies, as was the charity Kids Club Network. Kay Andrews was made a Baroness in 2000.

9 The chief inspector made no secret of his suspicion of LEA influence and his support for total devolution of funding to schools.

10 The leader of Manchester City Council accused Woodhead of pursuing a political agenda, telling the *Times Educational Supplement*: 'I think Woodhead should leave his post as soon as possible. He seems to have set himself a one-man target to destroy public education in this country as rapidly as possible' (Prestage 1998: 1).

11 There had been considerable discussion of a graded teaching profession in the early 1990s. Ross and Tomlinson (1991: 35) wrote that while there is a place for a tiered profession, 'appraisal and other devices are of limited value unless placed within a professional context. Teachers are not a workforce to be managed, but a profession to be respected'.

12 The first chair of the GTC in England was Lord Puttnam, well-known film producer, the vice-chair was Professor John Tomlinson, a long-time campaigner for a teaching council, and the chief executive was to be a former chief education officer Carol Adams.

Further reading

Ball, S.J. (1999) Labour, learning and the economy: a policy sociology perspective, *Cambridge Journal of Education*, 29(2): 195–206. This article discusses the education policy continuities between the Conservatives and New Labour in an international context, and argues that the stress on education's role in contributing to economic competitiveness is unlikely to lead to a high skill economy, because of an impoverished view of learning.

Barber, M. and Sebba, J. (1999) Reflections on progress towards a world class education system, *Cambridge Journal of Education*, 29(2): 183–93. In the same journal the head of the Standards and Effectiveness Unit at the DfEE and the unit's head of research describe the 'vision' of a world class education system and its key characteristics which they claim had driven New Labour's educational policy since 1997.

Docking, J. (ed.) (2000) *New Labour's Policies for Schools: Raising the Standard?*

London: David Fulton. This edited book, from the Roehampton Institute of Education Policy course team, discusses the policies pursued by the New Labour government in its first two and half years of office.

Gewirtz, S. (1999) Education Action Zones: emblems of the third way?, in H. Dean and R. Woods (eds) *Social Policy Review 11*. London: Social Policy Association. Gewirtz uses the 'innovation' of EAZs to point out that social justice, revived civil society, redistribution and teaching innovations are probably incompatible with markets, managerialism and privatization, and suggests the need for an examination of the effects of the range of reforms which characterize the pragmatism of contemporary social policy.

chapter
six

Diversity, selection and privatization 2000–2005

A New Labour government was re-elected in June 2001 and continued an evangelical emphasis on education as a major means of improving the nation's economic competitiveness and enhancing individual life chances. There was something of a slowdown in legislation, a White Paper on schools appearing two months after the election, and an Education Act incorporating some of its proposals in 2002. The year 2003 was blessedly free from Education Acts, although Green and White papers, statutory instruments, regulations, guidance and advice continued to flow from the centre, and the House of Commons Education and Skills Committee cautioned the DfES against introducing further initiatives until earlier ones had been properly evaluated.[1] However, the respite was brief and what McNamara and his colleagues (2000) had labelled 'the Blairite project of total schooling' continued from 2004 to produce legislation and initiatives. In July 2004, the government published, without previous consultation, a Five Year Strategy for Children and Learners (DfES 2004a), in effect a manifesto for a third term in office, and in April 2005, just before the end of the second term, passed the fifth longest education act ever.

In the second term the educational road had been littered with problems for some of the most senior figures. In February 2001 the Prime Minister's communications director Alastair Campbell claimed that some comprehensives in inner cities were 'bog-standard', a label and a claim that comprehensives supported a 'one-size-fits-all' curriculum, repeated by the press for several years. Estelle Morris, Secretary of State for Education from June 2001, referred during her tenure to 'some schools she would not touch with a barge-pole'. The then Shadow Conservative Shadow Home Secretary Oliver Letwin, added to the denigration of comprehensive schools by claiming, in October 2003, that he would 'rather go out on the streets and beg' than send his children to the local comprehensive school (Aaronovitch

2003). The Chair of the Qualifications and Curriculum Authority, Sir William Stubbs, resigned in September 2002 over A-level marking and assessment problems, followed by the resignation of the Secretary of State for Education herself in November 2002.[2] In April 2003 the new Secretary of State for Education, Charles Clarke, admitted that his Department had taken a 'bloody nose' over maladministration when the Individual Learning Accounts Scheme, set up to pay learning providers, collapsed amid allegations of fraud (Hook 2003). In November 2004 Clarke clashed with Prince Charles, heir to the throne, who had criticized a child-centred learning culture in schools.[3] By December 2004 Clarke had been made Home Secretary, and Ruth Kelly, a privately educated 36-year-old, became the third Secretary of State for Education in 26 months. Also in November 2004 the £129,000-a-year director of the National Assessment Agency – a part of QCA – resigned after flaws were found in tests for 14-year-olds. Despite the expansion of national testing and the competition this created among schools, parents and pupils, the Organisation for Economic Cooperation and Development (OECD) had to announce that the collection of attainment data for their three-yearly comparison study between countries could not be accepted from England for 2003, as the data were not reliable (DfES 2004b). Policy in the second term continued to emanate largely from a small group around the Prime Minister in 10 Downing Street.[4] The all-party House of Commons Education and Skills Committee was one of the few bodies openly holding the government to account. It produced a series of well-researched reports on the working out of educational policies and criticized particularly key policies which under the rubric of choice actually increased selection of pupils by schools (see House of Commons Education and Skills Committee 2004, 2005).

Despite the problems, public education continued its long, slow post-war improvement in terms of quality, with more attention paid to early years and childcare, and in terms of quantity as measured by numbers achieving literacy targets and public examination passes. But there was increased public unease that policies of school diversity, competitive marketization and privatization of schools and services, were helping to increase rather than diminish inequalities in both education and society. It was becoming clearer that the achievement of a meritocracy, to which the Prime Minister had committed himself (Blair 1999) was not compatible with an inclusive society, to which the government was also committed (Blair 1998c). The progressive abandonment of government involvement in social welfare provision and the increased role of the private sector appeared to be an electorally attractive way of enhancing 'choice' and reducing public spending, but it was creating huge anxieties for large sections of the middle and aspirant classes. Far from keeping key middle class groups happy, as New Labour educational policies were intended to do, there was dismay that competition for good schools and shifts in costs from the state to the individual were reducing benefits and privileges previously taken for granted. This chapter documents New Labour's commitment to the further development of a diversity of secondary schools as a way of 'modernizing the comprehensive principle' and the increased selection of young people by overt and covert means for different and unequally resourced schools; examines the encroaching privatization of schools, education services and LEAs and the further development of education as a commodity; and notes the positive developments and successes in early years' education and childcare, some policies on special needs and disability, and the continued central control and direction of teachers, testing and the curriculum. The policy story selectively presented in the chapter continues up to March 2005, when all the political parties were attempting to outbid each other with pre-election promises to improve education.

Box 6.1 Chronology of Acts, reports and events 2000–2005

2000   Race Relations (Amendment) Act; by May 2002 Public Bodies, including schools and LEAs, had a duty to promote racial equality (Home Office)

2000   (November) Chris Woodhead, Chief Inspector, resigned; Mike Tomlinson becomes Head of Ofsted

2001   (January) Green Paper *Schools: Building on Success: Raising Standards and promoting Diversity* (DFEE) 'Mission' to transform secondary schools set out; a revised Code of Practice on LEA/school relationships produced

2001   (June) New Labour elected for a second term; Estelle Morris Secretary of State for Education (David Blunkett made Home Secretary)

2001   (June) DfEE becomes DfES (Department for Education and Skills)

2001   (June) Racial conflicts in Bradford, Burnley and Oldham

2001   (July) Marking and timetabling problems with new A/S levels

2001   (September) White Paper *Schools: Achieving Success* (DfES); goal of a diverse secondary sector set out

2001   Special Educational Needs and Disability Act

2001   Special Education Needs: Code of Practice (DfES)

2001   (November) Education Bill

2001   National College for School Leadership set up

2002   David Bell appointed Chief Inspector of Schools

2002   (July) Education Act

2002   International Program for International Student Assessment (PISA) study demonstrates that countries with non-selective education systems achieve the highest education standards

2002   (August–September) A-level marking problems; Chair of QCA, Sir William Stubbs, resigns; enquiry into A-level standards set up (Chair. Mike Tomlinson)

2002 (September) Citizenship courses mandatory in National Curriculum
2002 (October) Secretary of State Estelle Morris resigns; Charles Clarke appointed Education Secretary with David Miliband as Schools Minister
2003 (January) *The Victoria Climbié Inquiry* Report of an inquiry by Lord Laming (DoH/Home Office)
2003 (February) Code of Practice on School Admissions
2003 (February) Building Schools for the Future (BSF) launched with first wave of funding for Private Finance Initiative (PFI) building projects
2003 Disability Discrimination (Amendment) Regulations
2003 (February) *Making Mathematics Count* Smith report on Maths teaching (DfES)
2003 *A New Specialist System: Transforming Secondary Education* (DfES)
2003 *Transforming London Secondary Schools* (DfES)
2003 (September) White Paper *Every Child Matters* (HM Treasury)
2004 (March) *Children Bill*
2004 (8 July) DfES Five Year Strategy for Children and Learners published; includes suggestion that all secondary schools become foundation schools
2004 (15 July) Labour Party National Policy Forum consultation on policy for next election manifesto
2004 (July) *Secondary Education: School Admissions* 4th Report of the House of Commons Education and Skills Committee
2004 (November) *School Admissions* The Government response to the Select Committee report (DfESc)
2004 (16 November) White Paper *Choosing Health* (DoH) Integration with Every Child Matters programme proposed
2004 (23 November) Three education-related Bills announced in the Queen's Speech to Parliament

- Education Bill (published by 30 November)
- School Transport Bill – cutting car use
- Child Benefit Bill – financial support for 16–19-year-olds

2004 (November) *Building Schools for the Future* (BSF); second wave of funding announced (DfES)
2004 (November) *Children Act*
2004 *Special Educational Needs and Disability: Towards Inclusive Schools* (Ofsted report)
2004 (December) Ruth Kelly appointed Secretary of State for Education; (Charles Clarke becomes Home Secretary; David Miliband moves to the Cabinet Office)
2005 (Jan) *Choice for Parents: The Best Start for Children* (DfES) A Ten-Year Strategy for children's services
2005 (April) Education Act

Secretaries of State for Education and Skills

Estelle Morris   June 2001–October 2002
Charles Clarke   October 2002–December 2004
Ruth Kelly   December 2004–

Shadow Education and Skills Secretaries

Damien Green 2001–2003
Tim Yeo 2003 (health and education)
Tim Collins 2003 –

Commitment to diversity

By 2001 a diversity of schools was well established. Overall there was
private schooling for some 7 per cent of pupils who constituted some
26 per cent of those staying on to take A-level examinations. For the majority in public sector education even primary schools had in some areas
become battlegrounds for parents anxious to get their children into desirable
schools. At secondary level there was overt selection for the remaining 164
grammar schools. The rest 'chose' ostensibly non-selective schools, except
where specialist schools selected up to 10 per cent of pupils by 'aptitude',[5]
religious schools selected mainly on the basis of faith, or other schools used a
range of covert methods (see Edwards and Tomlinson 2002). Selection by
mortgage continued, as those able to afford it moved close to desirable
schools. This was quantified by estate agents in Reading as a £42,000 pre-
mium to be near a good primary school and £23,000 to be near a good
secondary school (Garrett 2003). Post-1998, schools had designated themselves as foundation, voluntary aided/controlled or community schools.
Almost all secondary schools embracing the foundation label were former
grant-maintained schools which had benefited from superior resourcing during the 1990s, although some, on returning to the LEA post-1998, brought
debts which then became the responsibility of the LEA.

A Green Paper was published before the 2001 general election which
congratulated the government on 'getting the basics right in primary
schools' and listed government achievements so far. These included nursery
education for all 4-year-olds; cutting infant class sizes; increased funding
and school building; action on special educational needs; more computers
and a National Grid for Learning website; more Beacon schools; Learning
Support Units for disruptive pupils; fewer failing schools and poor lessons;
better progress on literacy and numeracy; improved exam results in deprived
areas; and the success of the Excellence in Cities programme. The Green

Paper criticized comprehensive schools for apparently not developing a 'distinctive character and mission' (DFEE 2001: 5), despite the largest ever study of comprehensive schools demonstrating that the schools were responding to their localities and developing a distinctive ethos (Benn and Chitty 1996). It set out plans for encouraging diversity among secondary schools as 'promoting diversity leads to greater flexibility, more opportunities for schools to learn from each other and . . . a wider range of choice for pupils and parents' (DFEE 2001: 17). Schools were to be encouraged to become specialist, and high performing schools could bid to be Advanced Specialist schools. By 2003, they were to be called Leading Edge schools. The City Academy programme, launched in March 2000, was to be extended. Private, voluntary and faith groups could take over weak or failing schools with greater autonomy for successful schools, and more vocational options were to be available from age 14 in schools or in further education colleges. Despite a rhetoric of mixing vocational and academic courses, the paper suggested more vocational links with CoVEs (Centres of Vocational Excellence) in further education for some pupils, while gifted and talented pupils went on to sixth form colleges. Far from suggesting an end to overt selection at 11 the Paper promised to encourage links between grammar schools and secondary modern schools.

By July 2001 this Paper had been rewritten into a White Paper (DfES 2001a) which was published in September 2001. The White Paper claimed that 'it was right to move away from the selective system which divided children into achievers and non-achievers . . . there can be no question of a two-tier system for tomorrow' (p. 6) and then went on to detail the 'flexible diverse system' which would guarantee a multiple tier school system with schools for 'achievers' highly sought after. In this paper at least half of secondary schools were to become specialist schools, with an expansion of Beacon schools, faith schools and City Academies ('Academies' in the 2002 Act), with successful schools allowed to innovate and change their curriculum, and expand their intake. Sponsors from private, voluntary or faith groups could establish new schools with running costs met by the State. The modest aim in this paper was 20 Academies by 2005. More partnerships between schools were envisaged with governing bodies of failing schools being replaced and LEAs expected to find external bodies to help turn round failing schools. The diverse system wanted was one where 'schools differ markedly from each other in the particular contribution they choose to make but are equally excellent in giving their students a broad curriculum' (DfES 2001a: 38). The Paper noted that GCSEs in vocational subjects would be available in all schools by 2003 and suggested an overarching award to recognize achievements in both academic and vocational subjects (see Chapter 7). The teaching profession was to be further reformed, with more support staff, performance related pay, support for professional development and recruitment, key roles for Advanced Skills teachers, and a Fast Track programme for new entrants. The Secretary of State was to take powers away from the School Teachers Review Body in order to change pay and conditions.

The 2002 Education Act, following this White Paper, and with 217 sections and 22 Schedules, was a complex mix of measures incorporating most of the White Paper proposals, and purporting to provide a new legal framework for schools. The first section gave the Secretary of State powers to allow schools to 'innovate' to raise educational standards – schools which 'earned autonomy' could change the curriculum and teachers' pay and conditions. Governing bodies could form or invest in companies to provide services to any schools. Schools could group in Federations and provide community services, and every LEA was to establish a Schools Forum to advise on budgets and an Admissions Forum to advise on local admissions. LEAs were required to organize competition for the establishment of new additional secondary schools. Headteachers were given more discretion to exclude pupils and the Secretary of State took further powers to close schools causing concern. Legislation created 'Academies' and schools formerly known as city academies or city technology colleges could become academies. The Learning and Skills Council could allow workplace training for 14–16-year-olds. There were attempts to tidy up some of the effects of previous initiatives and legislation. Section 38, for example, noted the 'desirability of avoiding sending excessive material' to schools and avoiding the 'imposition of excessive administrative burdens'. The overall effect of the Act was a further shift of powers from local authorities to the Secretary of State and to schools. Fowler (2002) noted that most innovations suggested in the Act had already come from local authority initiatives, and research from the 1990s had demonstrated that secondary schools were clinging more and more to tradition rather than innovation (Whitty *et al.* 1998).

Overt selection

The commitment to diversity included the retention of, and support for, a private sector which selected pupils by both income and ability. While the advantages and privileges of good private education have been well documented at a national level, privately educated pupils were increasingly part of a new global elite, moving on to world-class universities and top multinational jobs (Ong 2004). The major threat to private education offered by the government was a review of charities undertaken in 2002, although the DfES did offer a competitive grant of some £½ million annually to encourage partnerships between private and state schools. Private schools benefited financially from charitable status and the Independent Schools Council (ISC), eager not to lose funds, set out to demonstrate the public benefits private education offered in terms of shared facilities and joint activities with state schools. As Mitchell (2004) pointed out, most of these activities were designed to benefit the 'gifted and talented' or were peripheral to the activities of the private schools. He also pointed out that pretending that schools such as Eton, (attended by the Prince of Wales' sons) which had such large capital reserves that the school could afford to lose £4 million gambling on the Currency and Futures market, were charitable, 'is a peculiarly nauseating form of English hypocrisy' (Mitchell 2004: 2).

The major overt selection in state education in England continued to be the retention of 164 grammar schools which affected the intake of some 500 notionally comprehensive schools – 20 per cent of secondary schools. Although in 2003 Schools Minister David Miliband wrote 'the ending of the 11plus in most parts of the country was a victory over structural inequality of opportunity' (Miliband 2003), the 11+ examination continued to be an overt method of selection in 36 LEAs in England, with thousands of children still learning that they had 'failed' at 11. The permitted expansion of numbers in grammar schools meant that by 2003 the equivalent of eight more grammar schools had been created, and research into the development of Beacon schools indicated that some were recreating themselves as grammar-type schools (Hey and Bradford 2004). Arguments continued to be made that grammar schools had enabled educational and social mobility for working class children. The reality was that grammar schools had always predominantly educated middle class groups. In 2004 less than 2 per cent of pupils in grammar schools were eligible for free school meals compared to 18 per cent in all schools. These highly selective schools, oversubscribed by intensively tutored children, continue to educate the middle classes, and the government encouraged philanthropic schemes based on the notion of escape from supposedly less attractive non-selective schools.[6] A survey of parents in 2004 found that parents favoured local schools taking local children, with selection by ability even less popular than selection by lottery (Shaw 2004a).

From the 1990s evidence accumulated questioning the benefits of selective education even for the most able pupils (Edwards and Tomlinson 2002; Schagen and Schagen 2003), and poor but able children were unlikely to make it into grammar schools (Atkinson, Gregg, McConnell 2004). The international PISA study (OECD 2002) demonstrated that countries with non-selective systems achieved the highest performance standards overall, and a study in Northern Ireland documented that selection 'was socially divisive, damaged self-esteem, disrupted teaching and reinforced inequality of opportunity' (Gallagher and Smith 2001: 79). In 2002 the then Education Minster in Northern Ireland, Martin McGuiness, pledged to end selection in the Province. This pledge was reinforced by a working group and by the next Education Minister Barry Gardiner, although following the suspension of the Northern Ireland Assembly the date for ending selection was put back to 2008. In England, the government resolutely refused to consider even changing the complex balloting system put in place by the 1998 School Standards and Framework Act, which allowed parents with children at private schools to vote for retention of grammar schools, while disallowing many local parents. At the Labour Party National Policy Forum in July 2004, although many MPs, Trade Union representatives and local councillors were in favour of abolishing selection, the issue was thought by government to be an electoral liability.[7] The government also continued to encourage within-school selection, and continued to urge schools to set (track) pupils by ability. Via the Excellence in Cities programme, schools were to provide Learning Support Units and mentors for low-ability and disruptive pupils. The 'gifted and talented' were to attend summer schools, take more extra-curricular activities and study for 'world class tests'. In 2002 Warwick University won a bid to establish an Academy for Gifted and Talented Youth, at which the fortunate gifted would pay for courses. An early evaluation of the programme found white, middle class children more likely to be selected as gifted and in 2003 the Ofsted Chief Inspector reported that the programme had not raised standards overall (Bell 2003). However, those who had attended the Gifted Academy were able to report their attendance on their forms for University entrance as a way of demonstrating their giftedness (Bloom 2004).

Meanwhile, selection of pupils for vocational education from age 14 continued to develop, with over 120,000 14–16-year-olds 'training' in further education colleges each year. In early 2005 the Chief Inspector suggested that a new type of vocational school be created, causing critics to suggest he wished to return to the post-1944 tripartite system of schooling. The government White Paper of February 2005 (DfES 2005b), the response to the Tomlinson report on 14–19 education, also appeared to reinforce the separation of schooling for the 'academic' and the 'vocational'. The General Secretary of the Association of Teachers and Lecturers warned that plans for post-14 education threatened to 'turn the clock back by 50 years', reintroducing selection and dividing children along social class lines (Taylor 2005).

Specialist diversity

The specialist schools programme continued to be a major route to the government aim of 'modernizing the comprehensive principle,' although there was still no evidence of parental or student demand. In 2000 a government sponsored study had reported that 51 per cent of headteachers bid for specialist status for the extra money – £50,000 to be raised from business or the community matched by £50,000 from the government (West et al. 2000). At the end of 2004 a head of department in a school spending time bidding for specialist status wrote that 'My school wants specialist status because of the extra funding. Money, not educational aims . . . is behind our present work' (Savage 2004). Schools were required to meet performance standards to achieve specialist status, thus putting low achieving schools or those unable to raise £50,000 at a disadvantage. Nevertheless, even before the 2001 election the Prime Minister was announcing that half of all secondary schools would have a specialism by 2006. By 2003 there were some 992 specialist secondary schools, 443 specializing in technology, 173 in arts, 162 in sport, 157 in languages, 18 in business and enterprise, 24 in science, 12 in maths and computing, and 4 in engineering. Specialist schools, in common with all secondary schools, could admit 10 per cent of pupils by 'aptitude' although there was no consensus as to how aptitude could be measured at 11, or how this differed from 'ability' (see note 5). Specialist sports schools, were reported by Trudex Textile to be choosing a uniform of sweatshirts rather than the blazers and ties favoured by arts schools. They were intended to help transform the sporting prowess of English pupils despite a reportedly lower examination performance (Youth Sports Trust 2002). By the end of 2003, a paper announcing *A New Specialist System* (DfES 2003a) claimed that more schools were to be designated as specialist, bringing the total to over 1200. The goal was that by 2006 this would rise to over 2000. New specialisms in music, the humanities and rural studies were announced. Popular schools could expand and competitions to start new schools would be open to new and existing education providers. Schools were to be encouraged to work in Federations – groups of schools working in collaboration, even sharing governing bodies. Beacon schools were to be phased out, but high performing schools with a specialism could apply to be Leading Edge Schools with an annual £60,000 Leadership Incentive Grant to work with other schools. Private schools could also apply to be Leading Edge. A pilot of 240 extended schools acting as 'community hubs' offering childcare and other services were to create partnerships beyond the classroom. Adnett and Davies (2003: 394) pointed out that despite talk of partnership there had been little evidence of this as 'one school cannot at the same time compete and collaborate with another school in providing the same outcome'.

The 2003 paper made the claim, repeated often by Ministers, that performance in specialist schools outstripped that in non-specialist schools at GCSE. The evidence for this rested on surveys carried out by Professor David Jesson, in association with Cyril Taylor, Director of the Specialist Schools Trust, which had its genesis in 1987 under Mrs Thatcher as the Technology Colleges Trust. The surveys used DfES data to compare examination results of specialist and non-specialist schools and claimed that in 2003, 56 per cent of pupils in the 938 specialists schools gained five or more GCSEs at A–C grades compared to 47 per cent in all comprehensive and secondary modern schools (Jesson *et al.* 2004). The methodology of these surveys proved questionable. Even non-educationalists were able to point out that the surveys took no account of the extra money and attention the specialist schools had received. Glatter noted that the surveys were not peer reviewed but were disseminated in Specialist Schools Trust publications, and 'through skilful news management in media coverage' (Glatter 2004: 63). However, the Prime Minister was so impressed by the Trust that he gave Cyril Taylor, knighted by Mrs Thatcher under the Conservatives, a special knighthood for further services to education.[8] At a Specialist Schools conference in November 2004, the Secretary of State Charles Clarke, starting off his speech with 'Thanks to Cyril' claimed the schools offered 'the opportunity of a choice for parents between a range of strong, independent diverse, yet co-operating high quality schools' (Clarke 2004). However he did finally publicize the fact that there was no guarantee that specialist schools, with no uniform geographical or regional spread, could actually offer 'choice' to parents. By this time some 1968 schools were specializing in at least one curriculum subject, with the possibility of a second specialism about to be announced, and the target of two thousand schools was reached by early 2005.

Academies and admissions

The policy, which combined several agendas – providing a diversity of schools including more faith schools, improving inner city schools, reducing powers of local authorities, and bringing in private money – was encapsulated in the creation of Academies. Announced in March 2000 and making an initial appearance as City Academies in the 2000 Learning and Skills Act, the first three Academies opened in 2002. Academies were to be 'independent' semi-privatized schools sponsored by business, faiths or voluntary bodies, partly replacing the failing 'Fresh Start' policy for 'failing' schools, and partly modelled on the charter schools in the USA (Miron 2001). They were to be set up as limited companies with charitable status, in effect private schools publicly funded. Sponsors would contribute up to £2 million, and appoint a majority of governors who would control the school. Central government would contribute what turned out to be up to £25 million of tax payers money for each school and would transfer local authority owned land and buildings to the 'partnerships' which would own and run the schools. The schools were to be their own admissions authorities, taking advice from local admissions forums. They were to be specialist, able to admit 10 per cent of pupils on aptitude, have more autonomy over staffing and pay, and not be bound by the national curriculum. By early 2005 some 17 Academies were open or planned, the public cost being £475 million at this point, with 39 more planned. The Prime Minister was heavily committed to the Academy programme, proposing 30 Academies for London in a 2003 document on London Schools and claiming in his speech to the Labour Party conference in 2004 that 'parents have made the City Academy Schools so popular in areas of the greatest social disadvantage' (Blair 2004). The Five Year Strategy of July 2004 promised 200 Academies to be open by 2010. Despite problems with sponsors, Blair held 'breakfasts' in Downing Street for potential investors, including meeting American investment banker Bill Ruane, introduced to Downing Street by Cyril Taylor (Shaw and Paton 2004). Leading private schools were also approached to sponsor Academies, and two in London (Dulwich College and North London Collegiate) apparently had enough spare money to consider sponsorship (Crace 2004). Some 22 of the existing or planned Academies would be in the control of Christian organizations, including two evangelical sponsors. Teachers in Academies were not required to register with the General Teaching Council, a situation which led to a petition to Parliament by the GTC in 2005.

In their short history to 2005, Academies had mixed careers and receptions from parents. By the end of 2004 five Academy headteachers had resigned and been replaced, Greig Academy in Haringey having three heads in three years. The King's Academy in Middlesbrough, sponsored by millionaire car dealer and evangelical Christian Sir Peter Vardy, excluded 26 pupils in its first year, a 2.5 per cent rate compared with an English average of 0.23 per cent. The Vardy Foundation, already sponsoring a City Technology College in Gateshead which taught creationism alongside evolutionary theory, found its efforts to sponsor an Academy in Doncaster frustrated by local parents, who satirically put their school up for auction on the eBay internet auction site before it could be turned into an Academy (Shaw 2004b). Fashion designer Jasper Conran, who had considered sponsoring an Academy in Waltham Forest, London, was upset to find that local parents and teachers were against the plan (Conran 2004). In some cases, the cash promised by business sponsors took the form of services and consultancy (Stewart 2004a) and Academies excluding pupils were apparently not returning funding to the local authorities to educate them elsewhere (Stewart 2004b). Claims that Academies improved examination performance were questioned by research which indicated that they 'improved the intake', taking fewer children with special needs and excluding difficult pupils (Slater 2004a). Budge in 2001 had noted that the American Charter schools, intended to raise achievement in disadvantaged areas, were soon selecting pupils, taking fewer with special needs, and eroding local democracy as many were run by national education companies (Budge 2001; Miron 2001). The English *Independent* Newspaper asked in July 2004 whether sports agents, bankers, private school heads and evangelical creationist believers should be running state-maintained schools in England (Garner 2004).

With government encouraging a diversity of schools and referring to 'choice', which in reality was only a right to 'express a preference' for admission to a school, it was unsurprising that admissions increasingly became a source of confusion, anxiety and anger for many parents. In 2004 the Chief Schools Adjudicator reported that complaints against school admissions procedures had doubled over the past two years, many schools were failing to follow their own procedures and the rules on admission were overcomplicated and unclear. The Education Act 2002 required all LEAs to have an Admissions Forum, at which the LEA, as an Admissions authority, and those schools which were their own authorities (foundation schools, voluntary aided schools, CTCs and Academies) would meet to discuss problems in local school admission. A new non-statutory Code of Practice on Admissions was issued in 2003 (DfES 2003b) but by 2004 the House of Commons Education and Skills Committee had published a report on secondary school admissions which was highly critical of the admissions procedures and often covert selection procedures many schools used (House of Commons Education and Skills Committee 2004). Interviewing children and parents, disallowed by the Code of Practice after September 2005, was, for example, claimed by some schools to be only 'structured discussion' with parents. The Oratory School in London, attended by the Prime Minister's children 'had regard' to the Code and then decided to ignore it (Millar 2004). The government responded to the Select Committee in November 2004, rejecting criticisms of admission policies and claiming that the five-year strategy for schools, while setting out 'plans for greater diversity and freedom for schools' expected schools to 'work collaboratively and share their responsibilities for all pupils in their area' (DfES 2004c: introduction). By early 2005 the Select Committee had come to the end of a two-year inquiry into secondary education and was highly critical of the whole notion of diversity of provision.

> Diversity of provision: The Specialist schools programme and more recently the City Academy initiative have added new school types to an already diverse system of secondary education. The Government asserts that this policy will lead to a rise in standards, but it has failed to produce evidence to support the expansion of its diversity initiatives . . . expensive schemes are being rolled out before being adequately tested and evaluated compared to other less expensive alternatives.
>
> (House of Commons Education and Skills Committee 2005: 3)

Five-year strategies

In the summer of 2004 all major government departments were required to produce a five-year strategic plan, and the DfES responded by presenting their Five-year Strategy for Children and Learners (DfES 2004a) on 8 July, followed on 12 July by the Treasury Spending Review which promised £12 billion more for education by 2008, with education spending as a proportion of GDP rising to 5.6 per cent from 5.4 per cent in 2005 (HM Treasury 2004). The 100-page Strategy claimed five principles would underpin advances in education and children's services: greater personalization and choice; opening up services to new and different providers (privatization); freedom and independence for headteachers and managers with more secure funding; a commitment to staff development; and partnerships with parents, employers, local authorities and voluntary organizations. The plan covered all areas of education, from early years to further and higher education. It included plans for Children's Centres and 'educare', with 'wrap around' childcare in primary schools from 8am to 6pm.

The most contentious proposal was to create 'independent specialist schools in place of the traditional comprehensive'. All schools were to be guaranteed a three-year budget, still based competitively on pupil numbers, and passed on by the local authority. The LEA role was to be considerably diminished by the suggestion that all schools – apart from primary and voluntary-aided secondary schools – would be able, by a simple vote of their governing body, to become foundation schools taking on ownership of the land and employment of the staff and be their own admissions authority. Every secondary school up to standard was to be specialist by 2008, with possible second specialisms and able to open sixth forms, and popular schools could increase their intake within twelve weeks of making the request. The Academy programme, as noted above, was to be expanded and Foundation Partnerships of successful schools could take on extra responsibilities for teacher training, 14–19 curriculum sharing, provision for SEN and excluded pupils. Local authorities were to recast themselves as quality assurers of educational services, not as direct suppliers or managers of local schools and colleges. Consultation on the foundation school and school expansion proposals was put out by the DfES on 4 October 2004, and an Education Bill was presented to Parliament on 30 November despite the fact that the consultation did not close until 31 December. The proposed legislation appeared to suggest a system of 3000 separate secondary schools, each admitting the pupils they chose, but 'nationalized' under central control with funding for each school – including primary and special schools – determined by central government. An indication that all this was not too far from plans the Conservative opposition had for education was given by the Shadow Secretary of State for Education, Tim Collins, who wrote that the policies were 'the latest instances of New Labour mouthing Tory slogans 'although not offering schools the full independence a Conservative government would grant' (Collins 2005).

The final Education Act of the New Labour government's second term, passed in April 2005, turned out to be the fifth longest Act ever, with 124 clauses and 19 schedules. Of historic importance was section 101 in Part 4, which was concerned with the funding of maintained schools. Funding in the future was to come directly from the Secretary of State and not through local government financial settlements, thus overturning an arrangement dating back to the 1902 Balfour Education Act. There was still to be a minimum funding guarantee (MFG) and a funding period could be up to 48 months. Part 1 reduced school inspections, with more input from HMIs and inspections to start from school self-evaluations. The notion of 'schools causing concern' was to be replaced by 'schools requiring significant improvement'. Part 2 extended competition for all new schools to any 'promoters', for example religious or parent groups, and LEAs were required to take account of this new law on secondary school competition. Part 3 was concerned with 'training the workforce' giving more powers via the Secretary of State to the Teaching and Development Agency for Schools (TDAS), now overseeing the whole school workforce. Further sections required LEAs to set targets for the educational performance of all pupils in their maintained schools, required governing bodies to produce a school profile instead of holding annual parents meetings, gave more powers to governing bodies over excluded pupils, and gave schools powers to provide limited higher education courses, for example Open University courses. LEAs were to have more responsibility for children in care and for free school meals.

The origins for the unprecedented ending of local government control of education spending appeared to lie in a funding crisis in 2003–2004. From 1997 the government had undertaken several reviews of school financing, with changes made to allocations via the standard spending assessment (SSA) and the Additional Educational Needs Index (AEN), with funds increasingly diverted towards competitive initiatives. In 2002 the Chancellor of the Exchequer had announced an extra £15 billion for education over three years, but in early 2003 bitter arguments broke out between government, LEAs, schools and unions over school funding shortages (Crace 2003). Essentially, central allocation of funds to local authorities had not taken account of teachers' pay increases, pensions and national insurance costs, or of the required employment of more teaching assistants. The reduced allocation led some schools to reduce their teaching force and there was less money for special educational needs. The government initially attempted to blame LEAs for withholding money from schools but was eventually forced to concede under-funding and promised a rise of 4 per cent per pupil for 2004–2005. Travers, an expert on education funding, suggested that

> Ministers can't afford to preside over a funding muddle in 2005 – a general election year . . . Tony Blair could decide that direct Whitehall funding is the only answer and that would mean the final curtain for local government control of education.
>
> (Travers 2003)

It was then reported that policy advisers Andrew Adonis and Michael Barber were campaigning for Whitehall to take control of school budgets

(Smithers and White 2003). Since this actually came about it was yet another indication that unelected advisors in the New Labour central government had the power to change crucial parts of the education system in England with no democratic input.

Early years and childcare strategies

In contrast to the production of contradictory policies which increased competition between a diverse hierarchy of schools, while at the same time urging partnership and cooperation, policies on early years education and childcare were more coherent, and were in some measure based on research.[9] The government intentions were to reduce the numbers of children living in poverty, improve support for families with young children, and coordinate local services. The National Childcare Strategy, announced in 1998, brought in extra funding which was increased in the 2002 and 2004 Treasury Spending Reviews. In addition, nursery education places were available for all 3- and 4-year-olds by 2004; local authorities had set up Early Years Development and Childcare Partnerships; the 2002 Act had established a Foundation Stage for early education; QCA produced an early years qualifications and training framework; and Ofsted inspected early years services. Sure Start, a policy designed to improve the health and education of children in disadvantaged areas, appeared to be a success. By 2003 some 500 Sure Start programmes were in operation, bringing together midwives, health visitors and play workers to offer services to over 300,000 children in deprived areas (Ball 2002). It was noteworthy that this was one initiative that did not require competitive bidding between local authorities and did not appeal for private funding. It was supported from the outset by Norman Glass, a senior treasury civil servant later described as the architect of the programme, who made sure money was allocated to the scheme. A Sure Start Unit was set up in the DfES in 2003 to oversee early years and childcare initiatives and the development of Childcare Centres. A White Paper on health, published in 2004, claimed that by 2008 there would be 2500 Centres, bringing together health, social care and educational professionals (DoH 2004). However, by early 2005 Norman Glass had become concerned that the original aims of Sure Start had been subverted – the programme becoming part of the government agenda to provide childcare places while poor mothers went out to work (Glass 2005). The Public Accounts Committee of the House of Commons reported in 2004 on the progress in developing childcare, and concluded that while good progress had been made, a market in childcare had developed and more evidence was needed on care by private providers. They also found that provision was least developed in deprived areas (Public Accounts Committee 2004).

Childcare policies were treated with more urgency after the death, in

2000, of Victoria Climbié, an 8-year-old child of West African origin. A subsequent inquiry by Lord Laming blamed poor coordination between social, health and educational services, and in 2003 a Green Paper *Every Child Matters* set out a new framework of services for all children 0–19 in England (HM Treasury 2003). Proposals in this Paper included establishing a Minister for Children and Young People and Families, with a Director of Children's Services in each local authority to combine responsibility for education and children's services, overseeing Children's Trusts – bodies intended to integrate services including Children's Centres and extended schools. A Children's Commissioner would act as a children's champion independent of government. By November 2004 A Children Act had been passed legislating for a Children's Commissioner, Directors of Children's Services, a Lead Local Council Member to oversee the integration of services and a joint inspection service to check on this. Local authorities were required to put in place a Children and Young People's Plan by 2006. There was no requirement in the Act for schools to be included in the list of bodies required to cooperate and integrate, only that further guidance would be available. The contradictions between giving governing bodies and headteachers more 'independence' while requiring cooperation between all services for children were glaringly obvious.

Special educational needs

Policy initiatives in the New Labour's second term concerning children and young people with disabilities and special educational needs were aimed at making educational opportunities more widely available and Armstrong (2005) noted that the extent of policy intervention in this area far outstripped that of any previous government. A rhetoric of inclusion did, for some children, become a reality, as more children who would previously have been segregated were 'mainstreamed'. A revised Code of Practice on Special Educational Needs was issued in 2001, which provided a more concise managerial tool dealing with those with perceived learning and behavioural problems, followed by a Special Educational Needs and Disability Act. This Act, for the first time, linked special educational needs and disability issues, extending the power of the 1995 Disability and Discrimination Act to ensure that discrimination against disabled students is unlawful in any educational institution or service. In 2004 *Removing Barriers to Achievement* (DfES 2004e) linked special education to the 'Every Child Matters' agenda, offering early intervention, the removal of barriers to learning, improved teacher training and expectations, and improved partnerships with parents of all vulnerable children. The Paper claimed that more integrated children's services and early intervention would help reduce child poverty and educational disadvantage.

Inclusion, however, remained a contested concept. There was actually a 1 per cent increase in children 'statemented' as having special educational needs between 1999 and 2003, with noticeable local variations. Boys were more likely to have statements, accounting for 77 per cent of those with statements in secondary schools. Roma and Traveller's children were over-represented. African Caribbean boys continued to be excluded from main-stream schools in disproportionate numbers, being placed in schools for the emotionally and behaviourally disturbed and in pupil referral units. They continued to be four times over-represented in straight exclusions from school. The majority of pupils regarded as having learning difficulties, or being troublesome and disaffected, were, as always, predominantly from lower socio-economic backgrounds, although middle class knowledgeable parents continued to lobby for extra resources and segregated facilities for children with particular disabilities. Dyson (2004) researching inclusion and school achievement for the DfES, found that schools with higher levels of inclusion tended to serve more disadvantaged areas, further confirmation that in educational markets, schools serving advantaged areas were more likely to reject 'undesirable' pupils.

Privatization in public education

The privatization of public welfare provision intensified during the second term of the New Labour government, despite evidence that the introduction of market forces, competition and privatization was resulting in more edu-cational, social and economic inequalities (Pantazis and Gordon 2000; Ball 2003). Private incursions in education took several forms, particularly bringing in private providers to create a market in education support ser-vices. A DfEE paper in 2000 encouraged LEAs to trade services across local boundaries and promised extra funding for them to develop partnerships with private firms (DfEE 2000). Schools and LEAs regarded as failing were in danger of being taken over by private companies. Schools were encour-aged to become 'commodity producing enterprises' (Rikowski 2003), form-ing private companies and encouraging a business curriculum. Parents were increasingly under pressure to invest in their children's education by buying resources at home, computers and home tuition being the most obvious (Scanlon and Buckingham 2004). School building programmes were largely financed by PFI, whereby companies providing capital would eventually own the school buildings, and in 2003 the government announced a long-term 'Building Schools for the Future', programme of renewing secondary schools in England, with private capital of some £2.2 billion over ten years.

There was increased intervention by private companies and individuals in starting up fee-paying schools in the UK. A 'new species' of cheaper private education was planned by GEMS (Global Education Management Systems), a Dubai-based company operating 13 schools in England in 2004 and planning 120 more. GEMS included on its advisory board former Chief Inspector Sir Mike Tomlinson, knighted in 2005 for services to public education; Sir Michael Bichard, former DfES permanent secretary, knighted on leaving the DfES; and Elizabeth Passmore, former Director of Inspection at Ofsted (Shaw 2004c). Another former Chief inspector, Chris Woodhead, also chaired a private company, Cognita, which in 2004 purchased 17 private schools, causing the headline 'Ex-Inspectors in private wars' (Paton 2004). Private takeovers of state schools was slower to take off. In 2001 King's Manor School in Surrey became England's first 'privatized' comprehensive, a 'failing' state school taken over by a private company, 3E's Ltd, which proceeded to improve the school's performance by excluding more pupils with special needs.

However it was 'failing' local education authorities that were more at risk of being privatized. Islington, despite being the former home area of the Prime Minister, became the first LEA to have day-to-day running taken over by a private firm, Cambridge Education Associates. This firm was eventually penalized by the DfES for failing to meet agreed targets on pupil performance. Leeds LEA was taken over in 2001 by Education Leeds, run by the private company Capita – with Peter Ridsdale as the Chair of the board, being Chair of Leeds United Football club at the time. Capita was the company appointed by the DfES to run the Individual Learning Accounts for those taking vocational courses, a scheme which collapsed at some cost to the taxpayer after fraud investigations. Capita had failed to set up a proper computer system (Hook 2003). In 2004 Capita was also awarded an £178 million contract to support the national primary and Key Stage 3 strategies, causing the Liberal Democrat education spokesman, Phil Willis, to comment that as Capita already sponsored an Academy and was a large provider of education services, 'the whole thing stinks' (Mansell 2004: 15). Southwark LEA was forced to transfer its educational services to a private engineering company W.S. Atkins, but by the end of 2002 Atkins' performance was considered to be 'shambolic' (CPS 2003). The number of schools in special measures increased and the creditors even included the company that franked the mail. In March 2003 the company pulled out, and a team from Cambridge Education Associates was sent in. A journalist commented that 'what happened in Southwark is a bitter case study in how New Labour's political drive to involve private companies in education or health services can go badly wrong' (Toolis 2003).

Undeterred by the failings of Atkins, in 2003 the government awarded a £2 million contract to another engineering firm which had developed an interest in education, Jarvis Educational Services, to advise on the improvement of failing schools. Jarvis, the parent company, was under investigation for the rail crash at Potters Bar in 2002. Its share price fell when it accepted blame for this in 2004, putting at risk the company involvement in 19 PFI contracts in 120 schools (Slater 2004b). A headline in the *Times Educational Supplement* 'Nudists add to Jarvis's Woes' (Lee 2004) noted that under PFI, Northumberland Park School in North London had its swimming pool transferred to Jarvis who promptly banned a nude swimming group from bookings, causing some complaints. The government however, remained committed to increasing private involvement, with approved lists of contractors for the privatized inspectorate, for consultancy and other educational services, and there was considerable recycling of personnel from LEAs to private companies. There were, however, some successful partnerships between private companies and local authorities. The 2002 Act allowed schools to form companies, the Thomas Telford City Technology College in Shropshire being the most quoted example. This school had formed an online company to borrow money and make a profit selling educational services. Corporate influence and advertising in schools increased, notably in Academies, the Bexley Academy operating a business court with links to the London Stock Exchange. In attempting to explain the New Labour commitment to private sector involvement, Hatcher (2002) suggested that first, the government really believed private involvement increased efficiency, secondly that private involvement reduced state spending on education, and thirdly that government hoped a British education industry would participate in the global trade in education services.

More modernization

The 'modernization' of the teaching profession continued to preoccupy government, with Wragg noting that the word could actually encompass the reintroduction of old prejudices and economies with the truth (Wragg 2004).[10] Although a General Teaching Council had been set up, with teachers in state but not private schools required to register with the Council, central government continued to take over the regulation of teacher training and assessment. New entrants to teaching were required from February 2001 to pass skills tests in literacy and numeracy in addition to GCSE passes in English and maths. One consequence of this instant policy was that teacher recruitment fell, especially among ethnic minorities and those with English as an additional language. The tests were not required by those teaching in the private sector. Although this move was intended to raise standards, performance in Scottish schools, where teachers were not required to take the tests, continued to rise. Teacher's morale was raised in November 2000, when Chief Inspector Woodhead resigned his post,[11] to be replaced for two years by Mike Tomlinson, then David Bell. The system of performance related pay, particularly crossing the externally assessed 'threshold' of good performance after five years teaching, was researched by Mahoney and her colleagues between 2001 and 2003. They found that teachers largely resented the policy and that overall the process 'fitted into the existing context of pressure, surveillance and regulation' of teachers (Mahoney *et al.* 2003: 10). They also reported that the threshold process involved more contracts with private companies. Cambridge Education Associates and the Centre for British Teachers (CfBT) were initially awarded £36 million to train threshold assessors, the company being underwritten for the LEA by the global engineering company Mott Macdonald. They commented that 'in this context the meaning of "state education" has changed with the increased involvement of private sector involvement in making and implementing public policy for profit' (Mahoney *et al.* 2003: 16). One of the respondents in the study, employed privately, commented that the work was outsourced to prevent LEA involvement.

In 2003, teachers and their unions reached an agreement with government to cut their workload. Classroom assistants were to take over more administrative and clerical tasks. By September 2005 the workplace agreement was expected to be in place with teachers allowed more time for planning and assessment. The National Union of Teachers refused to sign the agreement as it suggested that teacher assistants could take over the supervision of whole classes. This suspicion appeared to be vindicated when at the end of 2003 a 'blue skies' paper circulating in the DfES suggested fewer qualified teachers and the employment of private agency unqualified staff in schools (Stewart 2003). The progressive removal of control of teacher education from institutions of higher education continued, with the Teacher Training Agency adding Continuing Professional Development (CPD) of all teachers, and training of classroom assistants to its portfolio. In 2005 the TTA became the Teaching and Development Agency for Schools (TDAS). The National College of School Leadership in Nottingham, opening in 2001, and costing £193 million in its first three years, was intended to become a key institution in the government agenda of improved management and leadership in school by providing a mandatory qualification for headteachers. The College had three heads in four years, one of whom had never been a headteacher, and in 2005 it lost some of its key functions. In the same year, the Standards and Effectiveness Unit in the DfES was closed down.

Developments in curriculum and assessment continued under tight central government control and direction. Even documents about primary schools read more like reports from Boards of Directors than educators. An Ofsted report on the primary school literacy and numeracy strategies solemnly reported that

The government's targets for 2002 – that 80 per cent of 11 year olds should gain at least Level 4 in English and 75 per cent should gain the same in mathematics were not met. Before the 2002 results were known

the government had already set higher targets for 2004 . . . it hopes
these targets will now be met by 2006.

(Ofsted 2003a: 4)

In 2002 one of England's academic experts on assessment – Dylan Wiliam –
declared that national tests at age 7, 11, and 14 were useless as measures of
progress and that rising scores reflected little more than teachers' ability to
teach to tests (Henry 2002). Meanwhile Katharina Tomasevski, a Swedish
professor of International Law and reporter to the UN Commission on
Human Rights, claimed in 2003 that the government was in breach of Article
29 of the UN Convention on Children Rights by its target and testing regime.
She argued that the current system was designed to fulfil political objectives
rather than children's needs (Woodward 2003; Tomasevski 2003).

The hasty introduction and assessment of A/S levels in 2001 – an examination between GCSE and A Level, with the A level becoming A2 – caused
considerable chaos and unforeseen changes. Students were overloaded with
examinations and examiners were confused about marking levels. In 2002
faulty grading caused 'what was arguably the worst education crisis to hit
any recent government' (Smithers 2003) with the resignations, already
noted, of the Chairman of QCA and the Secretary of State for Education.
The new Chairman was an Australian, Ken Boston. The problems with marking continued into 2004, despite the costs of testing having risen to over £30
million a year, and the head of the government agency responsible for
national testing, Jonathon Ford, resigned in 2004 after errors in marking
tests for 14-year-olds. One of the three major examination boards, Edexcel, was
handed over to a private company, Pearsons Publishing, without tenders or
discussion with the Qualifications and Curriculum Authority. Despite
national and international criticism and evidence of the negative effects of
testing on children and schools (Reay and Wiliam 1999), the government
resolutely defended its assessment regimes. The DfES did, however, produce
guidance on *Excellence and Enjoyment in Primary Schools* (DfES 2003c)
with accompanying videos on how to do it! A more reliable measure of
primary literacy progress was probably the Progress in International Reading Literacy study (PIRLS 2003), which reported England third out of
35 countries for reading at 10 years old. A strategy designed to raise the
attainments of students aged 11–14 at KS3, costing some £650 million, was
reportedly not reaching the set targets and actually reducing student motivation (Kirkman 2005). The curriculum developments implemented and proposed for students aged 14 and above are discussed in the following chapter.

In their second term of office New Labour certainly kept their promise to
create a diversity of schooling, but evidence that this had created more
choice was limited. Schools increasingly selected pupils and in some areas
had become a battleground for parents anxious to get their children into
desirable schools. Social and ethnic segregation was exacerbated, parental

pleas for a good local comprehensive school in every district went unheeded and the notion of a broad balanced curriculum for all pupils to 16 was disappearing under a plethora of specialisms. Policies of privatization affecting schools, LEAs and educational services had now moved to a global level, and the centralized control of teachers, curriculum and assessment processes continued.

Notes

1 The House of Commons Select Committee on Education and Skills, in their Seventh Report in 2003, cautioned the DfES against introducing further initiatives until earlier ones had been evaluated. This was accepted by the DfES in its reply to the Committee.

2 Estelle Morris felt that she had been unfairly blamed for the 2002 A/S level marking errors (Personal interview 18/10/04, and see Ward 2003).

3 A former staff member of the Prince of Wales, in a court case against another member of the Royal household, produced a handwritten memo from the Prince reading 'What is wrong with people now? Why do they all think they are qualified to do things far above their capabilities . . .? This is all to do with the learning culture in schools. It is the consequence of a child-centred education system which tells people they can become pop stars, high court judges, TV presenters or infinitely more competent heads of state without putting in the necessary work or having the natural ability' (see Smithers and Yafai 2004). The Secretary of State for Education Charles Clarke responded that Prince Charles' views were old-fashioned and out of date.

4 A major education advisor and author of Green and White papers continued to be Andrew Adonis, Head of the No. 10 Policy Unit from 2001, Oxford university graduate, former British Gas employee and journalist. A biography of David Blunkett (Pollard 2005) recorded that he was angry when ordered by the Prime Minister to keep Chief Inspector Woodhead, an ally of Adonis, asking 'Who is Education Secretary, me or Adonis?' Adonis was made a Lord and a junior education minister by Tony Blair in May 2005. Michael Barber, translated in 2001 from the DfES to head the Prime Minister's Delivery Unit charged with setting and delivering public service targets, continued to assist with education papers and initiatives. He was knighted in 2005. Peter Hyman, a young speechwriter for Tony Blair, claimed in 2005 that he had written a 'definition note' for Blair which was handed out to all Cabinet members to use in interviews which stressed that education had moved 'From the comprehensive era to the era of diversity' (Hyman, P. 2005: 256).

5 The House of Commons Select Committee on Education reported in 2003 that 'we are not satisfied that any meaningful distinction between ability and aptitude has been made and we have found no justification for reliance on the distinction between them (House of Commons Education and Skills Committee 2003a).

6 A scheme favoured by the government was run by millionaire businessman Peter Lampl, who set up the Sutton Trust dedicated to selecting 'bright' council estate children to prepare for selective examinations. However, Lampl did not approve of the Academies programme.

7 At the Labour Party National Policy Forum in July 2004, a policy document announced that 'we are pursuing a non-selective policy in secondary education' but an amendment to end all selection was defeated. MPs in constituencies retaining selection claimed that their electorate wanted this (Comprehensive Future 2004). Comprehensive Future, an organization set up in 2003, Chaired by David Chaytor MP, with Margaret Tulloch as Secretary (the author being a member) continued to campaign for total non-selection in schooling.

8 Cyril Taylor had his first job in the USA as a brand manager in advertising. Back in England he served as a conservative councillor in London and was an advisor to Secretary of State for Education Kenneth Baker. He supported the setting up of CTCs and chaired the Technology Colleges Trust. In 2003 this became the Specialist Schools Trust, with Taylor as Chair and an unspecified grant from the government. An article on Taylor in 2004 asked 'Does it matter that an unelected individual should wield such influence?' (Wilce 2004).

9 Early Years policy took note of the findings from a DfES funded study *Effective Provision of Pre-School Education* (EPPE), a longitudinal study of a national sample of children's development between the ages of 3 and 7, carried out by researchers at the Universities of Oxford and London (Birkbeck) and the Institute of Education (see Siraj-Blatchford *et al.* 2004).

10 Wragg noted that Tony Blair had attacked teachers and doctors in 1999 as being 'powerful forces of conservatism' and against modernization. He hoped that when the Prime Minister was subsequently treated for heart problems the doctors had not 'stuck leeches on his bum' (Wragg 2004: 25).

11 A group of professors (the author among them) were entertaining Secretary of State David Blunkett to dinner at the time Woodhead's resignation was announced. This led to general rejoicing.

Further reading

Oxford Review of Education (2005) Special Issue: Education and the Labour Government: an evaluation of two terms, 31 (1).

chapter

seven

Centralizing lifelong learning 1997–2005

This chapter documents post-16 education policies up to March 2005, covering the New Labour government's commitment to lifelong learning, and a skills revolution; disappointing if familiar policy on the education of 14–19-year-olds; and policies taking higher education completely into the marketplace. The chapter concludes with a brief overview of the effects of policy reform since 1997.

Continuities and similarities in post-16 and higher education policies marked the transition from Conservative to New Labour rule in 1997, the guiding ideology of both governments being expressed by Anthony Giddens as 'investment in human capital wherever possible, rather than the direct provision of economic maintenance' (Giddens 1998a: 117).[1] Education and training were to be subordinate to the needs of the economy, expressed in most documents as the needs of national and local employers and businesses, underpinned by anxieties about the skills required for competing in a global economy. Thus, a White Paper commissioned by John Major on *Competitiveness: Helping Business to Win* (DoE 1993) stressed that 'the most successful nations will be those which develop high quality, skilled and motivated workforces' (DoE 1993: 18), the theme being continued in a 1996 paper by future Chancellor of the Exchequer Gordon Brown and colleagues noting that in the new world economy a country's prosperity depended on the skills, knowledge and inventiveness of its people (Brown *et al.* 1996). Both governments quoted comparisons with other developed countries to claim that 'those that have a more concerted and co-ordinated approach to investment in human capital' had more successful economies (Hodgson and Spours 1999: 24).

Education as a means for people to contribute to the economy, the necessity for lifelong learning and acquisition of knowledge and skills, and the need to reduce the costs of welfare by moving people into work were recurring themes in the numerous papers and initiatives concerning post-compulsory education produced between 1997 and 2005. Colleges of further education were constantly mentioned as places where much of this education and training would take place, but despite nearly five million students being enrolled in these colleges by 2001, with a further million on adult education courses (Social Trends 2003), they struggled to cope with increased tasks and complex and inadequate funding. They received little thanks or recognition, and in 2004 were criticized for student failures by the Chief Inspector of schools (Clancy 2004). By this time over a hundred thousand pupils aged 14–16, the recipients of legislation disapplying them from the national curriculum, were undertaking some of their education in what was described as a 'vocational environment' in FE. Unsurprisingly they were mainly disaffected pupils from lower socio-economic groups.

Despite enthusiasm for higher skill levels for young people, the government in its first term continued to rely on the messy system of vocational education in schools and colleges, especially in the underfunded FE colleges. In attempts to raise levels of education and training in the workforce, it is also relied on TECs whose training policies had not been conspicuously successful (and which were soon to disappear); on voluntary groups; and on employers who continued to be reluctant training providers. But New Labour was concerned to end voluntarist policies and take more central control. A paper in 1997 placed the DfEE and Employment Service 'at the centre of an ambitious agenda for change' to help people develop their employability and match the performance of global competitors (DfEE 1997c: 11). The publication in 1999 of *Learning to Succeed: A New Framework for Post-16 Learning* (DfEE 1999e) and the subsequent publication of a Learning and Skills Bill, signalled that from 2000 a new framework and funding for all post-16 education and training (post-14 for the disaffected in work-related learning) would be developed. The framework would cover all existing further education, sixth form and tertiary colleges, all adult and continuing education and education–business links, giving the Secretary of State for Education and Employment, his Permanent Secretary and the DfEE unprecedented centralized control of all post-16 lifelong learning.[2]

In the first five years of the new century, the government promoted a 'skills revolution', taking central direction and coordination of a wide range of policies and practices. The aim was to develop a 'skills strategy' that would integrate phases of learning from early years and primary school, through secondary, further, higher and adult education, aiming to 'sustain a competitive, productive economy which delivers prosperity for all . . . and an ever growing proportion of skilled qualified people' (DfES/DTi 2003: 1). The focus was not to be on a job for life, but on employability for life. The curriculum and qualifications for the 14–19 age group moved towards the centre of attention when a working group was established under the Chairmanship of Mike Tomlinson to suggest more coherent reforms over a ten-year period (DfES 2004f). The government, however, managed to avoid any change in its response to the Group's report thus further cementing the academic–vocational divide in England.

By the second term, higher education was firmly linked into the lifelong learning agenda, a 2003 higher education White Paper asserting that 'Lifelong learning implies a fundamental shift in the "once in a lifetime" approach to higher education to one of educational progress linked to a process of continuous personal and professional development' (DfES 2003d: 16). Higher education was to expand to take in up to 50 per cent of 18–30-year-olds and universities were required to strengthen ties with business and the economy. Questions of access to university and a widening participation to include 'non-traditional' students were to be linked to funding, and there was to be a more stringent focus on including disabled students. Who should pay for university expansion became the subject of acrimonious parliamentary debate during 2003, and the government, with an overall majority of 155, was just five votes away from defeat over its Higher Education Bill in January 2004.

Box 7.1 Chronology of Acts, reports and events in post-16 education 1997–2005

1996 *Inclusive Learning: A Report of The Learning Difficulties And Disabilities Committee* (J. Tomlinson)

1997 (June) Kennedy Report *Learning Works: Widening Participation in Further Education*

1997 (July) Dearing Report *Higher Education in the Learning Society*

1997 (September) National Advisory Group for Continuing Education and Lifelong Learning Report *Learning for the 21st Century* (Fryer)

1997 (November) *Learning and Working Together for the Future: A Strategic Framework for the DfEE* (DfEE)

1997 Consultation paper on the Future of Post-16 Qualifications *Qualifying for Success* (DfEE)

1998 Minister for lifelong learning appointed

1998 *Opportunity Scotland: A Paper on Lifelong Learning* (DfEE)

1998 (February) Green Paper *The Learning Age: A Renaissance for a New Britain* (DfEE)

1998 (May) National Skills Task Force set up

1998 (July) Teaching and Higher Education Act

1998 (September) National Skills Task Force Report *Towards a National Skills Agenda* (DfEE)

1999 *Individual Learning Accounts: A Summary of Progress* (DfEE)

1999 Moser Report *Improving Literacy and Numeracy: A Fresh Start*

1999 *A New Way of Learning – The UfI Network. Developing the University for Industry Concept* (University for Industry Working Group)

1999 (June) *Learning to Succeed: A New Framework for Post-16 Learning* (DfEE)
1999 (December) Learning and Skill Bill
2000 SEN and Disability Bill
2000 Learning and Skills Act sets up a Learning and Skills Council and 47 local councils; TECs abolished
2001 Special Educational Needs and Disability Act
2001 Department for Education and Employment (DfEE) becomes Department for Education and Skills (DfES)
2001 *Skills for Life: Strategy for Improving Adult Basic Skills* (DfES)
2002 (February) Consultation Paper on 14–19 education *Extending Opportunities: Raising Standards* (DfES)
2002 (November) *Success for All: Reforming Further Education and Training. Our Vision* (DfES)
2003 (January) White Paper *The Future of Higher Education* (DfES)
2003 (January) *Opportunity and Excellence 14–19* (DfES)
2003 (March) *Draft Strategic Plan 2003–08* (Higher Education Funding Council for England)
2003 (March) 14–19 Working Group set up, Chair Mike Tomlinson
2003 (March) *Developing a National Skills Strategy and Delivery Plan: Underlying Evidence* (DfES)
2003 (July) Tomlinson Interim Report *Working Group on 14–19 Education: Principles of Reform* (DfES)
2003 (July) White Paper *21st Century Skills: Realising Our Potential* (DfES, DTi, HM Treasury, DWP); a National Skills Strategy set out
2004 (January) Higher Education Act, sets up an Office of Fair Access (OFFA)
2004 (October) *14–19 Curriculum and Qualifications Reform: Final Report of the Working Group on 14–19 Reform* (DfES)
2004 (October) Final Report on University Admissions (Steven Schwarz)
2004 (December) National Review of Further Education Colleges set up (Chair Sir Andrew Foster)
2005 (January) Conservatives promise to abolish Learning and Skills Councils if elected in the May General Election
2005 (February) White Paper *14–19 Education and Skills* (Government response to the Tomlinson report)

Lifelong learning

Husen (1974) proposed the idea that all citizens should participate in a learning society in which opportunities for lifelong learning were available to all. From the mid-1970s various versions of a learning society were produced by academics or embraced by governments (see Coffield 1997). Two contrasting versions were Ranson's visionary view that a learning society should be one in which a new moral and political democratic order took shape rather than one which only attempted to prepare people for a competitive economy (Ranson 1994), and Christopher Ball's (1999) view that governments should promote a learning society on the principles of individual responsibility, encouraging learners to invest in themselves, and promoting a learning market. New Labour embraced this latter view, and lifelong learning became a major theme in post-16 education and training policies. Individuals within a market economy were to be given greater responsibility for their own education and training. There were carrots such as Individual Learning Accounts (DfEE 1999f) – a scheme which rapidly failed – and the chance to participate in a University for Industry (University for Industry Working Group 1999). For not participating, there were the sticks of benefit withdrawals and unemployment. Coffield (1997) noted that lists of the desirable characteristics of lifelong learning, like lists of the world's best jokes, could all be revised and added to, but both UK and European lists ignored the structural barriers of race, class, gender and location which impeded many young people and adults from learning (Coffield 1997: 451). To this could be added the obsession of English education with progressively designating children and young people as failures. The contradictions of expecting enthusiasm for lifelong learning among people who had been subject to the selective and often alienating processes of formal education were treated by government as a problem of a 'lower class culture' that did not value education.

The incoming government in 1997 benefited from the reports of two committees set up by the previous government to consider widening participation in further education (Kennedy 1997) and to consider the role of higher education (Dearing 1997). In addition the first report from Labour's National Advisory Group for Continuing Education and Lifelong Learning was available towards the end of 1997 (Fryer 1997). The Kennedy report criticized the intense focus on preparation for the economy as the major rationale for further learning and training, pointing out that:

> Prosperity depends on there being a vibrant economy, but an economy that regards its own success as the highest good is a dangerous one . . . In a social landscape where there is a growing gulf between those who have and those who have not, the importance of social cohesion cannot be ignored.
>
> (Kennedy 1997: 6)

This report commented on the idea of 'social capital' – moral obligations, duties towards communities, and trust, which figured in much of Labour's writing about the 'Third Way' in politics (Blair 1998b; Giddens 1998a) – but which was not particularly apparent in education and training policy. In particular, although a rhetoric of inclusion of disabled people and those with special needs figured in papers on post-16 provision, much of it taken from an FEFC report on *Inclusive Learning* (Tomlinson 1996), the problems remained of ensuring that these groups had equal chances of education, training, employment or adequate living allowances if work was not a possibility. Riddell and her colleagues remarked in 1997 that human capital theory does not serve well the interests of young people and adults with learning difficulties (Riddell *et al.* 1997), and Walker (2005) commented that not being able to participate in the economy was itself socially excluding.

New Labour's 'radical vision' for lifelong learning was set out in a Green Paper *The Learning Age: A Renaissance for a New Britain* (DfEE 1998d), published nine months after taking office. Secretary of State Blunkett's introduction to this paper referred to the need for a well-educated, well-equipped and adaptable labour force to sustain economic growth (DfEE 1998d: 8). Funding and local planning of further education had been taken away from local authorities in 1992, with resulting waste and unnecessary competition between FE colleges and schools. This Green Paper urged more cooperation and partnership between what was still the Further Education Funding Council, and local government. Nine Regional Development Agencies were to be set up; one duty of these was ensuring that local labour needs meshed with local education and training provision, and these agencies began work in April 1999 (Baty 1999). Money was promised for a new Partnership Fund for learning partnerships between schools, colleges, LEAs, TECs and the careers service, and a Learning Direct telephone helpline would offer advice and guidance.

The DfEE had put out a consultation paper on the reform of post-16 qualifications, *Qualifying for Success* (DfEE 1997d) in which changes to A levels and GNVQs were suggested, plus a key skills qualification and the possibility of working towards the 'overarching certificate' for all post-16 qualifications, an idea explored by Labour while in opposition, and to reappear in the 2004 Tomlinson Report. These reforms and a possible credit framework for FE college work appeared briefly in the Green Paper, and figured in the 1999 White Paper (DfEE 1999e). A *Paper on Lifelong Learning* for Scotland was also produced (DfEE 1998e), the suggested broadening of post-16 qualifications in England being nearer to the Scottish model. By 1998 a Minister for Life-Long Learning had been appointed and a new field had opened up for professionals.

Learning to succeed

The White Paper *Learning to Succeed: A New Framework for Post-16 Learning* appeared in June 1999 (DfEE 1999e), and signalled considerable structural changes for the delivery of post-16 education and training, with heavily centralized funding, regulation and inspection. A major purpose of change appeared to be the familiar one of meeting the need for skills identified by employers and business in order to improve the economy; a second purpose was to encourage all young people to stay in education or training post-16; and a third purpose was to regulate the activities of those young people post-14 who were regarded as troublesome to the training and credentialling of the majority. The Secretary of State's introduction stated that:

> Lifelong Learning . . . will ensure the means by which our economy can make a successful transition from the industries and services of the past, to the knowledge and information economy of the future . . . contribute to sustaining a civilised and cohesive society . . . in which generational disadvantage can be overcome.
>
> (DfEE 1999e: 3)

This White Paper reiterated the 'Vision for the New Millennium' which was encapsulated in a set of principles underpinning the new framework for post-16 learning. The notion of leaving education at 16 'must pass into history' and new national targets were to be achieved by 2002. Individuals were to take responsibility for their own learning; employers were to improve the skills of their workforce; communities, especially LEAs, were to support and extend adult learning; and all 'providers' were to be accountable. The White Paper explained that change was considered necessary because the current funding and planning system had evolved piecemeal, with FE colleges funded by the FEFC, sixth forms via LEAs, and TECs directly by government.

The flagship policy of the new 'coherent' framework was to be a Learning and Skills Council (LSC) to take over funding, planning, management and quality assurance of all post-16 education and training, except HE. The secretary of state was to appoint the chair and members of this LSC, with employers being the largest group of members. The FEFC was to be dissolved; funding and responsibility for modern apprenticeships, national traineeships and other training courses taken from the 72 TECs, which would eventually be abolished; and the LSC was to work with LEAs and the pre-16 sector to ensure coherence across 14–19 education. A network of 47 local LSCs were to plan and coordinate local provision, again with majority employer and business representation. The White Paper promised £725 million to be given to FE colleges to widen participation, and successful colleges were to become 'beacons of excellence'. The Learning and Skills Council would control some £7 billion in funds from the DfEE, but a stringent accountability framework was suggested. The LSC was required to uphold principles of selflessness, integrity, objectivity, accountability, openness, honesty and leadership (DfEE 1999e). It would work in partnership with the University for Industry, the regional development agencies, LEAs, local learning partnerships, higher education, Investors in People, the Small Business Service and national training organizations. It was to develop a new national funding system but could vary funding to local councils. Poor

provision in some FE colleges, sixth forms and work-based routes was casti-
gated and a new inspection system set out. Ofsted would be responsible for
the inspection of provision for 16–19-year-olds in the 1800 school sixth
forms and 440 colleges, and an Adult Learning Inspectorate (ALI) would
inspect post-19 provision and work-based courses. A new-style Careers service, 'Connexions', was to provide learning mentors, and there were to be
educational maintenance allowances for students from low income families.

New arrangements for the 160,000 young people known to be neither in
education or training were promised and these were duly set out in July 1999
in a paper from the Social Exclusion Unit which demonstrated intense
anxieties over this group of young people, which included a large proportion
of African Caribbean, Pakistani and Bangladeshi young people (Social
Exclusion Unit 1999). Individual Learning Accounts, to which the government would give £150 for each individual plus contributions from employers, were noted as 'a major strand in the Government's programme for
life-long learning' (DfEE 1999e: 56). This scheme collapsed in 2003. There
was to be a new 'ONE Service' for benefit claimants, links with business
through the Small Business Service, trade unions and trade associations,
training organizations, Investors in People and the UfI.[3]

The 1999 White Paper was not without its critics. Lord Baker, a former
Conservative Education Secretary, was of the view that 'the enormous tiers
of quangos and interrelated bodies make Spaghetti Junction look like an
open road', and a *Times Higher Education Supplement* (*THES*) editorial
noted the absence of any reference to the staff who would provide these
courses, apart from threats of inspection. The *THES* editorial commented
that 'Contempt for the providers of education is a disease New Labour
seems to have caught from its Conservative predecessor' (*THES*, 2 July
1999). The assistant secretary of the Association of University Teachers
(AUT) noted that

> followers of government policy on post-16 education and training have
> a difficult task. Every few years a new review is announced, administra-
> tive arrangements, funding bodies, examination boards and qualifica-
> tions are invented or reinvented and a new set of acronyms have to be
> learned.
>
> (Cottrell 1999)

The model for post-16 education was one of top-down, enforced change,
professional disempowerment, heavy inspections by two inspection agencies,
institutions dependent on numbers passing exams for continued existence,
and the removal of the disaffected and troublesome from real education into
pseudo-education and potentially exploitative training. The assumption
made in the White Paper was that institutional reform could solve the
historical problem of providing a proper vocational education and training
system. The notion that partnership between a plethora of national, regional

and local statutory and voluntary bodies, plus business interests, all competing for funds and a clientele, would produce a vocationally educated workforce, was highly problematic. Keep (1999), a member of the National Skills Task Force set up in May 1998 to measure skills shortages and suggest ways in which education and training should respond to economic needs, pointed out that in any case the needs of the economy and the learning society are not necessarily compatible: up to 20 per cent of the workforce will continue to take jobs that do not require any qualifications, and others may find that their qualifications do not buy good jobs.

In December 1999 the Learning and Skills Bill was introduced in Parliament, and had its second reading in the House of Lords by January 2000. Before it had become law the Bill had its critics, notably from organizations responsible for the education and training whose views did not appear to have had any influence. The Association of Colleges (Further Education and Tertiary) was reported as claiming that the Learning and Skills Council, with members and chair appointed by the secretary of state, would have unprecedented and unconstrained powers of intervention and control of funding (Baty 2000: 4). In June 2000, Bryan Sanderson, a businessman and chair of Newcastle United Football Club, was appointed Chair of the LSC, leaving in 2004 to become Chair of Standard Chartered Bank. Any recognition of research which indicated that it was a shortage of jobs rather than poor education or skill levels which explained unemployment was absent from the 1999 White Paper and resulting legislation.

Twenty-first century skills

Reforms and initiatives designed to guarantee a future flow of higher skilled, better educated young people into the labour market, and raise skill levels of adults in work continued into the twenty-first century. In both the UK and the USA, as Hayward pointed out, policy was underpinned by a sense of long-term crisis, with an overemphasis on the work-related aims of learning, at the expense of general learning (Hayward 2004). Certainly the government remained concerned that 'our economic productivity and competitiveness remain well below those of our major competitor nations . . . one reason is the serious gaps in our national skills base' (DfES/DTI 2003: 11). Following the somewhat pessimistic report by Claus Moser on the supposed levels of adult illiteracy (Moser 1999) a *Skills for Life* strategy to boost adult basic skills was introduced in 2001. An Ofsted report in 2003 found that in pursuing targets set by government to remedy deficits in basic skills, colleges and other providers were signing on more people but offering lower quality courses with less qualified staff (Ofsted 2003a).

In 2002 *Success for All* (DfES 2002a), another vision and reform agenda for further education and training, addressed the 4000 providers of learning and skills funded by the LSC. These included further education colleges, sixth forms in schools and sixth form colleges, specialist further education colleges, HE institutions providing further education, local authority adult education, voluntary and community providers, the university of Industry, and all private sector providers and all employers. The largest ever investment in FE and training was promised, after the LSC had undertaken strategic area reviews and published a National Skills Strategy. New Sector Skills Councils (SSCs), employer bodies funded by the government, would improve business competitiveness and public service performance, and FE Colleges were urged to meet targets and improve 'customer focus'. Money from the Standards Fund was available for further FE staff training and productivity. This paper, however, noted that the government 'wanted to replace the destructive competition which exists beween providers' with more appropriate competition in a more collaborative environment (DfES 2002a: 5). Providers may have understood, but the general public may well have been mystified by the proliferation of centres and agencies all required to cooperate. Paragraph 45 (p. 23) notes that 'The government and LSC will make available funding to enable the development of 400 CoVES by 2006. The LSC will work closely with Regional Development Agencies (RDAs), the Sector Skills Development Agency (SSDA), SSCs, and UfI/learndirect to help ensure CoVE coverage is appropriate at each level.' This paper reiterated the view that 14–19 learners should have a greater choice of academic and vocational courses but otherwise barely referred to the flurry of activity on the 14–19 front taking place in 2002.

In 2003 the DfES published a Paper setting out the mode of delivery of a National Skills Strategy, and four months later the DfES, the Department for Trade and Industry, HM Treasury, and the Department for Work and Pensions published a joint paper on *21st Century Skills* (DfES/DTi 2003) describing a Skills Alliance which would bring government, employers and unions into a new social partnership, including the myriad other 'delivery agencies' as the various partners were described. This Paper lamented again the lower workforce skill levels in apprenticships, craft and technical compared to France and Germany and promised to 'give employers greater choice and control over the publicly funded training they receive' (DfES/ DTi: 13). Pring, commenting on the values underpinning the Skills Revolution, noted that while it was seen as the solution to the perceived problems in a competitive world, it did not appreciate the limitations of the concept of 'skill' (DfEE 1998f; Pring 2004: 113). The government continued to support the notion of a distinction between academic education and vocational skills, a distinction becoming less and less meaningful in a complex world. It was also noticeable that the *Five-year Strategy for Children and Learners* (DfES 2004a), coming a year after the papers on skills strategies, ignored the role of further education colleges in delivering much of post-16, and increasingly post-14 education and skills training, although a review of further education colleges was set up at the end of 2004, under the Chairmanship of Sir Andrew Foster, a Deputy Chair of the Royal Bank of Canada.

Policies and qualifications 14–19

Despite the focus on lifelong learning and the view that leaving education at 16 should 'pass into history', Labour's support for a coherent 14–19 curriculum, with a reformed unified qualifications system, remained minimal during the first term. It was not until the second term that the report of the Tomlinson Committee (DfES 2004f) made proposals very similar to those put forward in 1990 in an IPPR paper *A British Baccalaureate* (Finegold *et al.* 1990). This paper suggested that:

> the best way to open up intellectual and practical study lies in the creation of a unified qualification at 18-plus. It would replace existing qualifications, including 'A' levels and vocational awards like B-Tech Diplomas and Certificates.
>
> (Finegold *et al.* 1990: 5)

All students from age 14 would study a chosen mix of academic, vocational and work-based modular courses. Subsequent papers, including *Aiming Higher* (Labour Party 1996a), made detailed proposals for a reformed 14–19 curriculum and qualifications system, with an Advanced Diploma but retaining the A level and vocational routes. New Labour had decided by 1992 that there were no votes in the abolition of A levels, a position which persisted into their second term of office. The Conservative White Paper *Learning to Compete* (DfEE 1996a) suggested that, since a majority of young people stayed in education or training, the age of 16 was no longer a 'natural break'. By that time the track routes of A level, GNVQ and NVQs were developing, although NVQs found little favour with most young people. Sporadic proposals to abolish GCSEs came to nothing as the A–C economy of GCSE had become a major indicator of secondary school 'success' (Gillborn and Youdell 2000: 12).

It had become apparent by the 1980s that global, economic, technical and social changes meant that it no longer made sense to educate elite 'thinking classes' and offer only basic education and early vocational education to the rest, unless governments really were intent on sustaining hierarchical societies. There were choices to be made between preparing young people for a low-skilled undereducated society or a highly skilled informed learning society which educated everyone. Nevertheless despite a national curriculum supposedly offering 'a broad balanced curriculum' to 16 for all, there was an intensification of divisions between academic education and vocational preparation and occupational training routes (Tomlinson 1997c). Hodgson and Spours (1999) noted that there was an expectation, when Labour came to power, that it would build on Dearing's *Review of Qualifications for 16–19 Year Olds* (1996) and move towards the unified qualifications system. But lack of support for the overarching certificate and 'undisguised anxiety about reforming either GCSEs or A levels, gives rise to concern about New Labour's commitment to the vision of a coherent and unified 14+ qualifications system' (Hodgson and Spours 1999: 111). By 2000 curriculum reform had attempted to broaden sixth form study, A levels were to be broken down into two or three unit blocks of A/S and A 2 levels, and a key skills qualification was to be mandatory. By September 2000 schools and colleges were expected to have put into place arrangements for students to study up to five A/S levels and three A levels, and an Advanced Extension Award (a 'super A level') was being piloted (Woodward 2000b). By the turn of the century Labour was defending its 'evolutionary approach' to reforming the 14–19 curriculum and qualifications system, promising more action in its second term of office.

Action was certainly forthcoming, as the government proceded to produce and commission a series of papers and reports on the 14–19 age group, resulting, as noted by a Nuffield Review of 14–19 provision, in 'policy tensions, contradictions and evolving solutions to perceived problems' (Hayward *et al.* 2004: 13). It was unlikely that there would be much agreement on this highly contested area with many competing vested interests. The government, as one journalist put it, appeared unable to decide whether the aim of education was 'to get as many students as possible into universities or make sure we have enough plumbers' (Crace 2002: 9).

Meanwhile there followed a good deal of wrestling with attempts to upgrade the historically lower status of applied vocational courses. Most of the children of the middle classes – and the offspring of those in government – moved into academic courses. FE colleges struggled with lower achieving children on vocational courses supposedly serving their 'needs'. Alison Wolf, an expert on education and labour markets, was at this time warning that 'despite all the rhetoric about high-status vocational routes, policy is clearly aimed at the lower and indeed lowest-achieving young people' (Wolf 2002: 161). A consultation paper on extending opportunities for 14–19-year-olds appeared in February 2002 (DfES 2002b) which proposed new vocational courses to be available in schools, colleges or with other training providers, and more Modern Apprenticeships. Students would progress at different rates but all courses would lead to the award of an overarching diploma. There was a suggestion that the International Baccalaureate might be incorporated into a Matriculation Diploma, to be offered at intermediate, higher and advanced levels, with all existing courses, including work-related and citizenship activities fitting into this Diploma. Predictably, private and selective schools led with the charge that the 'gold standard' of A level was to be downgraded. They were given considerable ammunition in August 2002 when charges that A-level papers had been incorrectly marked and some students denied university places, led to the resignation – with some bitterness and threats of litigation – of the Chairman of the Qualifications and Curriculum Authority, Sir William Stubbs. His resignation was quickly followed, as noted, by that of the Secretary of State for Education herself. A committee of inquiry into A-level standards was set up, chaired by Mike Tomlinson, and a new Chief Executive of QCA, Australian Ken Boston, made it plain that he favoured A levels. Marking at A level in 2003 was less contentious but 110,000 test papers for 14-year-olds were submitted for re-marking.

A White Paper *Opportunity and Excellence 14–19* (DfES 2003e) appeared in January 2003, conceding to the A-level lobby that A levels and GCSE would continue, but with what was becoming familiar rhetoric 'a curriculum to combine breadth of study with more flexibility for schools and colleges to tailor programmes to individual needs and aptitudes' (p. 4). It rejected moves to the International Baccalaureate, reduced the compulsory national curriculum between 14–16 to English, maths, science, IT, and learning about work and enterprise. Foreign languages were to be optional and eight vocational GCSEs were to be supplemented by 'hybrid' GCSEs studied on either academic or vocational tracks. There was a suggestion that the 14–19 curriculum should be linked to local labour markets and pilot Pathfinder projects were to develop partnerships offering education and training. A Pathfinder case study in Lincolnshire was quoted, which, under the direction of the LEA, apparently brought together all schools and no less than ten other agencies – two Beacon Colleges, the local LSC, the local Learning Partnership, the local Education and Business Partnership, Connexions, the Consortium for Work-Based Learning, HE providers, adult education and youth services, and Scunthorpe United Football Club (p. 12). It was beginning to look as though running a football club was a precondition for involvement in education and training!

By the end of 2004 the myriad uncosted suggestions for reform were referred to by the new Chair of the Qualifications and Curriculum Authority, Sir Anthony Greener, in a New Year speech as 'wish-lists, not strategies . . . a jigsaw of activities that do not fit together' (Lepkowska 2004). 2004 was a year of waiting for Mike Tomlinson's final report, which duly appeared in October. This time a Diploma Framework formed the basis for 'a clear vision for a unified framework of 14–19 curriculum and qualifications' (DfES 2004f: 1). Within the framework some twenty 'lines of learning' would cover a wide range of academic and vocational disciplines, allowing specialization along different lines, but all forming a ladder of progression. The Diploma framework would encompass Entry, Foundation, Intermediate and Advanced levels, with core and main learning streams, and an extended project. The terminology of 'levels' taken from the National Qualifications Framework, would absorb existing GCSEs and A levels, allow students to continue to specialize but require all to have numeracy and communication skills. More teacher assessment, more use of e-assessment and less assessed coursework were also suggested, with a network of Chartered Assessors developing. Pupils under 16 would be able to opt for more vocational courses. All vocational programmes would be developed with the involvement of employers and higher education with 'coherent delivery of the knowledge and skills needed by different employment sectors' (DfES 2004f: 8). The report stressed that the needs of end-users, particularly employers and HE, were paramount, with employers apparently requiring not only specific skills but also the 'right attitude'. There was no cautionary note on the historically problematic relationships between education, skills and jobs (Keep and Mayhew 2000).

Education Secretary Charles Clarke introduced the Tomlinson report to the House of Commons on 18 October 2004 and the first comment from opposition benches was that it signalled the end of GCSE and A levels. The Prime Minister was not present, but by the evening had issued a statement saying that these qualifications would remain, and indeed by the end of February 2005 the new Education Secretary Ruth Kelly, introducing the White Paper responding to the Tomlinson proposals (DfES 2005) had announced in Parliament that GCSEs and A levels would indeed stay. A-level grades would be expanded to stretch the brightest, alongside fourteen new diplomas for vocational courses available by 2008. New Skills Academies and specialist schools offering vocational education through specialisms were also to be part of the package. GCSE maths and English were to be made harder and coursework reduced, but the overloaded exam system would essentially remain in place (DfES 2005b). Mike Tomlinson's comment was that 'What is proposed yet again risks emphasising the distinction between the vocational and the academic' (Smithers 2005) and a *Guardian* editorial noted that 'from every corner of the educational world came expressions of deep disappointment', as heads, teachers, unions, private schools, universities and employers (as represented by the British Chamber of Commerce), were united in the view that the Blair government had missed an opportunity to end an 'historic and crippling social divide dating back at least 150 years' (*Guardian* editorial 24/2/05). All the attention given to the 14–19 age group, including the £1 million Tomlinson Inquiry, appeared, according to one education journalist, to have been rejected because 'the government did not want to go into the election being accused by the Tories and the media of scrapping A-levels' (Mansell 2005: 13) – not a new situation for the New Labour government.

Higher education

Labour inherited a higher education system that had expanded dramatically since the Labour government of the 1960s oversaw a modest expansion after the Robbins Report's recommendations (Ministry of Education 1963b). The success of comprehensive education from the 1970s had resulted in a wider and more diverse qualified body of potential students, and expanding credentialism meant that degrees were increasingly needed to get jobs that previously lower level qualifications would have secured. All three major political parties backed an expansion of higher education, the Conservative target of one-third of 18–19-year-olds entering HE by the end of the 1990s having been achieved by the middle of the decade. However, expansion had been on the cheap, with a squeeze on the 'unit of resource' for each student and university staff pay held down. The Liberal peer Lord Russell described the early 1990s as the 'age of deferred expenditure' as although the 1995 HE costs were £5.6 billion, it was calculated that university staff would need a 37 per cent pay rise to return to their 1981 equivalent pay (CVCP and National Statistics Office 1996).

The abolition of the binary line between universities and polytechnics in 1992 led to considerable discussion as to the nature, purpose and funding of universities and the balance and quality of teaching and research. These issues led the Conservative government to set up the review chaired by Ron Dearing, which reported in July 1997 under the title *Higher Education in the Learning Society*. The brief of the committee had been to make recommendations on 'the purpose, shape, structure and funding of higher education, recognising that higher education embraces teaching, learning, scholarship and research' (Dearing 1997, para. 1 Introduction). The recommendations included raising the participation rate to 45 per cent of young people, with more sub-degree courses provided in FE colleges, and a substantial increase in public spending on higher education, with graduates in work contributing up to 25 per cent of their tuition costs.

The response to the Dearing Report was published with a foreword by David Blunkett, which referred to higher education as a vehicle for economic success and lifelong learning, using the metaphor which occurred in a number of government publications that while the 'power of the machine' ensured economic success in the nineteenth century, 'intellectual capital' was now required 'if this country is to remain internationally competitive'. The response accepted 'the provision of wider access for those traditionally under-represented in our Universities as a goal' (DfEE 1997e: 2), and rapidly made clear who would pay for the expanded access. Although up to 1997 Labour had consistently opposed the introduction of tuition fees for undergraduate students, by July 1998 the government had passed the Teaching and Higher Education Act, in which Sections 22–25 set out new and expanded arrangements for student loans and the abolition of maintenance grants, and Section 26 introduced student fees – the 'prescribed amount' of the fee referred to in this section working out at £1000 in up-front tuition fees. The Universities and Colleges Admissions Service promptly reported a decrease in the numbers of under-represented groups applying to universities – mature students, ethnic minorities and working class applicants (Goddard 1999). The Act also imposed fees on Scottish students, but one of the first Acts of the devolved Scottish Parliament in 1999 was to discontinue up-front fees. Barnett (1999), reviewing the Robbins and Dearing reports, pointed out that by the end of the twentieth century universities were no longer elite institutions, and competing interests – the state, the public, professional and corporate interests – had conflicting expectations of what they were for and who should pay for them.

Approaching a second term the government finally decided to take the lead in imposing a new structure and funding regimes on higher education. In February 2000, David Blunkett suggested a diversity of universities with three tiers of higher education – research being concentrated in top research-rated universities, some able to charge fees above the government-set rate, and some bidding to become e-universities, offering degrees online to overseas students. He also announced a two-year vocationally oriented foundation degree, and the renaming of GNVQs as vocational A levels, qualifications intended to provide access to the two-year degree. The 2001 Labour election manifesto, while promising to work towards a target of 50 per cent of young people going into universities, also promised that 'we will not introduce top-up fees' (Labour Party 2001: 20). The first announcement by the incoming Secretary of State for Education Charles Clarke in November 2002 back-tracked on this position and claimed that more money should come from students and alumni. He supported his claim with an OECD report which had surveyed graduate earnings in countries with widely differ-ent higher education systems, to suggest that graduates earned £400,000 more over a lifetime than non-graduates, a contentious figure which became widely quoted, but which earned some derision from graduate public service workers. The proposed expansion raised the issue of who exactly was bene-fiting from university expansion, young people in the top socio-economic groups being undoubted winners. In 2000, 72 per cent of young people in the highest socio-economic groups went on to university, with only 17 per cent from the lowest group. A five-year study by the Higher Education Funding Council, mapping the proportion of school leavers going to university in every region, found a distinct postcode effect, with those in advantaged areas six times more likely to attend university than those in deprived areas (HEFCE 2004). There was also considerable disjunction between govern-ment intentions and realities in universities. Despite a stated need for more scientists, four universities closed their chemistry departments in 2004, while student demand for media studies and psychology courses rose considerably.

Arguments as to whether private schools took up a disproportionate number of places in top research universities surfaced in 2000, when the Chancellor of the Exchequer Gordon Brown took up the case of Laura Spence, a comprehensive school student rejected for a place to study medi-cine at Oxford. The Deputy Prime Minister accused Oxford of elitism and publicized the fact that 40 per cent of students in the most prestigious universities were from private schools. The prestigious top twenty had indeed clubbed together in the 1990s styling themselves the Russell Group. The former polytechnics eventually formed the Coalition of Modern Universities. In 2003 Steven Schwarz, Vice-Chancellor of Brunel University, was asked to undertake a review of university access and admissions, a final report being produced in October 2004 and reducing the social class gap in university entry became a major policy focus. The 2003 White Paper on *The Future of Higher Education* (DfES 2003d), made widening access and participation a central aim. Universities would be required to draw up an Access Agreement for disadvantaged students before they could increase fees, extra funding being available for 'non-traditional students', and an Access Regulator was to be appointed to oversee agreements. The first Chief of what became OFFA, the Office of Fair Access, was Sir Martin Harris, former Vice-Chancellor of Manchester University. Laura Spence was meanwhile accepted to study in the USA at Harvard University.

Government plans for higher education, as set out in the White Paper, were to increase state support by 6 per cent per year, to some 0.8 per cent of GDP. This still compared unfavourably to the 1 per cent of GDP that France, Germany and the USA contributed. Up-front tuition fees were to be abolished but from 2006 students would pay back their fees via a Graduate Contribution Scheme, with universities able to charge up to £3000 annually per course, and to vary the fees. Students would continue to take out loans for their maintenance. This scheme 'allows universities the right to secure from graduates larger contributions to the cost of their education' (DfES 2003d: 9). The variable fees issue was regarded by many MPs, academics and others as confirming a hierarchy of institutions with top universities charging more and attracting richer students, while the two-year foundation degrees – explained in the White Paper as 'expansion through new types of qualifications, better tailored to suit the needs of students and the economy' (p. 7) were more likely to attract working class students. The National Union of Students President, giving evidence to the House of Commons Education and Skills Committee in their examination of the proposals (House of Commons Education and Skills Committee 2003b) commented that 'Differential fees are wrong and will create a two-tier elitist higher education system' (p. 66). For the whole of 2003 acrimonious discussion concerning university funding, top-up and variable fees occupied much space in the media and much political and academic time, with the Prime Minister supporting variable fees and allegedly influenced by Lord Jenkins, the then Chancellor of Oxford University. A Bill was introduced in January 2004 which included variable fees but with more concessions to poorer students. It was opposed by over one hundred Labour MPs and became a challenge to the Prime Minister's authority. In the event the Bill was passed on 27 January by five votes. In the future, universities are likely to retain their top position in the diverse system of higher education if they charge higher fees, attract endowments and gain more funding for research. An official from the Higher Education Funding Council, which published its own plans for higher education up to 2008 (HEFCE 2003) commented that 'There is a clear perception of a hierarchy of universities. This is well-known to students and employers and the institution attended makes a difference to your life-chances' (House of Commons Education and Skills Committee 2003b: 56). Universities had entered into an era of total marketization in the business of attracting students, and the less research intensive were to play a larger role in linking with business through Knowledge Exchanges and Knowledge Transfer Partnerships, to promote local and regional economies (DfES 2003d: 36). Surveying the move to mass higher education Mayhew *et al.* concluded that if the government was intent on expanding participation to 50 per cent it was probably best done via the two-year foundation degree, but concluded that 'worryingly, there is a danger that social and academic divides could be made even stronger and more immutable' (Mayhew *et al.* 2004: 79).

Box 7.2 Higher Education Act 2004

1 Part 1 makes provision for a new Arts and Humanities Research Council and the funding of arts and humanities research.
2 Part 2 sets out a scheme for reviewing student complaints, and ends the role of university Visitors over student complaints.
3 Part 3 enables HEIs to set their own fees, £3000 mentioned in regulations. Universities must submit their plans for fees to the Director of Fair Access. The plans must promote equality of opportunity and encourage wider participation of under-represented groups. Loans will be available to allow students to defer fees.
4 Part 4 allows for transfer of functions to the Welsh National Assembly, and refers to provisions on student loans. Loan payments can be made directly to institutions with students repaying later.
5 Part 5 includes provision for the appointment of a Director of Fair Access and reporting to the Secretary of State.

Continuity and change 1997–2005

Chapters 5, 6 and 7 have overviewed the continuity and the change in education policy as a Labour government took over after eighteen years of Conservative rule. In May 1997 hopes and expectations were high that, after seemingly endless educational legislation, policies imposed throughout the system with minimal or zero consultation, a denigration of teachers, local education authorities and academics, an immense centralization of power and control, and a stated withdrawal from egalitarian ideals, things would change. However, what followed over the next eight years demonstrated more continuity than change in the system. By early 2005 Neal Lawson, directing an organization supporting the 'democratic left' reported that focus groups considered that 'we have got two Tory parties . . . New Labour now means conservative' (Lawson 2005). Peter Hyman, a speechwriter for Tony Blair, confirmed in a book detailing ten years of New Labour policy that from 1994 policy was directed towards 'moving Labour ruthlessly to the centre ground and stealing back the clothes we had lost to the Tories . . . Tony was the master at stealing Tory clothes and Tory territory' (Hyman 2005: 54). Certainly a major educational continuity from Conservative years came about as New Labour abandoned any idea of a common educational experience for all young people and encouraged selective systems, hierarchies of schools and universities, a commercialization of education rather than supporting it as a public service, and a marginalization of local education authorities and local control. All of these were perfectly compatible with a Conservative agenda. Denis Lawton succinctly described the policies as 'bastard Thatcherism' (Lawton 2005: 154).

The New Labour government made education its 'number one priority' with the declared aim of preparing a more skilled and knowledgeable workforce, which had also been the declared aim of the Conservative government. A major continuity from Tory to New Labour policy was an ideological consensus which defined education as the key to future economic prosperity, allied to a refusal to evaluate the effects of their reforms in terms of continuing class stratification. Despite New Labour claims of commitment to social justice, education at the start of the twenty-first century was still a major agent in the social division of labour. Class, race, gender and disability were still reliable indicators of individual levels of economic prosperity. High status education and employment were still dependent on the right kind of schooling at the right kind of school and university, a situation exacerbated rather than diminished by the further marketization of schools and universities. Systems of selection and allocation to different sorts of school and college experiences, reduced to some extent between the 1960s and 1980s by the introduction of comprehensive schooling, continued to reproduce social divisions and economic inequalities into the 2000s. By 2005 the government was grudgingly conceding that 'comprehensive schools have raised standards and done well for many' (Kelly 2005: 20), but claiming that they had not brought about 'universal social mobility'. Policy ideology in a third New Labour term of office was to be based on the meritocratic notion of social mobility for some via what had become a commitment to a 'comprehensive education system'.

Despite the rhetoric, the retention and elaboration of market competition between schools, the expansion of selection under a language of diversity, and a continuation of strategies for the removal from mainstream schooling of disaffected lower class children, led to a more elaborate pecking order in schools and colleges than the grammar–secondary modern system had ever produced. Although the specialist school was originally Conservative policy, New Labour expanded this and other types of school to help create an education market, and those schools with superior finance and privileges inevitably attracted more knowlegable and aspirant parents. By 2005 young people could attend any of fifteen categories of schooling pre-16 – depending on their locality, parental income and knowledge of the system, and whether they were wanted as 'customers'. The categories are listed in Chapter 5 and include further education college courses for the disaffected and existing and planned academies. Comprehensive schooling as envisaged by Ministers from both Labour and Conservative parties in the 1960s and by most educationists and parents, and which had been successful in opening up opportunities for many, was effectively dead, and the higher education system was on its way to market-oriented reorganization. Despite using the slogan of 'standards not structures',[4] New Labour effectively elaborated on existing selective school structures. It also elaborated on the pernicious Tory policy of naming and shaming 'failing schools', to develop the notion of 'successful' schools allowed special privileges, ensuring that some schools were regarded as more desirable, rather than simply 'diverse', and some schools were shunned. New Labour's appropriation of the 1990s Conservative agenda of choice and diversity effectively destroyed the notion of good local schools for all, and ignored mounting evidence of social and ethnic divisions which the working out of 'choice' in schooling encouraged. The encouragment of more faith schools, particularly the expansion of Anglican schools and the sponsorship of the semi-privatized Academies by religious organizations, excited curiously little debate in a society increasingly riven by religious tensions.

Local education authorities, which had provided the infrastructure for local comprehensive education, were by 2005 responsible for ensuring high standards in a structurally fragmented school system in which equally high standards were impossible to achieve. The public education service had become a franchised set of competing institutions democratically accountable neither to the public nor to their staff. The government increasingly favoured privatization as a solution to historic public problems of schooling, a solution previously associated with the political right. Evidence of the failings and inefficiencies of private companies was ignored or down-played. There was marked continuity during the 2000s of centralized control of teachers, the curriculum, assessment and pedagogy, accompanied by more elaborate centralized inspection systems, although with the departure of Chief Inspector Woodhead in 2001 government was less inclined to treat teachers with contempt. Privatization and more stringent control of LEAs and of teachers' pay and conditions was described as 'modernization'.

A major reason for the raised hopes in 1997 that the Blair government would pursue more egalitarian as well as economically efficient education policies was New Labour's stated commitment to social inclusion and a return to social justice. There was much rhetorical commitment to the development and funding of new educational policies for the poor, and a plethora of initiatives undertaken with the proclaimed intention of improving education for the many. With many of the New Labour initiatives, the policies required some manipulation. As one headteacher noted, the replacement of her school's clapped-out old boiler was billed as having been part of a New Deal for Schools, with her LEA credited as having worked in partnership with the DfEE to 'invest in improvement and standards' (Newnham 2000: 14). In 2004 the author's daughter, as part of the new investment in Further Education Colleges, was, together with her teaching colleagues, given a wheely trolley to wheel her increasing amounts of paperwork around her college. New policies in the second term brought childcare and early years to the policy forefront, this area having been regarded by previous governments as relatively unimportant. The childcare policies were, however, linked with the work agenda, as women with very young children were increasingly encouraged to take employment to reach an economic participation rate common in other European countries, although those countries made better arrangements for childcare (Walker 2005). New policies to improve childcare included 'educare' and 'wrap-around childcare' plus Children's Centres and Children's Trusts. Significantly, early years' policies were ignored by the Conservatives until the run-up to the 2005 General Election. While the amalgamation of local education and social service departments, with an overall director, may have appeared a cohesive move, Crouch pointed out that social service departments are concerned with social repair and casualties (Crouch 2003). It appeared that Local Education Authorities were to become vehicles for social casualties, responsible for those excluded from school, children in local authority care, and those taking free school meals. Private, semi-privatized schools and selective schools, were unlikely to offer all-day 'educare', while schools in poorer areas were more likely to take on these tasks.[5] The public education service seemed set to become further divided and divisive as a section of schooling became associated with social care and repair rather than part of a universal high quality educational service.

Surprisingly, one of the policy changes from the previous Conservative government was that, despite the much hyped focus on 'Education, Education, Education' promised in 1997 by Tony Blair, spending on education as a proportion of GDP actually declined under Labour – from 4.8 per cent in 1996 to under 4.7 per cent in 1998 (Travers 1999: 2). New Labour was initially determined to shed its tax and spend image and, under Chancellor of the Exchequer Gordon Brown, embarked on a reduction of public expenditure. Thus, despite the extra £19 billion promised for education by

David Blunkett in July 1998, a figure endlessly repeated by politicians and the media and eventually a source of embarrassment to the government, New Labour's spending on education during their first two years in power was lower than under the Conservatives. By 2002 it was only marginally ahead of Conservative spending. Davies (2000a), in a thorough review of New Labour education spending, drew attention to a critical report by all-party MPs which noted the misleading accounting systems, with double and treble accounting in different budget streams, which concealed the reality of actual reductions in local authority and school budgets. Many of the initiatives announced required LEAs and schools to make competitive bids and LEA and school personnel wasted many hours in writing bids. Don Foster, a Liberal Democrat MP, reported that over two years 25,353 bids were made, of which only 8972 were successful, and 'the torrent of new money turned out to be little more than a trickle' (Davies 2000a: 11). The government budget in March 2000 promised another £1 billion for schools, to take the form of top-up grants to individual schools, bypassing local authorities, and for initiatives already announced. In July 2000, the Chancellor of the Exchequer announced large increases in public spending from 2001, including a £5 billion increase over three years for education which, however, only brought the total percentage of GNP spent on education to 5.1 per cent in 2003, a figure still below the average spending of 5.8 per cent in other OECD countries. The funding crisis in schools in 2002–2003 brought criticism from the government Audit Committee that central government's minimum spending guarantee for schools – about to be extended for three years to 'independent specialist schools' would not guarantee fair funding to areas of exceptional need (TEN 2004). The 2004 Spending Review enthused that total spending on education would be £12 billion more in 2008 than in 2004, a rise to 5.6 per cent of GNP (HM Treasury 2004). But this is still below the OECD average. While funding promises always prove variable, the question remains as to why the government of a rich country that had made education and training for global economic competition a major priority could not commit to more generous overall funding for all levels of education.

Notes

1 Anthony Giddens, eminent sociologist, former Director of the London School of Economics and Political Science, and an adviser to Tony Blair, provided much of the intellectual rationale for Labour's moves to dismantle the welfare state in favour of what he called a social investment state (Giddens 1998a). He was made a Lord in 2003.

2 According to Keep (1999) Michael Bichard, Permanent Secretary until 2001, believed strongly that, as in the civil service generally, all parts of the education and training system should be rewarded or penalized according to performance.

Pollard (2005) documented the influence of Bichard in developing and overseeing New Labour policies.

3 Much of the White Paper *Learning to Succeed* was credited to David Miliband, then Head of the Downing Street Policy Unit, later MP for South Shields, and a Minister for Schools, whose long-standing interest in post-16 education dated from his collaboration on the paper by Finegold *et al.* (1990) for the Institute for Public Policy Research.

4 Pollard (2005) provides insights into the policy-making process in 1995 when New Labour politicians and advisers wished to find a diplomatic way of appeasing the grant-maintained schools lobby while bringing the schools back under local authority funding. Michael Barber is credited with developing the mantra of 'standards not structures' which took media attention away from the hierarchical school structures proposed.

5 A survey by the Association of Teachers and Lecturers in 2005 found that private school teachers were also worried about their workload and extended hours (Kirkman 2005).

Further reading

Hodgson, A. and Spours, K. (1999) *New Labour's Educational Agenda*. London: Kogan Page. Drawing on interviews with ministers and advisers, this book offers a detailed analysis of New Labour policies for post-14 education, and suggested that the government needed to set a new agenda for the future.

Ranson, S. (1994) *Towards the Learning Society*. London: Cassell. This book is part of a project theorizing the politics of education since 1944. It argues that both Labour and Conservative governments have moved away from post-war social democratic beliefs in a fairer society, and that policymakers should now develop a 'learning society' which prepares individuals and institutions for democratic change.

Tomlinson, S. (ed.) (1997) *Education 14–19 Critical Perspectives*. London: Athlone. The contributors to this book argue for a unified curriculum and qualifications system post-14 for all young people and note that while educational credentials are no longer a certain guarantee of employment in an uncertain labour market, some are higher status than others and different groups of students are still unequally able to obtain them.

Hayward, G., Hodgson, A., Johnson, J. *et al.* (2004) *The Nuffield Review of Education and Training: Annual Report 2003–04*. The Trustees of the Nuffield Foundation established a review of education and training 14–19 in 2003. The first year report incorporated an historical and philosophical analysis of education and training, the skills debate and lifelong learning, and brings together much information from databases, literature and commissioned working papers.

chapter

eight

Education and the middle classes

Chapters 1–7 offered a necessarily selective descriptive analysis of educational policy, legislative change and underlying ideologies over 60 years, concentrating on the period 1997–2005. Policies have intended and unintended consequences, and this chapter examines the persistence of inequalities in educational outcomes by social class despite a half-century of dramatic social, economic and educational policy change and a more recent focus on poverty and social exclusion.

In the nineteenth and early twentieth centuries, education was openly intended to reinforce a class structure based on ascription by birth and wealth. 'The different classes of society, the different occupations, require different teaching', as a major *Schools Inquiry Report* put it in 1886 (Taunton Commission 1886). This translated into 'public' schools for the aristocracy and upper classes, minor public schools and a hierarchy of grammar schools for the middle classes, and an elementary education for the masses. Yet even at this time the expanding middle classes were demanding a replacement of ascription by 'achievement' as measured by a lengthy academic education and the acquisition of credentials. The 1886 report referred to 'a great body of professional men who have nothing but education to keep their sons on a high social level' (Taunton Commission 1886: 93). The subsequent elevation of a subject centred 'academic' curriculum and a disparaging of craft, vocational and technical education as suitable only for the lower classes set the scene for the twentieth-century two-tier system persistently associated with social class. However the idea of an 'educational ladder for the children of poorer parents' to climb their way out of the lower classes appeared in the Bryce Commission report on secondary education in 1895 (Bryce Report 1895).

Despite the post-war shift in Britain towards meritocratic and egalitarian ideals, embodied in the slogan 'equality of opportunity', and a focus on opportunities for previously marginalized groups – women, manual workers, ethnic minorities and disabled people – social class, that 'hereditary curse of English education' (Tawney 1931: 142) continued to affect educational policies and outcomes. While governments were encouraging more people to engage in the competitive attempt to improve their human capital potential by acquiring more qualifications, large numbers were still excluded from entering the competition on equal terms, and the class structure was proving remarkable resilient. To use popular football metaphors, there is no level playing field in a class society, and the goalposts are moved by pressures from, and attention paid to, the upper and middle classes. Educational policies, both deliberately and by default, have since Thatcher's first government in the 1980s, increasingly favoured groups already privileged or seeking privileges. The middle classes, described by historian Arthur Marwick (1998: 14) as 'not one middle class, but a range of middle classes, amazingly variegated in educational backgrounds, in burdens and privileges', became the major beneficiaries of market competition for the best schools, resources and funding. However, in the late twentieth and early twenty-first century, even belonging to elite middle class groups was no guarantee of success, and the middle classes were increasingly engaged in developing strategies and overcoming risks, to prevent any downward social mobility for their children.

Post-1997 government measures to tackle social exclusion in education and other areas were in conflict with the needs of old and new middle class and aspirant groups. By the 1990s, these groups felt increasingly insecure. Competition for the 'positional advantage' described by Hirsch (1977) created demands for the exclusion of as many competitors as possible, and led to contradictory policies, as the New Labour government preached inclusion, but pursued policies which ultimately ensured the exclusion of lower socio-economic groups. The Commission on Social Justice, set up by Labour leader John Smith in 1993, noted the way:

> the UK has wasted and continues to waste, much potential achievement through an inefficient and divisive education system which . . . sorts people as soon as it can into social classes in which, for the most part, they stay for the rest of their lives.
>
> (Commission on Social Justice 1994: 18)

These sentiments did not prevent the old and new middle classes pressurizing governments and developing strategies to ensure that their children retained advantages in any supposedly equal competitive situations. The New Labour governments produced an education system consistently favouring the middle classes, despite a constant rhetoric promising opportunity for the many not the few. They appeared pleased to collude with 'middle England' and policies of choice, selection, exclusion, and attention to the academic and the gifted and talented, resulted in the separation of vocational education and the denigration of schools largely attended by the poor. By the early twenty-first century disinterested observers could be forgiven for wondering whether it was a New Labour objective to eject troublesome lower class children and make schools safe for the middle classes.

Changing class structures

The persistence of class has meant that there is a very large literature on class formation, structures and the measurement of class (see Goldthorpe 1987; Halsey *et al.* 1997; Marshall 1997; Cannadine 1998; Crompton 1998; Savage 2000). Class origin continues to be a potent force for individuals and their educational chances and subsequent social and economic placement (Power *et al.* 2003b; Ball 2003). While during the 1990s both Conservative Prime Minister Major and New Labour leader Blair claimed that their goal was a classless society, inequalities of wealth and income, and of educational chances, have persisted, and Atkinson commented in 2000 'we are ending the century just as we began, with a widespread concern about poverty' (Atkinson 2000). However, ideologies of equality of opportunity, changing occupational structures and the reality of welfare state education, helped to create social mobility during the twentieth century, particularly from the 1960s. This situation, as noted in previous chapters, arose largely because increasing numbers of children in comprehensive schools were entered for public examinations. It was due to this success that higher education was able to expand. Changes in the economy resulted in more social mobility, as the proportion of unskilled jobs, particularly in manufacturing, was steadily reduced. The Registrar-General's classification of occupations into socio-economic groups, at what is now the Office for National Statistics (ONS), remained a major official measure of social class, dividing the population into a professional class, an intermediate or managerial class, skilled non-manual, skilled manual, semiskilled manual, unskilled and a residual category of those not in work. Academics and market researchers have produced different or more elaborated grades of class on the basis of (usually) male occupations. These gradings often exclude women, the retired, the unemployed and dependants (Marshall 1997: 86). The ONS produced a new system of classification in September 2000, involving 17 'classes'. It was greeted by one journalist with the comment that 'we are all middle class now. The government is to redefine the class structure . . . because so many people have joined the ranks of the upwardly mobile middle class' (Norton 1998). This was an exaggeration: the classes reflected changing occupational structures as manual jobs disappeared. However references to a working class had vanished from the political vocabulary by the mid-1990s, as politicians aimed their policies at the populist middle ground. The traditional manual working class had been redefined in the style of the Democratic Party strategies in the USA as the 'working middle class' (Gould 1998: 173). The Blair government made much use of the term 'hard-working families'. The partially employed or non-workers had become the socially excluded, the poor, or the underclass.

Adversarial Marxist notions of class, working class consciousness and class struggle, socialist beliefs in a mixed but managed economy and a welfare state had all but disappeared by the 1990s, although the hierarchical, three-layered model of an upper, middle and working class remained the way that most people conceptualized their society (Cannadine 1998). Both Conservatives and New Labour unashamedly aimed policies in the 1990s at 'middle England'. This description, derived from Richard Nixon's appeals to 'middle America' in the 1970s, had been described as 'A metaphor for respectability, the nuclear family, heterosexuality, conservatism, whiteness and the status quo' (Cannadine 1998: 183). But concern with the middle groups in industrial societies has a long history: the 'new middle classes' had been a feature of nineteenth-century Britain and North America, and middle class expansion had been much discussed since the 1930s (Vidich 1995). In Britain the successes of welfare state education through educational expansion and rising levels of qualifications had guaranteed entry to various middle class groups, notable via employment in the expanding public services. Attitudes to education in all classes changed as more people realized the importance of educational qualifications to obtain and retain any job. By the 1980s the expanding middle and aspirant classes were anxious that their children should obtain the credentials for good jobs, but aware that by then policies were rationing good education.

The major political parties sought to convey concern for the insecurity and anxiety that the middle classes displayed. They attempted to persuade individuals that their class-bound society was classless. Paradoxically, at the same time they stressed that individual effort and merit would bring social and occupational mobility. The electoral strategy of New Labour in 1997 was to appeal to a wider constituency than the Old Labour heartlands, and was aimed directly at the middle class and aspirant middle class Conservative voters. As Philip Gould, a Labour strategist, explained in his book: 'The middle class can no longer be viewed as a small, privileged sub-sector of society. Mass politics is becoming middle-class politics. Winning the century means winning middle-class support' (Gould 1998: 396). This sentiment translated into policies which reaffirmed educational privileges for the middle classes. The choices and trajectories of middle class groups were, as empirical research demonstrated, complex and diverse, but despite some 'losers and drop outs' mostly led via higher education to professional, managerial or good white-collar jobs (Power et al. 2003b).

Meritocracy and attainment

Previous chapters have indicated that educational reform, in Britain as in other developed countries, has seldom been effective in reducing advantages for middle class children, whose educational attainments have remained persistently higher than those of lower socio-economic groups. A longitudinal DfEE-funded Youth Cohort Study illustrated that at a time when educational achievement in terms of GCSE passes was rising for all pupils, inequalities of achievement between social classes also increased, particularly between manual and non-manual groups (Demack *et al.* 1998). There continued to be large differences in educational attainments across occupational groups.

Research continued to examine the ways in which educational advantage and disadvantage were reproduced, with some researchers pointing out that it was all too easy to update a deficit model of the working and non-working class and their classroom learning (Mac an Ghaill 1996; Duffield 1998). Research into the persistence of social class inequalities did, by the 1990s, focus much more on the strategies adopted by the middle classes to retain inequalities (Brown, P. 1997, 2000). This was the case in other countries as well as Britain, studies of the persistence of social inequalities in French education being noteworthy (Duru-Bellat 2000). Politicians however, continued to examine and deplore the achievements of the lower classes. In 2003 the DfES and HM Treasury commissioned a paper on socio-economic differences in educational achievement for a high level seminar, which again focused on the supposed deficiencies within families, especially poor parenting. It was equivocal as to whether low incomes led to low achievement. The paper concluded that socially segregated schooling due to the housing market and school allocation to low ability groups was detrimental to higher achievement (Hobbs 2003).

It was also the case that while participation in higher education rose considerably during the 1990s, young people from the lowest socio-economic groups remained under-represented. Although their participation in HE more than doubled from 6 per cent to 13 per cent over the 1990s, that of the children of professional parents went from 55 per cent to 72 per cent (*Social Trends 30* 2000: 56). The first analysis of universities by social class by the Higher Education Statistics Agency in 1999 showed that the professional and managerial classes dominated in the top twenty universities, headed by Oxford and Cambridge, which took half their home students from private schools, with lower socio-economic students predominantly attending former polytechnics. Subsequent HEFCE studies showed, via an examination of postcodes, the under-representation of students from disadvantaged areas (HEFCE 2004). Despite efforts by government and HEFCE to produce strategies that widen participation (Goddard 2000) the class inequalities and strategies that ensure this situation were unlikely to be eroded by higher education policies, particularly the payment of higher fees.

From the 1970s a mass of international evidence and literature was available describing the economic and cultural capital that parents in higher social classes were able to provide for their children (see Halsey *et al.* 1997). The higher achievements of those from the higher social groups were persistently rationalized by the myth of meritocracy – the notion that superior rewards are deserved because they reflect superior achievements. The notion of meritocracy had been boosted by the heavy reliance on mental testing throughout the twentieth century which encouraged the idea that selection for elite forms of education was meritocratic and that privileges were just and fair rewards for achievements.

This idea was satirized in 1958 by Michael Young, who pointed out that a meritocracy could mean downward mobility for some and sarcastically envisaged the upper classes admitting that they could produce dull children, who would then happily live in council housing, doing domestic service without resentment because 'the inferiors knew their superiors had a greater part to play in the world' (Young 1958: 122). However, this sad situation was never a reality; Goldthorpe and his colleagues demonstrated that attempts to provide legitimation for structures of inequality in modern societies do not work. Through painstaking social mobility studies, they showed that merit plays a limited role in class mobility and that children of lower socio-economic origins have to demonstrate much more 'merit' to enter desirable class positions (Goldthorpe 1997; Breen and Goldthorpe 1999). Analysis of the 40 richest young people in Britain in 2000, including internet entrepreneurs, showed that far from representing a classless generation, most were educated at top private schools and had rich and influential parents (O'Sullivan 2000).

Lawton (2005) brilliantly demonstrated the origins and persistence over the whole of the twentieth century of a Labour Party belief in the ideology of meritocracy, and the 'ladder of opportunity' by which a selected few of the working class could ascend into the middle classes. New Labour persisted in its ideological presentation of Britain as a meritocracy where even the socially excluded could rise into the middle class. Blair commented early in 1999 in a speech to the IPPR that his government had a ten-year programme to tackle poverty and social exclusion: 'At the end of it, I believe we will have an expanded middle class and ladders of opportunity for those of all backgrounds. No more ceilings that prevent people from achieving the success they merit'. Lawton's comment on this aim was that far from being a modernized aim 'New Labour's plans are extremely old-fashioned and unscientific. Blair's acceptance of a meritocracy and the "ladder of opportunity" are particularly objectionable' (Lawton 2005: 153).

School effectiveness

During the 1990s the realities of social class and education were obscured by governments which seized on school effectiveness research, which superficially supported the political message that 'poverty is no excuse' for schools in deprived areas obtaining low examination results, to create a blame and shame culture. Smith and Tomlinson, publishing a five-year study of multiracial comprehensive schools in 1989, were concerned to find their research eventually quoted in support of the 'no excuse' slogan (Smith and Tomlinson 1989). In March 2000 the secretary of state 'blamed' 530 secondary schools with low GCSE pass rates, a majority of them former secondary modern schools attended by poor pupils, claiming that school effectiveness research showed other schools with pupils in poverty (as measured by numbers receiving free school meals) performing better.[1] While school effectiveness debates were becoming increasingly acrimonious, numbers of pupils on free school meals increased by 590,379 between 1993 and 1997.

Governments from the 1980s believed that schools could be manipulated as technical systems (Lingard *et al.* 1998) to make a difference to performance, with individuals being responsible for their own levels of performance, and schools, whatever their history or clientele, being held responsible for failure to meet targets. School effectiveness research played down the impact of social and economic disadvantages on learning. Research in New Zealand carried out by Thrupp (1999), and published in a book aptly entitled *Schools Making a Difference: Let's Be Realistic* demonstrated the way in which schools with low socio-economic intakes struggled to improve, but were labelled as ineffective. In England the failure of technical solutions applied to so-called failing schools began to be apparent almost as soon as they were implemented. Three headteachers appointed under the Fresh Start programme to improve failing schools had resigned by early 2000. Nevertheless, politicians persisted in blaming schools for failure to overcome social and economic disadvantages, pretending that schools in class societies in which inequalities were widening could still be a major force in reducing rather than reproducing them. In particular, persistent evidence that a major way to raise standards and reduce inequitable school outcomes was to ensure those schools contained a balanced social and 'ability' mix (Duffield 1998; Paterson 1998) continued to be ignored in England, although such research did influence educational policy in Scotland. In England it was easier to focus on the supposed deficiencies of the excluded and continue nineteenth-century traditions of separate schooling for different social classes. The pretence, in the face of evidence to the contrary that a diversity of schools (including Academies) could reduce social class divisions, was more an exercise in hypocrisy than evidence-based policy. It was becoming more obvious in the early twenty-first century that the needs of the middle classes took precedence over social exclusion and social justice.

Middle class needs

Despite the political focus on social exclusion and inclusion – terms popularized after a 1995 European government summit in Copenhagen – a study of the needs of the middle classes proved more useful in explaining educational exclusion and the persistence of schools as places of class reproduction, than studying the characteristics of the excluded. In Britain the shift towards meritocratic and egalitarian ideals, embodied in the concept of 'equality of opportunity', characterized the period from the 1920s to the 1970s. The idea that there would be equal access to good credentials and jobs had a strong appeal for the middle classes, who either already possessed or quickly developed strategies to ensure that their children had advantages in any supposedly competitive examination. The move towards comprehensive education in the 1960s was supported by many middle class parents who realized that, despite cultural advantages, their children might be displaced in selective schools by 'able' working class children. But just as their children had dominated grammar schools in the selective system, the middle classes using state education became adept at seeking out the best comprehensives (particularly those retaining grammar streams), accessing resources and avoiding schools attended by the poor and by ethnic minorities.[2]

Despite the heterogeneous nature of the middle and aspirant classes a common characteristic had become a commitment to a social and political system that provided them with advantages and a 'good life', for many a better life than their parents, and a fierce determination to see their children reproduced into similar spheres. Middle class groups realized, long before the advent of new technologies, the increasing importance of access to knowledge and credentials. By the 1990s there was an important section of the middle class, educated in private or good state schools and 'good' universities, dominating the communications, information and propaganda industries, and the political arena, who were easily able to resist egalitarian and social democratic school organization. These and other knowledgeable groups were determined that their children would have similar access to privileged education. This entailed not only using traditional social networks and contacts with private schools and coaching children for the remaining grammar schools, but also using new market powers to 'choose' schools that would equip their children with the credentials to move on to the most prestigious universities. It also entailed equipping their children with what Philip Brown called the 'value-added curriculum vitae', a CV which demonstrated the right personal and social skills and cultural experiences. 'Within the middle classes, the development of the charismatic qualities of their children is becoming as important as arming them with the necessary credentials, contacts and networks' (Brown 1997: 744).

The importance of mothers in the reproduction and maintenance of class inequalities was cogently demonstrated by Reay (1998). In a study of the strategies adopted by middle and working class mothers to assist their children's educational achievements, she showed how the confidence and knowledge of the middle class mothers in their dealings with the school paid off. In addition, their children engaged in a 'social whirl' of contacts and extra-curricular activities, and dinner parties were devoted to discussing education. In 'acting in their own children's best interest' middle class mothers were inevitably acting against the best interests of less privileged mothers (Reay 1998: 165). The teachers were aware of the social class reproduction, but as the headteacher of a working class primary school remarked, 'What can we do? They want us to make their children middle class. We can't do that' (Reay 1998: 124). The need of the middle classes was not for equality of opportunity for meritocratic competition, but for making sure that their children mixed with others from the required social and familial backgrounds. There were also needs for the exclusion of students who were more difficult to teach and took teachers' time and resources, although by the 1990s the middle classes had realized the value of time and resources that could be claimed for some types of learning difficulty and numbers of children claimed as 'dyslexic' increased exponentially. The longitudinal work of Power and her colleagues (Power *et al.* 2003b) and Ball and his colleagues (Ball 2003) provided empirical confirmation of the way educational provision became almost literally a battleground in an educational class war!

The needs of less secure, lower-middle income and aspirant groups for the exclusion of those who might interfere with the acquisition of good credentials were even more intense. These groups did not have access to networks and contacts; their children were less likely to have acquired the value-added CV, and were thus more dependent on meritocratic competition. Governments in the 1990s and 2000s, responding to the fears and aspirations of these groups, adopted policies of reassurance: streaming, setting, specialist schools, and the exclusion of the troublesome lower classes in units, support centres, EBD schooling, and FE colleges. This all signalled advantages to aspirant classes. Aspirant minority ethnic groups, long-time critics of their stereotyping as low achievers, were also intended to be recipients of policies for improving inner city schools and catering for the 'able', in keeping with the low-key approach to race issues in the 1990s. There were, however, contradictions between the market policies which rationed good education for minorities (Gillborn and Youdell 2000) and attempts to mitigate this.

The educational needs of the middle classes, which by the 2000s incorporated the need to move away from meritocratic and egalitarian beliefs and exclude the disadvantaged and troublesome from interfering with their children's education, could be understood as a reaction to heightened insecurities, as global economic conditions, insecure employment, and a de-layering in public bureaucracies and private business affected middle class groups in ways they could not have envisaged up to the 1980s. The middle classes had largely become the anxious classes, certainly as far as their children's education was concerned. Particular ways in which their educational needs were satisfied were by the use of private education, by the advantages that choice policies delivered, by the avoidance of a vocational curriculum, and by avoidance of the poor and socially excluded.

Private advantage

Despite Conservative fears for over half a century that Labour would abolish private schooling, private education flourished in the final twenty years of the twentieth century.[3] New Labour Prime Minister Blair himself attended Fettes, a Scottish public school where his headmaster had previously been sacked from the headship of Eton for drunkenness (Morris 1995: 20). By the turn of the century some 2400 private schools were educating around 600,000 pupils, 7 per cent of the school population – up from 5.8 per cent when Mrs Thatcher came to power. The teacher:pupil ratio was 1:10. The schools, with an increase in day over boarding pupils, collected some £3.2 billion in fees. Foreign pupils contributing some £250 million and over 143,000 pupils received help with fees despite the boasted abolition of the assisted places scheme. The school sixth forms accounted for some 26 per cent of all those taking A levels (ISIS 1999; Davies 2000b). Using figures from Pollard and Adonis (1996), Davies documented the enormous power and influence that the products of top public schools subsequently wielded: 7 out of 9 senior army generals, 33 out of 39 senior judges, half of the eighteen permanent secretaries, and half of the 94 top civil servants, all had been educated privately. Private school pupils accounted for 75 per cent of those in professional or managerial jobs, compared to 40 per cent from state schools.

Clearly, private education continued to be important for those who could afford to buy competitive advantage for their children; the upper classes and old middle classes effortlessly reproduced most of their children into good social and economic positions, and new and aspirant groups were eager to grasp the advantages of both excellent resources and old boy networks, with the additional legitimacy of meritocracy. The top private schools, especially girls' schools, regularly featured at the top of school league tables from 1992, which, together with policies such as the assisted places scheme, encouraged aspirant parents to regard private schools as first rate and state schools as second rate. Philip Brown pointed out that an expanding section of both the old and new middle classes was undermining the principle of equality of opportunity by returning to the idea that educational outcomes should be determined by parental wealth and preference, rather than the ability and effort of pupils. 'This form of social closure is the outcome of an evaluation by the middle classes that educational success is too important to be left to the chances of a formally open competition' (Brown 1997: 402).

Giddens (1998b) put this in a slightly different way, rejecting the American scholar John Galbraith's (1992) thesis that there was a 'culture of contentment' among the middle classes. The middle classes, according to Giddens, were well aware of the hazards and risks of modern life, and opt out of public provision because they have a more active orientation to risk management. State education constitutes a risk; private education, if affordable, poses less risk. During the 1990s, politicians became worried that the private–public divide in education did pose considerable risk to social cohesion. George Walden (1996), former diplomat and Conservative MP, argued persuasively that although state and private education constituted a 'backward two-tier system based on class obsession rather than educational imperatives' (Walden 1996: 161), it was comprehensive schooling that had failed to offer high-level academic education, and encouraged the middle classes to escape into private schools. His solutions of diversification of schooling, more technical schools for inner city pupils and differential pay for teachers, were by and large adopted by New Labour, but without any noticeable reduction in the escapees into private education. New Labour was, however, concerned to promote partnerships between private and state education, setting up an advisory group in January 1999 to distribute over £1 million to encourage such cooperation (Passmore 1999). This largely took the form of private schools sharing playing fields with those whose sports facilities had been sold off during the 1980s. While in the 2000s private schools saw off threats to remove their charitable status, which saved them large amounts of tax, Hutton (2004) noted the 'intra-middle class warfare' that was developing as more competitors were delivered, via top state schools, to 'what has been a private school preserve' – privileged access to the top universities.

Choice and advantage

While private education depended on wealth, the policies that benefited all sections of the middle classes were the choice policies, which underpinned the marketization of education. Previous chapters have documented how the slow but steady progress towards a more equitable and an improving education system was denigrated post-1988 and an education market was introduced. The new framework for funding and administering all aspects of education and the competition between schools based on ostensible parental choice of school – fuelled by the annual publication of raw scores of examination results – introduced new modes of class disadvantage. Although free-market supporters, taking their cue from private education where the aim is to 'please the customer', paid some attention to the effects of markets on social equality (Chubb and Moe 1990; Tooley 1996), international studies demonstrated by the early 1990s that markets benefited the middle classes disproportionately. An OECD study in seven countries concluded that a major result of choice policies globally had been to increase social class segregation in schools:

> sometimes this is because more privileged groups are more active in choosing desired schools, sometimes it is because such schools are in more prosperous neighbourhoods whose residents continue to get more privileged access to them.
>
> (OECD 1994: 7)

Research in the UK certainly showed that social class difference enabled more privileged choosers to discriminate between schools, evaluate teachers and avoid schools with negative characteristics (Gewirtz et al. 1995; Ball et al. 1996). Privileged parents had the required cultural capital and educational knowledge for them to emerge as winners in local school markets, and 'the implementation of market reforms in education is essentially a class strategy which has as one of its major effects the reproduction of relative social class (and ethnic) advantages and disadvantages' (Ball 1993: 4). This appeared to be the case even in social democratic countries such as Sweden, where self-selection by parents and pupils resulted in social class differentiation in schools (Hatcher 1998).

The social polarization thesis did not go unchallenged in Britain. Researchers Gorard and Fitz, using data on free school meals in all LEAs in England and Wales, claimed that there was reduced class segregation among schools nationally (Gorard and Fitz 1998; Gorard 1999), a message which pleased politicians and the DfEE. However, Gibson and Asthana (1999) produced national data to show that social polarization was increasing locally and having a damaging effect on school performance and Noden (2000) also reported increasing levels of social segregation by school. A study commissioned by Ealing Council in London, examining the relationship between poverty and pupil performance of 5000 children, showed that the children from higher socio-economic groups attended the better schools and performed better, suggesting that 'social class is a crucial factor in determining whether a child does well or badly at school' (Dean 1998: 3). In 2001 Gorard and his colleagues concluded that while the school system in England and Wales was fairer than it was in 1989 the recent trend, once school choice processes had matured, was once again towards unfairness (Gorard et al. 2001).

Avoidance of the vocational

A major need of the middle classes had always been to avoid the relegation of their children to vocational education and practical training. The academic–vocational divide in Britain continued to be synonymous with a class divide into the twentieth-first century, with policymakers, politicians and professionals continuing to find reasons to legitimize the separation of some young people into high status education and others into lower status courses. Despite advances in understanding intellectual development and learning potentialities, the ideological belief persisted that only a minority of students were capable of abstract thinking, a minority in technical ideas and a majority in practical activities. The first post-war Labour government ensured a continuation of lower status practical education for working class children, and the middle classes developed strategies to avoid secondary modern schools. Comprehensive school reorganization, with some exceptions, continued to sort pupils into courses by criteria heavily influenced by class, race and gender (Benn and Chitty 1996, 2004).

Despite some moves towards a unified curriculum, or even the curriculum envisaged by Labour in the early 1990s whereby all pupils would study some academic, some vocational and some practical courses by 2000 (see Hodgson and Spours 1999), after eight years of New Labour government the academic–vocational divide was still in place. Schools and colleges were able to develop post-14 vocational courses, and the pupils who were encouraged to leave school and take up college courses were predominantly lower class disaffected students. The government rejection of the important recommendations for a unified and inclusive diploma system in the Tomlinson Report (DfES 2005b) led to a 'sense of betrayal . . . of the thousands who participated in the review process' (Hodgson and Spours 2005). Politicians continued to protect the A-level route, still regarded as a 'gold standard', confident that few middle class parents and students would be satisfied with other post-16 routes. For private, grammar, foundation and some other types of schools achieving places at Oxford or Cambridge remained the apogee of education. Green and Steedman (1997) had however pointed out that choosing the A-level route, rather than alternative vocational tracks, was a rational choice by parents and students, who rightly calculated that their chances of advancement in a competitive society lay in this direction. Growth in employment opportunities in business, financial and some public services, where the managerial and professional jobs were concentrated, encouraged aspirant groups to acquire academic qualifications if possible.

Avoiding the poor

In developing a theory of poverty and social exclusion, Jordan wrote that such a theory must explain not only why welfare systems designed to aid the poor were being dismantled, but also how this was exacerbated by the exit of the better off into private schemes, and the development of strategies for excluding the poor (Jordan 1996). This echoed the somewhat apocalyptic view of Robert Reich, former US Secretary of Labor, who was concerned that around one-fifth of the US population was able to command wealth through the value that the global economy placed on their skills and qualifications. The temptation for the fortunate few was not only to exclude others, but also to exclude themselves, withdrawing into their own schools, housing enclaves, health care and transport (Reich 1991). Giddens, in a public lecture in 1999, affirmed that this could happen in the UK, where 'social exclusion at the top' was practised by elites who sought to escape financial and social responsibilities and form their own communities (Giddens 1999b). The middle classes who could not afford private escape have usually had at their disposal strategies to avoid their children being educated with the poor, to ensure that their children attended well-resourced schools and avoided stigmatized forms of education.

The numbers of poor individuals and families, their increase during the final twenty years of the twentieth century, their living (and dying) conditions, health, housing and educational attainments, had all, by the early 2000s, been documented in astonishing detail (Acherson 1998; Social Exclusion Unit 1998; Power and Mumford 1999; Social Trends 2003; Brewer *et al.* 2004) and New Labour had committed itself to *Opportunities for All: Tackling Poverty and Social Exclusion* (DSS 1999). Since at that time nearly 20 per cent of households with children had no working adults (as compared with 8.8 per cent in France and 8.6 per cent in Germany) and 'the rise in income inequality in the UK over the past twenty years was virtually unparalleled among OECD countries' (DSS 1999: 30), the keynote policy was active intervention to help people get work. This involved (as has been documented in previous chapters) wide-ranging policy initiatives to improve levels of education and training. But raising skill and qualification levels among the poor inevitably led to even greater competitive anxiety among some sections of the middle classes. As Hirsch (1977) pointed out, there is a relative dimension to equality, in that quality of education, irrespective of content, consists of the advantage it gives over others. The resistance to attempts in the 1960s and 1970s in both the USA and Britain to integrate inferior with superior schools showed that former winners in educational markets were determined to retain their advantages (Hirsch 1977: 6). He pointed out that newcomers to the competition were likely to be frustrated and even 'Those in the middle-class elites may in time lose out . . . middle class moans may rest on objective experience' (Hirsch 1977: 173).

Middle class and aspirant groups, aided by market policies, continued to avoid or to move away from schools attended by the poor and disadvantaged. 'The poor academic performance of schools in poor neighbourhoods does have a strong deterrent effect on potential residents. It leads to families with high aspirations moving away' (Power and Mumford 1999: 37). In the internal selection in schools, the middle classes usually successfully avoided their children being relegated to lower streams, tracks and sets, or some forms of special education. Up to the 1980s some ingenious strategies were adopted to prevent children acquiring the stigmatized labels of 'educationally subnormal' or 'maladjusted' although the middle classes were willing to admit to producing children with sensory or physical disabilities (Tomlinson 1981). By the 1990s the concept of special educational needs had reduced the stigma associated with learning difficulty, and the middle classes were happy to take advantage of statements of SEN that guaranteed extra resources or teaching time, while still avoiding relegation to schools for children with learning difficulties or for emotional and behavioural disturbance. The reported over-representation of middle class children in programmes for the gifted and talented came as no surprise.

Globalization and the middle classes

By the 2000s higher status education and qualifications had effectively developed as rationed, positional goods, designed or redesigned to exclude as many potential competitors as possible who threatened already privileged or aspirant groups. The various middle class groups, depending on their levels of economic and cultural capital, struggled to maintain privileges for their children. The anxieties and risks generated by the choice and competition scenario had been well documented on a national level. As Ball noted: 'The demands and use of market rules of exclusion and a neoliberal risk management regime are challenges which the middle classes are well placed to meet, they are fearful, alert and strategic' (Ball 2003: 168). But the English middle classes were also faced with the challenge of an emerging global class structure, which mimicked national social structures. There are highly educated and qualified elites from developed and developing countries, often educated internationally at elite schools and universities, whose background and privileges guarantee them permanent wealth and employment. There are well-qualified groups dependent on their own efforts, some of whom may be employed around the world on short-term contracts, some of whom may be qualified people from developing countries willing to work for lower wages than their counterparts in the richer countries. There are qualified groups in service and routine jobs, and large groups with few or no qualifications whose chances of employment depend as much on international, national, and regional capital flows, on migration rules and other government policies, as on their own efforts.

The top groups constitute a new transnational capitalist class (Sklair 2001) whose members are the principal actors in the construction of a global economy. This class is composed of people who own or run major trans-national corporations, supported by globalized bureaucrats, financiers, technocrats, politicians, professionals and managers. A challenge for at least some of the English middle classes will be to equip their children to join the top layers of this global upper and middle class. Ong has pointed out that in the USA the rise of the 'global professional' is well established. The children of multinational employees, diplomats, the top military and others, usually speaking one or more languages other than English, are aiming for educa-tion at prestigious higher education institutions and seeking 'to accumulate world-class degrees and certificates that will open the door to a successful career in the international arena' (Ong 2004: 49). While the elites in the English middle class may increasingly become aware of the need for their children to compete in this arena, Room has pointed out that the positional competition allied to the costs of higher education and training, may 'threaten to bankrupt middle class families. For less advantaged families, even to enter this competition may seem too risky, given their fewer resources of both financial and social capital' (Room 2002: 45).

Class and the common good

The structural situation in the UK in the early twenty-first century, as in other developed countries, particularly the USA, was that there was a diverse and expanded middle class and aspirant classes whose needs took precedence in any competitive struggle for positional advantage in society. The political reality was that these groups, whose votes governments depended on, were catered for by the educational policies put in place from the 1980s which created and recreated social exclusion on a daily basis. Although some ameliorative strategies and initiatives were developed, gov-ernments were aware that any policies which threatened middle class advan-tages, threatened electoral advantage. In the later 1990s the New Labour government embarked on what Muller (1997: 15) called 'an honourable but diminished project of pragmatic amelioration'. The raft of social policies could be claimed to have had some effect on some of the poor and disadvantaged. They had little effect on the middle classes apart from ensur-ing that, more than ever before, the future status and security of their chil-dren would be a primary aim, and that their children would be educated, as far as possible, apart from the poor.

New Labour ideology, centred round the notion of a Third Way between capitalism and socialism, included the notion of a revitalized community and civic life, in which citizens and communities would take more responsibility for each other and work for a common good (Halpern 1998). The reality of a society still divided along class lines, in which education had become a competitive battleground, accorded more with social theorist Ferrara, who feared that modern societies would degenerate into exclusive enclaves and 'malignant forms of anomie' (Ferrara 1997: 395). Educational policies which seek to exclude potential competitors for social goods, and defend and extend privileges for some groups, are always more likely to support division and inequities than any common good.

Notes

1 During the later 1990s the slogan 'poverty is no excuse' for lower achievements in some schools became popular with politicians and Ofsted, as did talk of 'turning schools round' in months. Social, historical and economic analysis indicated the crudity, and indeed cruelty, of these slogans (see Slee *et al.* 1998; O'Connor *et al.* 1999).
2 See literature from Jackson and Marsden (1962) to Benn and Chitty (1996, 2004).
3 The European Convention on Human Rights makes it impossible to abolish the right of parents to educate their children privately. In most European countries private schooling is mainly religious schooling, usually subsidized by the state.

Further reading

Ball, S.J. (2003) *Class Strategies and the Education Market.* London: Routledge-Falmer. This book examines ways in which the middle classes maintain and improve their social position through education, identifying key moments in the decision-making process that sets middle class children on their largely successful educational path.

Cannadine, D. (1998) *Class in Britain.* Newhaven, CT: Yale University Press. This eminently readable history of class in Britain demonstrates that notions of a classless society are unrealized. Private and state education continue to perpetuate social apartheid, and no government can reform education so that it is both classless and meritocratic.

Halsey, A.H., Lauder, H., Brown, P. and Wells, A.S. (1997) *Education, Culture, Economy and Society.* Oxford: Oxford University Press. The contributors to this important 800-page book examine the major changes that took place in education and society in the late twentieth century, and establish that a social study of education is crucial to understanding the nature of post-industrial societies.

Power. S., Edwards, E., Whitty, G., Wigfall, V. (2003) *Education and the Middle Classes.* Buckingham: Open University Press. Based on the biographies of 350 young people, this book demonstrates the educational pathways chosen, and the successes and failures of the children of the middle classes. It discusses the meanings of academic selection and the limits of meritocracy.

Reay, D. (1998) *Class Work: Mothers' Involvement in their Children's Primary Schooling*. London: UCL Press. This excellent empirical study demonstrates the way that women's educational experience influences their involvement in their children's education and the crucial part that mothers play in social reproduction.

chapter

nine

Equity issues: race and gender

Efforts to eliminate racial and gender inequities in countries with well-developed school systems over the past half-century have been patchy and uneven but have achieved some success. How far this was the result of specific policies, and how far due to the determination and motivation of the groups involved and wider social and economic factors, is difficult to determine. In Britain up to the 1970s traditional expectations of women's subordinate role in all social classes and the inferior class position assigned to migrants from former colonial countries remained dominant forces (Rex and Tomlinson 1979; Weiner 1994). From the 1970s, legislation for equal opportunities and against discrimination via the Race and Sex Discrimination Acts set a liberal agenda, and changing economic conditions altered education and employment chances for men and women in all social classes and ethnic groups. Although outgoing Conservative Prime Minister Major asserted in 1997 that 'policies must be colour blind . . . and just tackle disadvantage' (Major 1997) by the 1990s a cultural change in the attitudes of educators and some policymakers towards ethnic minorities and girls was apparent.

New Labour was initially eager to affirm their view of a modern national identity which valued diversity and recognized the citizenship rights of settled minorities and the inequalities they faced. It attempted in its first term to tackle some long-running grievances and inequalities, notably passing a Race Relations (Amendment) Act in 2000, and taking on a recommendation of the Parekh Report (2000) that there should be a single Equalities organization. However by its second term contradictions and conflict due to hasty legislation and the gaps between policy rhetoric and practical reality were becoming more evident, particularly the rhetoric of 'inclusion' and a school system that increasingly separated different groups. Race riots in northern English towns, the events of 11 September 2001 in the USA, the 2003 war in

Iraq and increased racism against refugees and asylum seekers moved political rhetoric away from support for addressing inequalities towards new kinds of assimilationist policies (Back *et al.* 2002). In the weeks before the general election of 2005, both major parties competed to be 'tough' on immigrants and asylum seekers, and a respected black journalist asserted that 'New Labour had degraded the racial discourse in Britain' (Younge 2005).

The issue of girls' educational performance was assumed to have been settled as girls continued to outperform boys at GCSE level and by the end of the century over half of university undergraduates were women. However, girls continued to study mainly traditional 'female' subjects at A level and beyond, and their achievements did not necessarily translate into equal career opportunities. Osler and Vincent (2003) noted the intersection of ethnicity and gender in achievement as the overall improvement in girls' school performance masked the educational difficulties of significant numbers of girls from minority backgrounds. In both the USA and Britain, gender debate in 2005 appeared to have returned to older deterministic theories when the President of Harvard University, Lawrence Summers, speculated whether innate gender differences gave women less intrinsic aptitude for science and engineering (Walters 2005). This chapter briefly discusses how far racial and ethnic minorities have improved their position in education despite racism and xenophobia in the majority society,[1] and examines the achievements of girls as they began to be offered a more equitable education. The socio-economic background of girls and boys in all ethnic groups (including whites) has always been an important factor in access to and achievement in education, and into the 2000s in Britain there was considerable political anxiety about all low-achieving lower class boys.

Race and ethnicity

Minorities and education from the 1960s

From the 1960s to the 1980s the children of ethnic minority parentage entered a school system in which overt selection was disappearing and comprehensive education becoming the norm. Where selection remained, minorities were less likely to be successful (Rex and Tomlinson 1979; Walford and Miller 1991).

Policies to disperse them in order to prevent high concentrations of minority children in urban schools were soon abandoned and central and local government were, at least notionally, committed to widening access to a broad secondary education for all. Initial disadvantages faced by the children were associated with the need for English language teaching, selective systems which worked against minorities, lack of extra funding, an inappropriate curriculum, teachers who had no training or awareness of minority issues and the use of special education to remove black children from the mainstream. The hostility of some white parents to their children being educated alongside racial and ethnic minorities was an issue from the 1960s, still apparent at the turn of the century (Richards 1983; Gewirtz *et al.* 1995; Ball *et al.* 2000). Local authorities with high numbers of minority children made policy on an ad hoc basis and, other than encouragement from HMI and some funding via Section 11 of the Local Government Act 1966, there were no national policies to assist in the successful incorporation of the children.

In the 1970s it was official policy to subsume minority issues under disadvantage, a policy labelled by the American scholar Kirp (1979) as 'racial inexplicitness'. A DES (1974) reply to the House of Commons Select Committee on Race Relations and Immigration considered that the majority of 'immigrant' children shared with indigenous children the 'educational disadvantages associated with an impoverished environment' (DES 1974: 2) and a Home Office report noted that 'A good deal of the disadvantage that minorities suffer is shared by less well-off members of the indigenous population' (Home Office 1978: 1). Subsuming minority disadvantage under general disadvantage continued to underpin official views into the 1990s, despite evidence that minorities continued to experience problems considerably in excess of the majority. Census data in 1991 demonstrated housing overcrowding among Pakistani and Bangladeshi groups, rates of unemployment three times higher than whites for black Africans and Bangladeshis, and higher rates of long-term illness and poor health among minorities (Storkey 1991; Acheson 1998). In Tower Hamlets during the 1980s a severe shortage of school places, researched by the author, led to over five hundred Bangladeshi children being known to the local authority to have no school place – a situation which would never have been tolerated for white children (Tomlinson 1992). During the 1970s the lack of national policy for minority children became more obvious, particularly as their then lower school achievements became a cause for concern and minority parents pressured the government for action. The Race Relations Act 1976 included measures to combat racial discrimination in education, and in 1979 the Labour government set up an inquiry into the education of African Caribbean children. The interim report of this inquiry suggested that the education system incorporated both intentional and unintentional racism, and that teachers needed training to teach effectively in a multi-ethnic society (DES 1981a).

Minorities and education in the 1980s

In 1977 a Labour Green Paper on Education had noted that 'a curriculum appropriate to our Imperial past cannot meet the requirements of modern Britain' (DES 1977b: 4) and during the 1980s a considerable literature emerged, much of it produced by teachers, on multicultural and antiracist curriculum practice. Local authorities, notably ILEA, developed equal opportunities policies, appointed multicultural advisers, and set up curriculum projects. Teachers, particularly those working in multiracial schools, and minority parents were instrumental in beginning to change school practice to incorporate minority children fairly (see Craft and Bardell 1984; Arora and Duncan 1986; Tomlinson 1987). Despite the xenophobia and racism indicated by hostility toward any special focus on the education of minorities, advances were made during the 1980s. The final report of the Committee of Inquiry into the education of ethnic minority children, chaired by Lord Swann, was published in 1985, making 71 recommendations for improving education for all young people in a multiethnic society (DES 1985a). The report was given cautious approval by the then Education Secretary of State, Keith Joseph, although the Sun newspaper advised him to 'shove it in the Whitehall incinerator' and a right-wing commentator claimed that the report was 'a dangerous document aimed at reshaping British society' (Pearce 1986: 136). The part of the Swann Report that particularly upset traditionalists was the suggestion that a fundamental reappraisal of values and attitudes in education was needed and a 'redefined concept of what it means to live in British society' developed (DES 1985a: 8). Opposition to any moves towards making the curriculum more appropriate for a multicultural society was expressed by New Right politicians, academics and educationists. Multicultural education was denounced as left-of-centre egalitarianism, political subversion and a threat to British values, culture and heritage (Hillgate Group 1986; Palmer 1986). The tabloid media ran invented stories about the supposed activities of left-wing councillors – 'Loonies ban sexist Robin Redbreast' was a *Sun* headline (17 May 1987) – and in a speech at the Conservative Party Conference in October 1987 Mrs Thatcher expressed fears that multicultural and antiracist education lowered standards and led to left-wing extremism. In a subsequent article aptly entitled 'An episode in the thirty years war', Morrell (2000) examined why, despite its efforts to raise the achievements of ethnic minorities, girls and working class pupils, ILEA came under such virulent attack and was subsequently abolished.

Despite this the 1980s was a period of educational advance for minority education. Raised awareness among practitioners and teacher unions, the development of multicultural and antiracist policies by over two-thirds of local authorities, formal requirements by the Council for the Accreditation of Teacher Education for teachers to be trained for work in a multiethnic society, and projects run through Education Support Grants (ESGs) helped to improve practice (Tomlinson 1990). Pressure from minority communities and both national and international groups concerned with equity were all factors leading to the improved treatment and raised achievements of minority pupils. There continued to be resistance in 'white' areas to the idea that schools should take a lead in challenging racist and xenophobic attitudes (Gaine 2000).

Post-1988

Post-1988, however, the slow but steady progress towards the more equit-able incorporation of minorities into the education system was considerably impeded. Overt policies for dealing with race and minority issues were almost completely removed from the educational agenda and race became an 'absent presence' (Apple 1999: 12). Issues concerning racial and ethnic inequalities in education were certainly absent from political consideration between 1990 and 1997. The post-1988 framework for funding and admin-istering all aspects of education and competition between schools based on parental 'choice' introduced new ways of disadvantaging minorities. The location of minorities, concentrated in the most urbanized parts of Britain, meant that they largely attended schools which, though nominally com-prehensive, were former secondary modern schools never designed to pre-pare students for high level academic work. Although from their family backgrounds in the country of origin many minorities were of middle class origin, particularly East African Asians and Indian families, and almost all migrant parents held values about the worth of education that were dis-tinctly middle class, ethnic minority students were mainly located in working class areas, and had to contend with the lower expectations of government and teachers about their educational potential. Benn and Chitty (1996) showed that schools with black and other minority students had higher working class intakes and fewer middle class students.

Choice legislation enabled 'privileged choosers' (Gewirtz *et al.* 1995), largely middle class whites, to avoid schools with perceived negative charac-teristics – one of these being schools with high numbers of minority students. Schools, driven by the need to do well in the published examination league tables, began to search for desirable students and to avoid students with undesirable characteristics, such as being poor, from a minority, having refugee status, having special educational needs or second language needs. Racial and ethnic segregation was exacerbated by choice policies which offered white parents a legitimate way of avoiding schools with high intakes of minority students; a Conservative Education Minister, Lady Hooper, con-ceded in an interview in 1987 that 'racial segregation may be a price to be paid for giving some parents more opportunity to choose' (see Tomlinson 1988). However, the choices of an emergent black and Asian middle class mirrored white middle class choice, some parents preferring to send their children to predominantly white schools, although research by West and her colleagues found that, despite their expressed preferences and high aspir-ations, minority parents were less likely to get their children into schools with higher examination performance (Noden *et al.* 1998).

New Labour policy

In the first term of government New Labour attempted to deal with a number of issues relating to racial inequality in education (Tomlinson 2005). Policies included setting up a Social Exclusion Unit in 1998, which enquired into school exclusion and truancy, especially the over-representation of black boys in school exclusions; recognizing inequalities in achievement by different ethnic groups and lack of proper monitoring (DfEE 1997a); replacing the outdated Section 11 grant to local authorities with an Ethnic Minorities Achievement Grant; setting up an Ethnic Minorities Achievement Unit in the DfES; making the first positive decision to offer Muslim, Hindu and Greek Orthodox schools state funding similar to that given to existing Anglican, Catholic, Methodist and Jewish schools; and announcing the setting up of an inquiry into the murder in 1993 of black student Stephen Lawrence. The resulting MacPherson Report (1999) which made 70 recommendations, four of them concerning education, influenced the 2000 Race Relations (Amendment) Act, an Act which required all public authorities, including local education authorities, to eliminate unlawful discrimination and promote good race relations. This requirement meant that for the first time, schools, LEAs, and all other educational institutions were to be proactive in producing race equality policies, with the Commission for Racial Equality laying down guidelines. The Act also gave a major role in monitoring new policies to the schools inspectorate, Ofsted, which had not been particularly rigorous in monitoring racial equality to that date (Osler and Morrison 2000). The measures in the Act chimed well with assertions that the government was responding to claims for equitable treatment and a recognition of diversity.

Other urban policies, designed to mitigate some of the long-standing grievances of minority parents about the poor quality of their children's schools, had mixed results. The Education Action Zones, initiated in 1998 with some 73 zones eventually operating, were intended to improve the education of all children, but research into the zones was equivocal as to positive results for money spent (Power *et al.* 2003a). By 2004 the zones had been incorporated into the 1999 Excellence in Cities programme, which was largely intended to reassure inner city parents who could not 'take flight' that attention would be focused on attainment and behaviour. This programme offered support for the 'gifted and talented', learning support units for the disaffected and learning mentors for pupils. Warwick University won a bid for an Academy for the gifted and talented at which the fortunate gifted would pay for courses; an early check found white middle class children more likely to be selected as 'gifted'. The Chief Inspector of Schools reported in 2003 that the whole Excellence in Cities programme had given some pupils more self-confidence but had not noticeably raised educational standards (Bell 2003). The Sure Start programme, designed to improve the health, development and education of young children in areas of disadvantage, was generally recognized as successful, although up to 2005 there was no research on how it had impacted on minority families. In 2000, the torture and death of Victoria Climbie, an 8-year-old child of West African origin, led to a public inquiry into the failures of children's services, and the subsequent publication of the Green Paper *Every Child Matters* (HM Treasury 2003). A Children's Act was passed in 2004 which required schools, health and social services to work closely together.

In New Labour's second term, Home Office legislation affected education policy and arguably helped create a climate of antagonism towards settled minorities and potential new citizens. A White Paper *Secure Borders, Safe Haven* (Home Office 2002) outlined new policies for citizenship and nationality, followed by an Immigration and Asylum Act in 2002, which required future British citizens to pass an English language and a citizenship test. The Act also proposed building 'accommodation centres' for asylum seekers which would provide separate education for their children – a suggestion which led to debate as to whether this would breach the children's human rights (Rutter 2003). The White Paper and resulting legislation, although ostensibly concerned with new migrations,[2] was partly prompted by conflicts between white and Asian groups in the northern English towns particularly Bradford and Oldham. A Home Office report feared the loss of 'community cohesion' (Cantle 2001) and complained of the school segregation of pupils, which was in fact the result of patterns of settlement and 'white flight' over 30 years, exacerbated by school choice policies. In his response to the Report, the then Home Secretary, David Blunkett, presented long-settled members of the Asian communities as visitors rather than citizens. It was noteworthy however, that politicians were quick to embrace the 'Britishness' of Amir Khan, a 17-year-old from the northern town of Bolton, who won a silver medal for boxing in the 2004 Olympics.

Selection and diversity

In local school markets, both overt and covert selection by ability or aptitude for grammar or specialist schools and academies, selection for voluntary aided religious schools and streaming and tracking of pupils within schools, all worked against most minorities, particularly second language speakers and those lacking knowledge of the education process. Markets also encouraged schools to rid themselves of pupils who disrupted the smooth running of schools or who interfered with the credentialling of other pupils. Black students, four times over-represented in stigmatized special education categories up to the 1990s, were, in the 2000s, four times more likely to be excluded from school. By this time even black middle class parents were concerned that their boys were candidates for exclusion and some were sending their children back to the Caribbean for secondary schooling, the young people then returning to attend college or university (Goring 2004). A focus on schools described as failing and in need of special measures also disadvantaged minorities in that some 70 per cent of the schools identified during the 1990s had high proportions of minority students. The press coverage of the schools was negative and derisory, with responsibility for the schools problems assigned to the school, parents and pupils, rather than structural, economic or political factors.

In the desire to do well in GCSE league tables, many secondary schools adopted or continued practices that disadvantaged minorities. For example, Gillborn and Youdell (2000) found black pupils more likely to be entered for lower 'tiers' in the examination, and thus unable to achieve higher grades. They described the practice as 'educational triage' – a way of rationing support so that in the battle for standards some pupils are inevitable casualties. Despite government targets to reduce school exclusions, Osler and Vincent described a 'culture of exclusion' exacerbated by market forces which allowed 'successful' schools to reject, neglect or lose students whose education was resource intensive (Osler and Vincent 2003: 51).

Research in developed countries from the 1990s indicated that school choice policies tended to increase social and ethnic segregation (OECD 1994; Thrupp 1999; Duru-Bellat 2000), and the strongest evidence of the effects of school 'choice', selection and diversity suggests that many white parents have continued to move their children away from schools with large numbers of minorities. The emerging black and Asian middle classes adopt similar strategies to white parents, with expressed preferences for private or selective schools, even though despite high aspirations and expressed preferences they are less likely to get their children into selective or high performing schools (Noden *et al.* 1998; Abbas 2002). This mirrors the situation in the USA where an 'upwardly mobile section of the African-American population' is opting for private schools (Freeman 2004). In the UK, it is unsurprising that some minority parents are in favour of selection, in the hope that at least some of their children will have the benefits of superior resources and status, and MPs with large numbers of minorities in their constituencies are reluctant to support measures to end selection (Comprehensive Future 2004). In reality, children from minority groups have never done well in English selective systems. In Birmingham in the 1970s only 1 per cent of minority children attended the city's 21 grammar schools. In 2004, the remaining grammar schools were still 68 per cent white, and the city wards with the highest number of minority children had the lowest number selected for these schools. Abbas noted in his research that the relative success of Indian pupils compared to Pakistani and Bangladeshi owed more to social class position and material resources, and he documented the resentment of parents whose children were not successful in selective examinations (Abbas 2004).

But minority parents, especially African Caribbean, have always been enthusiastic for any form of schooling that would seem to offer communities some measure of control over the education of their children, and there has been some support for the development of Academies. Parents in Brixton, South London, raised £4 million towards an Academy, a plan supported by Nelson Mandela, but neither the local authority nor the government were willing to buy the required land. There were certainly no guarantees that the expanded Academy programme would offer places to local children who wished to attend. Despite the concern over 'community cohesion' the New Labour government promoted an expansion of faith schools. The Anglican Church after 2002 aimed to open 100 more schools, and 22 of the planned Academies were sponsored by Christian organizations. Only four schools had become state-maintained Muslim schools by 2005, although there were some 150 private Muslim schools. Early in 2005 the Chief Inspector criticized both Muslim and Evangelical Christian private schools for failing to promote tolerance and harmony (Slater 2005).

Achievement

Improvements in the education of ethnic minority young people were set in train well before the impact of market forces and the Education Reform Act 1988. Schools, teachers and local authorities had by the 1980s become more responsive to their needs; minority communities pressured governments for action and encouraged their children to stay in education. Despite all the difficulties the education system had presented to the children and their families, by the 1990s, a more promising picture of the educational achievements of various minority groups was beginning to emerge. A major problem in collecting information about minority attainment had always been the inadequate arrangements made at both local and central level for monitoring examination access and outcome. Where monitoring did occur, the ethnic categories were usually problematic, and generalizations made about performance – which did not take account of class and gender – were often misleading. In a review of research in the mid-1990s, Gillborn and Gipps (1996) suggested that while all pupils had improved their performance at GCSE level over a decade, there was a growing 'black–white' gap between African Caribbean pupils and their white peers. The achievements of some Pakistani and Bangladeshi pupils were also lower than white groups. This was still the same pattern in a later review published in 2000 (Gillborn and Mirza 2000). Data from a large government-funded Youth Cohort Study also indicated that white and Indian pupils achieved higher year-on-year improvements at GCSE level while black, Pakistani and Bangladeshi groups improved their pass rates at a lower level (Demack et al. 1998). This pattern of improvement continued into 2004, when some 37 per cent of pupils from African Caribbean families achieved the five good grades compared to 51.9 per cent of all pupils. But local differences in attainment were also apparent. A study of LEAs in the 1990s which were able to supply data in the London area, showed black children achieving well at KS2 (aged 11), but with much lower achievements at GCSE level, and in some areas Pakistani and Bangladeshi pupils doing well (Richardson and Wood 1999). In all groups the achievements of girls to GCSE level was higher than boys. There was little information on the education of refugee and asylum-seekers' children.

The New Labour government viewed the issue of minority achievement with concern, setting up what became an Ethnic Minority Achievement Division in the DfES and providing some £155 million annually for the Ethnic Minority Achievement grant. The White Paper preceding the 2002 Act (DfES 2001b) noted that while performance of all groups of pupils had improved, the children of Caribbean, Pakistani and Bangladeshi backgrounds were half as likely to achieve the five good grades at GCSE, and a consultation paper *Aiming High* (DfES 2003h) acknowledged that opportunities were unequal for one in eight of pupils from a minority background. The system still appeared to be failing young black pupils the following year, when a research report commissioned by the mayor of London, Ken Livingstone, documented again the negative experiences of these young people (London Development Agency 2004). In attempting to explain the differential performance of minority pupils – Chinese and Indian pupils achieving well – some facile comparisons were made, which ignored the educational and entrepreneurial background of these groups. The negative educational experiences of black pupils in the English education system continued to be researched, a study by Shotte (2002) finding that pupils relocated from the volcanic island of Montserrat, who were performing well in the island schools, lost motivation and achieved badly in London schools. Those Montserratian children relocated to the USA continued to do well.

Minority young people have always stayed in further education in greater proportions than whites, partly because of more difficulty in obtaining jobs, partly because of greater motivation to continue in education. In higher education the long-term persistence and motivation of minority students became apparent by the 1990s as they began to enter universities in greater numbers, aided by more encouragement from universities for 'nontraditional' students. By 1998 ethnic minorities accounted for 13 per cent of young HE students; Indian and Chinese groups were more likely to continue their education than other groups; Pakistani and Bangladeshi women and African Caribbean men were less likely to be at university; and all minorities were more likely to be studying in former polytechnics rather than 'old' universities (Social Trends 2000: 56). Indeed, Shiner and Modood found that 'when applying to old universities, there is evidence that minority students face an ethnic penalty, institutions in this sector are more likely to select white or Chinese candidates from among similarly qualified applicants' (Shiner and Modood 2002: 228). How far rates of success by various minorities will be affected by new policies and fees in higher education will be a matter for research. Despite Further Education Colleges being major education institutions for minority young people the Association for College Management accepted, in 2005, that there were 'serious problems with discrimination in the sector', particularly in the appointment of senior staff (Clancy 2005: 1).

Curriculum, refugees and racism

Possibly the most serious omission concerning the education of all young people in a multi-ethnic society was the failure of successive governments to encourage curriculum policies that would combat cultural ignorance, ethnocentric attitudes and racism. With the advent of the National Curriculum in 1988, Prime Minister Thatcher had attempted to impose her views of traditional British history (Phillips 1998). An official Task Group set up in 1989 to consider 'ways in which the national curriculum can broaden the horizons of all pupils' (the author being a member), had its report censored (Tomlinson 1993), and the first Chair of the National Curriculum Council reported that 'it was made starkly clear to him' that any reference to multicultural education would be unacceptable (Graham 1993). The New Labour government, while unafraid to take central control of curriculum delivery and assessment, was similarly reluctant to encourage curriculum change, despite the Macpherson Report recommending 'the amendment of the national curriculum aimed at valuing diversity and preventing racism' (MacPherson 1999: 334). The Qualifications and Curriculum Authority responded with assurances that in future the curriculum would help young people to become 'healthy, lively individuals capable of rational thought' (QCA/DfEE 1999), and much faith was placed in the statutory requirement for citizenship to be part of the national curriculum from 2000, a measure suggested by David Blunkett's old University tutor Bernard Crick (Crick 1998). Knighted for his services to education in 2002 Crick also recommended in a further report that those seeking British citizenship should show measurable progress in English, Gaelic or Welsh (Crick 2003). Although Blunkett was reported to consider the introduction of a citizenship curriculum a great success, and there was evidence that some schools introduced successful courses, a survey of pupils by the School Health Education Unit in 2004 found that they considered citizenship to be one of the most 'useless' subjects (Shaw 2004d).

Despite repeated assertions that teachers needed preparation to teach in a multi-ethnic society, during the 1990s many university and local authority courses for such preparation disappeared and student teachers were, in 2005, less likely to have any preparation in the area than in the 1980s. The Teacher Training Agency produced guidelines in 2000 which asserted that every trainee teacher needs to understand how to prepare pupils to live in a culturally diverse democratic society, but offered little advice on how to do this (TTA 2000). They later prepared a website in place of face-to-face courses. In 2005 the General Teaching Council prepared a more useful Archive Network to promote racial equality in schools (GTC 2005), but overall there had been little evidence that government was guiding the various agencies towards a curriculum to combat the racism and ignorance evident in the popular press and demonstrated in the increasing support for fascist political parties in Britain. Much of this racism impacted on refugee children. Contradictory policies claimed to offer a 'safe haven' to refugees and asylum seekers, but punitive policies affected the settlement and education of thousands of refugee children (Refugee Council 2000; Rutter 2003). All studies of refugee pupils' experiences indicated that a majority experienced harassment in school and in their neighbourhoods, the perpetrators mainly being other young people. Although in early 2005 controversial legislation was envisaged to counter incitement to religious hatred, there were no educational policies designed to counter a xenophobic nationalism exacerbated after September 11th 2001 – a situation which contributed to enhanced hostility against Muslims and media-fed antagonism to both economic migrants and refugees. Overall, the positive moves New Labour made towards race equality issues over their two terms of office appeared, in 2005, to have been largely cancelled out by negative policies targeting immigrants and refugees.

Gender

Gender and equity from the 1960s

Efforts to attain educational equality for women have a long history. In the UK and the USA struggles to gain access to secondary and university education during the nineteenth and early twentieth centuries, although benefiting mainly middle class women, contributed to changed attitudes towards the educational potential of women. Working class girls benefited from universal elementary education from 1870 in the UK, but continued until the 1960s to be directed towards a curriculum for domestic, factory and office work. In the 1950s middle class boys were 21 times more likely to attend a university than working class girls (King 1971). The post-war expansion of education, though supposedly gender-neutral, created tensions through expectations that women would be better educated and subsequently work outside the home but still care for families, and also play a major role in the education of their children (Arnot *et al.* 1999). This was very evident in a report by the Central Advisory Council for England in 1963, which, while recommending the raising of the school leaving age to 16, advocated a very different secondary modern curriculum for boys and girls. 'Girls know that whether they marry early or not, they are likely to find themselves eventually running a home' and were to be directed to housecraft activities, needlework and childcare, while 'A boy is usually excited by the prospect of a science course' (Ministry of Education 1963a: 142).

The movement towards coeducational comprehensive schooling for all assumed gender equity as a goal, although work by Dale (1974) and HMI (DES 1975a) showed that girls were still allocated to different subject areas, notably the humanities, languages and domestic sciences rather than maths, technical areas and the physical sciences. Major gender issues of the 1970s and early 1980s were the under-representation of girls in these subjects,[3] the attention paid to boys in classrooms at the expense of girls, and the directing of academically successful girls into the 'caring' professions – particularly via higher education where girls continued to be poorly represented in science, maths, engineering and medicine.[4] The post-education careers of girls, with middle class girls encountering male dominance, unequal pay and 'glass ceilings' at work, led to pressure on government to counter sex discrimination. An Equal Pay Act was passed in 1970 and a Sex Discrimination Act in 1975. The Equal Opportunities Commission (EOC) was set up, and the Act allowed for cases of both direct and indirect discrimination against women to be brought. The resurgent feminist movement from the late 1960s influenced teachers, some men as well as women, and, as was the case over race equality issues, it was teachers who took a lead in raising awareness about the effects of sexism in classrooms (Yates 1985).

Gender and market reforms

Just as there were considerable contradictions in policies and outcomes over race and multicultural issues in the Thatcher, Major and Blair governments, there were contradictions in the gender agenda which allowed for some progress to be made in terms of equity. Arnot *et al.* (1999) identified two aspects of Thatcherism which were unintentionally useful for women: the promotion of individualism rather than commitment to communities, and the production of flexible, qualified workers for a restructured economy, not necessarily defined by class, race or sex. A third area – the promotion of a moral, traditional family at a time when gender relations were undergoing a permanent change – was highly problematic for both girls and boys. Although the ideologies of marketization and managerialism which emerged in the later 1980s were distinctly male-oriented (Ball 1990), women promoted to managerial posts influenced practice in schools and LEAs. In their conclusions to research sponsored by the EOC on the impact of educational reforms on girls' education, Arnot, David and Weiner concluded that:

> Cultural, demographic and labour market changes have influenced the way students and teachers think about the schooling of girls and boys such that few now consider girls' education to be less important.

High scoring female students are proving attractive to schools in the competitive climate of the 1990s and it is poorly behaved and low-achieving boys who appear to be the subject of greatest concern.

(Arnot *et al.* 1996: 162)

The market certainly appeared to have both reinforced traditional notions of the greater 'respectability' and docility of girls, which together with their superior examination performance made them attractive to some schools. Ball and Gewirtz, examining the complexity of girls schooling in an educational market, noted the way in which schools can 'niche market' themselves to offer a particular middle class definition of femininity, school brochures showing girls operating industrial drills, but also shown 'in leotards and with violins' (Ball and Gewirtz 1995: 9). As always, issues relating to the education of girls in a reformed education system were cross-cut by social class and ethnic differences. Foster (2000) pointed out that it was misleading to assert that black girls were 'doing well' in education because they outperformed black boys. The overall 'success' of all pupils of Caribbean background in that year was still only 27 per cent achieving GCSE A–C levels, compared to nearly 50 per cent of all pupils. Considerable attention was given to the exclusion from school of male black students (Wright *et al.* 2000; Blair 2001) but Osler and Vincent, reporting a thorough study of the school exclusion of girls, noted that 'The rhetoric about boys' failure and girls' success masks a reality where there are vast differences in educational experiences and opportunities among girls' (Osler and Vincent 2003: 1).

Arnot *et al.* (1999: 101) eventually suggested that despite the Conservative governments' and the New Right influences of the 1980s and 1990s, and their concentration on gender and sex issues as part of a despised egalitarianism, much happened that was beneficial to girls' education, particularly the closer relationship between education and the economy. Women were being offered more opportunities to participate in the economy, even if in part-time low-paid jobs, and competition and performance tables led to the promotion of the 'good pupil', traditionally girls rather than boys. The benchmark of exam performance at 16 benefited girls, who had done well at this level for over twenty years, and girls staying on to take A levels were achieving as well or slightly better than boys in the new century.

Girls' achievements

As post-war research and policy documents record, girls had always outperformed boys in primary school tests and in public examinations at 16, a situation that went unremarked on or was actively resisted. One glossed-over disgrace was the adjustments made to 11+ scores from 1947. Girls outperformed boys at 11, but to ensure that grammar schools did not take more girls than boys, girls' scores were weighted. Similarly, although social and political expectations of what was appropriate for girls and boys to study persisted into the 1980s, schools actively reinforced the process. At the time Pratt *et al.* (1984) were recording that there were marked differences in subject choice for O levels, Tomlinson and Tomes (1986) were observing schools in which girls who had chosen to study woodwork and metalwork were being asked by teachers to give up their places to boys. The nonsense of asserting that girls had little interest in or aptitude for, scientific, mathematical, practical or other areas deemed 'male' has been obvious when the practices that denied girls the opportunities and resources to undertake the subjects were examined, and the negative attitudes which appear to still be prevalent in the twenty-first century described.

In 1976, when the Sex Discrimination Act was first implemented, 23 per cent of girls compared to 22 per cent of boys achieved five or more higher grades at O level or grade 1 in the CSE examination, the equivalent of the A–C yardstick at GCSE post-1986. By the mid-1990s, at a time when Arnot and her colleagues undertook a review of research into gender and educational performance for Ofsted, girls were achieving 48 per cent A–C passes, while boys achieved 39 per cent. Even in maths, the 'gender gap' had closed to the extent that 44 per cent of girls and 45 per cent of boys achieved higher passes in maths (Arnot *et al.* 1998: 9). The Arnot review noted that girls began to widen the achievement gap post-1987, a time when the new GCSE exam with a larger coursework element had been introduced, more pupils of both sexes were being taught and entered for exams and subjects were less likely to be dominated by one sex. However, during the 1990s boys continued to predominate in physics, CDT (craft, design and technology), economics, chemistry and computer studies; girls in home economics, social studies, modern languages, English and vocational studies. By 1999 just over half the girls entered for GCSE (51 per cent) achieved higher grades, compared to 44 per cent of boys. By 2004 girls had widened the gap slightly, achieving 57 per cent of higher grades to boys 49 per cent.

Post-16 more students than ever before stayed on to study at school or college in the 1990s, but gender disparities were much more in evidence. At A level boys dominated the traditional boys' subjects, girls the familiar subject areas of English, modern languages, social studies, art and design and biology rather than the other sciences. Similar patterns of gender stereotyping were apparent in vocational subjects studies. However, by 1995 girls and boys were achieving more or less the same A-level scores (14.5 average score for boys, 14.4 for girls), and in 2000 girls finally achieved marginally better points scores than boys. Girls were also more likely than boys to move into further education. By 2001 there were four times as many female FE students as in 1970, but only twice as many male students. Women made up just over half the university students by the end of the century, but were more likely to be studying arts and humanities, social sciences and languages, than maths, science and engineering. Social class and ethnicity continued to have powerful effects on examination performance. For those with professional parents, white girls achieved the highest scores, followed by Asian boys, then white boys, Asian girls, African Caribbean boys and African Caribbean girls. In the manual working class Asian girls did best, followed by Asian boys, white girls, white boys, then African Caribbean girls and boys (Arnot *et al.* 1998).

How far education reforms post-1988 contributed to improved examination performance by girls is (as noted previously) a debatable issue. The raised awareness of teachers, the development of the GCSE examination, the cult of individualism, women's demands and expectations, plus changes in employment patterns, were probably as influential as curriculum and assessment changes. Girls' enhanced educational performance and employment prospects increased their aspirations and young women appear to accept principles of equal opportunity for economic independence and personal respect (Wilkinson 1994). But the labour market realities confirm sex divisions, with women still in predominantly traditional female employment. Despite New Labour's female-friendly policies over childcare issues, which as noted had become important policy areas by 2004, Arnot *et al.* (1999) suggested that girls continued to resolve family–work dilemmas by opting for female occupations. By 2002 women's economic activity rate had increased to 73 per cent overall, with even 57 per cent of lone mothers working, but 52 per cent of working women were in administrative, secretarial, sales and personal service jobs (Social Trends 2003). The Equal Opportunities Commission continued to report that women were underrepresented in positions of influence – in 2004 just 9 per cent of business leaders and newspaper editors were women, 7 per cent of senior judiciary and police and 1 per cent of senior army personnel, and although more women were appointed directors of top companies six in every seven directors were men (Carvel 2004).

Boys' 'underachievement'

Despite the relatively recent improvements in girls' educational performance, and the reality that males still overwhelmingly dominated positions of power and influence, an alleged major problem in the 1990s and beyond became the supposed underachievement of boys. Sections of the media turned the issue into a 'moral panic' and linked it to the notion that there was a crisis in contemporary masculinity (Lucey and Walkerdine 1999). New Labour responded in 1998 with a 'co-ordinated plan of action to tackle the underachievement of boys' (DfEE 1998g). Explanations for slightly lower, but by no means dramatically lower attainment in key stage tests and at GCSE level, varied from resurgent biological explanations, to the construction of a 'male' identity by boys being anti-school, to female-dominated primary school environments, to curricula and assessment thought to favour girls (Pickering and Lodge 1998). On closer examination, the panic appeared to be related to the performance of working class boys, for whom there were now no traditional manual working class jobs available. As Wragg (1997) pointed out, the eruption of panic over boys' educational achievements was closely tied to the structural and social changes in the organization of work. 'Laddish' behaviour and physical strength did not guarantee jobs. 'No employer was about to get rid of two fork-lift trucks and drivers in order to employ twenty men with large biceps' (p. 4). Again, social class was the key to understanding both the construction of masculinity and related educational achievement. Lucey and Walkerdine (1999) demonstrated in their research that although both middle and working class boys exhibited the same stereotyped male behaviour, the middle class boys achieved well. 'To understand this apparent contradiction it is crucial to recognize the centrality of educational success in the construction of middle class hegemonic masculinity' (Lucey and Walkerdine 1999: 41). It was acceptable for middle class, and some Asian boys, to be both masculine and studious, in ways that had never been available to working class or black boys. Archer (2003) reminded readers that there was a range of 'masculinities', structured along lines of class, race and ethnicity and sexuality, but a common feature was an acceptance of the subordination of women and gay men. However it was working class and black males who were required, by the end of the twentieth century, to adapt to profound shifts in the economic and social organization of societies. It is these changes, and the links between education and employment, that are explored in the next chapter.

Notes

1 Groups are described in this chapter as racial or ethnic on the basis of characteristics imputed to them by others (see Rex 1986: ch. 1) and also on self-assignment in the 2001 Census. This indicated that the ethnic composition of the UK was just over 92 per cent white, white other or white Irish and 7.9 per cent (assumed non-white) ethnic minority, of whom 2.2 per cent defined themselves as black African, African Caribbean or black other; 4.4 per cent as South Asian, Indian, Pakistani or Bangladeshi; and 0.8 per cent as Chinese or other ethnic group. An important group described themselves as having mixed origins.

2 During the 1990s and 2000s new patterns of migration developed. The Single European Act allowed more movement of EU nationals, there was an increase in temporary skilled migrant labour with work permits, and an increase in transnational movements. Civil wars brought asylum seekers and refugees from Somalia, Sudan, Sri Lanka, Turkey, Bosnia, Kosova, Sierra Leone, Afghanistan and other places. The Office for National Statistics has noted that categories have

often been meaningless for any monitoring purposes. There is limited information on numbers of Gypsy and traveller's children. In 2002 there was an estimated number of 82,000 refugee children in school, 70 per cent in the London area.

3 Girls in single-sex schools were more likely to study the physical sciences to A level and at university.

4 Even in the 1970s it was noticed that South Asian girls were more likely to choose medicine and allied subjects on application to university.

Further reading

Arnot, M., David, M. and Weiner, G. (1999) *Closing the Gender Gap*. Cambridge: Polity. This book is an account of schooling for boys and girls since the Second World War explaining the closing of the gender gap in achievement and choices, and suggesting that educational reform, together with the women's movement, has reshaped gender identities irrevocably.

Gillborn, B. and Youdell, D. (2000) *Rationing Education*. London: Routledge. Based on research in two secondary schools, this book offers an excellent account of the way that educational reforms pressure teachers and ration educational opportunities. It demonstrates again that assumptions that some groups have more natural ability than others can institutionalize inequalities by race and class.

Parekh, B. (2000) *The Future of Multi-ethnic Britain*. London: Profile. This report is of a two-year study of the current state and future of Britain as a multi-ethnic community based on the principle that all individuals have equal worth irrespective of colour, gender, ethnicity, religion, age or sexual orientation. The Commission for Multiethnic Britain set up with government support (the author being a member) was met by 'a torrent of negative news media coverage and government handwashing' (McLaughlin and Neal 2004: 155).

chapter

ten

Education and the economy

In the introduction to this book a post-welfare society was defined as one where a work ethic and competition in education and the labour market dominate. It is also a society in which there is a restructuring or removal of welfare benefits on the grounds that excessive welfare provision leads to economic inefficiency. Individuals in post-welfare market societies are instructed to 'learn to compete' (DfEE 1996a) in education and the job market, both for their own economic futures and also to improve the competitiveness of the national economy. While these goals may seem self-evident, in particular the benefits to individuals who undertake more education and training, both propositions are debatable. Neither national government, employers nor individuals can be clear about what sort of education and skill acquisition will be needed in a globalized economy and by the turn of the century it was the case that even high levels of education were no guarantee of permanent employment. Both Conservative and New Labour governments were concerned to foster flexibility in job markets, but were also concerned that individuals losing out in the market should continually retrain to remain employable. But under both governments education and employment limits and possibilities continued to be affected by social class, gender, race, migration and disability. The impact of more education and training on the wider economy was unclear (Robinson 1991, 1997; Kelly 1999). The classical liberal economic assumptions that 'education is an investment which lifts individuals out of poverty by increasing their returns in the labour market' (Woodward 1997: 2) was fast becoming too simplistic an assumption in areas where labour markets were disappearing, and education had become a rationed positional good, effectively designed to exclude many potential competitors (Brown and Lauder 1996). This chapter reviews links between education and employment as work became more 'knowledge intensive' and affected by global economic factors, and looks at the prospects for the poor in a society increasingly divided by income and wealth and by the 'ability to consume' (Townsend 1993: 73).

Recent history

Education policy in the post-Second World War welfare state gradually recognized a clear relationship between education and the economy, once the chronic shortage of labour was addressed. The influence of academic economists, as noted in the introduction, convinced government that education expansion and recognition of new technologies was needed for the UK to compete in world markets (Vaizey 1958). Halsey and his colleagues wrote in 1961 that

> Education is a crucial type of investment for the exploitation of modern technology. In advanced industrial societies it is inevitable that the education system should come into a closer relationship with the economy ... as the proportion of the labour force engaged in manual work declines and the demand for white-collar, professional and managerial workers rises.
>
> (Halsey *et al.* 1961: 1–2)

Although policymakers routinely paid lip-service to the importance of education for social, cultural and personal reasons, in the post-welfare state the economic imperative came to dominate the political and educational agenda. Successive governments from the 1970s imposed economic priorities on education, accepting the received wisdom that formal education was fundamental to success and progress in a world dominated by free market economics (Porter 1999).

The right-wing Thatcher governments during the 1980s turned education into a quasi-market in which choice and competition were intended to make consumers select schools and courses which would maximize qualifications and job prospects, and drive uneconomical schools out of business. This strategy succeeded in polarizing the school system by social class at levels not seen since the 1950s. Overt and covert selective mechanisms advantaged middle class and aspirant groups and created more schools attended only by disadvantaged children, who continued to experience more difficulty in moving on to higher level education or training. Market reforms in education did indeed leave 'a large majority of the working population without the human resources to flourish in the global economy' (Brown and Lauder 1996: 8).

The centre-left 'modernizers', exemplified by the New Labour government elected in 1997, claimed to pursue both economic efficiency and social justice (Commission on Social Justice 1994), arguing that a better educated and trained workforce was the key to an economy which would induce investment and create more jobs. However, Labour's retention of the Conservative market principles in education plus an espousal of the long-held right-wing desire to return to selective policies, resulted in more social class polarization and affected the chances of many students in disadvantaged areas even to begin to join in what had become an intensive human capital competition. The well-intentioned palliative policies of Sure Starts, EAZs and New Deals appeared unlikely to affect class divisions in education and the labour market and create high skill 'employability' for all. In addition, as Brown and Lauder (1996: 12) pointed out, although the belief that in the global auction for jobs, western nations would dominate the market for highly paid and skilled jobs presented a 'comforting picture of the global economy', the picture was in fact an imperialist throw-back. Developing countries, especially those with expanded higher education systems, were creating a low-cost educated workforce which would be attractive to multinational companies.

New Labour ideologies

The Labour government's education policy from the early 1990s was driven by a micro-economic ideology which included the beliefs that a centrally prescribed curriculum from pre-school to higher education, an escalation of credentials and a commitment to lifelong re-skilling, would solve macroeconomic problems. While global economic changes and the influence of multinational companies and financial organizations were reducing the ability of national governments to control their own economies, Tory and Labour governments embraced the 'attractively simple explanation' (McCulloch 1998a: 203) that the British education system was at fault, and not designed to promote high economic performance. Post-1997 the New Labour government became a passionate advocate of the view that economic success depended on tight central control of education, meeting education and training targets, and persuading people to obtain more qualifications and skills. The assumption was that the more people invested in themselves as human capital and the more schools overcame their shortcomings in preparing pupils for economic success, the more competitive the economy would become. 'We cannot run a first-rate economy on the basis of a second-rate education system', as Gordon Brown, Chancellor of the Exchequer, observed in a 1997 speech in London's Guildhall. While this was unjust to an education system which for 20 years had been constantly 'reformed' by successive central government dictates, it also oversimplified the complex relationship between education and the economy. By the early twenty-first century it had become heresy to question whether or not the purpose of education should be primarily to enhance 'employability skills'. The Skills Strategy, as optimistically envisaged by the government, was to run from primary to higher and adult education, leading to increased productivity, wider employment and higher standards of living all round (Pring 2004).

Government assumptions were that skills and knowledge acquired at school, college and university would automatically translate into productive activities in the workplace, and that an emphasis on work-related aims in secondary and higher education would satisfy employers. The reality was that many employers, with a long history of deploring low levels of literacy, numeracy, communication or enterprise skills, continued to be deeply reluctant to invest in developing the skills of their own workforce and happy to pass responsibility on to the state. An additional problem was that employers were becoming even more uncertain as to which skills would be needed in the future. Gleeson and Keep (2004: 56) pointed out that even in the late 1980s the Confederation of British Industry had argued that 'few employers are able to predict their skill requirements with any confidence'. The uncertainties over technology, exchange rates and future corporate global strategies were too great to forecast the future of skills. Although greater roles for employers via new partnerships and Skills Councils was envisaged, they largely continued to demonstrate 'voice without responsibility' (Gleeson and Keep: 57) complaining if education failed to deliver the 'right' skills at the right price, while failing to provide sufficient work placements themselves. From the 1970s to the 2000s the plethora of training schemes and new qualifications, the reorganization of post-14 and post-16 education, the rise and demise of quangos, had not, in the early twenty-first century, had much effect on most parts of the British economy.[1] Economic successes were largely the result of financial and capital movement, and as Australian academic Marginson (1999: 29) pointed out, 'Education cannot in itself generate capital movements or create wealth'. The inevitable economic 'failure' of education associated with credentialism appeared to contribute to a recurring cycle of disillusion, blame and search for scapegoats. Ostensible meritocratic selective education policies, despite concerns over elitism in higher education (Ahmed *et al.* 2000: 2), continued in Britain to ensure a familiar social-class based system, divided between high status academic routes leading to professional, managerial and more secure jobs, the lower status vocational routes leading to less secure futures. The rejection, in 2005, of the Tomlinson Report and its attempts to break down the academic–vocational divide, provided yet more evidence that New Labour ideologies were firmly rooted in an old-fashioned meritocratic mode. A fortunate few could aspire to be professionals and managers, larger numbers would take the sales and services jobs and the rest would take an improved but still lower status vocational route into employment or the benefit office.

The labour market into the 2000s

By the late 1990s the British public was constantly assured that the economy was doing well, but the job market was characterized by insecurity and uncertainty. By 2002 more people were employed than ever before in the UK – some 27.7 million. One and a half million were officially unemployed but over four million who could have been 'economically active' were without work, according to a Treasury report in 1998 (Social Trends 2003: 66; Turok 2000: 59). A major change from the 1970s had been the entry of more women into the labour market, albeit mainly in part-time work and for lower pay than males. In 2002, 73 per cent of working age women were in the workforce, half in part-time work, and part-time workers received 33 per cent less per hour than full-time workers. There was a 43 per cent pay gap between male full-time workers and female part-time workers. The educational successes of girls, while opening up new opportunities, did not translate into high-level well-paid jobs for more than a few. 'Women part-timers stuck in low-paid jobs' (Ward 2005) accurately described the situation of nearly half the female workforce. Middle class women preferred to take professional rather than managerial jobs, a move that Crompton (1995) argued allowed them to reconcile family and work demands. For both middle class men and women, the status of university attended appeared more important to their level of occupation than school, but those working in the private sector were likely to earn more than those in public sector jobs (Power 2000). A relatively few women continued to break the 'glass ceiling' and move into male preserves. By 2004 one in seven directors of companies were female, but there was only one female chief executive of a FTSE 100 company. New Labour social policies post-1997 encouraged women, including single mothers, to find work, more young people stayed in education and training, and fewer older men were employed, including those classed as professional and managerial.

There were significant differences in the kinds of work available to ethnic minorities, who incurred an 'ethnic penalty' (Heath and McMahon 1997: 646; Performance and Innovation Unit 2003) which meant that they fared less well in the labour market than similarly qualified whites. Minorities were also more likely to live in cities, some 70 per cent of England's ethnic minority population living in the 88 most deprived wards in the country. It was these areas where jobs disappeared faster than in other areas. Between 1981 and 1996, 1.6 million jobs in manufacturing were lost in cities, which affected jobs in business, sales and other services. A direct effect of this was that more children of unemployed parents were attending city schools. Between 1980 and 1999 the proportion of people living in poor households doubled to nearly one-fifth of all households, and income inequalities widened. Despite working family tax credits and other measures to help the working poor, by 2001 some four million children were living in low income households (Social Trends 2003: 109). Disabled people were more likely to be unemployed or in low-level insecure employment, and were particular targets for welfare reform with reductions in eligibility for state support (Hyde 2000; Walker 2005).

There continued to be large regional differences in employment opportunities. The concentration of jobs in the south-east, even for those with low or no qualifications, became more intense during the 1990s. In 1999 over 70 per cent of poorly qualified people age 24–35 in the south-east had jobs. On Merseyside the figure was 43 per cent (Erdem and Glyn 2000). Encouraging people in depressed areas to train or retrain and persuading the unemployed and inactive to 'get on their bikes' to look for work does not guarantee more employment if jobs do not exist. Measures to help regional employment include getting firms to relocate, relocating public sector activity and improving regional infrastructure, all of which are as important in ensuring employment as education and training.

Jobs and education

When the actual structure of the economy and where jobs have been lost and gained is analysed, the levels of education and qualifications needed or demanded by employers can be better reviewed. Employers in the 1990s were increasingly demanding higher level qualifications for jobs not previously needing them, leading to the situation Dore (1976) described as 'Diploma Disease' when referring to developing countries. A prevailing government and business view was that the economy was structured around knowledge-intensive work, as website designers and ICT consultants took over from coalminers and steelworkers, and that education should prepare people for a 'knowledge economy'. Although a 1998 White Paper addressed the role of government in *Our Competitive Future: Building a Knowledge-based Economy* (DTI: 1998) there continued to be debate over how many would actually be employed in the new knowledge-based economy and how far the occupational structure had actually changed (Keep and Mayhew 2000; Gray and Flores 2000; Brown and Hesketh 2004). While New Labour promoted a knowledge economy – Blair endorsing *Living on Thin Air* (Leadbetter 1999), a book promoting the idea that livings are earned through service, analysis and information – new industries and their owners continued to behave in much the same way as traditional industries.

A Labour Force Survey in 1998 showed an increase in professional, managerial and technical jobs – up to 36 per cent of the workforce. This made it worthwhile for the middle and aspirant classes to adopt the strategies described in Chapter 8 and urge their children into higher education, although the increase in managers did include managing fast-food outlets. Clerical, sales, personal, administrative and secretarial jobs increased in the

1990s to 34 per cent of the workforce, some of which needed new-style qualifications (*Labour Force Survey* 1998). Hutton (2000) calculated that the number of hairdressing shops had risen from 15,000 in 1992 to 70,000 in 1999 – a possible 'hairdressing overkill' – but which had the merit of increasing the numbers of self-employed. Other fast growth areas were in telephone sales jobs, drivers' mates, nursery assistants, welfare workers, domestic staff and shelf fillers (Nolan 2001), where requirements are for personal qualities as much as for qualifications. Manufacturing employment continued to fall as governments failed to invest in both high- or low-technical areas. Multinational firms moved their factories anywhere labour was cheaper, and also employed 'knowledge workers' from countries with lower wages (Lind 1995; Klein 2001).[2]

In 1973 the American sociologist Daniel Bell suggested that a change in the structure of knowledge would form the basis for changed social and economic structural changes (Bell 1973). By the 1990s the terms knowledge economy and knowledge-intensive work had become 'buzzwords' for politicians, although these were seldom defined. Robinson (2000) defined knowledge-intensive work, which requires more intellectual capital, as 'the use of conceptual and analytical skills by individuals so that they can sift and arrange information to construct an argument or solve a problem' (Robinson 2000). This was not a new concept: workers by brain, as clause 4 of the Labour Manifesto of 1918 put it, had always relied on intellectual capital, but the shift from manufacturing to business, financial and professional jobs meant that more people were likely to be employed using these skills, plus new communication skills. In addition Thompson (2004: 13) pointed out that

> the real world, where tangibles such as sales, price and profits actually matter, has a tendency to catch up with the waffle . . . knowledge is not a resource in its own right separate from land, labour and capital – let alone one that is incapable of being measured.

But for the majority of workers, the relationship between education, skills and jobs remained problematic. Keep and Mayhew (2000) pointed out the risks of conflating the production of high-tech goods such as computers and IT equipment with a workforce of highly skilled knowledge workers. Employees may need a high level of manual dexterity to assemble electronic components but they do not need degrees or diplomas to do the work. Other writers pointed out that although there might be a skills shortage in the new high-tech areas, most employees in the UK at the end of the 1990s were still performing repetitive, closely supervised tasks (Thompson and Warhurst 1998). Employers, especially in the service sector, increasingly used personal characteristics – dress, appearance and accent – as proxy for 'skills' for employment. The move to 'competencies', more often a proxy for social skills than general and technical education based on knowledge, also shifted responsibility for training onto employees or the education system and away from employers (Thompson 2004).

A new economy?

Despite the claims that radical shifts were taking place in the national economy in the 1990s, the new economy and occupational structures turned out, at the end of the 1990s, to incorporate much continuity with the old economy. An IPPR economist noted in 2000 that 'although there have been significant shifts the labour market has not been transformed in the last ten years. The new economy still leaves the vast majority of us doing jobs that have been around for years' (Nick Burkitt quoted in Denny 2000: 17). The relationship between an individual's qualifications and their chances of finding work followed the trend since the 1960s, those with higher qualifications having better job prospects, and academic rather than vocational qualifications continuing to have a higher pay-off. In the UK, unlike other European countries, government pushed for 'starred A levels and world-class tests' rather than raising the status and resourcing of vocational qualifications. Evidence accumulated that the low-cost, poorly targeted training programmes adopted by governments over the previous twenty years had a poor record of helping individuals find jobs. The high expectations that the TECs (created at the beginning of the 1990s and abolished at the end) would improve training were disappointed, as funding policies and targets had encouraged a concentration on low-level, cheap programmes (Jones 1999). Similar expectations were then placed on the Learning and Skills Councils and Sector Skills Councils. It was also questionable as to what skills were actually being learned. Sennett provided a fascinating example of the changing work of bakers as more computerized technology was used in the baking industry. The problem was that if the technology broke down no one had hands-on knowledge. The outcome was that 'the bakers no longer know how to bake bread' (Sennett 1998: 68).

Although much research had attempted to identify links between education and training levels and global competitiveness, usually defined as growth in the economy, such links had proved difficult to establish. Politicians and sections of the media persistently attempted to make simplistic connections between pupil performance in international comparative studies in maths and science and growth per capita in GDP, but it was all mostly guesswork. Robinson (1997) pointed out that pupils in Bulgaria and the Slovak Republic did well in such tests but their economies did not exactly prosper, while the USA, low down in maths test scores, had the world's most successful economy. Ashton and Green (1996: 63) commented that if the link between education and economic growth was strong 'one would expect education's effects to shine through the empirical fog. It does not.'

The views of young people on the relationship between jobs, education and the economy were seldom sought, but Killeen *et al.* (1999), questioning students at two southern schools in the late 1990s, found that the young people adopted a thoroughly instrumental view of education. They believed strongly that qualifications were a paper currency that could be exchanged for work opportunities. They were also realistic about the lower status of vocational courses. The content of education was irrelevant and 'almost any kind of degree course seemed preferred to post-19 education and training routes' (Killeen *et al.* 1999: 113). For employers, education had fast become a potential screening device, and also a means of 'warehousing' potential employees until they could be selected for employment (p. 114).

At the local level, the disappearance of manufacturing and associated jobs appeared to affect the prospects and attitudes of young people. The threatened sale and closure of the Rover car plant in Birmingham by BMW (its German owners) early in 2000 had immediate repercussions for children at the main secondary school in the area. The headteacher reported that 'the atmosphere from Rover is definitely affecting them. You can see the older children thinking – what's the point? A lot of year 11 children have been dropping out, feeling, if jobs can disappear that easily, why bother?' (Matthew Brown 2000: 2). The threatened closure of the plant was averted when it was sold for £10 to a company which eventually changed its name to Phoenix Venture Holdings (PVH). Its directors, since their acquisition, took out £9.7m in salaries and set up a £16.5m pension fund for themselves and their families while the company made huge losses and the employees pension fund had a deficit of £400m (Milner 2004; Doward *et al.* 2005). The company began negotiations to create a joint venture with the Chinese Shanghai Automotive Industry Association but these failed and the company called in the receivers in April 2005. All this provided a good illustration of the difficulties for national governments in responding to the actions of the international business community and the insecure relationship between skills and employment at the local level.

The global economy and education

Definitions, debate and critique of 'globalization' entered business, political and academic thinking in the 1990s but public awareness of the meaning of a global economy and global communication remained low. Giddens, in a BBC Reith Lecture early in 1999, pointed out that 'every business guru talks about it [globalization], no political speech is complete without it, yet ten years ago the term was hardly used' (Giddens 1999a: 31). The term largely refers to processes of trade and financial flows, information and communications technologies, movement and migration of people and their labour, and cultural convergences between countries exemplified by, for example, music, jeans and McDonald's. It also signifies ways in which multinational businesses, and expanded capabilities for instant financial transactions, have reduced the power of governments in nation states to control their economies. Communication technologies have encouraged the translation of 'knowledge' into a saleable commodity (Reich 1991; Marginson 1999; Brown and Hesketh 2004). In a global economy, employers are no longer dependent on local, regional or even national labour. When capital and investment can move so easily, it will tend to move to countries where workers have the lowest wages (Gray 1998; Sivanandan 1999; Klein 2001).

Although the role of national governments in planning their education system and regulating and intervening in the economy remained important (Green 1997), globalization meant that relationships between education and employment continued to become more uncertain into the twenty-first century, and the relationship between a highly skilled workforce and national 'economic competitiveness' remained problematic. Lind (1995) pointed out that the world contained not only billions of unskilled workers, but also millions of scientists, architects, engineers and other professionals willing to do world-class work for a fraction of the payment that professionals in developed countries expected. If there is high-skill, low-wage competition from abroad, there can be no guarantees that even highly educated people in developed countries will find permanent work (Lind 1995: 203). The 2004 five-year plan produced by the Department for Trade and Industry noted that India produced three million graduates annually and China was the world's largest economy (DTi 2004). By the turn of the century the notion of a 'safe career' for many educated middle class people was no longer guaranteed but class was still a likely predictor of better jobs (Gray and Flores 2000). Mayhew and his colleagues questioned how, with an expansion of higher education, new graduates could be productively employed in the labour market (Mayhew *et al.* 2004). They concluded that 'Those from the lower socio-economic groups are as likely as not to be sorted into the lower reaches of the student population, obtaining lower end "graduate" jobs' (p. 79).

While there is an expanding literature attempting to explain the likely consequences of globalization, one of the most influential analyses in the 1990s was that provided by Reich (1991),[3] who was concerned that global economic forces would 'bestow even greater wealth on the most skilled and insightful, consigning the less skilled to a declining standard of living' (Reich 1991: 3). He described three categories of work emerging as that done by symbolic analysts (highly educated people such as biotechnology engineers and financial consultants), in-person service workers (waiters, security guards, etc.), and routine production workers. His major concern was that the rich and rewarded would withdraw into private enclaves, and questioned what happens in societies where people 'no longer inhabit the same economy' and where cosmopolitan elites 'could jettison the obligations of national citizenship' (Reich 1991: 303). Stiglitz, a Nobel Prize winner and former Chief Economist at the World Bank, also provided an influential critique of a globalized economy and offered positive suggestions for the development of global public institutions alongside global markets. He was concerned that 'for many people globalization has not worked. Many have been made worse off as they have seen their jobs destroyed and their lives become more insecure' (Stiglitz 2002: 248). He also reminded readers that the global economy was actually controlled by real, highly educated people, particularly unelected officials at the World Bank, the IMF and the World Trade Organisation. There are no 'hidden hands', but real people with vested interests who control the global economy.

Prospects for the poor

The employment prospects for the poor both in developed and developing countries continued to be analysed and theorized about in pessimistic detail into the twenty-first century. In Britain, Hutton (1995) in his best selling *The State We're In* described what he considered to be a divisive and destructive labour market, in which only around 40 per cent of the workforce enjoyed full-time employment or self-employment, 30 per cent were part-time or in insecure jobs, and the bottom 30 per cent were marginalized, working for poverty wages or unemployed (Hutton 1995: 14). The problems inherent in free market economies shifted more power to employers, more risks to those wanting work, and increased inequalities of job security, income and wealth. Hutton's view was that, far from education offering opportunities to all, it had become a creator of class division, and in the 1990s the growth in inequality had been the fastest of any advanced state. The plethora of national, European and international reports drawing attention to the growing divide between the rich and poor in the UK, confirmed the pessimistic conclusion that social justice, equality, economic redistribution and democratic participation were casualties of economic policies (Glyn and Miliband 1994; Acheson 1998; Hill 1998, 2004; Porter 1999; Pantazis and Gordon 2000; Sen 2000). The Thatcher governments of the 1980s deliberately followed strategies of inequality in the belief that economic efficiency would follow (Walker and Walker 1987). What actually followed was an increase in inequality in the distribution of household incomes (Barclay 1995). A Unicef report, using UK figures for 1997, estimated that one child in five was living in poverty, a similar proportion to that of Mexico (Dean and Thornton 2000).

New Labour came to power with a commitment to deal with poverty and inequality, but initially followed Conservative spending plans, sanctioned wide disparities in income, asserted that wealth creation was more important than redistribution, and reduced funding for a welfare state – none of which were likely to improve prospects for the poor. Tackling poverty and social exclusion became a matter for mapping areas where the poor lived, and a reliance on area-based policies to improve health, education, and employment in these areas. By the turn of the century, the Social Exclusion Unit, using new Indices of Deprivation, knew precisely which the poorest council estates were; the DfES and Ofsted knew which were the deprived 'failing' schools; the Office for National Statistics mapped the poorest wards in cities; and the Department for Work and Pensions knew how many parents and children lived in households with an income 60 per cent below the median income level – an official definition of poverty. New Deals for Communities and Education Action Zones and other area policies could never, in themselves, reduce the poverty in these areas, although New Labour claimed that by 2000, work-related policies such as the working families' tax credit had moved a million children out of poverty. This was difficult to quantify and by 2001 'the pattern of annual change (in numbers living on low incomes) had not changed over ten years and resulted in nearly 4 million children living in low income households' (Social Trends 2003: 109). Large-scale unemployment and poverty in the UK continued to be located in mainly urban areas, where targeting areas and individuals could not compensate for localized job shortages. No government had been willing to admit that the poor were poor largely because when working they were grossly underpaid. In 2003, by working at low-paid jobs, journalist Polly Toynbee graphically illustrated the poor living conditions of the one-third of the UK population left out of social progress but working hard for minimum wages. She concluded 'New Labour has not yet dared tell the majority of voters that to achieve it [the abolition of child poverty] they will have to hold back on their rising growth in living standards to allow those at the back to catch up' (Toynbee 2003: 227).

By the 1990s it had become clear that the poor in developed societies were no longer a reserve army of labour, as earlier analyses described them. Modern societies, as Bauman (1998) in another depressing comment had noted, do not need massive labour forces; profits can be increased while cutting down on labour, and grooming the poor to be a reserve army of labour no longer makes sense. The tragedy for the poor was that modern society engages its members mainly as consumers, and those lacking sufficient income, credit cards and bank accounts were flawed consumers. 'Decent and normal members of society, the consumers, want nothing from them and expect nothing. The poor are totally useless ... for them, zero tolerance' (Bauman 1998: 91). Bauman reminded his readers again that whereas a welfare state promoted the idea of collective insurance against individual misfortune, in the modern consumerist society, the poor once again are subject to means tests and charity, activities that originators of welfare states fought against. He also noted again that the 'welfare to workfare' programmes in the USA and the UK managed to remove the costs of the social effects of de-regulated markets from governments to employers via business subsidies and tax allowances. The effect on the poor was to dismantle the safety net and the certainty of social assistance, to be replaced by the vagaries of unstable job markets, and 'there is no better or more cruel way of making labour "flexible" – that is – submissive to the caprices of would-be employers' (Bauman 2002: 82).

A more optimistic and visionary discussion of the prospects for the poor emerged in William Wilson's (1996) account *When Work Disappears* of what happens to the urban poor in the USA. He researched the loss of manual jobs in American society and the 'suburbanization' of employment, which had left the black urban poor in areas of concentrated unemployment, alongside the growth of a black middle class. He demonstrated that the urban poor do not lack aspiration and motivation, but unlike the middle classes their desire for work and a stable life was constrained by lack of job opportunities as well as poor education and training opportunities. Public services and private employers had deserted cities; lack of transport had made journeys to work outside cities difficult. Blaming the poor, a favourite tactic of governments on both sides of the Atlantic, was pointless in the circumstances in which the poor lived, and those addicted to crime and drugs represented only a small segment of populations anxious and willing to work. Wilson (1996: 238) concluded that 'increasing the employment base [in cities] would have an enormous positive impact on the social organization of ghetto neighbourhoods'. Wilson proposed a series of related social and economic policies to enable people to live decently and avoid joblessness, while developing proper social benefit and health care programmes.

The enormous social and economic inequalities existing within countries and between countries remain a source of concern for national governments and international organizations, particularly since the late 1990s when 'global doubts' about the effects of a global economy manifested themselves in local and international protests. A major conclusion reached by commentators on the global economy was that if free market capitalism is to be the basis for a global economy it must be matched by a concern for democratic and civil and political rights for all. Economist and Nobel Prize winner Amartya Sen listed these, plus a free media, basic education and health care, economic safety nets and provision for women's freedom and rights, as crucial to any attempt to alleviate poverty and create a world where employment opportunities exist for all (Sen 2000: 29). Similarly Gray (1998) concluded that if market forces continued to be separated from democratic social and political control the age of globalization would become another turn in the history of servitude for the majority. If 'the planet is about to turn into one huge and indivisible playground of market forces' (Bauman 2002: 89) politicians' exhortations to individuals to regenerate their own communities, and empower themselves by education and training, are relatively meaningless.

The links between education and the national and global economies are not as simple as governments assert. Exhortations to obtain qualifications and skills and learn lifelong will be of use to individuals only if there are economic and political policies which aim for a secure and productive life for all members of a society. In the early twenty-first century in both developed and developing countries, free market policies in both education and the economy continue to have the effect of legitimizing continued inequality and the exclusion of weaker social groups.

Notes

1 Turok (2000) noted the evidence which suggested that most young people participate in temporary training programmes because of a lack of available local jobs.
   Keep and Mayhew (2000) and Gleeson and Keep (2004) have analysed the difficulties of matching skills and qualifications to jobs. Weir (1999), director of the
   Democratic Audit at Essex University, noted that private and business and city
   interests predominated in New Labour's quangos. Of 320 task forces, 71 per cent
   of members represented producer interests and 66 per cent of members were male
   (Weir 1999).
2 The term 'global outsourcing' began to be used by the end of the 1990s to refer to
   the use of highly qualified labour overseas who would receive and complete work
   sent online. High-tech industries in southern California became well known for
   outsourcing work to India.
3 Robert B. Reich, a Brandeis professor and major political economist in the USA,
   served for a period as US Secretary of State for Labor.

Further reading

Porter, J. (1999) *Reschooling and the Global Economic Future*. Wallingford: Symposium. This monograph documents the way the pursuit of free market policies
   have led governments to limit the capacity of schools to fulfil the social, political
   and cultural functions that are needed in democratic societies. The book vividly
   demonstrates that education has to be more than preparation for a job.
Reich, R. (1991) *The Work of Nations*. New York: Simon and Schuster. This book
   clearly indicates how the most fortunate are prospering in the global markets
   while the least skilled and privileged are growing poorer. The author calls for a
   recommitment to a productive status for all and an assertion of the mutual obligations of citizens to each other.
Sennet, R. (1998) *The Corrosion of Character*. New York: Norton. Brilliantly demonstrates the personal consequences of working in a new-style capitalist economy.
Thompson, P. (2004) *Skating on Thin Ice: The Knowledge Economy Myth*.
   Glasgow: University of Strathclyde. Originally an inaugural professorial lecture
   this pamphlet carefully demolishes the myth of the knowledge economy, and also
   usefully notes that the plethora of White Papers on education, training and the

economy, are predominantly 'boastful lists of unsubstantiated claims and assertions'.

Wilson, W.J. (1996) *When Work Disappears*. New York: Alfred Knopf. William Wilson, a Harvard professor and a US government adviser on urban poverty, has written a book which documents the devastating effects of the disappearance of work from inner cities.

Conclusion: education in a post-welfare society

> In 1900 the vast majority of Britons were elementary schooled proletarians . . . By the end of the century millions of children of manual workers had risen into non-manual jobs and many thousands had become the graduate children of butchers, bakers and candle-stick makers, following professional careers.
>
> (Halsey in *Social Trends 30* 2000: 17)

> A meritocracy where no one can remember what the moral bases for merit were, but where it can be measured and ruthlessly assessed nonetheless, promises a competitive dynamism that few nation-states could match today.
>
> (Bobbitt, P., *The Shield of Achilles*, 2002: 231)

This final chapter briefly assesses the positive and negative impact of educational policies from the late 1940s up to early 2005, and the effects of the short- and long-term educational agenda up to and beyond the end of the twentieth century. It was during the later twentieth century that the goal of educating the whole population of Britain rather than small elites began to be realized. A full primary education to 11 and a secondary education for all, to 16 by 1973, made education a key pillar of the welfare state. But by the 1970s, just as the idea of a common educational experience for all in equally-resourced schools was beginning to take root, the welfare rationale of nation states – that governments would seek the ever improving welfare of all citizens – began to disappear. Welfare states were evolving into competitive market states and post-welfare societies. Governments were to provide, via education and training unequally dispensed, the tools to 'empower individuals to take responsibility for their own futures' (Clinton 1994). Safety nets and welfare dependency were to be diminished, public services reduced in favour of private and business involvement and charity from the fortunate to the unfortunate encouraged. The polemical account of the moves towards meritocratic market states provided by Bobbitt (2002) helps to make sense of a major conclusion to this book – that education has moved from being a key pillar of the welfare state to being a prop for a global market economy.

Chapter 1 noted that in the post-war welfare state, education, along with other social policies, contributed to economic stability and attempts to create a more egalitarian distribution of life chances within a growing national economy. An expanding occupational structure and an expansion of opportunity, particularly through the development of comprehensive schooling, led to social mobility for larger numbers of those from manual working class backgrounds, who comprised the majority of workers in the 1960s and 1970s. However, the reproduction of privilege, especially by the upper classes, remained, and the idea that occupation and status would be determined solely by merit remained a myth (Halsey *et al.* 1997: 5). In England any supposed meritocracy remains influenced by advantages of birth, wealth, nepotism, patronage and purchase. The background to policies described in later chapters was the economic, political and cultural transformation of post-industrial societies. Beliefs in free market capitalism and privatization led to the dismantling of much welfare state provision, and global economic forces reduced the powers of national governments to control their own economies. In an effort to keep the UK economy competitive, education and training were elevated to key positions; 'raising standards', 'learning to compete' and getting education 'right' became major policy objectives. In the modernized Britain of the early twenty-first century, private business was designated a major role in the creation of wealth and employment and business models increasingly influenced education policy. Government had decided that its role was to encourage competitive markets in a deregulated economy and equip citizens with skills and aspirations to succeed in what was termed a flexible job market. Ensuring this meant tighter and tighter central control, the direction of the entire education and training system and an expansion of credentialism.[1] Those unlikely or unable to join the economy at any but the lowest levels, or whose presence interfered with the prescribed education for the majority, continued to be the recipients of special policies. Social justice was redefined as policy to alleviate the growing divisions and inequalities which market policies were creating. Education had become narrowed to an economic function, and governments were effectively neutralizing schools, colleges and universities as independent and democratic institutions (Porter 1999). The idea that free universal education was a democratic right and a common good was disappearing.

Positive aspects

Although the negative effects of educational market reforms have hampered progress since 1979, any long-term view of education over the second half of the twentieth century demonstrated widening opportunities and growing aspirations. In 1939 the majority of pupils were still the 'elementary schooled proletarians' described by Halsey (Social Trends 2000: 17). By 1946, some 4.5 million English school pupils and subsequently their children were democratically entitled to a secondary education initially to 15, albeit on a selective basis. Gradually the right to prepare for entry to public examinations, further and higher education was extended. By 2001 over nine million pupils (92 per cent of all pupils) attended state-maintained schools from 4 to 16 or 18, with 6 per cent in private schools and 1 per cent in special schools. Ninety-eight per cent of 4-year-olds were in early years education, with 74 per cent of 16–18-year-olds staying in education or training. Some five million students were enrolled full- or part-time in further education colleges, 58 per cent of them female. Over 2 million students were enrolled on higher education courses, 55 per cent of them female, and 13 per cent from ethnic minorities, and 1.1 million were on adult education courses (Social Trends 2003). Information and communications technology was becoming more equitably shared, with nearly all secondary schools connected to the internet by 2002. A National Grid for Learning linking schools, colleges, universities and libraries was in development. The success of comprehensive education, as both an education project that raised standards, and to a lesser extent, an egalitarian project, had been remarkable. Standards, as measured by those prepared for, entered for and passing in public examinations rose steadily from the 1960s. In 1962, when some 20 per cent were selected for grammar schools, 16 per cent obtained five O level passes. In 2004, 55 per cent obtained the equivalent five GCSE passes. The A-level exam, originally designed in 1952 for less than 10 per cent of the school population was achieved in two or more subjects by 37 per cent of young people in 2001. In 1970, 47 per cent left school without a qualification; by the turn of the century this had fallen to less than 10 per cent. In the early 1960s less than 10 per cent went on to higher education; by 2002 this had increased to over 40 per cent with a government target of 50 per cent.

Dramatic shifts in attitudes towards the education of girls over the half-century had led to a closing of the gender gap in school achievement and 'in the UK schooling appears to have broken with the traditions of the gender order' (Arnot *et al.* 1999: 156). Girls' success was still strongly linked to social class, and educational success, while benefiting middle class women, had not ensured much wider occupational changes for all women. However, girls' aspirations overall had been raised to a level which affected all other social and economic institutions, especially their role in families. The education of minority groups gradually became a serious issue for successive governments from the 1970s, and some minority groups, overcoming continued racism and xenophobia, began to achieve well. A Commission on the Future of Multiethnic Britain, reporting in October 2000, made 18 recommendations to government to counter racial inequalities in education (Parekh 2000), and four years later tentative moves had been made to address around half of these.

Social class, rooted in economic and power inequalities and partially reproduced through education, remained a powerful predictor of life chances. Some 72 per cent of young people with parents in the higher professional class obtained the five A–C GCSEs which allowed them to move into higher education but only 29 per cent of routine manual workers' children obtained these. However wider working class attitudes to education were changing. A political consciousness was developing which recognized the importance attached to qualifications and credentials. A final decline in the kind of deference which led pre-war parents to consider education as 'not for the likes of us' ensured that governments would in future need to take working class educational aspirations seriously. The promotion of lifelong learning was slowly becoming part of what Raymond Williams (1965) had termed *The Long Revolution*, a process which included an aspiration for universal education and the extension of active learning to all, not just to selected groups. Civil and human rights awareness and legislation were affecting access to, treatment within, and outcomes of education. As always, those affected by inequalities, discrimination and control attempted to develop strategies to resist or subvert regressive policies. Short-term ameliorative policies in socially disadvantaged areas, particularly those stemming from New Labour's 'initiatives' post-1997, had positive effects for many individuals. Schools had become less repressive institutions than earlier in the century, and much learning was taking place outside formal educational structures.

Negative aspects

A long-term view of negative consequences of educational reforms over the past half-century must give pride of place to the obsession with selection and segregation of children into different schools or different curricula within schools. This was usually based on spurious notions of ability, which effectively mirrored the social class structure. The political project of the right throughout the second half of the twentieth century was to avoid any recognition of the limited successes of democratic educational reforms and to seek to reintroduce selective mechanisms, which would work for the social reproduction of an hierarchical society. While overt selection had largely become unacceptable by the 1980s, the application of market principles to education proved extraordinarily effective in reintroducing a complex system of selection, passing as 'diversity' in which, as intended, the greatest beneficiaries were the middle classes. The New Labour government pursued market policies, claiming that parental choice, competition, testing, targets and central control of curriculum, teachers and funding were the only route to a 'world class' education system that would retain the loyalty of those middle class parents who would otherwise use private education.[2]

The results of market competition did indeed work to the benefit of middle class and aspirant groups, and despite a rhetoric of inclusion, continued to perpetuate a divided and divisive system. Governments, as Jordan (1998: 137) pointed out, can announce that opportunities are formally open to all but cannot control jockeying for positional advantage. In the USA, the UK and other countries whose educational systems embraced market forces, markets were dysfunctional in terms of 'raising standards' for all. As a wealth of research demonstrated (see, for example Willms and Echols 1992; Gewirtz *et al.* 1995; Levačić and Hardman 1998; Thrupp 1999; Edwards and Tomlinson 2002) the market success of some schools enabled them to select their customers; choice became a sham for many parents. In the UK, under pressure from league table comparisons, schools selected children who would enhance their league table position and were easy to teach. Those with special educational needs, second language needs or learning and behaviour problems were unwanted in oversubscribed schools. Competition for 'able students' exacerbated existing divisions between academic and vocational routes, and vocational qualifications, even to degree level, were still assigned a lower status.[3] A nineteenth-century subject-centred curriculum, controlled and evaluated by central diktat, left schools with a limited capacity for critical reflection. Examination technique, rote learning and revision replaced much substantive teaching.

By 2005 it was clear that Prime Minister Blair and his advisers were totally committed to selective policies in education, with academic schools to be part of a diverse multi-tiered system. The policies of the two main political parties had become more or less indistinguishable. References to comprehensive education had become references to a 'comprehensive system of education' (Millar 2005). Evidence that the majority of parents wanted a broad education for their children regardless of presumed abilities, aptitudes and skills, at least to 16, was ignored. Also ignored was evidence that education markets did not encourage social balance in schools, equalize opportunities or help the socially excluded, and social segregation in education worked against the possibility of preparing good citizens who cared about each other. On the global level in both developed and developing countries, increased numbers of highly educated professional and managerial elites – successful in state school competition or privately schooled – were by the twenty-first century contributing to what Reich (1991: 282) described as the politics of secession. This meant 'undoing the ties that bind them to their undesired compatriots' and creating new global structures of inequality.

A further major negative aspect of educational reform was the increasing deprofessionalization of teachers, as they increasingly came under central control and direction, government exerting detailed control of practice hitherto regarded as the responsibility of those teaching in and running schools and colleges. While Etzioni (1969) famously described teachers as 'semi-professionals', the post-war generation of teachers were credited with the major characteristics of professionalism – an ideal of service and a degree of control over their own practice. By the latter part of the twentieth century teachers had been reduced to technician status, 'delivering' a prepared curriculum, policed by an unpopular inspectorate and publicly criticized by ministers. There was much evidence of lowered morale and a continuing crisis in teacher recruitment. A management ethos dominated schools, or 'human service organisations' as one book described them (MacGilchrist et al. 1997: 111). The creation of a General Teaching Council notionally returned some professional control to teachers, but the drive for centralized control, inspection and direction of activities was extended to all post-16 education and training. University staff were also increasingly deprofessionalized, as their activities became subject to measurement, control and external direction.

Market forces, centralized control of education and the subservience of educational ends to economic priorities combined, by the end of the century, to diminish schools as independent, creative and democratizing institutions. Schools were places where 'tougher targets' were to raise standards to give 'competitive advantage in the modern economy' (Blair 1998b: 11). Universities had largely lost their critical functions and were required to market themselves to students and business, becoming, according to Lord Sainsbury, the Minister for Science, institutions 'at the centre of our productive capacity and powerful drivers of technological change . . . Central to local and regional regeneration' (*Oxford University Gazette*, 3 August 2000: 1). The notion that educational institutions had any purpose other than an economic function had almost completely disappeared from policymaking discourse.

Education in a post-welfare market state

Right-wing ideological beliefs in education as a mechanism for the development of an hierarchical society, in which a differentiated school and higher education system creates a stratified workforce, explains much of Conservative education policy during the twentieth century, with some acceptance of a meritocratic position. Mrs Thatcher's introduction of the Assisted Places scheme in 1980 was to 'enable talented children from poorer backgrounds to go to private schools . . . to ensure that families like my own had the chance of self-improvement' (Thatcher 1993: 39). Influential Labour politicians, as Lawton (2005) demonstrated, had also clung to the notion of meritocracy and selection of the 'able' for a superior education, a position which in 2005 still dominated New Labour education policy. Although the Labour Party had historically also regarded education as a means to improve society in terms of social justice and equality of opportunity – demonstrated in New Labour's rhetorical commitment to social inclusion and community empowerment – explanations for current early twenty-first century policies must be linked to wider issues relating to the management of economic and social change in a global economy. New Labour policies had changed the welfare state into a competition state (Cerny and Evans 2000, 2004), 'pushing marketisation and privatisation as zealously as the Conservatives did' (Marquand 2004: 118) and created a society centred around consumption rather than production in which the poor could never fully participate (Bauman 2002).

Philip Bobbitt's (2002) polemical view of the transformation of nation states into market states goes some way towards explaining current policies, as he believes that while in the UK and the USA Thatcher and Reagan laid the groundwork for market states and 'did much to discredit the welfare rationale for the nation-state', it is Bush and Blair who 'are the first market state political leaders, offering to improve and expand the opportunities offered to the public' (Bobbitt 2002: 222). The improvement of opportunities comes via enterprise, human capital development, tax incentives for business and meritocratic education. Market states must maximize opportunities by encouraging competition, providing incentive structures and draconian penalties – especially the threat of unemployment and loss of income – for individuals. Because multinational companies evaluate states for their workforce capabilities and other attractions for capital, market states must educate and train their populations for a global job market, but are not in the business of the redistribution of jobs or money and can no longer guarantee the welfare of all citizens. Indeed, market states are no place for mutual assistance and 'are largely indifferent to the norms of justice' (p. 230). They require more centralized government but governments can reduce the scope of their activities by handing out former responsibilities to private, charitable and other organizations. Market states encourage meritocracies where 'ruthless assessment' is the norm and any 'choices' in, for example, education, are in fact strategies in a competitive market place. Bobbitt goes further in his analysis of the endpoint of market policies in education – he envisages that 'the days of mass public education are unlikely to continue' (p. 242) as various types of privatization take over. The Academies programme in England was certainly an illustration of a partial handover of state schools to privatization. Crouch had commented on all this in 2003, asking 'once public services are treated in most respects as commodities . . . how long will it be possible to defend their being subsidised and not bought or sold in the market like other commodities?' (Crouch 2003: 25).

A major casualty of the ceding of public services to the market is democracy itself. Individuals are urged to be consumers, but have little power to influence their society. In early twenty-first century England democracy was in retreat (Lawson 2005). Despite a political rhetoric of social justice there was little realization of a common good. A democracy presupposes responsible civic-minded citizens who are bound together by commitment to common institutions. Democratic societies cannot be based on Bobbitt's notion of a social contract – that governments exist only to maximize opportunities for individuals. It is through social institutions that democratic communities are created, and for governments to sell off welfare and assert that they are no longer in the business of caring for all citizens is an affront to democracy. John Dewey wrote that schools must educate for democracy (Dewey 1966). Education should help create a society 'in which every person shall be occupied in something which makes the lives of others better worth living, and which accordingly makes the ties which bind people more perceptible' (Dewey 1966: 316). If schools and universities are predominantly about jobs, business, enterprise and competition, education for democracy comes a poor second. If governments were serious about social inclusion and social justice they would seek to reinvigorate the public sphere and provide some leadership towards redeveloping the notion of the common good. The politics of special interests, with government conceding to groups they consider give electoral advantage, continue to contribute to civic decay rather than civic vitality.

The future

Predictions about the future direction of education have always proved particularly problematic, change depending on political prejudice, powerful vested interests and pressure groups. Although as Heller (1988: 24) remarked, 'politics and good intentions do not mix' New Labour's plans for education appeared replete with good intentions. Barber (2000), describing UK government strategy for education into the twenty-first century in a speech to policymakers in the USA, claimed that 'our [New Labour] vision is a world class education service'. While few would dispute the desirability of improving the education service for all, a serious question raised by the notion of global competition for world class education is 'Whose world?'

Examination of the beneficiaries of 'high quality education', however it is defined, indicate that this kind of education has always been monopolized by higher socio-economic groups with some concession to social mobility for lower class 'gifted' individuals. The restriction of access to particular forms of education has always acted as a dominant form of social exclusion. New Labour, as with governments around the world at the end of the twentieth century, was grappling with a situation in which more and more people were engaged in a competitive attempt to gain qualifications and employment, large numbers were excluded from entering the competition on equal terms, and others, driven by heightened insecurities, were intent on retaining or gaining positional advantage. In this situation good intentions for reducing inequality and exclusion were balanced by the political reality that policies which threatened the middle and aspirant classes could threaten the government's electoral base. In addition all social groups, while told by government they had choices as consumers, increasingly felt powerless to shape their society and its institutions (Bauman 2004). In the demolition of the welfare state, a major casualty has been the abolition of a collective voice from all those who believed that a common educational experience, equally resourced and based on shared values, was a democratic right. But despite the dominant influence of market state ideologies of meritocracy, selection and privatization in the early twenty-first century, there may eventually be effective opposition to selection, a centrally imposed curriculum, never-ending rigid assessments, central control of educational institutions and a narrow economic view of the purpose of education.

Any real change in the structure, content, governance and organization of education systems in developed countries in the twenty-first century may well depend on forces beyond national educational planning. Freeing education to serve goals other than economic will depend on restraint of the global free market system, which Neal Acherson (1998) described as 'the most powerful and arrogant order in human history . . . a form of capitalism too unfair and callous to last, too unequal to be tolerated and too recklessly greedy to be sustainable'. Acherson was optimistic that there are now millions of people worldwide, formerly the 'docile masses' who by now have sufficient education and a sense of their own rights and dignity, to challenge educational inequalities, poverty and injustice. If some form of global cooperation replaced the seemingly irreplaceable economic competitiveness, then it would be possible to consider other functions for education.

Critiques of the narrowing of education to economic ends want to reclaim education as a humanizing, liberalizing, democratizing force, directed, as the UN (1948) Universal Declaration of Human Rights put it, to 'the full development of the human personality and a strengthening of respect for human rights and fundamental freedoms'. Education must also help people to make sense of the impact of global changes, combat resurgent xenophobic nationalism, recreate the idea of the common good and move beyond a tawdry subservience to market forces.

Notes

1 Smithers (2000b) commented in the *Guardian* (Education section) on surveys by teaching unions showing that school students faced some 75 tests between

5 and 16. The increased numbers of young people passing GCSEs and Advanced GCE levels have led to the creation of 'starred A levels'.

2 This argument was promoted by Hutton (1995), Walden (1996) and Barber (2000) who were either unaware of all the evidence demonstrating the educational advantages permanently accruing to the middle classes in state education and the subtle use made by some of both state and private education, or were supporting a familiar class-based selective system.

3 In August 2000 the Chief Inspector of Schools, Chris Woodhead, continued to lament the introduction of vocational courses to degree level on the grounds that they were not academically rigorous (Woodhead 2000). In his post-inspectorate incarnation as a professor at the private University of Buckingham and a newspaper columnist, Woodhead continued to urge a 'traditional' curriculum.

References

Aaronovitch, D. (2003) The Real Class Issue, *Observer*, 12 October.

Abbas, T. (2002) The home and the school in the educational achievements of South Asians, *Race Ethnicity and Education*, 5(3): 292–316.

Abbas, T. (2004) *The Education of British South Asians*. Basingstoke: Palgrave MacMillan.

Acherson, N. (1998) We live under the most arrogant of world orders, but it will not last, *Independent on Sunday*, 25 January.

Acheson, D. (1998) *Inequalities in Health: Report of an Inquiry*. London: Stationery Office.

Adler, M., Petch, A. and Tweedie, J. (1989) *Parental Choice and Education*. Edinburgh: Edinburgh University Press.

Adnett, N. and Davies, P. (2003) Schooling reforms in England: from quasi-markets to competition, *Journal of Education Policy*, 18(4): 393–406.

Adonis, A. and Pollard, S. (1997) *A Class Act*. London: Hamish Hamilton.

Ahmed, K., Bright, M. and Hinsliff, G. (2000) PM to wade in with assault on elitism, *Guardian*, 4 June.

Ainley, P. (2004) The new market state and education, *Journal of Education Policy*, 19(4): 497–514.

Aldrich, R. (1997) Labour strains for that elusive goal, *Guardian* (Education), 8 July.

Anderson, P. and Mann, N. (eds) (1997) *Safety First: The Making of New Labour*. London: Granta.

Apple, M. (1999) The absent presence of race in educational reform, *Race Education and Ethnicity*, 2(1): 9–16.

Archer, L. (2003) *Race, Masculinities and Schooling*. Buckingham: Open University Press.

Argyropolu, D. (1986) Tribute to Keith Joseph, *Education*, 16 May.

Armstrong, D. (2005) Reinventing inclusion: New Labour and the cultural politics of special education, *Oxford Review of Education*, 30(1): 135–52.

Arnot, M., David, M. and Weiner, G. (1996) *Educational Reform and Gender Equality in Schools*. Manchester: EOC.

Arnot, M., Gray, J., James, M. and Ruddock, J. (1998) *A Review of Recent Research on Gender and Educational Performance*. London: Ofsted.

Arnot, M., David, M. and Weiner, G. (1999) *Closing the Gender Gap*. Cambridge: Polity Press.

Arora, R. and Duncan, C. (1986) *Multicultural Education: Towards Good Practice*. London: Routledge.

Ashton, D. and Green, F. (1996) *Education, Training and the Global Economy*. London: Edward Elgar.

Atkinson, B. (2000) Distribution of income and wealth, in A.H. Halsey and J. Webb (eds) *Twentieth Century Social Trends*. London: Macmillan.

Atkinson, A., Gregg, P. and McConnell, B. (2004) *The Result of 11+ Selection: An Investigation into the Equity and Efficiency of Outcomes for Pupils in Selective LEAs*. Leverhulme Centre for Markets and Public Organisation. Bristol: University of Bristol.

Audit Commission (1992) *Getting In on the Act – Provision for Pupils with Special Educational Needs: The Natural Picture*. London: HMSO.

Auld, R. (1976) *William Tyndale Junior and Infant School Public Inquiry*. London: ILEA.

Back, L., Solomos, J. and Shukra, K. (2002) Challenge to unrest brings out Labour's true colours, *Times Higher Educational Supplement*, 14 June.

Baer, K.S. (2000) *Reinventing Democrats: The Politics of Liberalism from Reagan to Clinton*. Lawrence, Kansas: University of Kansas Press.

Baker, K. (1993) Kenneth Baker, in P. Ribbins and B. Sherratt (eds) *Radical Education Policies and Conservative Secretaries of State*. London: Cassell.

Ball, C. (1999) *Our Learning Society*, 4(1): 83–90.

Ball, M. (2002) *Getting Sure Start Started*. London: DfES publications.

Ball, S.J. (1990) *Politics and Policy-making in Education*. London: Routledge.

Ball, S.J. (1993) Educational markets, choice and social class: the market as a class strategy in the UK and USA, *British Journal of Sociology of Education*, 14(1): 1–20.

Ball, S.J. (1999) Labour, learning and the economy: a policy sociology perspective, *Cambridge Journal of Education*, 29(2): 195–206.

Ball, S.J. (2003) *Class Strategies and the Education Market*. London: Routledge/Falmer.

Ball, S.J. and Gewirtz, S. (1995) *Girls in the Education Marketplace; competition and complexity*. (Unpublished paper). London: Kings College, London.

Ball, S.J., Bowe, R. and Gewirtz, S. (1996) School choice, social class and distinction: the realisation of social advantage in education, *Journal of Educational Policy*, 11(1): 89–112.

Ball, S.J., Maguire, M. and Macrae, S. (2000) *Choice, Pathways and Transitions*. London: Falmer.

Banks, O. (1955) *Parity and Prestige in English Secondary Education*. London: Routledge and Kegan Paul.

Barber, M. (1996) *The Learning Game*. London: Cassell.

Barber, M. (2000) High expectations and standards for all – no matter what, *Times Educational Supplement*, 7 July.

Barber, M. and Dann, R. (1996) *Raising Educational Standards in Inner Cities*. London: Cassell.

Barber, M. and Sebba, J. (1999) Reflections on progress towards a world class education system, *Cambridge Journal of Education*, 29(2): 183–93.

Barclay, P. (1995) *Income and Wealth*, vol. 1. York: Joseph Rowntree Foundation.

Barnard, N. (1999) Where are business bids for zones? *Times Educational Supplement*, 28 May.

Barnard, N. (2000) Assessors reap rewards, *Times Educational Supplement*, 21 January.

Barnett, R. (1999) The coming of the global village: a tale of two inquiries, *Oxford Review of Education*, 25(3): 293–306.

Barton, L., Barrett, E., Whitty, G., Miles, S. and Furlong, J. (1994) Teacher education and teacher professionalism in England: some emerging issues, *British Journal of Sociology of Education*, 15(4): 529–44.

Baty, P. (1999) Power players for the regions, *Times Higher Education Supplement*, 1 January.

Baty, P. (2000) Post-16 Bill muddies waters, *Times Higher Education Supplement*, 21 January.

Bauman, Z. (1998) *Work, Consumerism and the New Poor*. Buckingham: Open University Press.

Bauman, Z. (2002) Searching for politics in an uncertain world, *Renewal*, 10(1): 78–90.

Bauman, Z. (2004) *Identity*. Cambridge: Polity Press.

Becker, G. (1964) *Human Capital*. New York: National Bureau of Economic Research.

Bell, Daniel (1973) *The Coming of Post-industrial Society*. New York: Basic Books.

Bell, David (2003) Education Action Zones and Excellence in Cities, *Education Review*, 17(1): 10–15.

Benn, C. and Chitty, C. (1996) *Thirty Years On: Is Comprehensive Education Alive and Well or Struggling to Survive?* London: David Fulton.

Benn, Melissa and Chitty, C. (2004) *Education and Democracy – A Tribute to Caroline Benn*. London: Continuum Press.

Benn, C. and Simon, B. (1970) *Half Way There*. London: McGraw-Hill.

Benn, T. (1994) *Years of Hope: Diaries, Papers and Letters 1940–1962*. London: Arrow.

Bennet, C. (2000) Schools Fresh Start goes stale, *Guardian* (G2), 16 March.

Blackburne, L. (1996) Labour threat to nursery vouchers, *Times Educational Supplement*, 22 November.

Blackstone, T. (1999) Closer links reap mutual benefits, *Times Educational Supplement* Business Links, 4 June.

Blair, M. (2001) *Why Pick on Me? Schools Exclusion and Black Youth*. Stoke on Trent: Trentham Books.

Blair, T. (1994) *Socialism*. London: Fabian Society.

Blair, T. (1996) The new age of achievement, extracts from the Labour leader's speech to conference, *Times Educational Supplement*, 4 October.

Blair, T. (1998a) *Leading the Way: A New Vision for Local Government*. London: IPPR.

Blair, T. (1998b) *The Third Way: New Politics for a New Century*. Pamphlet no. 588. London: Fabian Society.

Blair, T. (1998c) Forging an inclusive society, *Times Educational Supplement*, 11 September.

Blair, T. (1999) Speech to Labour party Conference, Bournemouth, 8 October.

Blair, T. (2004) Speech to Labour Party Conference, Brighton, 28 September.

Bloom, A. (2004) Gifted club eases path to universities, *Times Educational Supplement*, 3 December.

Blunkett, D. (2000) Transforming secondary education, speech to Social Market Foundation, London, 15 March.

Boaler, J. (1997) *Experiencing School Mathematics: Teaching Styles, Sex and Setting*. Buckingham: Open University Press.

Bobbitt, P. (2002) *The Shield of Achilles: War, Peace and the Course of History*. London: Allen Lane.

Bolton, E. (1994) Alternative policies: school inspection, in S. Tomlinson (ed.) *Educational Reform and its Consequences*. London: Rivers-Oram Press/IPPR.

Bosely, S. (1994) Labour's class question, *Guardian*, 7 December.

Bowe, R., Ball, S.J. and Gold, A. (1992) *Reforming Education and Changing Schools*. London: Routledge.

Boyson, R. (1975) *The Crisis in Education*. London: Woburn Press.

Brace, A. (1994) Is this the worst school in Britain?, *Mail on Sunday*, 20 March.

Brain, J. and Klein, R. (1992) *Parental Choice: Myth or Reality?* Social Policy Paper 21. Bath: University of Bath.

Breen, R. and Goldthorpe, J. (1999) Class mobility and merit: the experience of two British birth cohorts. Paper to seminar at Nuffeld College, Oxford, May.

Brewer, M., Goodman, A., Myak, M., Shaw, J. and Shephard, A. (2004) *Poverty and Inequality in Britain*. London: Institute for Fiscal Studies.

Bright, M. (1996) Brighter students deserve elite exam, say heads, *Observer*, 16 September.

Bright, M., McHugh, J. and Brace, A. (1998) Dear Mr Blunkett, Please don't force us to play the free market in schools. Just build a good local comprehensive for our kids, *Observer*, 5 April.

Brivati, B. and Bale, T. (1997) *New Labour in Power*. London: Routledge.

Brown, G., Blunkett, D. and Harman, H. (1996) *Equipping Young People for the Future: From Welfare to Education*. London: Labour Party.

Brown, Margaret (1998) The tyranny of the international horse race, in R. Slee, G. Weiner and S. Tomlinson (eds) *School Effectiveness for Whom?* London: Falmer.

Brown, Matthew (2000) A long shadow, *Guardian* (Education), 16 May.

Brown, Michael, with Chope, C., Fallon, M., *et al.* (1985) *SOS Save Our Schools*. London: Conservative Political Centre.

Brown, P. (1997) The third wave: education and the ideology of parentocracy, in A.H. Halsey, H. Lauder, P. Brown and A.S. Wells (eds) *Education, Culture, Economy and Society*. Oxford: Oxford University Press.

Brown, P. (2000) Globalisation of positional competition, *Sociology*, 34(4): 633–54.

Brown, P. and Hesketh, A. (2004) *Playing to Win: Managing Employability in the Knowledge-based Economy*. Oxford: Oxford University Press.

Brown, P. and Lauder, H. (1996) Education, globalisation and economic development, *Journal of Education Policy*, 11(1): 1–26.

Bryce Report. (1895) *Secondary Education in England*. London: HMSO.

Budge, D. (2001) Private troubles nag model Academies, *Times Educational Supplement*, 8 January.

Bynoe, I., Oliver, M. and Barnes, C. (1991) *Equal Rights for Disabled People*. London: IPPR.

Caldwell, B. and Spinks, J. (1988) *The Self-Managing School*. Lewes: Falmer.

Campbell, J., Little, V. and Tomlinson, J. (1987) Multiplying the divisions, intimations of educational policy post 1987, *Journal of Educational Policy*, 2(4): 369–78.

Cannadine, D. (1998) *Class in Britain*. Newhaven, CT: Yale University Press.

Cantle, T. (2001) *Building Community Cohesion*. London: Home Office.

Cantor, L., Roberts, K. and Pratley, B. (1995) *A Guide to Further Education in England and Wales*. London: Further Education Unit, DfE.

Carr, W. and Hartnett, A. (1996) *Education and the Struggle for Democracy*. Buckingham: Open University Press.

Carvel, J. (1997a) Name and shame policy goes on, *Guardian*, 11 November.

Carvel, J. (1997b) Time to pick up the pieces, *Guardian* (Education), 6 May.

Carvel, J. (1998) Barbed school report brings battle between advisors out into the open, *Guardian*, 6 February.

Carvel, J. (1999a) Grammar schools no escape for poorer children, *Guardian*, 29 May.

Carvel, J. (1999b) Failing schools privatised, *Guardian*, 12 May.

Carvel, J. (2004) Cracks in the glass ceiling as women managers win pay breakthrough, *The Guardian*, 15 September.

Central Advisory Council for England (1963) *Half Our Future*. London: The Stationery Office.

Cerny, P.G. and Evans, M. (2000) New Labour, globalisation and the competition state, *Harvard Papers 70*. Cambridge MA: Center for European Studies, Harvard University.

Cerny, P.G. and Evans, M. (2004) Globalisation and public policy under New Labour, *Policy Studies*, 25(1): 51–66.

Chew, J. (1990) *Spelling Standards and Examination Results among 6th Formers 1984–90*. York: Campaign for Real Education.

Chitty, C. (1989) *Towards a New Educational System: The Victory of the New Right*. London: Falmer.

Chitty, C. (2004) *Education Policy in Britain*. London: Palgrave-Macmillan.

Chubb, J. and Moe, T. (1990) *Politics, Markets and American Schools*. Washington, DC: Brookings Institution.

Clancy, J. (2004) Failing colleges judged inadequate. *Times Educational Supplement*, 26 November.

Clancy, J. (2005) Race bias still rife, *Times Educational Supplement* (FE FOCUS), 25 January.

Clarke, C. (2004) Speech to Annual Conference of Specialist Schools, Birmingham, 25 November.

Clinton, B. (1994) Remarks on the reinventing government initiative, *Weekly Compilation of Presidential Documents*, 30: 1763. Washington.

Clinton, B. (2004) *My Life*. London/NY: Hutchinson.

Coffield, F. (1997) Introduction and overview: attempts to reclaim the concept of the learning society, *Journal of Educational Policy*, 12(6): 449–55.

Collins, T. (2005) Opinion, *Guardian* (Education), 24 January.

Commission for Racial Equality (CRE) (1996) *Exclusions from School and Racial Equality*. London: CRE.

Commission on Social Justice (1994) *Social Justice: Strategies for National Renewal*. London: Vintage.

Comprehensive Future (2004) National Policy Forum Meeting – The Outcome, *Newsletter*. London: Comprehensive Future.

Conran, J. (2004) My support for academy schools, Letter to the *Guardian*, 13 December.

Conservative Education Association (CEA) (1992) *Choice and Diversity: The CEA Response to the White Paper*. London: CEA.

Cosgrave, P. (1978) *Margaret Thatcher: A Tory and her Party*. London: Hutchinson.

Cottrell, P. (1999) Learning to succeed, *AUT UPDATE*, 61, November.

Cox, C.B. (1995) *The Battle for the English Curriculum*. London: Hodder and Stoughton.

Cox, C.B. and Boyson, R. (eds) (1977) *Black Paper 1977*. London: Temple-Smith.

Cox, C.B. and Dyson, A.E. (eds) (1969) *Black Paper One*. London: Critical Quarterly Society.

CPS (2003) *Mortgaging Our Children's Future*. Sheffield: Centre for Public Services.

Crace, J. (2002) What's the point? *Guardian* (Education), 3 December.

Crace, J. (2003) Bare coffers, *Times Educational Supplement*, 20 May.

Crace, J. (2004) Academy Fervour, *Guardian* (Education), 20 July.

Craft, A. and Bardell, G. (1984) *Curriculum Opportunities in a Multicultural Society*. London: Harper.

Crick, B. (1998) *Education for Citizenship and the Teaching of Democracy in School: Final Report of the Advisory Group on Citizenship*. London: QCA.

Crick, B. (2003) *The New and the Old: Interim Report: Living in the United Kingdom Group*. London: Home Office.

Critchfield, R. (1990) *Among the British*. London: Hamilton.

Crompton, R. (1995) Women's employment and the middle class, in T. Butler and M. Savage (eds) *Social Change and the Middle Class*. London: UCL.

Crompton, R. (1998) *Class in Britain*, 2nd edn. Cambridge: Polity Press.

Crouch, C. (2003) *Commercialisation or Citizenship: Education Policy and the Future of Public Services*, Fabian Ideas 606. London: The Fabian Society.

CVCP (1993) *Draft Response to the Government Proposals for the Reform of Initial Teacher Training*. London: CVCP.

CVCP and National Statistics Office (1996) *Earnings Survey*. London: CVCP.

Dale, R. (1974) *Mixed or Single-sex School*, vol. 3. London: Routledge.

Daniels, J.C. (1961) Effects of streaming in primary schools, *British Journal of Educational Psychology*, 22(3): 69–78 and 119–27.

Davies, M. and Edwards, G. (1999) Will the curriculum caterpillar ever learn to fly? *Cambridge Journal of Education*, 29(3): 265–76.

Davies, N. (1999) Political coup bred educational disaster, *Guardian*, 6 September.

Davies, N. (2000a) Blunkett's magic tricks and the £19 billion boost for education that doesn't exist, *Guardian*, 7 March.

Davies, N. (2000b) State of despair as public schools get the cream, *Guardian*, 8 March.

Davies, N. (2003) *Inside the Laboratory: The New Politics of Public Service in Wales*. London: Catalyst Press.

De Haviland, J. (1988) *Take Care Mr. Baker*. London: Fourth Estate.

Dean, C. (1998) 5000 pupils prove social class matters, *Times Educational Supplement*, 25 September.

Dean, C. and Thornton, K. (2000) Teachers forced to do too much social work, *Times Educational Supplement*, 16 June.

Dearing, R. (1993) *The National Curriculum and its Assessment* (final report). London: SCAA.

Dearing, R. (1996) *Review of Qualifications for 16–19 Year Olds*. London: SCAA.

Dearing, Sir Ron (1997) *Higher Education in the Learning Society: Report of the National Committee of Inquiry into HE*. London: The Stationery Office.

Demack, S., Drew, D. and Grimsley, M. (1998) Myths about underachievement: gender, ethnic and social class differences in GCSE attainment 1988–93. Paper presented to the British Educational Research Association Annual Conference, Belfast, August.

Denny, C. (2000) Job descriptions, *Guardian*, 6 June.

DES (1967) *Children and their Primary Schools: A Report of the Central Advisory Council for Education* (Plowden Report). London: HMSO.

DES (1968) *Public Schools Commission: First Report*. London: HMSO.

DES (1970) *Public Schools Commission: Second Report* (Donnison Report). London: HMSO.

DES (1972) *Education: A Framework for Expansion*, Cmnd 5174. London: HMSO.

DES (1974) *Educational Disadvantage and the Needs of Immigrants*, Cmnd 5720. London: HMSO.

DES (1975a) *Curricular Differences for Boys and Girls*, Education Survey 21. London: HMSO.

DES (1975b) *A Language for Life* (Bullock Report). London: HMSO.

DES (1977a) *A New Partnership for our Schools* (Taylor Report). London: HMSO.

DES (1977b) *Education in Schools: A Consultative Document*. London: HMSO.

DES (1980) *A Framework for the School Curriculum*. London: HMSO.

DES (1981a) *West Indian Children in our Schools* (Rampton Report). London: HMSO.

DES (1981b) *The School Curriculum*. London: HMSO.

DES (1982) *Mathematics Counts* (Cockcroft Report). London: HMSO.

DES (1983) *Teaching Quality*. London: HMSO.

DES (1984) *Parental Influence at School*, Cmnd 9242. London: HMSO.

DES (1985a) *Education for All* (Swann Report). London: HMSO.

DES (1985b) *Better Schools*, Cmnd 9469. London: HMSO.

DES (1986) *Education and Training: Working Together*, Cmnd 9823. London: HMSO.

DES (1989a) *Our Changing Schools*. London: HMSO.

DES (1989b) *Your Child and the National Curriculum*. London: Department of Education and Science.

DES (1991) *You and Your Child's Education* (Parents' Charter). London: DES.

DES/DoE (1991) *Education and Training for the 21st Century*, Cmnd 1536. London: HMSO.

Dewey, J. (1966) *Democracy and Education*. New York: The Free Press.

DfE (1992) *Choice and Diversity: A New Framework for Schools*, Cmnd 2021. London: HMSO.

DfE (1994a) *Our Children's Education* (updated Parents' Charter). London: DfE.

DfE (1994b) *Code of Practice on the Identification and Assessment of Special Educational Needs*. London: DfE.

DfEE (1996a) *Learning to Compete: Education and Training for 14–19 Year Olds*, Cmnd 3486. London: HMSO.

DfEE (1996b) *Self Government for Schools*. London: HMSO.

DfEE (1996c) *Nursery Education: The Next Steps*. London: DfEE.

DfEE (1997a) *Excellence in Schools*, Cmnd 3681. London: The Stationery Office.

DfEE (1997b) *Excellence for All Children: Meeting Special Educational Needs*. London: The Stationery Office.

DfEE (1997c) *Learning and Working Together for the Future: A Strategic Framework for the DfEE*, Consultation Document. London: DfEE.

DfEE (1997d) *Qualifying for Success*, Consultation Paper on the Future of Post-16 Qualifications. London: DfEE.

DfEE (1997e) *Higher Education for the 21st Century*. London: DfEE.

DfEE (1998a) *Meeting Special Educational Needs: A Programme for Action*. London: DfEE.

DfEE (1998b) *Teachers: Meeting the Challenge of Change*. London: DfEE.

DfEE (1998c) Circular letter to providers of initial teacher training in all LEAs in England and Wales, 25 November.

DfEE (1998d) *The Learning Age: A Renaissance for a New Britain*, Cmnd 3790. London: The Stationery Office.

DfEE (1998e) *Opportunity Scotland: A Paper on Lifelong Learning*, Cmnd 4048. London: The Stationery Office.

DfEE (1998f) *Towards a National Skills Agenda*, First Report of the National Skills Task Force. London: DfEE.

DfEE (1998g) Byers outlines coordinated action to tackle boys' underachievement, press release. London: DfEE.

DfEE (1999a) *School Exclusions and Pupil Support*. Circular, October. London: DfEE.

DfEE (1999b) *Sure Start: A Guide for Trailblazers*. London: The Stationery Office.

DfEE (1999c) *Excellence in Cities*. London: The Stationery Office.

DfEE (1999d) *Code of Practice on LEA–School Relationships*. London: DfEE.

DfEE (1999e) *Learning to Succeed: A New Framework for Post-16 Learning*, Cmnd 4392. London: The Stationery Office.

DfEE (1999f) *Individual Learning Accounts: A Summary of Progress*. London: The Stationery Office.

DfEE (2000) *The Role of the Education Authority in School Education*. London: DfEE.

DfEE (2001) *Building on Success: Raising Standards and Promoting Diversity*, Cmd 5050. London: The Stationery Office (Green Paper).

DfES (2001a) *Schools: Achieving Success*, Cmd 5230. London: The Stationery Office (White Paper).

DfES (2001b) *Skills for Life: Strategy for Improving Adult Basic Skills*. London: DfES.

DfES (2002a) *Success for All: Reforming Further Education and Training. Our Vision*. London: DfES.

DfES (2002b) *14–19 Extending Opportunities: Raising Standards*. London: The Stationery Office.

DfES (2003a) *A New Specialist System: Transforming Secondary Education*. London: DfES.

DfES (2003b) *School Admissions: Code of Practice*. London: Department for Education and Skills.

DfES (2003c) *Excellence and Enjoyment in Primary Schools*. London: DfES.

DfES (2003d) *The Future of Higher Education*, Cmd 5735. London: The Stationery Office.

DfES (2003e) *Opportunity and Excellence 14–19*. London: The Stationery Office.

DfES (2003f) *Working Group on 14–19 Reform. Principles for Reform of 14–19 Learning Programmes and Qualifications*, Interim Report. Nottingham: DfES.

DfES (2003g) *Developing a National Skills Strategy and Delivery Plan: Underlying Evidence*. London: DfES.

DfES (2003h) *Aiming High: Raising the Achievement of Minority Ethnic Pupils*. London: DfES.

DfES (2004a) *Five-year Strategy for Children and Learners*, Cmd 6272. London: The Stationery Office.

DfES (2004b) *OECD Programme for International Student Assessment: Treatment of UK Data*, press release. London: Department for Education and Skills.

DfES (2004c) *The Government Response to the Education and Skills Committee Report on Secondary School Admissions*, Cmd 6349. London: The Stationery Office.

DfES (2004d) *Building Schools for the Future* (BSF). Second wave of funding announced. London: DfES.

DfES (2004e) *Removing Barriers to Achievement*. London: DfES.

DfES (2004f) *14–19 Curriculum and Qualifications Reform: Final Report of the Working Group on 14–19 Reform* (Tomlinson Report). Nottingham: DfES.

DfES (2005a) *Choice for Parents: The Best Start for Children*. (A Ten-Year Strategy for Children's Services.) London: DfES.

DfES (2005b) *14–19 Education and Skills*, Cmd 6476. London: The Stationery Office.

DfES/DTi, HM Treasury, DWP (2003) *21st Century Skills: Realising Our Potential*. London: The Stationery Office.

Dodd, V. (2000) Head defies the statistics to give school a fighting chance, *Guardian*, 2 March.

DoE (1981) *The New Training Initiative*. London: HMSO.

DoE (1993) *Competitiveness: Helping Business to Win*, Cmnd 2536. London: HMSO.

DoH/Home Office (2003) *The Victoria Climbie Inquiry*. Report of an Inquiry by Lord Laming. London: The Stationery Office.

DoH (2004) Choosing Health. London: Department of Health (White Paper).

Dore, R. (1976) *The Diploma Disease*. London: Allen & Unwin.

Doward, J., Morgan, O., Asthana, A. (2005) Brown signals probe on Rover bosses' millions, *The Observer*, 10 April.

Driver, S. and Martell, L. (1998) *New Labour: Politics after Thatcherism*. Cambridge: Polity Press.

DSS (1999) *Opportunities for All: Tackling Poverty and Social Exclusion*. London: The Stationery Office.

DTI (1998) *Our Competitive Future: Building a Knowledge-based Economy.* London: The Stationery Office.

DTI (2004) *Five-Year Plan.* London: Department for Trade and Industry.

Duffield, J. (1998) Unequal opportunities or don't mention the class war. Paper presented to Scottish Educational Research Association Annual Conference, Dundee, September.

Duru-Bellat, M. (2000) Social inequalities in the French education system: the joint effect of individual and contextual factors, *Journal of Educational Policy*, 15(1): 33–40.

Dyson, A. (2004) *Inclusion and Pupil Achievement* @ www.dfes.gov.uk/research

Edwards, T. (1998) *Specialisation without Selection, Rise Briefing no. 1.* London: Research and Information on State Education Trust.

Edwards, T., Fitz, J. and Whitty, G. (1989) *The State and Private Education: An Evaluation of the Assisted Places Scheme.* London: Falmer.

Edwards, T. and Tomlinson, S. (2002) *Selection Isn't Working: Selection, Diversity and Inequality in Education.* London: Catalyst Publications.

Ellison, N. (1997) From welfare state to post-welfare society: Labour's social policy in historical and comparative perspective, in B. Brivati and T. Bale (eds) *New Labour in Power.* London: Routledge.

Elton Committee (1989) *Discipline in Schools: Report of a Committee of Inquiry Chaired by Lord Elton.* London: HMSO.

Erdem, E. and Glyn, A. (2000) Northern exposure, *Guardian*, 4 April.

Esping-Anderson, G. (1996) *Welfare States in Transition: National Adaptation in Global Economies.* London: Sage.

Etzioni, A. (1969) *The Semi-professions and their Organisation.* New York: Free Press.

European Commission (1997) *Accomplishing Europe through Education and Training*, Report of a Study Group on Education and Training. Luxembourg: European Commission.

Ferrara, A. (1997) The paradox of community, *International Sociology*, 12(4): 395–408.

Ferrera, M., Hemerijck, A. and Rhodes, M. (2000) *The Future of European Welfare States. Report for the Portuguese Presidancy of the European Union.* Brussels: European Union.

Finch, J. (1984) *Education as Social Policy.* London: Longman.

Finegold, D., Keep, E., Miliband, D., *et al.* (1990) *A British Baccalaureate*, Education and Training Paper No. 1. London: IPPR.

Fitz-Gibbon, C. and Stephenson-Foster, N. (1999) A poor report, *Guardian* (Education), 5 October.

Floud, J. (1963) *Further Memorandum on Higher Education*, Evidence to Robbins Committee on Higher Education. London: HMSO.

Floud, J., Halsey, A.H. and Martin, F.M. (1956) *Social Class and Educational Opportunity.* London: Routledge and Kegan Paul.

Flude, M. and Hammer, M. (1990) *The Education Reform Act 1988.* London: Falmer.

Foster, M. (2000) A black perspective, in K. Myers (ed.) *Whatever Happened to Equal Opportunities in Schools?* Buckingham: Open University Press.

Fowler, J. with Evans, E. (2002) *A Guide to the 2002 Education Act.* London: Advisory Council for Education/TEN.

Freeman, S.G. (2004) Increasingly, African-Americans take flight to private schools, *New York Times*, 18 May.

Fryer, R. (1997) *Learning for the 21st Century*, First Report of the National Advisory Group for Continuing Education and Lifelong Learning. London: NAGfCELL.

Fullan, M. (1991) *The New Meaning of Educational Change*. London: Cassell.

Gaine, C. (2000) Anti-racist education in white areas: the limits and possibilities of change, *Race, Ethnicity and Education*, 3(1): 65–82.

Galbraith, J. (1992) *The Culture of Contentment*. London: Sinclair-Stevenson.

Gallagher, T. and Smith, A. (2001) The effects of selective education in Northern Ireland, *Education Review*, 15: 74–81.

Gamble, A. (1988) *The Free Economy and the Strong State*. London: Macmillan.

Gardiner, J. (1996a) A hit squad's target wins reprieve in climbdown, *Times Educational Supplement*, 6 July.

Gardiner, J. (1996b) Break out those whips and canes, *Times Educational Supplement*, 1 November.

Gardiner, J. (1997) Blunkett to continue shaming, *Times Educational Supplement*, 14 November.

Garner, R. (2004) Should these people be running state schools? *Independent*, 8 July.

Garrett, A. (2003) Top dollar to be top of the class, *Observer (Property)*, 21 September.

Gewirtz, S. (1999) Education Action Zones: emblems of the third way?, in H. Dean and R. Woods (eds) *Social Policy Review 11*. London: Social Policy Association.

Gewirtz, S., Ball, S.J. and Bowe, R. (1995) *Markets, Choice and Equity in Education*. Buckingham: Open University Press.

Gibson, A. and Asthana, S. (1999) Schools, markets and equity: access to secondary education in England and Wales. Paper presented to the American Education Association Annual Conference, Montreal, Canada, 21 April.

Giddens, A. (1998a) *The Third Way*. Cambridge: Polity Press.

Giddens, A. (1998b) Risk society, the context of British politics, in J. Franklin (ed.) *The Politics of the Risk Society*. Cambridge: Polity Press.

Giddens, A. (1999a) New world without end, *Observer*, 11 April.

Giddens, A. (1999b) ESRC Tenth Annual Lecture. London: Economic and Social Research Council.

Giddens, A. (2002) *Where Now for Labour?* Cambridge: Polity Press.

Gillborn, D. and Gipps, C. (1996) *Recent Research on the Achievements of Ethnic Minority Pupils*. London: Ofsted.

Gillborn, D. and Mirza, H. (2000) *Educational Inequalities: Mapping Race, Class and Gender*. London: Office for Standards in Education.

Gillborn, D. and Youdell, D. (2000) *Rationing Education*. London: Routledge.

Glass, N. (2005) Surely some mistake, *Society Guardian*, 5 January.

Glatter, R. (2004) Choice and diversity of schooling provision: does the emperor have any clothes? *Forum*, 46(2): 63–9.

Gleeson, D. and Keep, E. (2004) Voice without accountability: the changing relationship between employers, the state and education in England, *Oxford Review of Education*, 30(1): 37–64.

Glyn, A. and Miliband, D. (1994) *Paying for Inequality*. London: IPPR/Rivers-Oram Press.

Goddard, A. (1999) Costs thwart broader access, *Times Higher Education Supplement*, 8 October.

Goddard, A. (2000) Unequal opportunities: a university challenge, *Times Higher Education Supplement*, 10 March.

Goldthorpe, J. (1997) Problems of meritocracy, in A.H. Halsey, H. Lauder, P. Brown and A.S. Wells (eds) *Education, Culture, Economy and Society*. Oxford: Oxford University Press.

Goldthorpe, J. (with Llewllyn, C. and Payne, C.) (1987) *Social Mobility and Class Structure in Modern Britain*, 2nd edn. Oxford: Clarendon.

Gorard, S. (1999) Well, that about wraps it up for school choice: a state of the art review, *School Management and Leadership*, 19(1): 25–47.

Gorard, S. and Fitz, J. (1998) The more things change . . . the missing impact of marketisation, *British Journal of Sociology of Education*, 19(3): 365–76.

Gorard, S., Fitz, J. and Taylor, C. (2001) School choice impacts: what do we know?, *Educational Researcher*, 30(7): 18–23.

Gordon, P., Aldrich, R. and Dean, D. (1991) *Education and Policy in England in the 20th Century*. London: Woburn Press.

Goring, B. (2004) The perspectives of Caribbean parents on schooling and education: continuity and change. Unpublished PhD, University of the South Bank.

Gould, P. (1998) *The Unfinished Revolution: How Modernisers Saved the Labour Party*. London: Little, Brown.

Graham, D. (1993) *A Lesson for Us All: The Making of the National Curriculum*. London: Routledge.

Grant-Maintained Schools Trust (GMST) (1989) *The New Choice in Education*. London: GMST.

Gray, J. (1998) *False Dawn: The Delusions of Global Capitalism*. London: Granta.

Gray, J. and Flores, F. (2000) *Entrepreneurship and the Wired Life*. London: Demos.

Green, A. (1997) *Education and Globalisation and the Nation State*. London: Macmillan.

Green, A. and Steedman, H. (1997) *Into the 21st Century: An Assessment of British Skill Profiles and Prospects*. London: Centre for Economic Performance.

GTC (General Teaching Council) (2005) GTC Petition on registration of teachers in Academies @ www.gtce.org.uk/achieve. London: General Teaching Council.

Hackett, G. (1994) Peace and passion by the sea, *Times Educational Supplement*, 7 October.

Hackett, G. (1996) Bill would extend selection, *Times Educational Supplement*, 1 November.

Hackett, G. (2000) Islington firm faces big penalty, *Times Educational Supplement*, 14 January.

Hall, J. (1985) The centralist tendency, presidential address to the Society of Education Officers, January. *Forum*, 28(1).

Halpern, D. (1998) *The Third Way: A Summary of Nexus On-line Discussion*. London: Nexus.

Halpin, P. (1998) *Tackling Educational Disadvantage through Collective Action: Social Capital and Labour's Education Action Zone Policy*. London: Education Department, Goldsmiths College.

Halsey, A.H. (1972) *Educational Priority*, vol. 1. London: HMSO.

Halsey, A.H., Floud, J. and Anderson, C.A. (eds) (1961) *Education, Economy and Society*. London: Free Press.

Halsey, A.H., Lauder, H., Brown, P. and Wells, A.S. (1997) *Education, Culture, Economy and Society*. Oxford: Oxford University Press.

Hamilton, D. (1996) *Peddling Feel-good Fictions*. Liverpool: School of Education, University of Liverpool.

Hannon, V. (1999) On the receiving end: New Labour and the LEAs, *Cambridge Journal of Education*, 29(2): 207–17.

Hardy, J. (1997) Selective schools? Just try to find one that isn't, *Guardian*, 29 November.

Hatcher, R. (1994) Market relationships and the management of teachers, *British Journal of Sociology of Education*, 15(1): 27–40.

Hatcher, R. (1998) Class differentiation in education: rational choices, *British Journal of Sociology of Education*, 19(1): 5–24.

Hatcher, R. (2002) *How Business Agendas Drive Labour's Policies for Schools*. London: Socialist Education Association.

Hattersley, R. (2000) How to cheat at 11+ ballots, *Observer*, 12 March.

Hayward, G., (2004) Foreword: a century of vocationalism, *Oxford Review of Education*, 3(1): 3–12.

Hayward, G. Hodgson, A., Johnson, J., *et al.* (2004) *The Nuffield Review of 14–19 Education and Training: Annual Report 2003–04*. Oxford: Department of Educational Studies, University of Oxford.

Heath, A. and McMahon, D. (1997) Educational and occupational attainments: the impact of ethnic origins, in A.H. Halsey, H. Lauder, P. Brown and A.S. Wells (eds) *Education, Culture, Economy and Society*. Oxford: Oxford University Press.

HEFCE (2003) *Strategic Plan 2003–08*. Bristol: Higher Education Funding Council for England.

HEFCE (2004) *Entry to Higher Education by Post Code*. Bristol: Higher Education Funding Council for England.

Heim, A. (1954) *The Appraisal of Intelligence*. London: Tavistock.

Heller, J. (1988) *Picture This*. New York: Ballantine.

Henry, J. (2002) Welcome leap in inner city results, *Times Educational Supplement*, 12 April.

Hetherington, P. (2000) Jobless forced to take lessons, *Guardian*, 12 January.

Hey, V. and Bradford, S. (2004) Successful subjectivities: the beaconisation of class, ethnicity and gender positions. Paper to conference on New Labour's Education Policy and Social Justice, Northampton, University College, April.

Hill, J. (1998) *Income and Wealth*, vol. 1. York: Joseph Rowntree Foundation.

Hill, J. (2004) *Inequality and the State*. Oxford: Oxford University Press.

Hillgate Group (1986) *Whose Schools? A Radical Manifesto*. London: Hillgate Group.

Hirsch, F. (1977) *The Social Limits to Growth*. London: Routledge.

HM Treasury (1999) *Public Expenditure Statistical Analysis*, Cmnd 4201. London: The Stationery Office.

HM Treasury (2003) *Every Child Matters*, Cmnd 5860. London: The Stationery Office.

HM Treasury (2004) *2004 Spending Review*, Cmnd 6237. London: The Stationery Office.

HMI (1981) *Aspects of the School Curriculum*. London: HMSO.

Hobbs, G. (2003) Understanding socio-economic group differences in educational achievement: a literature review. Paper for DfES/HM Treasury seminar, 24 November.

Hodge, M. (1999) What a difference a year makes, *Childcare Quarterly*, 2: 8–9.

Hodgson, A. and Spours, K. (eds) (1997) *Dearing and Beyond*. London: Kogan Page.

Hodgson, A. and Spours, K. (1999) *New Labour's Educational Agenda: Issues and Policies for Education and Training from 14+*. London: Kogan Page.

Hodgson, A. and Spours, K. (2005) Divided we fall, *Guardian* (Education), 1 March.

Hofkins, D. (1996) Literacy framework gains early welcome, *Times Educational Supplement*, 6 December.

Home Office (1978) *Proposals for Replacing Section 11 of the 1966 Local Government Act*. London: Home Office.

Home Office (1998) *Supporting Families: A Consultation Document*. London: The Stationery Office.

Home Office (2002) *Secure Borders, Safe Haven; Integration with Diversity in Modern Britain*, Cmnd 5387. London: The Stationery Office.

Honeyford, R. (1988) *Integration or Disintegration?* London: Claridge Press.

Honeyford, R. (1990) The National Curriculum and its official distortion, *Salisbury Review*, 8(4): 6–9.

Hook, S. (2003) Learning Accounts give us a bloody nose, *Times Educational Supplement*, 11 April.

House of Commons Education Committee (1995a) *Fifth Report on Educational Expenditure Plans (1995–98)*, Report no. N/95/202. London: HMSO.

House of Commons Education Committee (1995b) *Performance in City Schools* (Third Report). London: HMSO.

House of Commons Education and Employment Committee (1996) *Education and Training for 14–19 Year Olds*, vol. 1. (First Report). London: HMSO.

House of Commons Education and Employment Committee (1998) *Disaffected Children* (Fifth Report). London: HMSO.

House of Commons Education and Skills Committee (2003a) *Secondary Education: Diversity of Provision*, Fourth report Session 2002–03. London: The Stationery Office.

House of Commons Education and Skills Committee (2003b) *Fifth Report: Higher Education*. London: The Stationery Office.

House of Commons Education and Skills Committee (2004) *Secondary Education: School Admissions*, Fourth report Session 2003–04. London: The Stationery Office.

House of Commons Education and Skills Committee (2005) *Secondary Education*, Fifth report Session 2004–05. London: The Stationery Office.

House of Commons Select Committee (1977) *The West Indian Community*. London: HMSO.

Howie Committee (1992) *Upper Secondary Education in Scotland*. Edinburgh: Scottish Office.

Howson, J. (1999) When fund-raising is not enough, *Times Educational Supplement*, 8 October.

Hughill, B. (1994) Left to rot in secondary school free-for-all, *Observer*, 4 December.

Husen, T. (1974) *The Learning Society*. London: Methuen.

Hutton, W. (1995) *The State We're In*. London: Cape.

Hutton, W. (2000) The murder of manufacturing, *Observer*, 7 May.

Hutton, W. (2004) Good for Oxford . . . but for the rest? *Observer*, 10 October.

Hyde, M. (2000) From welfare to work: social policy for disabled people of working age in the UK, *Disability and Society*, 15(2): 327–41.

Hyman, P. (2005) *1 Out of 10: From Downing Street Vision to Classroom Reality*. London: Vintage.

Institute for Public Policy Research (2003) *Opportunity and Inclusion*. Forum on Mobility and Social justice. Newcastle, England, 6/7th November.

ISIS (1999) *Independent Schools Census*. London: ISIS.

Jackson, B. (1964) *Streaming: An Education System in Miniature*. London: Routledge.

Jackson, B. and Marsden, D. (1962) *Education and the Working Class*. London: Routledge and Kegan Paul.

Jackson, B. and Segal, P. (2004) *Why Inequality Matters*. London: Catalyst Publications.

Jacques, M. (2005) When the Party is over, *Guardian*, 16 February.

James, E. (1947) The challenge to the grammar school – an attack upon standards and values, *Times Educational Supplement*, 1 February.

Jarvis, F. (1995) *Education and Mr. Major*. London: Tufnell Press.

Jesson, D. with Taylor, C. and Ware, J. (2004) *Educational Outcomes and Value-added by Specialist Schools*. London: Specialist Schools Trust.

Jones, M. (1999) *New Institutional Space: TECs and the Remaking of Economic Governance*. London: Jessica Kingsley.

Jordan, B. (1996) *A Theory of Poverty and Social Exclusion*. Cambridge: Polity Press.

Jordan, B. (1998) *The New Politics of Welfare*. London: Sage.

Joseph, K. (1975) Speech to Birmingham Conservative Association, 17 October. Report in the *Sunday Times*, 20 October.

Joseph, K. (1985) Speech to North of England Conference, Sheffield, January.

Judd, J. (1997) Caning for 3000 bad headteachers, *Independent*, 5 February.

Karabel, J. and Halsey, A.H. (1977) *Power and Ideology in Education*. Oxford: Oxford University Press.

Keep, E. (1999) Seminar, Department of Education, University of Oxford, November.

Keep, E. and Mayhew, K. (2000) Towards the knowledge-driven economy, *Renewal*, 7(4): 50–9.

Kelly, K. (1999) *New Rules for the New Economy*. London: Fourth Estate.

Kelly, R. (2005) Beyond Crossland's vision, *Guardian*, 30 March.

Kennedy, H. (1997) *Learning Works: Widening Participation in Further Education*. Coventry: FEFC.

Killeen, J., Turton, R., Diamond, W., Dosnon, O. and Wach, M. (1999) Education and the labour market: subjective aspects of human capital investment, *Journal of Education Policy*, 14(2): 99–116.

King, R. (1971) Unequal access in education: sex and social class, *Social and Economic Administration*, 5(3): 287–303.

Kirkman, S. (2005) Halt the secondary slide, *Times Educational Supplement*, 14 November.

Kirp, D. (1979) *Doing Good by Doing Little: Race and Schooling in Britain*. Berkeley, CA: University of Californian Press.

Klein, N. (2001) *No Logo*. London: Flamingo Press.

Knight, C. (1990) *The Making of Tory Education Policy in Post-War Britain 1950–1986*. London: Falmer.

Labour Force Survey (1998) London: Office for National Statistics.

Labour Party (1989) *Meet the Challenge, Make the Change*, Policy Review Document. London: Labour Party.

Labour Party (1990) *Looking to the Future*. London: Labour Party.

Labour Party (1994) *Opening Doors to a Learning Society*. London: Labour Party.

Labour Party (1995a) *Diversity and Excellence: A New Partnership for Schools*. London: Labour Party.

Labour Party (1995b) *Excellence for Everyone: Labour's Crusade to Raise Standards*. London: Labour Party.

Labour Party (1996a) *Aiming Higher: Labour's Proposals for the Reform of the 14–19 Curriculum*. London: Labour Party.

Labour Party (1996b) *Early Excellence: A Headstart for Every Child*. London: Labour Party.

Labour Party (1996c) *Learn as You Earn: Labour's Plans for a Skills Revolution*. London: Labour Party.

Labour Party (1996d) *Lifelong Learning at Work and in Training*. London: Labour Party.

Labour Party (1997) *A New Deal for Britain: Proposals for Youth and Long-term Unemployment*. London: Labour Party.

Labour Party (2001) *Election Manifesto*. London: Labour Party.

Lawlor, S. (1990) *Teachers Mistaught: Training in Theories or Education in Subjects?* London: Centre for Policy Studies.

Lawrence, I. (1992) *Power and Politics at the Department of Education and Science*. London: Cassell.

Lawson, N. (2005) *Dare More Democracy*. London: Compass Publications.

Lawson, M. (1999) Designer drivel; Blair's third Way, *Guardian*, 9 January.

Lawton, D. (1980) *The Politics of the School Curriculum*. London: Routledge.

Lawton, D. (1992) *Education and Politics in the 1990s: Conflict or Consensus?* London: Falmer.

Lawton, D. (1994) *The Tory Mind on Education 1979–1994*. London: Falmer.

Lawton, D. (2005) *Education and the Labour Party: Ideologies 1900–2001 and Beyond*. London: Routledge/Falmer.

Leadbetter, C. (1999) *Living on Thin Air*. London: Viking.

Lee, J. (2004) Nudists add to Jarvis woes, *Times Educational Supplement*, 15 October.

Lepkowska, D. (2004) Exam chief slams wishlist waste, *Times Higher Education Supplement*, 23 January.

Levačić, R. and Hardman, Y. (1998) *Competition as a Spur to Improvement: Differential Improvement at GCSE Level*, International Congress on School Effectiveness. Manchester: University of Manchester.

Levin, B. (1998) An epidemic of educational policy-making: what can we learn from each other? *Comparative Education*, 34(2): 131–42.

Lewis, O. (1968) The culture of poverty, in D. Moyniham (ed.) *On Understanding Poverty*. New York: Basic Books.

Liell, P.M., Coleman, J.E. and Poole, K.P. (1998) *Laws of Education*, 9th edn. London: Butterworth.

Lind, M. (1995) *The Next American Nation: The New Nationalism and the Global American Revolution*. New York: Free Press.

Lingard, B., Ladwig, J. and Luke, A. (1998) School effects in postmodern conditions, in R. Slee, G. Weiner and S. Tomlinson (eds) *School Effectiveness for Whom?* London: Falmer.

Lloyd, C. and Payne, J. (2003) What is the High Skills Society? Some reflections on current academic and policy debates in the UK, *Policy Studies*, 24 (2/3): 115–34.

London Development Agency (2004) *Rampton Revisited: The Educational Experiences and Achievements of Black Boys in London*. London: London Development Agency.

Lowe, R. (1988) *Education in the Post-War Years*. London: Routledge.

Lucey, H. and Walkerdine, V. (1999) Boys' underachievement, social class and changing masculinities, in T. Cox (ed.) *Combating Educational Disadvantage*. London: Falmer.

Mac an Ghaill, M. (1996) Sociology of education, state schooling and social class: beyond critiques of new right hegemony, *British Journal of Sociology of Education*, 17(2): 103–76.

MacPherson, Sir W. (1999) *The Stephen Lawrence Enquiry*, CM 4262. London: The Stationery Office.

McClean, M. (1990) *Britain and a Single Market Europe: Prospects for a Common School Curriculum*. London: Kogan Page.

MacCleod, D. (1996) Clampdown on schools in inner city, *Guardian*, 7 May.

MacClure, S. (1988) *Education Reformed*. London: Hodder and Stoughton.

McCulloch, G. (1998a) Education and economic performance, *History of Education*, 27(3): 203–6.

McCulloch, G. (1998b) *Failing the Ordinary Child*. Buckingham: Open University Press.

MacGilchrist, B., Myers, K., Reed, J. (1997) *The Intelligent School*. London: Paul Chapman.

McKie, D. (1997) Plenty of rapid action but how tough is tough? *Guardian*, 9 August.

McLaughlin, E. and Neal, S. (2004) Misrepresenting the Multicultural Nation, *Policy Studies*, 25(3): 155–74.

McNamara, O., Hustler, D., Stonach, I., Rodrigo, M., Beresford, E. and Botcherby, S. (2000) Mobilising the active partner in home-school relations, *British Journal of Educational Research*, 26: 273–89.

Maden, M. (1999) A piece of the action, *Education Today and Tomorrow*, 50(1): 13–14.

Mahoney, P. (1998) The rise and fall of standards in teaching. Paper presented to the Professional Standards Conference, Edith Cowan University, Perth, Australia, 24 February.

Mahoney, P., Menter, I. and Hextall, I. (2003) *The Impact of Performance Threshold Assessments on Teachers' Work*. Summary Report for the ESRC. Surrey: University of Roehampton.

Major, J. (1997) Speech given at the Commonwealth Institute, London, 18 January.

Mansell, W. (2004) Capita's contract award stinks, *Times Educational Supplement*, 8 October.

Mansell, W. (2005) Playing politics with our exams, *Times Educational Supplement*, 25 February.

Marginson, S. (1999) After globalisation: emerging politics of education, *Journal of Education Policy*, 14(1): 19–31.

Marquand, D. (2004) *The Decline of the Public*. Cambridge: Polity Press.

Marr, A. (1999) The times they really are a-changing, *Observer* (Review), 26 December.

Marshall, G. (1997) *Repositioning Class*. London: Sage.

Marwick, A. (1998) Class of 98, *Observer* (Review), 11 October.

Mayhew, K., Deer, C. and Mehak, D. (2004) The Move to mass higher education in the UK: many questions and some answers, *Oxford Review of Education*, 30(1): 65–82.

Mays, J.B. (1962) *Education and the Urban Child*. Liverpool: Liverpool University Press.

Miliband, D. (2003) Class that haunts the classroom, *Guardian*, 18 September.

Millar, F. (2004) Guidance is not going to make school admissions fairer, *Guardian* (Education), 9 November.

Millar F. (2005) Opinion: selection is back on the agenda, *Guardian* (Education), 15 March.

Millett, A. (1997) Partners in the classroom (letter), *Times Educational Supplement*, 21 February.

Milner, M. (2004) Rover chiefs attacked for disgusting salaries, *Guardian*, 13 November.

Minister for the Disabled (1996) *Booklet D-100: Requirements of the 1995 Disability Discrimination Act for Schools, Further Education Colleges and Higher Education*. London: HMSO.

Ministry of Education (1944) *The Public Schools and the General Education System* (Fleming Report). London: HMSO.

Ministry of Education (1945) *The Nation's Schools*. London: HMSO.

Ministry of Education (1947) *School and Life*, First Report of the Central Advisory Council for Education (England). London: HMSO.

Ministry of Education (1954) *Early Leaving*, Report of the Central Advisory Council for Education (England). London: HMSO.

Ministry of Education (1959) *Fifteen to Eighteen*, Report of the Central Advisory Council for Education (England) (Crowther Report). London: HMSO.

Ministry of Education (1963a) *Half Our Future*, Cmnd 2165, Report of the Central Advisory Council for Education (England) (Newsom Report). London: HMSO.

Ministry of Education (1963b) *Higher Education* (Robbins Report). London: HMSO.

Miron, G. (2001) *What's Public about Charter Schools?* The Evaluation Centre, Western Michigan University, Kalamazoo: Michigan.

Mitchell, D.T. (2004) A commentary on Good Neighbours: ISC schools and their communities. Bedford: Bedfordshire County Council.

Morrell, F. (2000) An episode in the thirty years war: race, sex and class in the ILEA 1981–90, in K. Myers (ed.) *Whatever Happened to Equal Opportunities in Schools?* Buckingham: Open University Press.

Morris, M. (1995) Elite strangleholds, *Education*, 31 March.

Morris, R., Reid, R. and Fowler, J. (1993) *Education Act 1993: A Critical Guide*. London: Association of Metropolitan Authorities.

Mortimore, P. (1998) A big step backwards, *Guardian* (Education), 24 March.

Mortimore, P. (2000) Does educational research matter? *British Journal of Educational Research*, 26(1): 5–24.

Moser, C. (1999) *Improving Literacy and Numeracy: A Fresh Start*, Report of a Working Group. London: DfEE.

Muller, J. (1997) Social justice and its renewals: a sociological comment, School of Education, University of Cape Town, South Africa.

National Commission on Education (1993) *Learning to Succeed*. London: Heinemann.

Newnham, D. (2000) No reply, *Times Educational Supplement*, 18 February.

Noden, P. (2000) Rediscovering the impact of marketisation: dimensions of social segregation in England's secondary schools 1994–99, *British Journal of Sociology of Education*, 21(3): 371–90.

Noden, P., West, A., David, M. and Edge, A. (1998) Choices and destinations of transfer to secondary schools in London, *Journal of Education Policy*, 13: 221–36.

Nolan, P. (2001) Shaping things to come, *People Management*, 27 December.

Norton, C. (1998) Upwardly mobile Britain split into 17 new classes, *Sunday Times*, 13 September.

Norwood Committee (1943) *Curriculum and Examinations in Secondary Schools* (Norwood Report). London: Ministry of Education.

NUT (1979) *Special Educational Needs: The NUT reply to Warnock*. London: NUT.

NUT (1993) *Union Response to the proposals for the Reform of Initial Teacher Training*. London: NUT.

O'Connor, M. (1990) *Secondary Education*. London: Cassell.

O'Connor, M., Hales, E., Davies, J. and Tomlinson, S. (1999) *Hackney Downs: The School that Dared to Fight*. London: Cassell.

OECD (1994) *School: A Matter of Choice*. Paris: OECD.

OECD (2002) *Programme for International Student Assessment* (PISA Study). Paris: OECD.

Ofsted (1993) *Access and Achievement in Urban Education: A Report from HMI*. London: Ofsted.

Ofsted (1995) *Ofsted Handbook Pt 5: Technical Paper 13 – Schools Requiring Special Measures*. London: Ofsted.

Ofsted (1996a) *The Implementation of the Code of Practice for Pupils with Special Educational Needs*. London: Ofsted.

Ofsted (1996b) *The Teaching of Reading in 45 Inner London Primary Schools*. London: Ofsted.

Ofsted/OECD (1995) *The Improvement of Failing Schools: UK Policy and Practice 1993–95*. London: DfEE.

Ofsted (2003a) *The National Literacy and Numeracy Strategies and the Primary Curriculum*. London: Office for Standards in Education.

Ofsted (2003b) *Report on Further Education Colleges*. London: The Stationery Office.

Ong, A. (2004) Higher learning: educational availability and flexible citizenship in global space, in J.A. Banks (ed.) *Diversity and Citizenship Education*. San Francisco, CA: Jossey-Bass.

ONS (Office for National Statistics) (1998) *Britain: An Official Handbook*. London: The Stationery Office.

Osler, A. and Morrison, M. (2000) *Inspecting Schools for Race Equality*. Stoke on Trent: Trentham Books.

Osler, A. and Vincent, K. (2003) *Girls and Exclusion*. London: Routledge/Falmer.

O'Sullivan, T. (2000) The young rich, *Observer* (Review), 12 March.

Oxford Review of Education (2005) Special Issue: Education and the Labour Government: an evaluation of two terms, 31 (1).

Palmer, F. (1986) *Anti-racism: An Assault on Education and Value*. London: Sherwood.

Pantazis, C. and Gordon, D. (2000) *Tackling Inequalities*. Bristol: Policy Press.

Parekh, B. (2000) *The Future of Multi-ethnic Britain*. London: Profile.

Passmore, B. (1999) Divided sector, equal partners, *Times Educational Supplement*, 22 January.

Paterson, L. (1998) You take the higher road, *Times Educational Supplement*, 9 October.

Paton, G. (2004) Ex-Inspectors in private war, *Times Educational Supplement*, 10 December.

Patten, J. (1992) Parents must have choice of school, *Forward*, Magazine of the Conservative Way.

Pearce, S. (1986) Swann and the spirit of the age, in F. Palmer (ed.) *Anti-racism: An Assault on Education and Value*. London: Sherwood.

Performance and Innovation Unit (2003) *Ethnic Minorities and the Labour Market*. London: Cabinet Office.

Phillips, R. (1998) *History Teaching, Nationhood and the State*. London: Cassell.

Phillips, R. and Furlong, J. (eds) (2001) *Education, Reform and the State: Twenty-Five Years of Politics, Policy and Practice*. London: Routledge.

Pickering, J. and Lodge, C. (1998) Boys' underachievement: challenging some assumptions about boys, *Improving Schools*, 1(1): 54–60.

PIRLS (2003) *The 2001 Progress in International Literacy Study*. Slough: National Foundation for Educational Research.

Pollack, A.M. (2004) *NHS plc: The Privatisation of our Health Care*. London: Verso.

Pollard, S. (1995) *Schools, Selection and the Market*. Memorandum no.16. London: Social Market Foundation.

Pollard, S. (2005) *David Blunkett*. London: Hodder and Stoughton.

Pollard, S. and Adonis, A. (1996) *A Class Act*. London: Macmillan.

Porter, J. (1999) *Reschooling and the Global Economic Future*. Wallingford: Symposium.

Power, A. and Mumford, K. (1999) *The Slow Death of Great Cities*. London: Joseph Rowntree Foundation.

Power, S. (2000) Education and the middle classes, *British Journal of Sociology of Education*, 21(2): 133–45.

Power, S., Whitty, G., Gewirtz, S., Halpin, D. and Dickson, M. (2003a) *Paving A Third Way; A Policy Trajectory Analysis of AEZs*, Final Report to the ESRC. London: Institute of Education, University of London.

Power, S., Edwards, T., Whitty, G. and Wigfall, V. (2003b) *Education and the Middle Classes*. Buckingham: Open University Press.

Pratt, J., Bloomfield, J. and Seale, C. (1984) *Option Choice: A Question of Equal Opportunity*. Slough: National Foundation for Educational Research.

Prestage, M. (1998) Woodhead must go says council chief, *Times Educational Supplement*, 26 June.

Pring, R. (1995) *Closing the Gap*. London: Hodder and Stoughton.

Pring, R. (2004) The Skills Revolution, *Oxford Review of Education*, 30(1): 105–16.

Public Accounts Committee (2004) *Early Years: Progress in Developing High Quality Childcare and Early Education Accessible to All* (35th Report HC444). London: House of Commons.

Pyke, N. (1993) Fear for future of objective research, *Times Educational Supplement*, 12 November.

Pyke, N. (1996) Schools focus on D-graders, *Times Educational Supplement*, 22 November.

QCA/DfEE (1999) *A Review of the National Curriculum in England and Wales: The Consultation Materials*. London: QCA.

Ranson, S. (1984) Towards a tertiary tripartism: new codes of social control and the 17+, in P. Broadfoot (ed.) *Selection, Certification and Control*. London: Methuen.

Ranson, S. (1994) *Towards the Learning Society*. London: Cassell.

Ranson, S. (1990) From 1944 to 1988: education, citizenship and democracy, in M. Flude and M. Hammer (eds) *The Education Reform Act 1988*. London: Falmer.

Ranson, S. and Tomlinson, J. (1994) *School Co-operation: New Forms of Local Government*. London: Longman.

Reay, D. (1998) *Class Work: Mothers' Involvement in their Children's Primary Schooling*. London: UCL Press.

Reay, D. and Wiliam, D. (1999) I'll be a nothing; structure, agency and the construction of identity through assessment, *British Educational Research Journal*, 25(3): 343–54.

Rees, G., Williamson, H. and Istance, D. (1996) Status zero: a study of jobless school leavers in education, *Research Papers in Education*, 11(2): 219–35.

Refugee Council (2000) *Helping Refugee Children in Schools*. London: The Refugee Council.

Reich, R. (1991) *The Work of Nations*. New York: Simon and Schuster.

Rex, J. (1986) *Race and Ethnicity*. Buckingham: Open University Press.

Rex, J. and Tomlinson, S. (1979) *Colonial Immigrants in a British City*. London: Routledge.

Reynolds, D. (1989) Better schools? Present and potential policies about the goals, organisation and management of secondary schools, in A. Hargreaves and D. Reynolds (eds) *Education Policies: Controversies and Critiques*. London: Falmer.

Reynolds, D. and Farrell, S. (1996) *Worlds Apart: A Review of International Surveys of Educational Achievement Involving England*. London: Ofsted.

Ribbins, P. and Sherratt, B. (1997) *Radical Education Policies and Conservative Secretaries of State*. London: Cassell.

Richards, K. (1983) A contribution to the multicultural debate, *New Community*, 10(2): 222–5.

Richardson, R. and Wood, A. (1999) *Inclusive Schools: Inclusive Society – Race and Identity on the Agenda*. Stoke-on-Trent: Trentham.

Riddell, S., Baron, S., Stalker, K. and Wilkinson, H. (1997) The concept of the learning society for adults with learning difficulties: human and social capital perspectives, *Journal of Educational Policy*, 12(6): 473–84.

Rikowski, G. (2003) The business takeover of schools, *Media-Active*, 1: 91–108.

Robinson, J. (1994) *The Legal Framework for Education*. Buckingham: University of Buckingham.

Robinson, K. (1999) *All Our Futures* (Robinson Report). London: HMSO.

Robinson, P. (1991) Education, training and economic performance: what do we need to know? Paper to International Labour Organisation Conference on Global Economic Change, London, 25 November.

Robinson, P. (1997) *The Myth of Parity of Esteem: Earnings and Qualifications*, discussion paper no. 34. London: Centre for Economic Performance.

Robinson, P. (1999) The tyranny of league tables: international comparisons of educational attainment and economic performance, in R. Alexander, P.M. Broadfoot and D. Phillips (eds) *Learning from Comparing: Part 1*. Wallingford: Symposium.

Robinson, P. (2000) Measuring the knowledge economy: employment and qualifications, in D. Robertson (ed.) *The Knowledge Economy*. London: Routledge.

Room, G. (2002) Education and welfare: recalibrating the European debate, *Policy Studies*, 23(1): 37–50.

Ross, A. and Tomlinson, S. (1991) Teachers for tomorrow, in *Teachers and Parents*, education and training paper no. 7. London: IPPR.

Rudd, W.C.A. (1960) The effects of streaming – a further contribution, *Educational Research*, 2(3): 225–8.

Rutter, M.L. and Madge, N. (1976) *Cycles of Disadvantage*. London: Heinemann.

Rutter, J. (2003) *Supporting Refugee Children in 21st Britain*. Stoke-on-Trent: Trentham Books.

Sallis, J. (1994) *Free for All: A Brief History of State Education*. London: Campaign for State Education.

Sammons, P., Hillman, J. and Mortimore, P. (1995) *Key Characteristics of Effective Schools: A Review of School Effectiveness*. London: Institute of Education.

Savage, D. (2004) Becoming a specialist school, *Times Educational Supplement*, 12 November.

Savage, M. (2000) *Class Analysis and Social Transformation*. Buckingham: Open University Press.

Scanlon, M. and Buckingham, D. (2004) Home learning and the Education Market Place, *Oxford Review of Education*, 30(2): 287–303.

Scarman Committee (1982) *The Brixton Disorders 10–12 April 1981*. Harmondsworth: Penguin.

Schagen, I. and Schagen, S. (2003) Analysis of national value-added data sets to assess the impact of selection on pupil performance, *British Educational Research Journal*, 29(4): 561–82.

Schwartz, S. (2004) *Final Report on University Admissions*. Bristol: HEFCE.

Scruton, R., Ellis-Jones, A. and O'Keefe, D. (1985) *Education and Indoctrination*. London: Education Research Centre.

Sen, Amartya (2000) Freedom's market, *Observer*, 25 June.

Sennett, R. (1998) *The Corrosion of Character*. New York: Norton.

Shaw, M. (2004a) Put local children first, *Times Educational Supplement*, 24 September.

Shaw, M. (2004b) School put up for internet auction, *Times Educational Supplement*, 3 September.

Shaw, M. (2004c) Tobacco firm to help fund private schools, *Times Educational Supplement*, 20 August.

Shaw, M. (2004d) Citizenship education leaves pupils cold, *Times Educational Supplement*, 20 August.

Shaw, M. and Paton, G. (2004) Blair courts US for academy funding, *Times Educational Supplement*, 29 October.

Shephard, J. and Vulliamy, G. (1994) The struggle for culture: a sociological case study of the development of a national music curriculum, *British Journal of Sociology of Education*, 15(1): 27–40.

Shiner, M. and Modood, T. (2002) Help or hindrance? Higher education and the route to ethnic equality, *British Journal of Sociology of Education*, 23: 209–32.

Shotte, G. (2002) Education, migration and identities: relocated Montserratian children in London schools. Unpublished PhD thesis, Institute of Education, University of London.

Silver, H. (1980) *Education and the Social Condition*. London: Methuen.

Silver, H. (1990) *Education, Change, and the Policy Process*. London: Falmer.

Simon, B. (1988) *Bending the Rules: The Baker 'Reform' of Education*. London: Lawrence and Wishart.

Simon, B. (1991) *Education and the Social Order 1940–1990*. London: Lawrence and Wishart.

Siraj-Blatchford, I., Sylva, K., Taggart, B., Melhuish, E., Sammons, P. and Elliot, K. (2004) *EPPE: The Final Report*. Technical Paper no 12. London: Insitutute of Education, University of London.

Sivanandan, A. (1999) Globalism and the Left, *Race and Class*, 40(2/3): 5–20.

Sklair, L. (2001) *The Transnational Capitalist Class*. Oxford: Blackwell.

Slater, J. (2004a) Special Needs pupils barred, *Times Educational Supplement*, 10 December.

Slater, J. (2004b) Jarvis problems add to private finance fears, *Times Educational Supplement*, 9 July.

Slater, J. (2005) Christian schools fail test of tolerance, *Times Educational Supplement*, 21 February.

Slee, R., Weiner, G. and Tomlinson, S. (1998) *School Effectiveness for Whom?* London: Falmer.

Smith Report (2003) *Making Mathematics Count*. London: DfES.

Smith, D.J. and Tomlinson, S. (1989) *The School Effect: A Study of Multiracial Comprehensives*. London: Policy Studies Institute.

Smith, T. and Noble, M. (1995) *Education Divides. Poverty and Schooling in the 1990s*. London: Child Poverty Action Group.

Smithers, R. (1999a) A barren timetable, *Royal Society of Arts Journal*, 4(4): 8–11.

Smithers, R. (1999b) Sink schools should be shut to help others, *Guardian*, 29 September.

Smithers, R. (2000a) Setback for Labour on staff selection, *Guardian*, 15 January.

Smithers, R. (2000b) You're not alone, *Guardian* (Education), 15 August.

Smithers, R. (2003) On your marks, *Times Educational Supplement,* 29 April.

Smithers, R. (2004) Teaching in 1960s crackers says inspector, *Guardian*, 6 October.

Smithers, R. (2005) Outcry at Kelly reforms, *Guardian*, 24 February.

Smithers, R. and White, M. (2003) Blair faces new row over school funds, *Times Educational Supplement*, 31 December.

Smithers, R. and al Yafai, F. (2004) Old fashioned, out of time; Clarke dismisses Princely views of education, *Guardian*, 19 November.

Social Exclusion Unit (1998) *Truancy and Exclusion from School*. London: The Stationery Office.

Social Exclusion Unit (1999) *Bridging the Gap: New Opportunities for 16–18 Year Olds not in Education, Training or Employment*, Cmnd 4405. London: The Stationery Office.

Social Trends (2000) No. 30. London: The Stationery Office.

Social Trends (2003) No 33. London: The Stationery Office.

Spencer, S. (2000) Making race equality count, *New Economy*, 7(1): 35–40.

Stanton, G. (1997) Patterns in development, in S. Tomlinson (ed.) *Education 14–19: Critical Perspectives*. London: Athlone.

Stewart, W. (2003) Storm out of blue skies, *Times Educational Supplement*, 5 December.

Stewart, W. (2004a) Miliband faces quiz over Academy cash, *Times Educational Supplement*, 20 August.

Stewart, W. (2004b) Academy profits from exclusions, *Times Educational Supplement*, 24 September.

Stiglitz, J. (2002) *Globalisation and its Discontents*. London: Penguin Books.

St John-Brooks, C. (2000) Education is still my number one priority, *Times Educational Supplement*, 21 January.

Storkey, M. (1991) *London's Ethnic Minorities*. London: London Research Centre.

Straw, J. and Blair, T. (1991) *Today's Education and Training: Tomorrow's Skills*. London: Labour Party.

Sukhnandan, L. and Lee, B. (1998) *Streaming, Setting and Grouping by Ability*. Slough: National Foundation for Educational Research.

Taunton Commission (1886) Report of the Royal Commission known as the *Schools Inquiry Report*, vol. 1. London.

Tawney, R.H. (1931) *Equality*. London: Unwin.

Taylor, M. (2005) School plans turn the clock back by 50 years, *Guardian*, 25 March.

TEN (2004) Speak up for funding flexibility, *The Education Network*, 36: 1.

TGAT (1987) *Report of the Task Group on Assessment and Testing*. London: Department of Education and Science.

TTA (2000) *Raising the Attainment of Minority Ethnic Pupils; Guidance and Resource Materials*. London: Teacher Training Agency.

Thatcher, M. (1993) *The Downing Street Years*. London: HarperCollins.

Thrupp, M. (1999) *Schools Making a Difference: Let's be Realistic*. Buckingham: Open University Press.

Thompson, P. (2004) *Skating on Thin Ice: The Knowledge Economy Myth*. Glasgow: University of Strathclyde.

Thompson, P. and Warhurst, C. (1998) *Workplaces of the Future*. London: MacMillan.

Tomasevski, K. (2003) *Education Denied*. London and New York: Zed Books.

Tomlinson, J. (1996) *Inclusive Learning: A Report of the Learning Difficulties and Disabilities Committee*. Coventry: FEFC.

Tomlinson, S. (1981) *Educational Subnormality: A Study in Decision Making*. London: Routledge.

Tomlinson, S. (1987) *Ethnic Minorities in British Schools: A Review of the Literature 1960–1982*. London: Heinemann.

Tomlinson, S. (1988) Education and training, *New Community*, 15: 103–9.

Tomlinson, S. (1989) The expansion of special education, in B. Cosin, M. Flude and M. Hales (eds) *School, Work and Equality*. Sevenoaks: Hodder.

Tomlinson, S. (1990) *Multicultural Education in White Schools*. London: Batsford.

Tomlinson, S. (1991) Home–school partnerships, in *Teachers and Parents*, education and training paper no. 7. London: IPPR.

Tomlinson, S. (1992) Disadvantaging the disadvantaged: Bangladeshis and education in Tower Hamlets, *British Journal of Sociology of Education*, 13(2): 337–46.

Tomlinson, S. (1993) The Multicultural Task Group: the group that never was, in A. King and C. Reiss (eds) *The Multicultural Dimension of the National Curriculum*. London: Falmer.

Tomlinson, S. (ed.) (1994) *Educational Reform and its Consequences*. London: Rivers-Oram Press for IPPR.

Tomlinson, S. (1997a) Sociological perspectives on failing schools, *International Studies in Sociology of Education*, 7(1): 81–98.

Tomlinson, S. (ed.) (1997b) *Education 14–19 Critical Perspectives*. London: Athlone.

Tomlinson, S. (1997c) Education 14–19 divided and divisive, in S. Tomlinson (ed.) *Education 14–19 Critical Perspectives*. London: Athlone.

Tomlinson, S. (2001) Education policy 1997–2000: the effects on Top, Bottom and Middle England, *International Journal of Sociology of Education*, 11(3): 261–77.

Tomlinson, S. (2005) Race, ethnicity and education under New Labour, *Oxford Review of Education*, 31(1): 153–71.

Tomlinson, S. and Tomes, H. (1986) *Curriculum Option Choice in Multiracial Schools*. London: Department of Education and Science.

Tooley, J. (1996) *Education without the State*. London: Institute for Economic Affairs.

Toolis, K. (2003) Will they ever learn, *Guardian*, 22 November.

Townsend, P. (1993) *The International Analysis of Poverty*. Milton Keynes: Harvester.

Toynbee, P. (2003) *Hard Work: Life in Low-pay Britain*. London: Bloomsbury.

Toynbee, P. (2004) Blair trashed the 60s for the sake of a Tory one-liner, *Guardian*, 21 July.

Travers, T. (1999) Squaring the circle, *Guardian* (Society), 22 September.

Travers, T. (2003) Opinion, *Guardian* (Education), 11 November.

Trow, M. (1994) Managerialism and the academic profession: the case of England, *Higher Education Policy*, 7(2): 1–15.

Turner, M. (1990) *Sponsored Reading Failure*, Education Unit, Warlingham, Surrey.

Turok, I. (2000) Inequalities in employment: problems of spatial divergence, in C. Pantazis and D. Gordon (eds) *Tackling Inequalities*. Bristol: Policy Press.

United Nations (1948) Universal Declaration of Human Rights, Article 26. Geneva: UN.

University for Industry Working Group (1999) *A New Way of Learning – The UfI Network. Developing the University for Industry Concept.* London: DfEE.

Vaizey, J. (1958) *The Costs of Education.* London: Allen and Unwin.

Vidich, A.J. (1995) *The New Middle Classes.* London: Macmillan.

Walden, G. (1996) *We Should Know Better: Solving the Education Crisis.* London: Fourth Estate.

Walford, G. and Miller, H. (1991) *City Technology College.* Buckingham: Open University Press.

Walker, R. (2005) *Social Security and Welfare.* Berkshire: Open University Press/ McGraw-Hill.

Walker, A. and Walker, C. (1987) *The Growing Divide: A Social Account 1979–1987.* London: Child Poverty Action Group.

Walker, A. and Walker, C. (1997) *Britain Divided.* London: Child Poverty Action Group.

Walters, N. (2005) A Challenge to Sexual Mumbo-Jumbo, *Guardian*, 21 February.

Ward, L. (1999) Outrage over Tories' school plans, *Guardian*, 6 October.

Ward, L. (2003) Why I said sod it, *Guardian* (Education), 9 January.

Ward, L. (2005) Women part-timers stuck in low paid jobs, *Guardian*, 9 March.

Warnock, M. (1978) *Special Educational Needs.* Report of the Committee of Inquiry into the Education of Handicapped Children and Young People (Warnock Report). London: HMSO.

Warnock, M. (1980) A flexible framework, *Times Educational Supplement*, 26 September.

Webb, B. (1926) *My Apprenticeship.* London: Longman.

Weiner, G. (1994) *Feminisms and Education.* Buckingham: Open University Press.

Weir, D. (1999) The city has taken over the quangos under New Labour, *Independent* (Tuesday Review), 23 November.

West, A., Noden, P., Kleinman, M. and Whitehead, C. (2000) Examining the impact of specialist schools performance. Research report 196. London: DfES.

White, R., Pring, R. and Brockingham, D. (1995) *14–19 Education and Training: Implementing a Unified System of Learning.* London: Royal Society of Arts.

Whitty, G. (1989) The New Right and the National Curriculum: state control or market forces, *Journal of Education Policy*, 4(4): 329–42.

Whitty, G. (2002) *Making Sense of Education Policy.* London: Paul Chapman.

Whitty, G., Power, S. and Halpin, D. (1998) *Devolution and Choice in Education.* Buckingham: Open University Press.

Wilce, H. (2004) Prophet of the specialist schools, *Times Educational Supplement*, 19 November.

Wilkinson, H. (1994) *No Turning Back: Generations and the Genderquake.* London: Demos.

Williams, R. (1965) *The Long Revolution.* Harmondsworth: Penguin.

Willms, J.D. and Echols, F. (1992) Alert and inalert clients: the Scottish experience of parental choice of school, *Economics of Education*, 11(4): 339–50.

Wilson, W.J. (1996) *When Work Disappears: The World of the New Urban Poor.* New York: Alfred Knopf.

Wintour, P. (1999) Blair turns the heat on teachers, *Observer*, 17 October.

Wintour, P. (2003) Left told to earn the right to be heard, *Guardian*, 14 July.

Wolf, A. (2002) *Does Education Matter?* London: Penguin Books.

Woodhead, C. (2000) Degrees with a mark of failure, *Sunday Times* (News Review), 13 August.

Woodward, D. (1997) Economic dimensions of education and the role of the World Bank, Paper to NGO Economic Forum, London, October.

Woodward, W. (2000a) Blunkett humiliated in pay row, *Guardian*, 15 July.

Woodward, W. (2000b) Brave new world, *Guardian* (Education), 18 July.

Woodward, W. (2003) School tests break UN Convention, *Guardian*, 14 July.

Wragg, E.C., Haynes, G.S., Wragg, C.M. and Chamberlain, R.P. (2000) *Failing Teachers*. London: Routledge.

Wragg, T. (1997) Oh boy, *Times Educational Supplement*, 16 May.

Wragg, T. (2004) Opinion: not all that modernisation is good, *Guardian* (Education), 7 December.

Wragg, T. (ed.) (2005) *Letters to the Prime Minister*. London: New Vision Group.

Wragg, T. and Jarvis, F. (eds) (1993) *Education: A Different Vision*. London: IPPR.

Wright, C., Weekes, D. and McGlaughlin, A. (2000) *Race, Class and Gender in Exclusions from School*. London: Falmer.

Yates, L. (1985) Is girl-friendly schooling really what girls need?, in R. Deem, L. Kant and M. Cruikshank (eds) *Girl-friendly Schooling*. London: Methuen.

Young, D. (1990) *The Enterprise Years*. London: Headline Publishing.

Young, M. (1958) *The Rise of the Meritocracy*. Harmondsworth: Penguin.

Young, S. (1996) Heads' nightmare vision of selection, *Times Educational Supplement*, 11 October.

Younge, G. (2005) We can't vote Labour, *Guardian*, 21 February.

Youth Sports Trust (2002) *Best Practice in Sports Colleges: A Guide to School Improvement*. Loughborough: Youth Sports Trust.

Index

A levels, 64, 85, 86, 151, 152–3, 154,
176, 196, 217
A/S levels, 138, 152
Aaronovitch, D., 117
Abbas, T., 189
academic-vocational divide, 43, 46, 64,
84–6, 86–7, 151–2, 176
academies, 122, 123, 127–9, 130, 190,
221
Academy for Gifted and Talented Youth,
125, 187
Access Agreement, 157
Access Regulator, 157
accommodation centres, 188
Acherson, N., 223
Acheson, D., 35
achievement/attainment, 168–9
boys' underachievement, 197–8
girls', 195–7
race and ethnicity, 190–2
Additional Educational Needs Index
(AEN), 131
admissions, 45–6, 100, 127–9
Admissions Forum, 123, 129
Adnett, N., 126
Adonis, A., 79, 88, 131, 139
Adult Learning Inspectorate (ALI), 148
Advisory Committee on the Supply and
Education of Teachers, 41

Advisory Group on Citizenship, 113
advisory groups, 94–5
Ahmed, K., 203
aided schools, 98
Aiming High, 191
*Aiming Higher: Labour's Proposals for
the Reform of the, 14–19
Curriculum*, 86–7
Ainley, P., 6
Aldrich, R., 96
Allen, L., 87, 88
Andrews, K., 115
Apple, M., 38, 186
Archer, L., 198
Archive Network, 193
Argyropolu, D., 42
Armstrong, D., 133
Arnot, M., 193, 194–5, 196, 197, 217
Ashton, D., 207
assessment, 137–8
assessors, 112, 154
assisted places scheme, 34, 77, 95, 220
Association of Local Authority
Education Committees, 41
Asthana, S., 35, 175
asylum seekers, 188
Atkins, W.S., engineering company, 135
Atkinson, B., 166
Atkinson, W., 97

attendance, 59, 61
Attlee, C., 16
Audit Commission, 60
Auld, R., 25

Back, L., 183
back-to-basics curriculum, 56
Baer, K.S., 5
Baker, K., 31, 41, 45, 51, 52–3, 61, 148
Balchin, R., 110
Ball, C., 145
Ball, M., 132
Ball, S.J., 90, 175, 178, 195
Banks, O., 17
Barber, M., 67, 88–9, 91, 98, 115, 131,
    139, 222
  influence over appointments, 114
  Literacy Task Force, 83
  Standards and Effectiveness Unit, 60,
    94
Barclay, P., 210
Barnard, N., 107, 112
Barnett, R., 64, 156
baseline assessment, 77
Baty, P., 149
Bauman, Z., 211–12, 221, 223
beacon schools, 103, 124
beacons of excellence, 147
Bell, Daniel, 206
Bell, David, 22, 187
Benn, C., 20, 122, 176, 186
Benn, M., 101
Benn, T., 16–17
Better Schools, 38, 43–4
Bichard, M., 135, 162–3
'Black Papers', 21
Blackburne, L., 76
Blackstone, Baroness, 68, 70, 103
Blair, T., 70, 79, 94, 118, 127, 173, 219,
    220, 221
  academic-vocational divide, 86
  academies, 127–8
  demonization of education, 22
  education as priority, 83
  employment, 7
  Euan sent to Oratory School, 60
  'forces of conservation', 111
  inner city schools, 102

Labour Education Summit, 96
LEAs, 109, 110
  poverty and social exclusion, 169
  and reform of qualifications, 69, 154
  SEU, 91
block grant, 40
Bloom, A., 125
Blunkett, D., 6, 51, 70, 74, 86, 89, 94,
    162
  Asian communities, 188
  citizenship education, 192
  Dearing Report, 155
  Diversity and Excellence, 87
  Excellence in Schools, 96
  failing schools, 95
  higher education, 156
  The Learning Age, 146
  selection, 72
  specialist schools, 102–3
Bobbitt, P., 5–6, 215, 221
Bolton, E., 58
Booklet D100, 81–2
Boston, K., 138, 153
Bowe, R., 54
Boyle, E., 19
boys' underachievement, 197–8
Boyson, R., 21, 25
Brace, A., 79
Bradford, S., 124
Brain, J., 57
Brewer, M., 4
Brighouse, T., 54, 94
Bright, M., 84, 102
Britain 1998: An Official Handbook, 91
British Educational Research
    Association, 67
Brown, G., 141, 161, 162, 202
Brown, Margaret, 84
Brown, Matthew, 208
Brown, P., 168, 171–2, 173–4, 200, 201,
    202
Bryce Report, 164
Buckingham, D., 134
Budge, D., 128
'Building Schools for the Future'
    programme, 134
Building on Success, 121–2
Bullock Report, 24

Burkitt, N., 207
Burnham Committee, 41
Bush, G.W., 221
Butler, R.A., 51
Byers, S., 95, 109
Bynoe, I., 81

Callaghan, J., 25–6
Cambridge Education Associates, 110,
    112, 135, 137
Campaign for State Education, 27, 102
Campbell, A., 117
Campbell, J., 53
Cannadine, D., 167
Cantle, T., 188
Capita, 110, 135
Carlisle, M., 31, 33, 42, 57
Carr, W., 14, 26
Carvel, J., 80, 94, 102, 110, 170, 197
CEM Consortium, 110
Central Advisory Council for Education
    (CACE), 16, 41, 193–4
centralization of control, 2, 4, 39–40
Centre for British Teachers (CfBT), 137
Centre for Policy Studies, 24
Centres of Vocational Excellence
    (CoVEs), 122
Cerny, P.G., 221
Certificate of Secondary Education
    (CSE), 18, 20, 196
charities, 123–4
Charles, Prince, 94, 118, 139
charter schools, 127, 128
chartered assessors, 154
Child Poverty Action Group, 78
childcare centres, 132
childcare champions, 106
childcare policies, 106, 132–3, 161
Children Act 1989, 54
Children Act 2004, 133, 188
Children and Young People's Plan, 133
Children's Commissioner, 133
children's trusts, 133
Chitty, C., 20, 101, 122, 176, 186
Choice and Diversity, 9, 55–7, 58
choice policies, 35, 219
    Conservative governments, 51–2,
    54–7

effects of, 77–9
    middle class and, 174–5
    New Labour, 101–2
    race and ethnicity, 186, 189–90
Circular 10/65, 20
Circular 10/70, 23
circulars, 8, 12
cities, 107–9, 212
citizenship education, 113, 192
city academies, 103, 122, 127
city technology colleges (CTCs), 44–5,
    53, 54, 97
Clancy, J., 142, 192
Clarke, C., 118, 121, 127, 139, 156
Clarke, K., 51, 56, 66
class sizes, 95, 99
classroom assistants, 137
Climbié, V., 132–3, 188
Clinton, B., 5, 215
Coalition of Modern Universities,
    157
Cockcroft Report, 42–3
Code of Practice on Admissions, 129
*Code of Practice on LEA–School
    Relationships*, 109
Code of Practice on SEN, 61, 82, 133
Coffield, F., 145
Cognita, 135
Collins, T., 121, 130
Commission on the Future of
    Multiethnic Britain, 218
Commission for Racial Equality, 187
Commission on Social Justice, 165
Committee of Inquiry into the Education
    of Ethnic Minority Children, 37–8,
    184
Committee of Vice-Chancellors and
    Principals (CVCP), 67
commodification of education, 2, 32
commodity producing enterprises, 134
common good, 179–80, 222
community hubs, 126
community schools, 98, 99
*Competitiveness: Helping Business to
    Win*, 141
Comprehensive Future, 140
comprehensive education, 3, 17, 23, 42,
    122

'bog-standard' comprehensive
schools, 117
demonisation of, 21, 24–5
introduction, 18–20
middle class and, 171
New Labour and, 159–60
Thatcher government, 32–3
Confederation of British Industry, 203
Connexions, 148
Conran, J., 128
Conservative Party policies, 3, 88,
220
1950s and 1960s, 18–19
1970 government, 23
1980–87 governments, 9, 29–47
1988–94 governments, 9, 48–71
1994–97 government, 9, 72–89
consolidating acts, 74–6, 88
consumers, 211
Continuing Education Advisory Group,
95
control, centralization of, 2, 4, 39–40
core curriculum, 42
Cornford, J., 68, 70
Corrigan, P., 70
Coryton, D., 49
Cosgrave, P., 23
Cottrell, P., 148
Council for the Accreditation of Teacher
Education (CATE), 41, 67, 185
Council for National Academic Awards
(CNAA), 64
Cox, C.B., 21, 22, 62–3
Crace, J., 128, 131, 152
creativity and culture, 113
Crick Reports, 113, 192
Crompton, R., 204
Crosland, A., 19
Crouch, C., 161, 221
'Crown schools', 35
Crowther Report, 18
curriculum, 17–18, 69
control of in 1980s, 42–4, 61–2
critiques, 62–4
gender and, 193–4
governing bodies and, 38–9
issues in the mid-1990s, 82–4
National *see* National Curriculum

New Labour and, 112–14, 137–8
and racism, 192–3

David, M., 194–5
Davies, B., 87
Davies, M., 114
Davies, N., 4–5, 52, 53, 162, 173
Davies, P., 126
Day, G., 66
De Haviland, J., 46, 51
Dean, C., 175, 210
Dearing, R.
higher education review, 85, 145, 155
review of National Curriculum, 63,
64, 83
Demack, S., 168
democracy, 222
Department for Education and
Employment (DfEE), 74, 95, 97,
111, 114
see also under individual papers
Department for Education and Science
(DES), 42
Department for Trade and Industry
(DTi), 209
deprofessionalization of teachers, 220
Dewey, J., 222
differentiated curriculum, 42–3
differentiation, 35
Diploma framework, 153–4
direct grant schools, 24
Disability Discrimination Act 1995,
81–2
disabled people, 205
disaffection, 107–9
discipline, 77
diversity
Conservative governments, 54–5, 57
New Labour and, 121–3, 129, 159–
60
selection and, 188–90, 218–19
specialist schools, 125–7
Diversity and Excellence, 87–8
Dodd, V., 97
Dore, R., 205
Douglas-Home, A., 19
Downing Street Policy Unit, 95, 114
Duru-Bellat, M., 168

dyslexia, 81
Dyson, A., 22, 134

early excellence centres, 96
Early Learning, 18
Early Years Development and Childcare
    Partnerships, 132
early years forums, 96
early years policy, 96, 132–3, 161
Eccles, D., 18–19
economy, 6–8, 11, 195, 200–14, 216,
    220
Edexcel, 138
Education Act 1944, 1, 3, 13, 15, 51
Education Act 1976, 24, 36
Education Act 1979, 32
Education Act 1980, 24, 33–5, 38
Education Act 1993, 9, 36, 56, 58–61,
    105
Education Act 1994, 67–8
Education Act 1997, 77
Education Act 2002, 10, 123, 129
Education Act 2005, 130–1
Education Action Forums, 107
Education Action Zones (EAZs), 97, 99,
    107, 187
education associations, 56–7, 60, 80
Education Bill 1979, 24
Education Extra, 106, 115
Education (Grants and Awards) Act
    1984, 40
Education (Handicapped Children) Act
    1970, 23
Education Network, The, 110
Education (no.1) Act 1986, 40, 41
Education (no.2) Act 1986, 38–9
Education Reform Act 1988, 8, 9, 46,
    51–3, 54
Education (School Inspections)
    Regulations 1993, 58
Education in Schools, 26
Education (Schools) Act 1992, 58
Education (Schools) Act 1996, 74–5
Education (Schools) Act 1997, 95
Education (Schools Inspection) Act
    1996, 75–6
Education (Special Education) Act 1981,
    36

education spending, 24, 40, 74, 129–30,
    161–2
Education (Student Loans) Act 1990,
    64–5
Education (Student Loans) Act 1996,
    74
education support grants (ESGs), 38, 40,
    185
*Education and Training: Working
    Together*, 44
Educational Priority Areas (EPAs),
    21–2, 107
Edwards, G., 114
Edwards, T., 34, 103
effective schooling, 46, 170–1
egalitarianism, 19
eleven plus (11+) exam, 16, 124, 195–6
Ellison, N., 8
Elton Committee, 48
employment, 6–8, 25–6, 43, 197, 198,
    200–14, 216
Employment Zones, 107
Equal Opportunities Commission
    (EOC), 194, 197
Equal Pay Act 1970, 194
Equal Rights for Disabled People, 81
equality of opportunity, 2, 15–18,
    164–5, 171
Erdem, E., 205
ethnic minorities *see* race and ethnicity
Ethnic Minorities Achievement Grant,
    187, 191
Ethnic Minorities Achievement Unit,
    187
Etzioni, A., 220
European Inquiry Team, 69
Evans, M., 221
Every Child Matters, 133, 188
*Excellence for All Children: Meeting
    Special Educational Needs*, 104
Excellence in Cities, 108–9
Excellence in Cities programme, 108–9,
    187
*Excellence and Enjoyment in Primary
    Schools*, 138
Exellence for Everyone, 88
Excellence in Schools, 10, 96–9
exclusion, social, 4, 8, 104–9

expenditure on education, 24, 40, 74, 129–30, 161–2

failing schools, 56, 59, 60, 79–81, 95, 97, 170, 189
faith schools, 187, 190
Farrell, S., 84
Fatchett, D., 69, 70
federations, 126
Ferrara, A., 180
Ferrera, M., 7
Finch, J., 8
Finegold, D., 151
Fitz, J., 175
Fitz-Gibbon, C., 58
Five Year Strategy for Children and Learners, 10, 117, 129–30, 150
Fleming Report, 16–17
Flores, F., 209
Floud, J., 17, 19
Ford, J., 138
Foster, A., 151
Foster, D., 162
Foster, M., 195
Foundation Partnerships, 130
foundation schools, 98, 99, 101, 121, 130
Foundation and Voluntary Aided Schools Association (FVASA), 101
fourteen education professors' letter, 2, 11
14–19 policies, 10, 84–6
    see also post-16 education
Fowler, J., 123
Framework for the School Curriculum, A, 42
free school meals, 34
Freeman, S.G., 189
Fresh Start, 97, 170
Funding Agency for Schools (FAS), 56, 58, 59, 75, 101
funding for maintained schools, 130–1, 131–2
further education, 10, 18, 52, 53, 142, 217
    gender and, 196
    race and ethnicity, 191–2

Further Education Funding Council (FEFC), 147
Further and Higher Education Act 1992, 65, 84
Future of Higher Education, The, 157

Gaine, C., 186
Gaitskell, H., 16–17
Galbraith, J., 174
Gardiner, B., 124
Gardiner, J., 80, 95
Garner, R., 128
GEMS (Global Education Management Systems), 134–5
gender, 10–11, 182, 183, 193–8, 217
    and labour market, 197, 204
General Certificate of Secondary Education (GCSE), 42, 43, 151, 154, 189, 217
    girls' achievement, 196
    race and ethnicity and attainment, 190–1
    specialist schools and results, 126–7
general national vocational qualifications (GNVQs), 63–4, 85, 156
General Teaching Council (GTC), 72–3, 98, 111–12, 128, 136, 193, 220
Gewirtz, S., 54, 186, 195
Gibson, A., 35, 175
Giddens, A., 5, 141, 162, 174, 177, 208
gifted children, 125, 187
Gillborn, D., 151, 172, 189, 190
Gipps, C., 190
girls' achievement, 195–7
Glass, N., 106, 132
Glatter, R., 127
Gleeson, D., 203
global economy, 202, 208–10, 212
global free market system, 223
globalization, 178–9, 219
Glyn, A., 205
Goddard, A., 168
Glenemara, Lord, 67–8
Goldthorpe, J., 169
Gorard, S., 175
Goring, B., 189
Gould, P., 5, 69, 167

governing bodies, 24, 38–9, 100
Graduate Contribution Scheme, 157
Graham, D., 61, 62, 192
grammar schools, 33, 42, 189
  New Labour, 102, 124–5
  postwar consensus, 16, 17–18, 19, 20,
    21, 23–4
grant-maintained (GM) schools, 9, 76,
  80, 101
  increasing number of, 56–7, 59,
    59–60
  introduction of, 45–6, 52, 53, 54–5
  New Labour, 69–70, 87–8
Grant-Maintained Schools Trust, 52
Gray, J., 209, 212
Great Debate on education, 25–6
Green, A., 176, 209
Green, D., 121
Green, F., 207
Greener, A., 153
Griffiths, Lord, 70
Guardian, 2, 11, 154

Hackett, G., 70, 76, 110
Hall, J., 45
Hall, P., 113
Halpern, D., 180
Halpin, P., 107
Halsey, A.H., 201, 215, 216, 217
Hamilton, D., 81
Hannon, V., 109
Hardy, J., 101–2
Harris, M., 157
Hartnett, A., 14, 26
Hatcher, R., 66, 136, 175
Hattersley, R., 102
Hayward, G., 149, 152
Headmasters' Conference, 84
headship qualification, 111, 112
Headstart, 21–2, 106–7
Health Action Zones, 107
Heath, E., 24
Heim, A., 16
Heller, J., 222
Her Majesty's Inspectorate (HMI), 42,
  58
  see also Office for Standards in
    Education

Hetherington, P., 106
Hey, V., 124
higher education, 10, 13, 92, 217, 220
  centralizing control, 40
  Education Reform Act, 52, 53
  expansion in 1960s, 19
  gender and, 196–7
  New Labour, 143, 154–8
  1990s, 64–5
  participation and class, 168
  race and ethnicity, 191–2
Higher Education Act 2004, 10, 157–8
Higher Education Funding Council
  (HEFC), 65, 156, 158, 168
Higher and Further Education Act 1992,
  65, 84
Hirsch, F., 8, 165, 177
Hobbs, G., 168
Hodge, M., 106
Hodgson, A., 86, 141, 151–2, 176
Hofkins, D., 83
home background, 21–2
Honeyford, R., 38, 62
Hook, S., 118, 135
Hooper, Lady, 186
House of Commons Education
  Committee, 74, 78
House of Commons Education and
  Employment Committee, 85, 108
House of Commons Education and
  Skills Committee, 117, 118, 129,
  139
House of Commons Select Committee,
  37
Howarth, A., 35
Howson, J., 60
human capital, 2–3, 6–8
Husen, T., 144
Hutton, W., 79, 174, 206, 210
Hyman, P., 139, 159

ideology
  New Labour, 179–80, 202–3
  in the 1970s, 26–7
Immigration and Asylum Act 2002, 188
inclusion, 4, 118, 134, 145–6, 161
Independent Schools Council (ISC),
  123–4

Independent on Sunday, 57
individual education plans (IEPs), 82,
  103
Individual Learning Accounts, 118, 145,
  148
individualism, 32
inequality, 3–4, 159, 210
  see also poverty; social exclusion
information and communications
  technology (ICT), 97–8, 113, 217
inner city schools, 107–9
Inner London Education Authority
  (ILEA), 25, 52, 53, 185
inspection, 58, 75–6
  LEAs, 97, 109
  post-16 education, 148
Institute for Public Policy Research
  (IPPR), 68, 87
integration, 36
intelligence, 19
international comparisons, 83–4
International Monetary Fund (IMF),
  210
Islington LEA, 135

Jackson, B., 17, 20
Jacques, M., 5
James, E., 13
Jarvis, F., 2, 11, 68
Jarvis Educational Services, 135–6
Jenkins, R. (later Lord), 37, 157
Jesson, D., 126
jobs *see* employment
Jones, M., 207
Jordan, B., 6, 106, 177, 219
Joseph, K., 24–5, 31, 35, 40, 41, 42–3,
  185
Judd, K., 110

Keep, E., 149, 154, 203, 206
Kelly, R., 121, 139, 154, 159
Kennedy Report, 145
Khan, A., 188
Kids Club Network, 106, 115
Killeen, J., 208
King, R., 193
Kinnock, N., 25–6, 31, 69
Kirkman, S., 138

Kirp, D., 184
Klein, R., 57
knowledge economy, 205
Knowledge Exchanges, 158
knowledge-intensive work, 206
Knowledge Transfer Partnerships, 158

labour market *see* employment
Labour Party policy, 17, 27, 72–3,
  220–1
  assisted places scheme, 34
  early 1990s, 68–70
  National Policy Forum, 125, 140
  New Labour *see* New Labour policy
  1960s government, 20, 21
  1970s government, 24, 37
  standards, 46, 49
Laming Report, 133
Lampl, P., 139
language, 24
Lauder, H., 200, 201, 202
Lawlor, S., 41
Lawrence, I., 95
Lawrence, S., 187
Lawson, M., 5
Lawson, N., 159, 222
Lawton, D., 25, 35, 42, 49–50, 55, 159,
  169, 221
Leadbetter, C., 205
Leading Edge schools, 122, 126
league tables, 55, 83–4
Learn as You Earn, 87
*Learning Age, The: A Renaissance for a
  New Britain*, 146
*Learning to Compete: Education and
  Training for 14–19-Year-Olds*, 7,
  85–6, 151
Learning Direct helpline, 146
Learning and Skills Act 2000, 10, 149
Learning and Skills Council (LSC), 123,
  147, 149, 150, 207
learning society, 144–6
*Learning to Succeed: A New Framework
  for Post-16 Learning*, 142, 146–9
learning support units, 125
Lee, J., 136
Leeds LEA, 135
left-wing extremists, 24–5

Letwin, O., 117
Levin, B., 90
Lewis, O., 21
liberal individualism, 32
Liell, P.M., 30
lifelong learning, 10, 144–6, 218
Lifelong Learning, 87
Lind, M., 209
Lingard, B., 170
literacy, 83–4, 91, 113–14
literacy hour, 94–5, 96
literacy strategy, 137–8
Literacy Task Force, 83, 94, 94–5
Lloyd, C., 7
local education authorities (LEAs), 3
    central control and powers of, 40
    Education Act 1986 and, 38, 39
    introduction of comprehensive
        education, 20, 23, 24
    Major government and, 75
    milk and meals, 34–5
    New Labour and, 96–7, 99, 109–10,
        123, 130, 131, 161
    privatization, 110, 135
    reversal of comprehensive education,
        33
Local Government Act 1966, 40
Local Government Act 1980, 40
local management of schools (LMS),
    45–6, 52, 52–3, 54, 100
Lodge, C., 198
London Development Agency, 191
Lower Attaining Pupils Programme
    (LAPP), 43
Lucey, H., 197, 198

MacCleod, D., 83
MacClure, S., 54
MacGilchrist, B., 220
MacGregor, J., 51, 56, 66
MacPherson Report, 187, 192
Maden, M., 107
Madge, N., 21
Mahoney, P., 111, 136–7
Major, J., 55, 56, 60, 78, 88, 182
Major governments, 55–68, 72–86
Manpower Services Commission
    (MSC), 24, 43

managerialism, 66
Mansell, W., 135, 154
Marginson, S., 203
Margrave, R., 70
market reforms, 3–5, 201, 219
    effects of market forces, 77–9
    gender and, 194–5
    regressive vision of Thatcher
        government, 31–2
market state, 5–6, 215–16, 220–2
Marquand, D., 221
Marr, A., 92
Marshall, G., 166
Marwick, A., 165
May, T., 94, 101
Mayhew, K., 154, 158, 206, 209
Mays, J.B., 18
McCulloch, G., 17–18, 202
McGuinness, M., 124
McKie, D., 95
McNamara, O., 117
meals, school, 34–5
*Meeting Special Educational Needs: A
    Programme for Action*, 104
meritocracy, 2, 14, 17, 27, 203, 216,
    220–1
    and attainment, 168–9
    and inclusion, 4, 118
middle classes, 2, 8, 11, 79, 164–81, 198
    needs of, 171–3
migration, 188, 198–9
Miliband, D., 70, 87, 114, 124, 163
Millar, F., 129, 219
Miller, H., 45
Millett, A., 94, 110–11
Minister for Children and Young People
    and Families, 133
Miron, G., 127
Mirza, H., 190
Mitchell, D.T., 124
modernization, 136–9, 160
    curriculum, 112–14, 137–8
    LEAs, 109–10
    teaching profession, 110–12, 122–3,
        136–7
Modood, T., 191
Morrell, F., 185
Morris, E., 104, 108, 117, 118, 121, 139

Morris, M., 173
Morris, R., 59
Morrison, M., 187
Mortimore, P., 91–2, 102
Moser, C., 49, 149
mothers, 172
Muller, J., 179
multicultural education, 185
multicultural society, 37–8
Multicultural Task Group, 62, 192
Mumford, K., 178

nation state, 5–6
National Advisory Group for
    Continuing Education and Lifelong
    Learning, 145
National Advisory Group on SEN, 104
National Assessment Agency, 118
National Childcare Strategy, 106, 132
National College for School Leadership,
    111, 112, 137
National Commission on Education, 49
National Council for Vocational
    Qualifications (NCVQ), 44, 63, 77,
    85
National Curriculum, 32, 61–2, 82–3,
    192
  critiques, 62–4
  introduction of, 45–6, 51, 53, 55
  New Labour, 112–13
National Curriculum Council (NCC),
    51, 56, 61, 62, 63
National Grid for Learning, 97–8, 113,
    217
National Health Service, 6
National Health Service Act 1948, 1
National Insurance Act 1946, 1
National Literacy Project, 83
National Skills Strategy, 150, 202–3
National Skills Task Force, 149
National Union of Teachers (NUT), 36,
    137
national vocational qualifications
    (NVQs), 44, 64, 85
New Deal Advisory Group, 95
New Deal for Communities, 107
New Deal for 18–24-year-olds, 106
New Deal for New Britain, A, 87

New Deal Task Force, 95
New Labour policy, 3–4, 8, 72, 210–11,
    219, 221, 222–3
  continuity and change, 158–62
  economy, 201–2, 202–3, 210–11
  human capital, 7–8
  ideologies, 179–80, 202–3
  mid-1990s, 86–8
  1997–2000 government, 9–10,
    90–116
  post-16 education, 10, 141–63
  and poverty, 105–7, 177, 210–11
  private school-state school
    partnerships, 174
  race and ethnicity, 182–3, 187–8,
    191, 193
  and social class, 165–6, 167, 169
  2000–05 government, 10, 117–40
New Opportunities Fund, 113–14
New Right, 29, 35, 37, 185
New Specialist System, A, 126
New Training Initiative, The, 44
Newnham, D., 161
Newsom Report, 18
No Turning Back Group, 45
Noden, P., 175, 186
Nolan, P., 206
'non-exam' children, 20
non-interventionist state, 14
Nord Anglia, 110
Northern Ireland, 124
Norton, C., 166
Norwood Report, 16, 42
numeracy, 83–4, 113–14
numeracy strategy, 137–8
Numeracy Task Force, 94–5, 96
Nursery Education: The Next Steps, 76
Nursery and Grant-Maintained Schools
    Act 1996, 76

O levels, 20, 196, 217
O'Connor, M., 20, 21, 57, 60, 80, 97
Office of Fair Access (OFFA), 157
Office for National Statistics (ONS), 166
Office for Standards in Education
    (Ofsted), 78, 137–8, 187
  Code of Practice on SEN, 82
  criteria for failing schools, 79

establishment of, 58
inspection of LEAs, 97, 109
politicization, 75–6
and post-16 education, 148, 149
teacher training institutions, 67
Woodhead's amendment of report, 83
Ong, A., 123, 179
open enrolment, 51–2, 53, 54–5
Open University, 21
Opening Doors to a Learning Society,
70, 86
opportunities, improvement of, 221
*Opportunities for All: Tackling Poverty
and Social Exclusion*, 177
Opportunity and Excellence, 153
Organisation for Economic Cooperation
and Development (OECD), 118,
175
Osler, A., 183, 187, 189, 195
O'Sullivan, T., 169
Our Changing Schools, 54
*Our Competitive Future: Building a
Knowledge-Based Economy*, 205
Ouseley, H., 113
overseas students, 40

Parekh Report, 182, 218
parental choice *see* choice policies
Parental Influence at School, 38
parents, 98
Parents' Charter, 55
Partnership Fund for learning
partnerships, 146
Pascall, D., 70
Passmore, B., 174
Passmore, E., 135
Pathfinder projects, 153
Paton, G., 128, 135
Patten, C., 56
Patten, J., 51, 56, 63
pay, teachers', 41, 66, 112, 136–7
Pay Review Body, 41, 66
Payne, J., 7
Pearce, S., 185
performance-related pay, 66, 112,
136–7
personal, social and health education
(PSHE), 113

Phillips, R., 63, 192
Phoenix Venture Holdings (PVH),
208
Pickering, J., 198
Plowden Report, 22
Pollack, A.M., 6
Pollard, S., 79
Polytechnic and Colleges Funding
Council, 64
polytechnics, 64, 65
Porter, J., 201
post-16 education, 10, 64, 141–63,
196–7
see also further education; higher
education
postwar consensus, 3, 8–9, 13–28
post-welfare market society, 5–6, 200,
215–16
education in, 220–2
human capital in, 6–8
poverty, 21–2, 77–8, 80, 204–5
middle class and avoiding the poor,
177–8
New Labour policies, 105–7, 177,
210–11
'no excuse', 170, 180
prospects for the poor, 210–13
Power, A., 178
Power, S., 167, 187, 204
Pratt, J., 196
Prestage, M., 109
Pring, R., 43, 150, 203
private finance initiative (PFI), 134
private schools, 14, 16, 33–4, 121
assisted places, 34, 77, 95, 220
New Labour and, 123–4
social class and, 173–4
and university admissions, 156–7
privatization, 32–5, 109–10, 134–6,
160, 221
Progress in International Reading
Literacy Study (PIRLS),
138
progressive education, 22, 24–5
Public Accounts Committee, 132
public schools *see* private schools
Public Schools Commission, 23
pupil referral units (PRUs), 61

qualifications, 7
  Dearing review, 85, 145, 155
  and labour market, 205, 207
  Labour Party policy, 86–7, 151–4
  unified structure, 69, 151–2
  see also under individual
    qualifications
Qualifications and Curriculum
  Authority (QCA), 77, 113, 138,
  192
Qualifying for Success, 146

race and ethnicity, 11, 37–8, 105, 172,
  217–18
  equity issues, 182–3, 183–93
  and gender, 195, 197, 198
  labour market, 204
  school exclusions, 134
Race Relations Act 1976, 24, 184
Race Relations (Amendment) Act 2000,
  182, 187
race riots, 37
racial inexplicitness, 184
racism, 192–3
Radice, G., 31
Rampton Report, 37–8, 184
Ranson, S., 33, 54, 109, 144–5
rate capping, 40
Reagan, R., 221
Reay, D., 138, 172
Red Tape Working Group, 95
Rees, G., 108
refugees, 192–3
Regional Development Agencies, 146
regressive vision, 31–2
regulations, 8, 12
Reich, R., 177, 209–10, 213, 219
Removing Barriers to Achievement, 133
research assessment exercise (RAE), 65
Reynolds, D., 46, 84
Riddell, S., 146
Rikowski, G., 134
Robbins Report, 19
Robinson, J., 74
Robinson, P., 7, 206, 207
Room, G., 179
Rover, 208
Ruane, B., 128

Ruskin College speech, 25–6
Russell, Lord, 155
Russell Group, 65, 157
Rutter, J., 188
Rutter, M.L., 21

Sainsbury, Lord, 220
Sanderson, B., 149
Savage, D., 126
Scanlon, M., 134
Scarman Report, 37
school-based teacher training, 66, 68
School Curriculum and Assessment
  Authority (SCAA), 56, 77
school effectiveness, 46, 170–1
School Examinations and Assessment
  Council (SEAC), 51, 56
school exclusions, 105, 188, 189
School Exclusions and Pupil Support,
  105
school leaving age, 13, 18, 24, 84
school meals, 34–5
School Performance Award Scheme,
  112
School Standards and Framework Act
  1998, 10, 99–100, 109, 125
School Support Fund, 112
Schools: Achieving Success, 122–3
Schools Council for the Curriculum, 20,
  22, 40, 41
Schools Forum, 123
Schools Framework and Consultative
  Group, 95
Schools Standards and Effectiveness
  Unit, 69, 94, 137
Schwarz Report, 157
Scotland, 4, 29, 146, 156
Scruton, R., 39
Sebba, J., 98
secondary education, 15–16, 217
  see also under individual types of
    school
Secondary Heads Association, 76–7
secondary modern schools, 16, 17–18,
  19, 33, 42
Section 28, 39
Sector Skills Councils (SSCs), 150, 207
Secure Borders, Safe Haven, 188

selection, 14, 20, 218–19
  Conservative governments, 32–5, 57,
    60, 76–7
  New Labour, 72, 97, 100–4, 121,
    123–5, 159–60
  race and ethnicity, 188–90
  Thatcher and, 23, 32–3
  tripartite system, 16
Sen, A., 212
Sennett, R., 207
Sex Discrimination Act 1975, 24, 194
Shaw, M., 124, 128
Shephard, G., 72, 74, 75, 77
Shepherd, J., 63
Shiner, M., 191
Shotte, G., 191
Silver, H., 40
Simon, B., 16, 19, 20, 23, 24, 34, 35, 39,
    52
Skills Alliance, 150
Skills for Life strategy, 149
Skills Strategy, 150, 202–3
skills revolution, 142, 149–51
Sklair, L., 179
Slater, J., 128, 136, 190
Smith, D.J., 170
Smithers, R., 22, 132, 138, 154
social capital, 145, 171–2
social class, 11, 46, 164–81, 218
  changing class structures, 166–7
  economy and, 209
  tripartite system, 16, 17
social democratic consensus, 3, 8–9,
    13–28
social exclusion, 4, 8, 104–9
Social Exclusion Unit (SEU), 91, 105,
    148, 187
social inclusion, 4, 118, 134, 145–6, 161
social justice, 91, 216
social mobility, 166
social polarization, 175
Social Priority Areas, 107
Social Security Act 1986, 34
social services departments, 161
SOS Save Our Schools, 45
Southwark LEA, 135
special educational needs (SEN), 8
  Education Act 1993, 59, 60–1

  mid-1990s, 81–2
  middle class and, 178
  New Labour, 104–5, 133–4
  1980s, 36
*Special Educational Needs: A Guide for
    Parents*, 82
special educational needs coordinators
    (SENCOs), 61, 82, 105
Special Educational Needs and
    Disability Act 2001, 133
Special Educational Needs Tribunal,
    61
Special Needs Advisory Group, 95
Special Needs Educational Training
    Consortium, 105
specialist schools, 97, 98, 102–3, 125–7,
    130
Specialist Schools Trust, 126–7, 140
Spence, L., 156, 157
Spours, K., 86, 141, 151–2, 176
St John-Brooks, C., 110, 111
Standard Assessment Tasks (SATs), 62
standard spending assessment (SSA), 74,
    88, 131
standards, 21, 72, 217
  Callaghan's Ruskin speech, 25–6
  Conservative governments, 33, 43,
    48, 49
  New Labour, 91–2
Standards and Effectiveness Unit, 69,
    94, 137
Standards Task Force, 94, 97
statements, 134
statutory instruments (SIs), 8, 12
Steedman, H., 176
Stephenson-Foster, N., 58
Stevenson, Lord, 113
Stewart, W., 128
Stiglitz, J., 210
Straw, J., 31, 49, 51, 69
streaming (primary schools), 17, 20
Stuart, N., 47
Stubbs, W., 118, 153
student loans, 64–5
Student Loans Company, 74
student unions, 67, 68
Success for All, 149–50
Summers, L., 183

Sure Start programme, 106–7, 132, 187–8
Sure Start Unit, 132
Swann Report, 38, 185

targets, 96, 137–8
task forces, 94–5
Task Group on Assessment and Testing (TGAT), 45, 62
Tate, N., 94
Taunton Commission, 164
Tawney, R.H., 54, 165
Taylor, Andrew, 70
Taylor, Ann, 51, 70, 86
Taylor, C., 126, 127, 128, 140
Taylor, M., 125
Taylor Report, 24, 38
teacher training, 66–8, 137
Teacher Training Agency (TTA), 67–8, 94, 105, 110–11, 137, 192–3
teachers
    Conservative governments and control of, 41–2, 66–8
    deprofessionalization of, 220
    New Labour and, 98, 110–12, 122–3, 136–7
Teachers: Meeting the Challenge of Change, 112
Teachers' Pay and Conditions Act 1987, 41
Teachers' Pay and Conditions Act 1991, 66
Teaching and Development Agency for Schools (TDAS), 131, 137
Teaching and Higher Education Act 1998, 74, 111–12, 155–6
Teaching Quality, 41
technical schools, 16, 17
Technical and Vocational Educational Initiative (TVEI), 43, 85
Thatcher, M., 29, 38, 48, 185, 221
    assisted places scheme, 220
    Education Secretary, 8, 23–4
    educational advisers, 49
    GM schools, 52
    National Curriculum, 63, 192
    selection, 32–3
    Victorian values, 32

Thatcher governments, 9, 14, 27, 29–55, 194, 201, 210
Third Way, 5
Thompson, P., 206, 206–7
Thornton, K., 210
3E's Ltd, 135
thresholds, performance, 112
Thrupp, M., 170
Times Educational Supplement, 95, 96
Times Higher Education Supplement (THES), 148
Tomasevski, K., 138
Tomes, H., 196
Tomlinson, J., 109
Tomlinson, M., 10, 12, 135
Tomlinson, S., 3, 54, 62, 64, 68, 80, 95, 151, 170, 178, 184, 185, 187, 192, 196
Tomlinson Report, 10, 142–3, 151, 153–4, 176, 203
Toolis, K., 135
Townsend, P., 201
Toynbee, P., 22, 211
Training and Enterprise Councils (TECs), 44, 142, 147, 207
transnational capitalist class, 179
Travers, T., 131, 161
Treasury Comprehensive Spending Review 1998, 91
Treasury Spending Review 2004, 129–30
tripartite system, 16, 17–18
Trow, M., 65
tuition fees, 155–6, 157
Tulloch, M., 103
21st Century Skills: Realising Our Potential, 10, 150

underachievement, boys', 197–8
United States (USA), 5, 212
Universal Declaration of Human Rights, 223
universities *see* higher education
Universities and Colleges Admissions Service (UCAS), 155
Universities Funding Council, 64
University Grants Committee (UGC), 64
University for Industry, 95, 145

Vaizey, J., 201
value-added CV, 171–2
Vardy Foundation, 128
Victorian values, 32
Vidich, A.J., 167
Vincent, K., 183, 189, 195
vocational A levels, 156
vocational education, 219, 224
  academic-vocational divide, 43, 46,
    64, 84–6, 86–7, 151–2, 176
  Conservative governments, 44–5,
    63–4
  middle class and avoidance of, 176
  New Labour, 108, 122, 125, 152
voluntary schools, 75, 98, 99, 101
voucher schemes, 35, 76
Vulliamy, G., 63

Walden, G., 174
Wales, 4
Walford, G., 45
Walker, A., 210
Walker, C., 210
Walker, R., 146
Walkerdine, V., 197, 198
Ward, L., 10, 110, 204
Warhurst, C., 206
Warnock Report, 36
Webb, B., 21
Weiner, G., 194–5
Weir, D., 213
welfare state, 1, 13, 215, 216
  reforms, 3–4, 5–6
welfare to workfare programmes, 211–
  12
West, A., 125
White, M., 132
White, R., 85
Whitty, G., 123
Wiliam, D., 138
Wilkinson, H., 197

Willetts, D., 94
William Tyndale primary school, 25
Williams, R., 218
Williams, S., 26, 37
Willis, P., 135
Wilson, H., 21
Wilson, W., 212
Wintour, P., 5, 111
Wolf, A., 152
Woodhead, C., 58, 94, 136, 160, 224
  amendment of Ofsted 1996 report, 83
  Manchester City Council and, 109,
    115
  1994–5 report, 75–6
  privatization, 110, 135
Woodward, W., 112, 152, 200
work, 6–8, 25–6, 43, 197, 198, 200–14,
  216
working class, 166–7
  see also social class
World Bank, 210
World Economic Forum *World
  Competitiveness Report*, 87
World Trade Organisation, 210
Wragg, T., 11, 68, 110, 136, 140, 198
Wright, O., 48

Yates, L., 194
'Yellow Book', 25
Yeo, T., 121
Youdell, D., 151, 172, 189
Young, D., 43
Young, M., 169
Younge, G., 183
*Your Child and the National
  Curriculum*, 61
youth training schemes (YTS), 24, 44,
  84
youth unemployment, 24, 27, 44, 106

zones, 107